Religion
in Education: 2

The Religion in Education Series

a programme for professional development

in religious education and in church school education

is edited by

The Revd Dr William K. Kay

and

The Revd Canon Professor Leslie J. Francis

from

The Centre for Theology and Education

Trinity College

Carmarthen

The development of the series has been supported by grants from St Gabriel's Trust, Hockerill Educational Foundation, All Saints Educational Trust and St Luke's College Foundation. The collaborative nature of the project has been supported by a co-ordinating committee, including staff from the Church Colleges, Anglican Dioceses and The National Society: Ruth Ackroyd (University College Chester), the Revd Marian Carter (College of St Mark and St John, Plymouth), Dr Mark Chater (Bishop Grosseteste University College, Lincoln), the Revd Professor Leslie J. Francis (Trinity College, Carmarthen), the Revd Dr John D. Gay (Culham College Institute, Abingdon), Dr Fred Hughes (Cheltenham and Gloucester College of HE), Dr Sheila Hunter (University College of St Martin's, Lancaster), the Revd Dr William K. Kay (Trinity College, Carmarthen), Dr Anna King (King Alfred's College, Winchester), David W. Lankshear (Secretary, The National Society, London), Ruth Mantin (Chichester Institute of HE), Carrie Mercier (College of Ripon and York St John, and National Society RE Centre, York), the Revd Canon Alan Nugent (Diocesan Director of Education, Durham), the Revd David Peacock (Roehampton Institute, London), Dr Christine Pilkington (Christ Church, Canterbury), Gaynor Pollard (University College Chester), the Revd Canon Robin Protheroe (Diocesan Director of Education, Bristol), the Revd Alex M. Smith (Hope University College, Liverpool).

Religion in Education: 2

Teaching about the Bible

Spiritual and Moral Development

Christian Values and the Curriculum

Church School Management

edited by

William K. Kay

and

Leslie J. Francis

First published in 1998

Gracewing
2 Southern Avenue
Leominster
Herefordshire HR6 OQF

UK ISBN 0 85244 426 5

Typesetting by Anne Rees

Printed by Cromwell Press
Trowbridge, Wiltshire, BA14 OXB

Contents

Foreword

The National Committee of Inquiry into Higher Education chaired by Sir Ron Dearing published its report in July 1997. Among its 93 recommendations (with a further 29 for Scotland!) are that the number of students, funded through loans, should rise and that a much greater proportion of the population should benefit from university level qualifications.

As part of these proposed changes, this is the second volume of a series designed to meet the needs of a growing number of people in Britain who are embarking on higher degrees in religion and education. When the working population needs constantly to be 're-skilled', distance learning provides the most painless method of progress. Learning materials come to your own home. You may work at your own pace. You can work in your own way. All you lack is the immediate stimulus of a lecturer or teacher and other students off whom you can bounce your ideas. So, to try to compensate for the lack of a teacher, most distance learning institutions provide a tutor, someone who is available to give technical and academic help.

To compensate for the lack of fellow students, there are various strategies, but whatever your college offers, a web site has been designed to use the capacities of the Internet to enhance the electronic presence of your resources. Contained within these pages and the resources of this project, then, are ideas which should make you a better teacher, lecturer, diocesan adviser, parent, governor or cleric.

This book is the outcome of an imaginative collaboration between representatives of the Anglican colleges in England and Wales and the church college trusts. In this connection, thanks should go to John Gay of Culham College Institute and to Ruth Ackroyd of University College Chester for their patient work in putting together the team and the funding that were necessary for all these materials to be written.

The work of editing these volumes has been undertaken within the Centre for Theology and Education at Trinity College, Carmarthen, a research centre stimulated by the Principal and Governors of the College specifically to facilitate developments of this nature. The editors record their gratitude to Diane Drayson, Anne Rees and Tony Rees for their help in shaping the manuscript.

William K. Kay
Leslie J. Francis
Easter, 1998

Introduction

Overview

This book, the second in a planned set of four, contains four modules, each of which is broken down into three units. As they are presented there is clear progression within the modules. For example the module *Teaching about the bible* starts with an overview of biblical scholarship and then moves from a general engagement with children's understanding of texts to the specifics of Agreed Syllabuses and biblical writings. The module *Spiritual and Moral Development* begins with the way that spirituality and morality are linked in official documentation and then moves to the research that supports, in the first instance, spirituality in the form of faith development and, in the second instance, morality as a developmental process. The module *Christian Values and the Curriculum* looks first at the curriculum and the ways it may be structured, then at how knowledge and values meet and relate in the school and finally at the process of education, both organisational and curricular, and the perspective Christian values bring to bear on it. The module *Church School Management* starts with theory and ends with practice.

Each unit, however, is written by a separate author and is to some extent independent of the others. Although we anticipate you would choose a pathway through this material that would lead you to work through all the units in a particular module consecutively, other options would also make sense. In other words, the materials given here are designed to be as flexible as possible within the constraints of a modern British degree at Master's level.

All the writers have been asked to write in a way that conforms to *Level M descriptors*. These descriptors express in a standardised way the 'operational contexts', 'cognitive activities' and 'transferable skills' which would normally be found in work at Master's degree level. In terms of evaluation, these descriptors require students to be able to weigh the strengths and weaknesses of alternative approaches and accurately assess and report on their own. For this reason the materials often include an outline of more than one standpoint on contentious issues. This allows student activities to be built into the text that encourage the evaluative process or, fulfilling another M level descriptor, to synthesise information and ideas so as to develop new approaches in new situations.

Similarly, since M level work requires 'depth of knowledge in complex and specialised areas', no concessions have been made to the detailed and sometimes demanding technical debates that the topics of these units cover. Moreover, M level asks students to be responsible within bounds of professional practice, to be autonomous in the use of resources and in the resolution of problems. We have sought to achieve the balance between supporting students and encouraging autonomy. Our pilot testing of the materials suggests we have been successful.

These distance learning materials, so far as possible, are free-standing - they should not require you to obtain vast numbers of extra books. Nevertheless, it has proved impossible to do without reference books altogether but, to help you, and in the realisation that not all students will be able to obtain all books, we almost always include summaries of the texts to which you are pointed, so that you have at least an outline of what these texts say.

In addition, these materials have been written with a view to the Readers edited by Francis and his collaborators and published by Gracewing. Each of these Readers contains about thirty original papers that have been carefully selected and reprinted from a wide range of journals across the world. The Readers therefore function like a miniature library and will save you many hours of tracking down important but out-of-the way literature. The Readers are:

- L.J. Francis and A. Thatcher (eds) (1990), *Christian Perspectives for Education*, Leominster, Gracewing.
- J. Astley and L.J. Francis (eds) (1992), *Christian Perspectives on Faith Development*, Leominster, Gracewing.
- L.J. Francis and D.W. Lankshear (eds) (1993), *Christian Perspectives on Church Schools*, Leominster, Gracewing.
- J. Astley and L.J. Francis (eds) (1994), *Critical Perspectives on Christian Education*, Leominster, Gracewing.
- J. Astley, L.J. Francis and C. Crowder (eds) (1996), *Theological Perspectives on Christian Formation*, Leominster, Gracewing.

At the end of each unit, you will find a reference to the most helpful sections of the Readers and a full bibliography of other books either referred to by the author of the unit or to give you further lines of research on particular topics.

We recognise that distance learning students will be increasingly people who rely on electronic means of communication. The day of the 'electronic campus' has already arrived. Consultations by e-mail, the collection of resources using Internet search engines and video conferencing are being used by increasing numbers of students. *This project therefore has a web site specifically constructed to service its students and provide additional help for them.* Your college will be able to give you the information necessary to access the web site.

The next sections provide an overview of the modules in the order in which they appear and details of activities and assessment.

Teaching about the Bible

Unit A provides a compressed and comprehensive synopsis of the development of biblical scholarship. It shows not only what the differences between fundamentalists and liberals might be, but also the basis of their disagreements and the subtler variants of more recent positions. It considers how the bible may be treated by children and within education. Two sections then follow that summarise debates on the authorship and reliability of the Old Testament and on the construction of the synoptic gospels, the quest for the historical Jesus and the apparent differences between John and Paul. The tools of biblical criticism are explained and then the relationship of the bible to religion and to theology is discussed. Finally, both biblical theology and the diversity within the bible are brought into view.

Unit B considers children's understanding of language and words, their gradual ability to comprehend texts, and the literary abilities expected of children within the National Curriculum. Such abilities include the grasp of meanings beyond the literal and the grasp of narrative conventions. From here the unit considers aspects of current literary theory and then discusses the place of story in religious education before looking at research on children's understanding of metaphor in general and religious metaphor in particular. The unit concludes by looking at a study of children's ability to understand parables and the implications of this for more general understanding of the bible.

Unit C considers the teaching of the bible in the light of the requirements of the National Curriculum and of Agreed Syllabuses. It shows that there is considerable scope for teaching the bible even within non-religious subjects of the National Curriculum (for instance in history) and by using methods for dealing with texts that are familiar through the teaching of English. Taking three modern Agreed Syllabuses it shows how their construction in each case might have an effect on the presentation of the bible in the classroom. It outlines approaches to the life of Christ and discusses bible teaching in GCSE examination syllabuses.

Spiritual and Moral Development

Unit A addresses the meaning of spirituality and argues that it is found in the 'lived experience of religion' and has corporate as well as individual dimensions. It then traces the course of legislative directives and official guidelines and attempts, from this perspective, to find how spirituality should be interpreted in an educational context. It concludes that only when OFSTED began its work did the previous confusion begin to subside.

It compares religion and spirituality and shows what conditions need to be fulfilled for non-religious spirituality to exist. It takes note of criticisms of OFSTED's guidance about spirituality and introduces SCAA's attempt to take the debate forward. But it notes criticisms of SCAA's proposals and the relevance of a theological framework in which education might be placed. This leads to an examination of three recent research projects on spirituality, those of Robert Coles, David Hay and the Children and Worldviews Project, and to case studies on the possible conflict between religion and science.

Unit B introduces Piaget's theory of mental development and gives a thorough introduction to Fowler's six stage theory of faith development building on its Piagetian foundations. It also considers empirical and psychological criticisms of Fowler's work before turning to the problems raised by any theory of development and to the variant forms of developmental theory. It concludes by comparing the operation of logic in Piaget and Fowler and by pointing to the hard questions such a comparison raises.

Unit C introduces Piaget's pioneering work on moral development. It shows how Piaget was able to integrate mental development with a series of moral stages that led to the appreciation of reciprocal moral obligations and to a conception of justice. Following this the unit shows how Kohlberg elaborated and extended Piaget's work, especially in its relation to moral education. After this Gilligan's feminist critiques of Kohlberg and, by implication, Piaget are given. Gilligan argued on the basis of evidence she collected that the psychological development of females took a different course from that typically experienced by males and that Piaget's and Kohlberg's work was therefore inappropriate and unhelpful as a universal description. A series of counter-critiques of Gilligan, however, suggest that her views need amendment. Lastly, the unit considers classroom approaches and techniques in the field of moral education.

Christian Values and the Curriculum

Unit A of this module introduces the concept of curriculum and curriculum theory. It shows how society and curriculum are related and how curriculum may be structured in a variety of ways: by reference to the internal logic of the subject areas it contains, or according to the cognitive needs of children, or by using epistemological considerations implied in recent philosophical changes heralded by the arrival of the post-modern era or, finally, by assessment needs. A discussion of the control of the curriculum follows and this leads into a review of the key features of the National Curriculum, SATS, school league tables and possible areas where change will be needed in future.

Unit B introduces a distinction between objectivist and constructivist approaches to knowledge. It shows the strengths and weaknesses of each and proposes a middle path, referring also to the virtues of constructivism for the classroom. From there it moves to a focus on values. It defines values as 'principles or fundamental convictions which act as general guides to behaviour or as points of reference in decision-making' and discusses whether they may be absolute or whether they are subjective and without an objective reality. It asks if private and public values must be identical and considers how, in general, values may be categorised (by subject matter or by ideology, for instance). This leads to a focus on the shared values that would find a place in a common framework for maintained schools as expressed in the work of the SCAA National Forum on Values in Education. It concludes by exploring methods in values education and distinguishing between tolerance and neutrality.

Unit C explores the presence of Christian values in the process of education. It begins by taking three Christian areas of doctrine (Trinity, human nature and beliefs about the world) and drawing out their value implications for education. Subsequently it considers how Christian values are maintained in a world that opposes them. From here consideration is given to Christian values within the subject areas of the curriculum and then within the human relationships (staff to staff, pupil to pupil and staff to pupil) that the educational process necessarily involves.

Church School Management

Unit A introduces concepts of management and makes use of the classic texts of management theory to discuss not only what managers do but the different styles by which they try to achieve their objectives. There is certainly a responsibility, or accountability, faced by the manager and there is an equally obvious need for the manager to make strategic decisions about the future direction, scope and functioning of an institution. But in schools the concept of management is diversified because there is a sense in which every teacher is a manager of one kind or another. While the headteacher may manage finance in relation to external bodies, the classroom teacher manages resources in relation to the learning of children. While the headteacher's management cycle may follow patterns established by the financial year, the classteacher is more likely to be affected by the academic year. Moreover the variations in management styles may also be influenced by the indicators and targets that are used to measure managerial success. Thought needs to be given to this issue because it is possible that the dangers of turning people into units of production may be forgotten in the drive to attain institutional goals. Leadership may therefore also be seen as a form of relationship and management may be seen as the empowerment of people to handle change on the basis of an agreed vision.

Unit B explores the philosophical meaning of management and the interrelationship between the means and ends of management. This leads to a discussion of how management is related to values and, in a church school, to Christian values. A differentiation between distinctively Christian values and characteristically Christian values and between these and spiritual values follows, and this leads to an outline of 'three ages of school management'. These are the earlier age where headteachers were expected to show moral leadership in their schools, where this sort of leadership was often wedded to a fixed social and political order based on class. More recently, between the 1940s and 1970s, professional leadership came to the fore. This sort of leadership tended to be democratic and influenced by the ideal of public service. Since the late 1980s, management has been influenced by the philosophy of the market, where educational goods are offered for the least cost, and the techniques of commerce have seemed appropriate.

This leads Astley to a consideration of mission statements, the hidden curriculum and moral education and the democratic or autocratic style of leadership and learning adopted by a school. But his powerful final sections are devoted to an examination of market philosophy on educational management and he concludes that, for a school with a Christian basis, the philosophy of service is preferable.

Unit C discusses many of the practicalities of church school management. It relates school effectiveness to the roles of the headteacher and shows how Ethos Statements, which are likely to shape the organisation of schools, will help determine particular policies in the future. It then considers the task of turning a failing county school into a successful or effective church school and outlines strategies that would work under various circumstances. It relates the unit's content to the National Professional Qualification for Headship and gives examples of the application of the professional knowledge of headteachers to typical management tasks. It also shows how the practical day-to-day problems of the headteacher in handling staff may be solved using the Christian values that church schools are intended to exemplify.

Activities and assessment

Your assessment will be based on a piece of work carried out by you at the end of the module. The activities that punctuate these materials are not intended to be assessable, though in some cases your tutors may base an assessment around them. But your tutor will tell you *in advance* what your assessable assignment will be. Do not, however, treat the activities as an optional extra. They are designed to consolidate and deepen the learning process, to make you benefit more fully from the information and the processes laid before you.

Each activity is followed by a 'Comment' in which the unit's author has given an opinion on the kinds of things you might have thought or written in response to the stimulus you were given. The comment should be taken as just that, a comment, and not a definitive answer to the activity's stimulus.

All modules are broken into three units, A, B and C. All the activities are labelled by a letter and a number and indicated by double parallel lines in the margins. Activity A1 is the first in unit A, activity B3 is the third in unit B, and so on. The units themselves are broken into sections, each prefixed by the unit's identifying letter. A3 is the third section of unit A, B2 is the second section of unit B, and so on. This means that it is easy to refer to any part of a module in an assignment: *all you need is the module's name and a letter and a number*. For example, 'Parable comprehension' is found at B6 in the module *Teaching about the Bible*.

Contributors

The twelve units in this book have been written by the following contributors.

- *Revd Professor Jeff Astley* is Director of the North of England Institute for Christian Education and Honorary Professorial Fellow in Practical Theology and Christian Education at the University of Durham.
- *Mr Clive Erricker* is Reader in Theology and Religious Studies at Chichester Institute of Higher Education.
- *Ms Jane Erricker* is Research Director at the School of Education, King Alfred's College, Winchester.
- *The Revd Canon Professor Leslie J. Francis* is D.J. James Professor of Pastoral Theology at Trinity College, Carmarthen, and University of Wales, Lampeter.
- Mr Roger Goulden is Principal Lecturer and Head of In-Service Teacher Education at Trinity and All Saints University College, Leeds.
- *Dr Mark Halstead* is Reader in Moral Education at the Faculty of Arts and Education, University of Plymouth.
- *The Revd Dr William K. Kay* is Senior Research Fellow at the Centre for Theology and Education, Trinity College, Carmarthen.
- *Mr David W. Lankshear* is Deputy Secretary and Schools Officer of the National Society and Schools Officer of the General Synod Board of Education.

- *Ms Gaynor Pollard* is Senior Lecturer in Theology and Religious Studies at University College, Chester, and Religious Education Adviser for Chester Diocese.

Activity symbols

This book is designed to be read interactively: there will be things you are asked to do while reading it. Sometimes you are asked simply to read a text, or re-read information given in the activity section, and then to think about it and write down what you think. At others the assumption is that you will work with a group of children or with a friend. The symbols shown below are placed in the text's wide margin to alert you to the activity you will be asked to undertake.

Read

Reflect

Write

Work with a group

Teaching about the Bible

Teaching about the Bible

Unit A

Overview of biblical scholarship

Revd Professor Jeff Astley

North of England Institute for Christian Education

Durham

Contents

Introduction

Aims

After working through this unit you should be able to:

- understand the major insights of biblical scholarship over the last century;
- critically evaluate different positions on the relationship between historical criticism and personal belief;
- critically evaluate various attitudes to scripture.

Overview

We begin with some reflections on the problem of the 'historian and the believer', as this applies to scripture, and examine a variety of ways of approaching scripture. Two sections on the history of biblical scholarship follow, together with an account of the tools used by biblical critics. A final section returns to more theological concerns relating to the use of scripture.

A1 'Studying the bible': religion and criticism

Modern biblical scholarship is inextricably linked with the phrase 'biblical criticism'. Of course 'criticism' is not necessarily 'critical'. The word derives from the Greek *krisis*, meaning 'judgement', and is used in academic and educational circles to label a species of scholarly study in which the student exercises a reflective, intelligent, informed, evaluative judgement of the matter in hand.

'To read/study the bible critically' is to apply a critical attitude and critical skills to the text of scripture. It may produce results that seem to religious people to be either negative or positive, but its aim, methods and motivation should in fact be *neutral* with respect to faith and piety. Biblical criticism is often described as 'rational', in the sense that it applies the same criteria of reasonableness to scripture that we find in disciplines such as history, literary studies, archaeology, etc. Again, 'rational' - in the sense of being 'in accordance with reason' - should properly be seen as a neutral term.

The critical study of the Christian bible in fact goes back to the early fathers of the church, but it is true to say that up until about 1750 such study was piece-meal and remained very restricted by ecclesiastical concerns about orthodoxy. From the eighteenth century 'Enlightenment' onwards these restrictions were increasingly ignored by scholars, and biblical study took on a life separate from, and sometimes in opposition to, the life and doctrines of the church[1]. The mainstream Protestant denominations soon accepted this state of affairs, but the Roman Catholic Church's official hostility to the critical investigation of the bible continued well into the twentieth century[2].

Activity A1

Take some time to think about *how* you were taught about the bible (at home, school or church) and *what* you were taught. As an adult, how has your understanding of the bible changed? How do you feel about those changes?

Comment on activity A1

Many Christians were taught - or assumed - a position that linked 'taking the bible seriously' either with 'taking it literally' or with defending it as a source-book of historical and scientific, as well as religious and moral truths.

Adults often have problems with such a position, as they come to face the challenges to traditional biblical understanding provided by geology (over the age of the earth), biology (the evolution of species) and history (scepticism about miracle stories). Those who are more familiar with the contents of the bible itself are also forced to recognise the diversity of genres and theologies presented there, and the existence of many inconsistent accounts of the same event. For some, these factors result in their taking the bible less seriously, shaking their belief in its veracity. For others, such reflections are liberating, as they begin to rediscover divine revelation as something that can take place through these very human documents.

Religious and scholarly 'use of the bible'

There is no doubt that the rise of an increasingly independent community of scholars working from a critical standpoint has posed difficulties for the church. The bible may be 'the church's book' in origin and theological status, but scholars now pay little heed to any restrictive covenants that the church would wish to impose on those who claim to have a squatter's right to this particular

---

[1] See the texts in J.M. Creed and J.S. Boys Smith (eds), *Religious Thought in the Eighteenth Century*, (Cambridge, Cambridge University Press, 1934) and B.M.G. Reardon (ed.), *Religious Thought in the Nineteenth Century*, (Cambridge, Cambridge University Press, 1966).
[2] See R.A. Dyson and R.A.F. Mackenzie, S.J., 'Higher criticism of the bible', and E.F. Sutcliffe, S.J., 'The replies of the biblical commission', in Dom B. Orchard *et al.* (eds), *A Catholic Commentary on Holy Scripture* (Edinburgh, Nelson, 1953), pp 61-75.

property. Critical scholarship is today an autonomous study, which may be appropriately designated as 'secular' (i.e. not under religious control or influence). Does this matter?

There is a *prima facie* clash between the religious use of the bible by Christians in their private devotions and their public worship and witness, and the ways in which the bible is analysed and critiqued by contemporary scholars. What are the problems here? If the bible is to be studied 'like any other book'[3], does it not lose its authoritative power to command, convict and illuminate us, in the way that the Word of God should? As the bible is first and foremost the book of and for a religion, it must still be possible 'to read the bible religiously (on the assumption that it speaks of God)', that is to read it *as scripture* (Morgan with Barton, 1988, pp 36, 38). But if the bible is to be used in this way in preaching, evangelism and nurture (to arouse, deepen and strengthen faith) and in worship (to help express and evoke attitudes of devotion, commitment and fellowship), can we also hold it at arm's length for a critical appraisal? Would that be to 'murder to dissect' it?

These are important questions, but perhaps they cannot be answered theoretically. Christians need rather to engage in some critical study of the bible *and* use the bible in pew and pulpit. Only then will they discover whether it is possible for the two uses to co-exist for themselves.

We meet here the problem of 'the historian and the believer'. Different individuals and different Christian spiritual traditions will find different ways of resolving this problem, or at least of living with the tension of it. They will have to do one or the other, since most scholars would argue that *not* to study the bible critically is no longer a live option for educated, thinking adults - nor perhaps for (educating, thinking?) children who will become educated, thinking adults.

From fundamentalists to liberals, and beyond

It is a common misunderstanding that the proper and original Christian treatment of the bible is represented by 'fundamentalism'. In fact, that label itself is of comparatively recent coinage and marks a reaction against modern biblical criticism and liberal theology. It originated in a series of tracts reaffirming central Christian doctrines, *The Fundamentals*, from the pen of conservative Protestants in the early decades of this century. The most pronounced characteristics of fundamentalism as it exists today have been described (Barr, 1981, p 1) as:

---

[3] This is Benjamin Jowett's phrase, from his essay in the notorious collection *Essays and Reviews* (1860), p 338.

- a very strong emphasis on the inerrancy of the bible, i.e. the absence from it of any sort of error;
- a strong hostility to modern theology and to the methods, results and implications of the modern critical study of the bible;
- an assurance that those who do not share their religious viewpoint are not really 'true Christians' at all.

Three points may be made straight away. First, inerrancy is more crucial to fundamentalists than 'taking the bible literally' (Barr, 1973, chapter 10). In order to preserve this claim to inerrancy fundamentalists often have to interpret certain texts figuratively (e.g. the references in Genesis 1 to the 'days' of creation). Second, fundamentalism is an all-or-nothing doctrine. If one tiny historical mistake is found in scripture, the whole position collapses. It is therefore extremely vulnerable to criticism. Third, fundamentalism is based on a particular kind of religious tradition. Despite its claims, it does *not* dispense with tradition in order to approach the bible naked of presuppositions.

Let us take up this third point in more detail. A church's tradition is the place where its view of the authority of scripture is to be found. Claims about the inerrancy of scripture logically cannot just be read out of scripture, for the argument would be circular: 'This text is true because it is in the bible. This text says that all scripture is true. Therefore all scripture (including this text) is true.' Surely, the texts that make such a claim must first themselves be accepted as authentic if they are to be of any use in the argument? Isn't the fundamentalist bringing his or her belief about scripture *to* scripture?

In any case, the texts that might be read in this way are rare and very late (e.g. 2 Timothy 3.16, 2 Peter 1.21)[4]. Despite the claims of extreme Protestants that the bible is sufficient in all things and any human traditions only detract from it[5], we may agree with Richard Hanson that 'tradition is a necessary part of historical Christianity, and no Christian denomination or communion has existed, or could have existed, without tradition'[6]. In the religious tradition of fundamentalism, the bible is 'the supreme religious tangible sacred reality' and the 'symbol of the religious pattern' (Barr, 1981, pp 36, 37). Inerrancy is thought to be essential to that perspective.

Fundamentalism is often associated with an extreme understanding of the *inspiration of scripture*, in which God dictates his word through umpteen infallible secretaries. However, the concept of divine inspiration is construed very differently by others - even by some fundamentalists and other

---

[4] Further, they almost certainly 'do not mean what fundamentalist apologists have taken them to mean' (Barr, 1981, p xviii).

[5] See, e.g., A. Wallis, *The Radical Christian* (Eastbourne, Kingsway, 1981), pp 109-110. This view was *not* held by the classical Reformers or the mainstream Protestant traditions.

[6] Although a particular church might have a tradition of 'dispensing with [other people's] tradition'! (Hanson, 1983, p 574).

conservatives - so as to avoid such an implausible picture. Most students of scripture understand inspiration in a way that accommodates some human (and therefore fallible) dimension in the receiving, interpreting and recording of the biblical revelation. More liberal scholars extend this human dimension very much further (cf. Borg, 1994, pp 174-179)[7]. Geoffrey Lampe asserted that the notable lesson taught by the development of criticism in the past century was:

> that God speaks to us in a manner congruous with the Incarnation itself, through human words and human minds conditioned by the circumstances of place and time, subject to our ordinary limitations. They are human minds peculiarly able, as our experience and the collective experience of the Church can testify, to discern the true spiritual significance of history, which is to say that they are inspired; but they are none the less liable to error and ignorance. There is no mechanical inspiration of the words they use, and we must beware of any attempt to find a substitute for verbal inerrancy in the idea that the images in which their thoughts are given pictorial expression, ... or the structure of Hebraic language and the psychology of its thought-forms are a specially designed instrument for the direct utterance of the voice of God.

These things are very important, in Lampe's view, for our understanding of what the biblical writers have to tell us. But in his study of the church's use of the bible Lampe (1963, p 142) continues:

> They do not, however, form a direct channel of divine inspiration, and the 'images' which guide the thinking of the prophets and poets of the scriptures are no more exempt from human error and limitation than their words.

This metaphor of incarnation ('enfleshing') picks up a general theological theme, expressed in the words of St Paul in the claim that we hold divine treasure 'in earthen vessels' (2 Corinthians 4.7). Such a doctrine of inspiration accepts that God was in contact with people in the formation of the biblical tradition, but that 'the mode of this contact was not different from the mode in which God has continued to make himself known' (Barr, 1973, p 18). Scripture is special, but it is not totally different in kind from any other medium of revelation.

Spectrum of attitudes to scripture

If a spectrum of views on the bible were to be drawn, *fundamentalism* would appear at the extreme (right wing?) end of it. Fundamentalism is the limiting case of a much broader position that can be called 'conservative'. Many

---

[7] Kenneth Cragg, a Christian scholar and bishop who is also an expert on Islam, recognises that fundamentalism fits the Qur'anic concept of revelation, with its notion of verbatim dictation independent of the receptive will of its recipient and without a period of oral tradition. But he argues that it is applicable to the Christian bible and that a more incarnational doctrine of inspiration would better capture the sense of how the words of Jesus were disseminated and mediated ('hazardously', 'housed within the reverent recollection... of disciples'). He concludes that 'one cannot well infallibilize what does not come that way' (Cragg, 1981, p 25).

conservatives clearly distinguish themselves from fundamentalists. Although they also have a high view of the authority and trustworthiness of the bible (in moral and theological matters certainly, but often when it makes claims about history too), they would refuse to go so far as to describe it as 'inerrant' (particularly, perhaps, with regard to any implications for science). *Liberals* appear to the left of conservatives in the spectrum. They are less sure of the trustworthiness of the bible across a wider range of topics, while accepting its general authority - and often its centrality - for Christian believers. Beyond the liberals lie the *radicals*, many of whom adopt a highly relativist view of the meanings and truth of scripture (as we shall see), and are willing to dispense with large parts of both Old and New Testaments in reconstructing their doctrinal system. Extreme radicals, such as the eighteenth century Deists, regard revelation and scripture as wholly secondary to reason, a mere 'republication' of the beliefs that could be discovered by reason alone. Some might be willing to dispense with scripture altogether.

David Kelsey's *The Uses of Scripture in Recent Theology* (Kelsey, 1975; cf. Kelsey, 1968 and Farley and Hodgson, 1983) offers us a more detailed analysis of how many modern theologians use scripture. He distinguishes seven uses in all. You may care to try to plot your own view of scripture on the following spectrum of positions.

The first three ('conservative') uses of scripture treat it as authoritative by virtue of its *content*, although only (1) focuses on the actual words of scripture. All three assume that the role of theology is that of translating and citing scripture. The fourth position is rather betwixt-and-between, a 'mediating' position. The last three ('liberal') interpretations treat scripture as authoritative because of its power to 'express' past revelatory events and to give rise to new occasions of revelation and salvation. For the last three types theology has the task of redescribing (not directly translating), in contemporary thought-forms, what was expressed in the bible in its own language.

- Scripture as containing inspired, inerrant *doctrine*. (This is often termed fundamentalism.)
- Scripture as containing inspired, authoritative *concepts*. (This is one variant of the position known as 'biblical theology'; see Section A5 below.)
- Scripture as the recital of *salvation history*. (This is expressed by those 'biblical theologians' for whom the bible is the book of the 'acts of God in history'.)
- Scripture as the (human, fallible) *medium through which God may disclose himself in his Word.* The text is therefore not authoritative by virtue of its content, but only because of the way it *functions* as the medium for a new encounter with God. (This is the view of the great Swiss theologian Karl Barth, the most influential Protestant theologian of the twentieth century.)

- Scripture as expressing past revelation and occasioning a present revelation through *poetic images* (as in the theology of the English scholar Austin Farrer).

- Scripture as expressing past revelation and occasioning a present revelation through *religious symbols* (as in the theology of the influential German-American liberal theologian Paul Tillich).

- Scripture as expressing past revelation and occasioning a present revelation through *kerygmatic statements* of the proclamation of faith (as in the theology of the German New Testament scholar and existentialist theologian, Rudolf Bultmann).

Kelsey makes clear in this analysis the extent to which a wide variety of theologians adopt a *functional* view of scripture. For them, the bible is treated as scripture in terms of its function - how it *works*, rather than in terms of its nature. There is great religious strength in this functionalist position. If it is taken to extremes, however, scripture may become merely a medium or catalyst for some effect in us: our contemporary discernment, inspiration or understanding. The particular nature or original meaning of the bible will soon then be a matter of no real significance. For many Christians, such a view would be too relativistic and not authoritative enough.

As liberal a theologian as Maurice Wiles admits that we can still find great value in the 'scripture principle' (treating the bible *as* authoritative scripture). Not only does it create in us a respect for antiquity and a focus for the community (the 'unity' of the church is traditionally said to be symbolised by its possession of one bible), it also offers us an escape from our subjectivity and a witness to what he calls the 'over-against-ness' of God (Wiles, 1975). Others have stressed the 'necessity and centrality of scripture', while insisting on a distinction between scriptural traditions and revelation itself (thus Morgan with Barton, 1988, p 181, cf. p 272).

Whose meaning?

The art and science of interpreting texts ('hermeneutics') has become a major focus of theological interest over recent decades. In particular, the earlier concern of scholars such as the great F. D. E. Schleiermacher (1768-1834), that we should come to know the 'true meaning' of a text by and through recovering the author's own intended meaning, has been strenuously challenged by Hans-Georg Gadamer (who was born in 1900) and many others. Gadamer recognised that the interpreter has her own contribution to play. We can only understand a text such as scripture when the 'horizon' (world-view, assumptions, culture) of the text is in a conversational dialogue with our own horizon of understanding, and can thus speak to us through interpretation (see

Gadamer, 1982, pp 271-274, 327-338, 358). Gadamer also argued that the text from the past is open to a great variety of new interpretations. These are themselves *creative* dialogues between text and interpreter in which proper meanings, other than those intended by the author, are released from the text.

The English biblical scholar and radical theologian Dennis Nineham once wrote, 'I should like to see Christians nowadays approach the bible in an altogether more *relaxed* spirit', accepting it as an ancient story told by people with a very different world-view and giving it a chance to speak to us (Nineham, 1976, p 196). This comment comes in a book that espouses a particular *relativistic* view of the bible. Nineham argues: 'There is nothing properly described as "*the* meaning of the bible", no fixed quantum of truth which it contains and which we have only to take over as it stands.' He adds that 'it is perfectly legitimate to find in a document meanings which go beyond what the original author consciously intended' (Nineham, 1976, p 262; cf. Barr, 1973, chapter 3). On this account, the truth and meaning of the bible are not objective and independent features of scripture. Different ages and people will find differing meanings there, and the 'truth of scripture' for me will not be its (your) truth for you - let alone for St Paul. As you might expect, such a view is more welcome to liberals and radicals than to conservative or fundamentalist readers of scripture. (See also Section A5 below.)

Bible, children and education

The difficult pedagogical issues of how to teach about the bible (and, even more difficult, how to teach *from* the bible) in schools are tackled in units B and C of this module. Two rather more theological points are made here.

First, although the bible has presumably always had some sort of educational function, there are grave dangers in using it for that purpose. Karl Barth argued that the bible's 'strange world' (for it is not of this world) offers little of value to *our* concerns about history, morals or even religion. He claimed that 'large parts of the bible are almost useless to the school in its moral curriculum', because they are lacking in practical wisdom and examples of moral excellence. 'The bible is an embarrassment in the school and foreign to it' (Barth, 1957, p 38). Less extremely, we may note that the bible's 'diversity of material makes it possible to support any number of opposing positions', at least in ethical matters and with regard to the Old Testament (Rogerson, 1983, p 150). But even this author recognises on the next page some measure of agreement within the Old Testament in particular areas, such as its attitude to justice and compassion.

Second, a related point is that the bible is a book for *adults*, 'and crystallizes the religious experience of adults'. Hence, as one New Testament scholar claims, 'if taught to children [the bible] is either talking about experience which is beyond what they have or ought to have, or it is disembowelled in various ways in an attempt to bring it within what is supposed to be their experience' (Evans, 1971, p 40; cf. Dewey, 1903). We may contrast this view with that of many religious educators who affirm that children *can* 'learn from the bible about themselves', relating the biblical world and its theological insights to their own experiences, hopes and needs (see Furnish, 1975; Hull, 1992; Cully, 1995). You should draw on your own knowledge of children's religious understanding in reflecting on this debate.

A2 History of Old Testament study

In this section and the next I intend to give a sketchy overview of the history of the critical study of the Old Testament and (in somewhat more detail) of the New. I hope that these surveys will provide a general picture of some of the vast amount of work that has been published in these areas, while dropping some important names along the way!

According to John Rogerson, 'the main reason for the rise of biblical criticism was the severing of the link between the Old Testament and the New Testament, and the investigation of the former without regard to the latter' and its theological agenda (Rogerson, in Coggins and Houlden, 1990, p 84). The sense of the historical and theological *particularity* of the Old Testament was strengthened, and doubts about its status as divine revelation increased, for three main reasons:

- it began to be seen as the literature of an ancient oriental people;
- doubts were raised about the traditional attributions of authorship of many of its books;
- historical, scientific - and sometimes moral - criticisms of the miraculous events it recounted were increasingly voiced.

These criticisms began to emerge towards the close of the seventeenth century, in part under the influence of rationalist English Deism. From the mid eighteenth century onwards they had developed such energy that the limiting restrictions of Christian orthodoxy were thrown off entirely, and critical scholarship galloped forward, especially on continental Europe.

'Books of Moses'

In the nineteenth century the critical method flourished most in Germany, where it was particularly marked by new thinking about the documentary sources of the Pentateuch, new studies of the history of Israel (derived from a critical evaluation of material in the Old Testament itself), and some speculative reflection on the evolution of Israelite religion. These critical methods and conclusions gradually permeated both England and the USA, although not without resistance from more traditional scholars and clerics (see Rogerson, 1983, pp 19-23).

Many people think that research on the Old Testament is largely a matter of digging up relevant remains of cities and discovering old documents in Israel or Egypt. Although archaeological and (particularly) comparative historical studies in the Ancient Near East have made considerable contributions, new ways of handling the literature itself have been far more fruitful. Over a hundred years ago a major breakthrough in this area resulted from an analysis of the *Pentateuch* (the first five books) which, according to the 'Graf-Wellhausen hypothesis', isolated four possible documents from different periods, labelled 'J', 'E', 'P' and 'D' (the Book of Deuteronomy).

The traditional authorship of Moses had long been questioned - after all his death is recounted in Deuteronomy 34.5. Julius Wellhausen (1844-1918), drawing on the earlier work of the schoolmaster-scholar K.H. Graf and others, confirmed that the so-called Priestly Document ('P') with its great collection of cultic laws[8] was the latest of these sources. The Law, it appeared, came *later* than the Prophets. Further, this source-criticism of the Pentateuch neatly revealed a development in Israelite religious thinking itself, as the anthropomorphic figure of Yahweh (the God of Israel) from the early source 'J' (as in Genesis 2.4b to 4.25) evolved into the transcendent, divine ruler and lawmaker of the later 'P' source (e.g. as in Genesis 1.1 to 2.4a, Exodus 25.9 to 31.18, and most of Leviticus).

This early literary criticism has since been criticised, and is rejected by I. Engnell and other scholars who would place all their reliance on blocks of *oral* tradition that need to be understood by a form critical account of the shaping of traditions (see below section A4). On this interpretation, none of the sources are thought of as having been written down until c. 540 to 450 BC, after the return from Exile. Nevertheless, the variety of different *strands* of the Pentateuch is still recognised.

---

[8] The *cultus* is the system of worship.

Activity A2

Look carefully at the following texts in a modern translation:

- Genesis 1.1 to 2.4a ('P') and Genesis 2.4b-24 ('J')
- Genesis 6.1-5 and 7.1-5 ('J') and Genesis 6.9-22 ('P')

What are the main differences in content, style and theological tone between the 'J' and 'P' traditions?

Comment on activity A2

Different aspects will strike different readers. The usual account of distinctions between the Pentateuchal sources includes the following two points.

First, the 'J' tradition presents in vivid, concrete stories an anthropomorphic picture of God, who is consistently referred to as *Yahweh* (often translated 'the LORD'). It probably originated earliest, about 850 BC, in Judah. It is supplemented by the sparser 'E' tradition, which is perhaps a hundred years later and originated in the Northern Kingdom of Ephraim. 'E' presents a more reverent, awesome, transcendent view of God, influenced by Israelite prophecy. In 'E' God is called *Elohim*. (For examples of E material, see Genesis 20.1-18; most of Exodus chapters 20 to 23).

Second, the 'P' source, unlike 'J', recognises that the divine name *Yahweh* was not known before the theophany to Moses (Exodus 6.2-3). This strand originated during the Exile in Babylonia, and is often written in a dry, technical, ordered style with masses of material of interest mainly to priests and interpreters of the Law. Forming a framework for the earlier traditions, 'P' tells the history of Israel from the priestly standpoint (e.g. no sacrifice takes place before the priesthood has been instigated), and reflects a high transcendent monotheism.

Other books

The *Psalter* is another part of the Old Testament that has been subjected to form criticism, with the German scholar H. Gunkel and the Norwegian scholar S. Mowinckel tracing different genres of Psalm back to their context in liturgical temple worship, a context that included, for Psalms 47, 93 and 97, a supposed annual New Year Festival of the enthronement of Yahweh (a hypothesis strongly criticised by Claus Westermann). This work nicely illustrates the way in which biblical criticism can operate in a positive way by raising the status of certain parts of the bible. According to Clements (1983, p 118):

[The Psalms] were looked upon simply as reflecting the undercurrent of personal piety and hope which flourished when the main creative impulses of Israel's religion had ebbed away. As a result of the work of Gunkel and Mowinckel, however, the Psalms were elevated to a new position of priority as a witness to the groundwork of cult and piety which underlie the formation of the historical books as well as the phenomenon of prophecy in Israel.

Hermann Gunkel also did much pioneering work on the *Prophetic Books*, recognising the rhythmic prophetic oracle as the basic (oral) unit of prophecy. Although a great deal of research relevant to these books has focused on the phenomenon of prophecy and the nature of the prophetic experience itself, the analysis of the relationship between the prophetic tradition and the Israelite cult has been of more significance. Prophecy and cultus were once thought to be diametrically opposed and unrelated dimensions of Hebrew religion. Although many of the prophets criticised the cult, it is now clear that this was no 'radical Protestant' overturning of cultic practice as such. Israelite religion was more of a piece than many had suspected.

Other work on the oral and written sources, editorial structure and presuppositions underlying the books of the great 'writing prophets' (such as Isaiah and Jeremiah) has revealed the long and complicated processes that have given rise to these books, as well as underscoring the difficulty of reconstructing the meaning (or perhaps meanings?) of their prophecies in their original contexts. This has made Christian commentators more chary of simplistic accounts of the prophets as predictors of the mission of Jesus, rather than as inspired revealers of God's demands for their own time.

The discovery of Egyptian parallels to the Book of Proverbs and the form critical and traditio-historical analysis of other types of *Wisdom Literature* has considerably advanced the study of this part of the Old Testament (as in the work of J.H. Breasted and J. Fichtner). A positive account of the *religious* dimension of Israelite wisdom, which is often castigated as essentially 'secular' (see Ecclesiastes), has been given by Gerhard von Rad. The Book of Job is now acknowledged to be composed of a separate poem about a puzzled Job who challenges God, which has been built into an earlier prose story of the saintly 'patient' Job. It is often cited as particularly relevant to present day religious concerns.

History and theology

A convincing historical framework of the life and times of Israel is essential background to an analysis of all the biblical books. The study of *Old Testament history* as such was taken forward significantly by Albrecht Alt and his pupil Martin Noth. Noth's work on the political structure of early Israel, in terms of a union of independent tribes united by common worship at a central shrine (modelled on the ancient Greek 'amphictyonies'), has been very influential but (inevitably!) also criticised.

Much Old Testament study involves a 'scientific', scholarly, reconstruction of cultural background and historical events. Nevertheless, the last hundred years of Old Testament study has also produced works of *Old Testament theology*. Descriptive accounts of the variety of Israelite beliefs may not properly count as 'theology', but this term surely does apply to the work of a scholar like Walter Eichrodt (Eichrodt, 1961, 1967), who reacted against mere 'historicist' concerns with factual history alone, and offered a more unified treatment around the concept of covenant. Von Rad is famous for producing a rich account of the theology of the historical traditions of the Old Testament, yet many believe that his work still remains at the level of 'historical theology' (von Rad, 1962, 1965; Gunneweg, 1978, pp 82-92; Morgan with Barton, 1988, pp 98-104).

There is nowadays more concern to move beyond 'the mesmeric power' that history has exercised over biblical scholars, towards more directly theological concerns. The tension between the history and theology of the Old Testament has been expressed by R.E. Clements (1983, p 178) along the following lines. We shall return to these concerns later.

> It is evident that the progress and achievements of Old Testament criticism have not always produced the kind of results that theologians would regard as most desirable.... The historical conclusions reached by this enquiry have seldom been able to solve theological questions.... On the other side it is . . . unsatisfactory to try to find in the Old Testament a body of timeless doctrines which can be easily and smoothly set apart from the connection with particular people, events and institutions.

A3 History of New Testament study

For many Christians, the real 'problems of biblical criticism' arise with its application to the New Testament. The traditional pictures of the New Testament and its authors, and particularly of the historical Jesus, were soon undermined with the application of new critical methods used without dogmatic presuppositions. Eighteenth century German scholars such as Michaelis, Lessing and Schleiermacher paved the way for the influential work of F.C. Baur (1792-1860) and the Tübingen School. They also led to David Strauss' monumental and extreme *Life of Jesus Critically Examined* (1835-6), which declared the Gospels to be without historical foundations (cf. Kümmel, 1973, part 4). In Britain our biblical critics were less outrageous. More orthodox biblical scholars such as J.B. Lightfoot, B.F. Westcott (both later Bishops of

Durham) and F.J.A. Hort ploughed the furrow of New Testament criticism here in the latter half of the nineteenth century, at a time when Christian orthodoxy was also struggling to come to terms with the new insights of Darwinism (Neill and Wright, 1988, chapters 1 and 2; Chadwick, 1970, chapters 1 and 2).

As with the Old Testament, archaeological discoveries, even of the Dead Sea Scrolls of the Qumran community and the apocryphal 'Gospel of Thomas' (which contains early, independent sayings of Jesus), have not been as significant as new methods of study applied to the text itself, and new insights into the Jewish and Hellenistic (Greek) background to its history. The contribution of Jewish scholars and secular historians has been important, prompting many New Testament scholars to recognise both the extent to which both Paul and Jesus himself were products of the essential genius of Judaism (itself very varied), and that Jewish and Hellenistic thought and authors were neither as different nor as separate as many had believed[9]. Most recently, the sociological and political context of the New Testament material has been more fully recognised (Borg, 1994, chapter 5), with painstaking reconstructions of the 'social world' of the early Christian communities and of the ways their beliefs functioned within them[10]. One danger in this approach, however, is that of constructing out of the text itself a picture of the society for which a text was created, and then interpreting the text in the light of that society. Such circular argumentation is an ever-present temptation in biblical studies, as we shall see.

Synoptic gospels

In New Testament studies, as in the analysis of the Old Testament, *textual criticism*[11] has made careful, mostly unspectacular progress. While patient scholarship is continually improving the translation of the Greek text, reconstruction of the original Aramaic traditions of the words of Jesus himself has been particularly illuminating (Neill and Wright, 1988, chapters 3 and 5). Study of the Synoptic Gospels (Matthew, Mark and Luke) took a leap forward with the advent of a *source critical analysis*, whose 'fundamental solution' was enshrined in B.H. Streeter's *The Four Gospels: a study in origins* (1924). His four document hypothesis recognised Mark as the earliest Gospel (against the

[9] See C.H. Dodd, *The Bible and the Greeks* (1935); W.D. Davies, *Paul and Rabbinic Judaism* (1949) and *The Setting of the Sermon on the Mount* (1964); D. Daube, *The New Testament and Rabbinic Judaism* (1956); J. Daniélou, *The Theology of Jewish Christianity* (in French 1958); J. Barr, *The Semantics of Biblical Language* (1961); G. Vermes, *Jesus the Jew* (1973); E.P. Sanders, *Paul and Palestinian Judaism* (1977) and *Jesus and Judaism* (1985).

[10] For example, G. Theissen, *Sociology of Early Palestinian Christianity* (1978); W.A. Meeks, *The First Urban Christians: the social world of the Apostle Paul* (1983); R. Horsley and J.S. Hanson, *Sociology and the Jesus Movement* (1989).

[11] For further details of the different types of biblical criticism, see section A4 below.

church's tradition that placed Matthew earliest), and argued that it was independently drawn on by both Luke and Matthew. These two evangelists also utilised a common source of sayings (now otherwise lost) labelled 'Q', in addition to documents containing some at least of the material peculiar to their own books (Matthew's 'M' material and Luke's 'L' material). (Streeter thought that L and Q were first combined into 'Proto-Luke' by that Evangelist, who later added his infancy narratives and passages from Mark.)

Form criticism exploded onto the world of New Testament studies with the work of K. L. Schmidt, Martin Dibelius (*From Tradition to Gospel*, German second edition 1934) and Rudolf Bultmann (*The History of the Synoptic Tradition*, first German edition 1921). The forms of the oral units ('pronouncement-stories', 'miracle-stories', etc.) were declared to be largely determined by their use in the preaching, instruction, controversy and apologetic of the early Christian church. The older, easy assumption of eye-witness historical reliability behind the gospel accounts was replaced by a *functional* account of how such stories served the purposes of the first Christians, and became smoothed and polished by such oral use - rather like pebbles in a fast flowing stream - before they were written down. The *Sitz im Leben* ('setting in life') of the stories was now seen primarily as the life of the church - a church that selected the material, as relevant to its own needs, and shaped each story. These stories, we should note, may or may not go back to the time of the historical Jesus; some could have been entirely creations of the church. Form criticism was usually less interested in 'what really happened' than in the religious faith of the church expressed in these traditions.

The later development of *redaction criticism* encouraged scholars to concentrate more on how the oral and written sources were adapted to fulfil the theological and evangelistic purposes of the gospel writers themselves, often by being given a literary setting and final form - and therefore another meaning and function - that was different both from that of the tradition and from whatever its historical origin might have been. Much recent work in New Testament studies has involved careful analysis of the theological presuppositions lying behind the editorial ('redaction') work of those responsible for the final form of the synoptic gospels (cf. Rohde, 1968). William Wrede's account of Mark's invention of a 'Messianic Secret' (that Jesus strove to keep his messianic identity a secret) has been very influential since its first publication in German in 1901. Wrede argued that this hypothesis was Mark's attempt to reconcile his own Christological views with the absence of Messianic material in the tradition, the real explanation of which was that Jesus had not thought of himself as Messiah. This theory has been given a historical basis by some scholars, but it has also been much criticised by others. Since Wrede's time, Mark's theology has been extensively studied, recently in substantial works by Ernest Best and H. Räisänen.

Studies of the gospels of Matthew (e.g. by Kilpatrick, Stendahl, Bornkamm, Barth and Held) and Luke (especially by Conzelmann and Haenchen) have presented detailed pictures of the theology of these books. Controversies over the historical trustworthiness of Luke's second volume, the Book of Acts, have continued (it is difficult to reconcile with Paul's own account of his work). At the same time there has been a developing recognition of the theological character of the text. Work on Acts is particularly associated with the names of Dibelius, Haenchen and Conzelmann.

Questing for Jesus

The title of the English translation of Albert Schweitzer's (1875-1965) classic *The Quest of the Historical Jesus* (published in German in 1906) captures in a phrase the New Testament scholar's search to recover some sort of picture of the life, ministry and teaching of Jesus, by burrowing behind the obscuring-but-revealing veils of written documents and hypothetical written and oral traditions. In his survey Schweitzer rejected many 'liberal' reconstructions of Jesus, such as the portrait of the moral preacher of the 'Fatherhood of God and the Brotherhood of Man' painted by the Liberal Protestant Adolf Harnack. In their place Schweitzer substituted his own (equally partial) picture of a tragic figure driven by 'apocalyptic' beliefs about the end of the world[12].

The work of Rudolf Bultmann (1884-1976) strengthened the attitude of historical scepticism among many scholars. For Bultmann, what was important was the church's proclamation about Christ - the *kerygma* - and the existential challenge this confronts us with today, rather than any 'mere history'. Bultmann's influence was felt for a considerable time. Eventually, however, a 'New Quest' of the historical Jesus brought the pendulum back from this extreme swing. This movement acknowledged that a continuity could be traced between the Christ of the kerygma and the Jesus of history, and showed more confidence in filling out the gaps left in earlier accounts (Morgan with Barton, 1988, pp 104-124). It insisted that the assumption of the earlier form critics that the early church was not at all interested in historical truth was too extreme. The New Quest was associated with names such as E. Käsemann, E. Fuchs, G. Ebeling, G. Bornkamm and J. Jeremias. A subsequent 'Third Quest' (by M. Borg, E.P. Sanders, B. Meyer, A.E. Harvey, etc.) is even more sympathetic to the possibility of historical (and political) realism about the facts of Jesus (see Neill and Wright, 1988, pp 379-403; Riches, 1993, chapter 6),

---

[12] See A. Harnack, *What is Christianity?* (ET 1958). Others before Schweitzer had argued for the centrality of the eschatological themes of divine judgement and the end of history, e.g. J. Weiss, *Jesus' Proclamation of the Kingdom of God* (German, 1892) and G. Tyrrell, *Christianity at the Crossroads* (1909). Today many New Testament scholars are highly sceptical of any reading of Jesus as an eschatological figure - see Borg, 1994, chapters 3 and 4. Jesus is now often presented more as a teacher of subversive wisdom and a social prophet.

although the majority of present day Jesus scholars seem to accept only a small part of the recorded *teaching* of Jesus as his authentic words (see Borg, 1994, chapter 8).

John Riches (1993, pp 121-122) has summarised the current state of the debate in a useful way by distinguishing between three areas. First, he lists a number of points of *scholarly agreement about the figure of Jesus*, including the fact that he associated with tax collectors and sinners and that this caused offence to some of the Jewish devout. Second, he identifies 'fruitful areas' of *debate and disagreement*, which include:

> The extent to which Jesus did or did not advocate views that were essentially at odds with the Law, either in the sense that they proposed alternative courses of action which were acceptable or unacceptable to God, or indeed that they specifically challenged established interpretations of the Law.

Third, he notes *more detailed points of contention*, including questions like:

> Did Jesus expect an imminent end to the present age? To what extent would the new age be continuous with the old? How far would Jesus and his followers be responsible for 'bringing it in'?

Morgan with Barton (1988, pp 121-124) make an interesting point relevant to such 'questing'. They argue that Christology[13] 'does not depend on reconstructing the history of Jesus', rather 'Christology expresses God's concern with the world today by pointing to Jesus of Nazareth'. The New Testament helps us to recognise that 'concern' in Jesus. That is all we need; we do not need detailed reconstructions of Jesus' life:

> To abandon the historical quest would be to break with something that has always been important for Christianity. This 'something' is not the so-called 'historical Jesus', i.e. modern historians' critical reconstructions of Jesus, but the largely inaccessible earthly historical reality of Jesus himself.

You might reflect whether this idea of historicity is sufficient for Christian faith.

John and Paul

Progress in understanding the 'Fourth Gospel' (the gospel according to John) waited until the recognition of its distinctiveness from, and independence of, the synoptics. John is more obviously a theological treatment than the other gospels[14], and has its own anti-gnostic[15] and anti-Jewish apologetic axe to

---

[13] Christology is the doctrine of the person, nature and significance of Christ.

[14] But note that redaction critics stress the extent to which the synoptic Evangelists were also theologians.

[15] The gnostic movement of the second century of the Christian era was anticipated by earlier, less developed systems of religious beliefs that incorporated a secret knowledge (*gnosis*) that could deliver salvation by allowing the spiritual part of human beings to escape from the prison of the body and the world. Unlike mainstream Judaism and early Christianity, it disparaged history and the earthly life.

grind. Bultmann's major commentary on John (in German, 1941), discerned different sources for the gospel, including actual gnostic ones. Later scholarship, including the work of the English scholars C.H. Dodd, C.K. Barrett and J.A.T. Robinson, has focused more positively on a range of issues such as the (independent) historical tradition behind the gospel, the gospel's relationship to the synoptics, its origins in the tension between Christianity and Judaism, and its date. Nevertheless, few scholars today regard the sayings of Jesus contained in this gospel as authentic.

Bultmann was also very influential through his Lutheran and existentialist study of Paul, worked out especially in the first volume of his *Theology of the New Testament* (in German, 1948). More recent work, by E. P. Sanders and others, has attempted to rescue Paul from those who would read his theology *solely* through the eyes and theological concerns of Luther (see Neill and Wright, 1988, pp 403-430; Riches, 1993, chapter 7). The recognition of the Jewish context of and influence on Paul's theology has already been noted. The older picture of Pauline thought as a complete overturning of the concepts and values of Judaism has thus been tempered by a careful, scholarly revealing of this situation of continuity-with-discontinuity.

A4 Tools of biblical criticism

Many of the main approaches to the critical study of the bible have already been noted. I offer here a summary, with some additional material, of some of these, together with a couple of illustrative activities.

Textual criticism (sometimes called 'lower criticism')

This is a foundational discipline. It attempts to reconstruct the original wording of the biblical text by comparing existing manuscript readings (there are over five thousand extant manuscripts containing parts of the New Testament) so as to develop a 'critical text', with variant readings listed in a 'critical apparatus'. Most variations are likely to be caused by accidental omissions and other mistakes in copying by scribes, but some are most plausibly explained as deliberate alterations to clarify or 'correct' the text. Few are of major historical or theological significance. Manuscripts are evaluated by both 'external criteria' ('families' of manuscripts are assessed genealogically) and 'internal criteria' (such as 'prefer the more difficult reading' and 'prefer the shorter reading').

We may note in this context not only the existence of a vast technical literature on *translating the biblical text*, but also such rich studies as G. B. Caird's *The Language and Imagery of the Bible* (1980), which provides much detailed and subtle analysis of the variety of *forms of scriptural language* (including the language of myth, metaphor and anthropomorphism).

Source criticism (sometimes called 'literary criticism')

This seeks to uncover written sources (documents) behind the books, or in some cases collections of books, in the bible. Theories about the composite nature of the Pentateuch were described in section A2. In the last section we saw how the first three gospels have been particularly subject to this sort of study. Source criticism also identifies later additions to an original text, or non-authorial insertions, often by differences in vocabulary, style or theology (see John 21; 2 Corinthians 6.14 to 7.1; and the ending(s) to Mark's gospel).

With regard to the synoptics, the main point to be made is that the *resemblances* among the synoptic gospels, which are especially clear in the original Greek, are too close to be explained on any other theory than that of interdependence amounting to copying from each other, or from common sources that are no longer extant. The *differences* between the gospels are also most plausibly explained by this hypothesis.

The priority of Mark has been criticised, however, as most of the data that suggests that Matthew and Luke have copied from Mark could also be adduced to support the view that the gospel was *created* from Matthew and Luke, partly by omitting the material they have in common[16]. But there are other factors to take into account. In a much-quoted comment one scholar writes, 'Given Mark, it is easy to see why Matthew was written; given Matthew, it is hard to see why Mark was needed' (Styler, 1966[2], p 231; cf Styler, 1982[3]). The existence of 'Q' *as a separate document* is now routinely challenged, although 'Q material' is apparently readily identifiable.

Activity A3

Note the close similarity between these texts in the synoptic gospels. To begin with here are two examples of Matthew and Luke copying from Mark, with some variation.

- Mark 4.30-32 // Matthew 13.31-32 // Luke 13.18-20
- Mark 11:27-33 // Matthew 21.23-27 // Luke 20.1-18

---

[16] Cf. W.R. Farmer, *The Synoptic Problem* (1964); H. Palmer, *The Logic of Gospel Criticism* (1968).

Second, here are two examples where Matthew and Luke apparently draw on a common 'Q' source, with some variation.

- Matthew 3.7-10 // Luke 4.1-3
- Matthew 7.3-5 // Luke 6.41-42

Now try to identify some material in Luke and Matthew that is *not* common to them both, i.e. the so-called 'L' and 'M' material.

Comment on activity A3

While noting similarities, you will also have noticed differences. If both Matthew and Luke have copied from Mark, why are all three versions not identical? Most scholars regard the changes as attempts to 'improve' Mark's version in different ways (see below). In the Q material, Matthew has Jesus criticising the Jewish leaders, whereas in Luke the words of Jesus are directed to the crowds.

You probably noted that the material at the beginning of the gospels of Luke and Matthew is different, as is much of their Passion narratives. Notice also the distinctive L material in Luke chapters 15 and 16; and the M material in Matthew 18.23-35, 20.1-32 and 25.1-13, 31-46.

Form criticism (German, *Formgeschichte*)

Form Criticism traces the 'tradition' (literally, 'that which is handed on') back behind the text, its authors and written sources, to a history of oral transmission. This has been described as 'the living traditions of common people, traditions of shared experience and belief as varied as life itself' (Soulen, 1977, p 62; see also Neill and Wright, 1988, chapter 7). The oral forms or 'literary types' recognised by Form Criticism are indeed very varied, but even so the method has been challenged for over-simplifying matters both in this area and in its account of their setting or life situation (*Sitz im Leben*).

Used on its own, form criticism underestimates the contribution of the biblical authors. There is also a danger that it may 'reconstruct the life-setting from the form and then . . . explain the form by appeal to its life-setting', thus arguing in a circle (Muddiman, in Coggins and Houlden, 1990, p 241). Some form critics have been unnecessarily sceptical about the reliability of the oral tradition and the possibility of checks on it through deliberate memorisation and eye-witness testimony. Many extravagant claims for this method of study have been made, particularly in its application to the New Testament (where the time available for oral transmission is very short).

Redaction criticism

Form criticism tends to adopt a fragmentary approach to the gospels, focusing on the individual, self-contained units of tradition that eventually crystallised in written form as *pericopes*. Redaction criticism is a more holistic investigation of the final stage of the tradition. It involves studying the ways in which this oral material (together with any written sources) is utilised by the final 'redactor' (editor), who selects, rewrites and re-unites the material and provides it with a redactional framework. (It is clearly more difficult to engage in such a study where an author is drawing on a hypothetical, extinct document such as 'Q'.)

In this critical perspective the biblical editors are truly authors in their own right, with their own theological concerns and emphases. They are no longer seen merely as scissors-and-paste hacks. Redaction criticism of the synoptic gospels asks such questions as (Soulen, 1977, p 143; cf. Tuckett, in Coggins and Houlden, 1990, pp 580-581):

- Why does Luke alter the Markan tradition concerning John the Baptist as Elijah? (Cf. Mark 6.15-16 with Luke 9.7-9; Mark 6.17-29 and 9.9-13 are absent from Luke.)
- Why does he have Satan present at the beginning and end of Jesus' ministry and not during it? (Luke 4.1-13; 22.3, but cf. Mark 8.31-33 with Luke 9.21-22.)
- Why does he restrict the appearances of the risen Lord to Jerusalem and its environs? (Cf. Mark 16.7 with Luke 24.6-7, 46-49; Acts 1.4.)

Activity A4

Look up the appropriate texts to try and answer Soulen's questions in the examples above, both from your own resources and by referring to some modern commentaries.

Comment on activity A4

The following points have been made by some redaction critics of Luke.

- Luke portrays Jesus himself as a prophet like Elijah (see 1 Kings chapters 17 to 19; 2 Kings chapters 1 to 2), raising a child from death (7.11-17) and ascending into heaven (Acts 1.9).
- Luke sees Jesus' ministry as a very special time of divine salvation, protected from the ravages of the Evil One (unlike the history of Israel and of the early church).

- Jerusalem has a special place in Luke's theology of Jesus (see 2.22-52, 24.13-53) and of the church (most of the first half of Acts is the story of the Jerusalem church; the Christian Way is traced as it moves triumphantly from Jerusalem to Rome).

Rhetorical criticism and narrative criticism

The energy and output of biblical scholars has been impressive. In particular, no books have ever been studied so minutely as the slim volumes that represent the library of the New Testament. Some may say, however, that they have been 'over-researched'. We may perhaps criticise the critics for picturing the Evangelists and other early Christians too much in their own image: 'in the guise of Oxford scholars, poring over their sources, meticulously piecing together the evidence... and taking care to record all available material and to lose no scrap of evidence' (Hooker, 1975, p 29). This scenario is profoundly anachronistic, to say the least. Other ways of studying the bible have amended this picture, including rhetorical criticism and narrative criticism.

The bible is a religious, theological and (partly) historical text. But it is always also a *text*, a piece of literature. Recently scholars have drawn on insights from literary criticism to understand these texts further. Rhetorical criticism attempts to exhibit the structural patterns used in the composition of the literary units in the bible, by concentrating on the individual text and its rhetorical 'occasion', structure and effects, as in the work of H.-D. Betz and G.A. Kennedy. This is a form of scholarship that fades into other species of 'literary criticism' - the older term being confusingly reapplied here - that are sometimes influenced by structuralism (briefly) and by the philosophy of language. For some literary critics of the bible, the author's original intention and meaning is less relevant than the meaning given in the text in its relation to other texts, or the meanings created by the *reader* in responding to and construing the text. Others continue to test biblical interpretations against the author's presumed intentions.

Narrative criticism is the term used to label the study of a biblical narrative as a whole text interacting with its reader/hearer. The author as narrator is seen as structuring his tale to produce an effect that is much more than just the communication of theological ideas. This has resulted in some very illuminating recent work on both Old and New Testaments (cf. Alter and Kermode, 1987). In the past the literary skills of the authors of the biblical books have been largely ignored in the interests of defending or attacking the historicity of their work. Current biblical scholarship is redressing the balance.

A5 Theology, religion and the bible

Bultmann was both a first-rank New Testament scholar and a modern critical and constructive theologian concerned to find and communicate the heart of the Christian gospel. This latter task led him to argue for a programme of *demythologising* the pre-scientific 'mythological' language of the New Testament, especially its talk of heaven and hell, angels and devils, the pre-existence of Christ, miracles and cosmic acts of incarnation and salvation[17]. This treats such myths as challenges to make an existential decision in favour of an 'authentic' existence through faith, involving our 'turning our backs on self and abandoning all security' (Bultmann, 1964, p 19). Bultmann's position draws on existentialism and Heidegger, and influenced by Luther. Many argue that it is a theology that is brought to the New Testament, rather than derived from it.

Bultmann pioneered a distinction between mere history (*historie* in German) and significant event (*geschichte*). The death of Christ is mere history, and therefore of no religious value, unless and until its meaning is realised, as we awaken to it as it is addressed to us in the preaching (*kerygma*) of the church. 'The meaning in history', Bultmann (1957, p 155) wrote, 'lies always in the present'. For Bultmann, the resurrection of Christ was not an historical (*historisch*) event at all. Rather, Christ 'comes alive' in the church's preaching of Christ. We 'believe in the resurrection' by accepting this word as directed to ourselves. Bultmann (1964, p 42) wrote:

> The real Easter faith is faith in the word of preaching which brings illumination. If the event of Easter Day is in any sense an historical event additional to the event of the cross, it is nothing else than the rise of faith in the risen Lord, since it was this faith which led to the apostolic preaching. The resurrection itself is not an event of past history.

In short, the resurrection is but the Easter faith of the disciples, which itself is a way of preaching the salvific significance of the cross.

Activity A5

Reflect on Bultman's views and then consider the following questions.

- How do you respond to Bultmann's position?
- What are its implications for the relationship between history and faith?
- What do *you* think about the nature of that relationship?

---

[17] A 'myth' is technically a story about the actions of God or the gods that represents these events as if they were observable on the human stage (e.g. God walks in the Garden of Eden in the cool of the day, or shuts the door of the Ark). They are story-metaphors, 'moving pictures of the sacred' (Smart, 1973, p 79). Although in common parlance the word 'myth' is used to imply an untruth, theologians use it to label a story which when literally understood (and, perhaps, historically understood) is 'untrue', but which expresses a 'deeper' theological truth about God's relationship to the world.

Comment on activity A5

Some people find Bultmann invigorating. He seems to offer an account of faith that is highly personal and contemporary, but which releases us from worrying about the problems of miracle, myth or history. But others are disturbed by his cavalier approach to 'what actually happened'.

Bultmann offers us radical theology with a vengeance! Most Christian theologians and New Testament scholars prefer to build their theological interpretations on the back of historical events. New Testament scholars who follow a Bultmannian line are nowadays rather few and far between. Besides, 'to be blunt, Bultmann's way, with its philosophical basis, is a way for intellectuals, and is far more difficult to understand than the New Testament' (Leaney, in Davidson and Leaney, 1970, p 339).

The two tasks

Nevertheless, at least Bultmann showed a willingness to hold together the two tasks of biblical exegesis (discovering the original meaning of the texts) and theology (expressing the Christian faith in modern terms), by doing 'theology through scriptural interpretation' (Morgan with Barton, 1988, p 111). Others have instead worked hard to keep them separate, perhaps partly in response to Bultmann's own enterprise. Most recently, however, scholars have begun to bring the two activities back together again. This is in part the hermeneutical task that Gadamer described as a 'fusion of horizons' between text and interpreter (see above, section A1 'Whose meaning?').

Patently, two very different exercises face the informed reader of the bible. The *historical-critical* task has been described as seeking 'to give an - objective - account of developments in religious faith and practice' in the bible traditions, an account that 'is guided and tested by analogy with human experience' and is 'prepared to argue its case in the humanistic circles of modern academia'. The other, *theological-interpretative* task is very different: 'it seeks to read the texts in such a way that they may address the reader's deepest concerns', so that she hears the Word of God speaking through them in judgement and redemption (Riches, 1993, p 198). This broad distinction is elsewhere classified (e.g. by Krister Stendahl, who is one of those who argued that the two should be kept separate) as a distinction between what the text *meant* and *what it means*, or between *historical descriptive theology* and *(modern) confessional theology*. It is the distinction between secular, critical scholarship and committed religious faith, with which we began this unit.

Biblical commentators today are taking more interest in the theological value and status of the biblical texts and are less purely historicist. The path trodden by Bultmann in this direction may now be regarded as a cul-de-sac, but there are other tracks of theological appraisal that have shown more promise. Brevard Childs' distinctive commentary on Exodus is unashamedly intended 'to interpret the book . . . as canonical scripture within the theological discipline of the Christian church'. He is (perhaps unnecessarily) critical of historical scholarship, and argues for a more theological reading of scripture. The usual textual and contextual commentary, concentrating on the final form of the text, is thus followed in his book by sections on the New Testament's treatment of the passage, the later history of its exegesis and Childs' own Christian theological reflections. Child (1974, p xiii) writes that he:

> does not share the hermeneutical position of those who suggest that biblical exegesis is an objective, descriptive enterprise, controlled solely by scientific criticism, to which the Christian theologian can at best add a few homiletical reflections for piety's sake. In my judgement, the rigid separation between the descriptive and constructive elements of exegesis strikes at the roots of the theological task of understanding the bible.

Childs and others (e.g. J. A. Sanders) are sometimes said to be engaged in *canonical criticism*, in the sense of taking seriously the bible in its present ('canonical') form, rather than chasing it back through its written or oral sources. One advantage of such an approach is that this is the form in which scripture is read and used by most Christians.

The problem of biblical interpretation is the subject of Robert Morgan and John Barton's book of that name (Morgan with Barton, 1988). Morgan writes of 'the value of an independent historical research', but adds that this 'does not preclude a different style of interpretation in which historical and theological interests are fused' (p 179). In a powerful metaphor, he likens a biblical text to an electric wire. The 'text has no life of its own'; its power comes from its human author, but it only comes 'alive' when it contacts a human reader (sometimes giving 'a nasty shock', p 269). He calls for a *literary reading of the text* to supplement its historical study, on the grounds that it is literary study that can provide the necessary creative stimulus for the church's contemporary theological thinking.

This distinction between a purely historical, secular scholarship and theological reflection is clearly important. These are two very different tasks performed by two different communities. But they are tasks that must somehow be connected. In order to do this, it is claimed, believers must approach the work of historical criticism with a theory of religion that is open to the existence and power of the transcendent (Morgan with Barton, 1988, pp 184-185; cf. 174, 281). The interpreter's own religious interests (and those of the readers of scripture) must in this way be taken very seriously. The bible is then read both *for itself*, with an openness to all the historical and critical problems that it raises, and *for a religious purpose*, with an openness to its being taken seriously as a religious text that 'speaks to us'. But is this still a 'neutral approach' to biblical criticism (see section A1)?

On this view, theological interpretation must approach the bible with a religious aim. Others prefer to keep a distinction between a religious use of scripture, bearing directly on 'the religious life of the user of scripture', and a theological use, bearing directly on a theological analysis of this understanding of self and world (Kelsey, 1968). The religious impact of scripture is of course primary for theology, but unless it continues into the testing provided by *critical theological* reflection, many scholars see real dangers in that influence (Barr, 1973, pp 100-102). After all, fundamentalism is a clear example of a religious interpretation that badly needs the sensible correctives provided by a critical theology.

Biblical theology and biblical diversity

'Biblical theology' is a phrase that has shifted in meaning from 'theology that accords with the bible' to 'the theology [rather, theologies] contained in the bible' (Morgan, in Coggins and Houlden, 1990, p 87; see also Morgan, 1973, part 1). Karl Barth argued that biblical scholarship did not sufficiently engage with the theological content of the bible - the living God confronting those who hear. Barth's influence has been profound, and for some time it extended to a 'biblical theology' that rejected philosophical and contemporary interpretation in favour of a straightforward repetition of biblical categories and (overused) concepts such as 'the God who acts' and 'salvation history'. Some critics of the whole idea of biblical theology point out that the biblical 'revelation as such is not theological and faith as such is not belief in theological propositions' (Ebeling, 1960, p 63). 'Theological interpretation of the bible' is often the preferred phrase today, 'biblical theology' being open to the criticism of giving the impression of digging theological information out of texts. Interpretation requires a more personal metaphor: Barton and Morgan suggest 'spinning wool'.

A further significant issue for theology, which is fatal to the idea of a unified biblical theology, is the scholar's recognition of the *diversity* of religious expressions in both Old and New Testaments. This is perhaps not surprising in the Old Testament, which was written over a period of nearly a millennium and incorporates a vast range of genres (legal material, historical narrative, prophetic oracles, hymnody, legends, proverbial and speculative wisdom, etc.). But the New Testament is a much shorter work, with much less diversity of form, and was written over a period of perhaps less than fifty years. Yet even there Dunn (1977, pp 373-374) notes that:

> When we ask about the Christianity of the New Testament we are not asking about any one entity; rather we encounter different types of Christianity, each of which viewed the others as too extreme in one respect or another . . . [and] each 'type' of Christianity was itself not monochrome and homogeneous, rather more like a spectrum.

There might be an identifiable unity discernible among this variety, Dunn admits, 'but orthodoxy, whether in concept or actuality, no' (p 374). This raises problems for the sort of biblical theology that insists on reading the bible 'as a whole'. The diversity and disagreement found within the bible may be 'a more sure characteristic of its nature' (Barr, 1973, pp 6, 181).

In her devotional and theological use of scripture, the reader must strive to produce a single coherent, unified viewpoint. But this is inevitably the *reader's own* unity, rather than that of the bible. In the end, we cannot slough off our responsibility to think for ourselves in religion and theology. Scripture cannot provide us with a single, consistent, ready-made framework of beliefs. It can only offer us a diversity of materials from which we can construct our *own* house of meaning. This is a very important principle to bear in mind when we come to attempt any educational use of the bible.

Reading

Three books that offer an overview of developments in biblical criticism are R.E. Clements (1983), *A Century of Old Testament Study*, Cambridge, Lutterworth; S. Neill and T. Wright (1988), *The Interpretation of the New Testament 1861-1986*, Oxford, Oxford University Press; and J.K. Riches (1993), *A Century of New Testament Study*, Cambridge, Lutterworth. These all give a detailed account of the periods they cover, with some reflective comments.

More authorial reflection is provided by the very good general text by R. Morgan with J. Barton (1988), *Biblical Interpretation*, Oxford, Oxford University Press. A valuable work of reference is R.J. Coggins and J.L. Houlden (eds) (1990), *A Dictionary of Biblical Interpretation*, London, SCM.

Bibliography

Alter, R. and Kermode, F. (eds) (1987), *The Literary Guide to the Bible*, London, Collins.

Barr, J. (1973), *The Bible in the Modern World*, London, SCM.

Barr, J. (1977, 1981[2]), *Fundamentalism*, London, SCM.

Barth, K. (1957), *The Word of God and the Word of Man* (ET by D. Horton), London, Hodder and Stoughton.

Borg, M.J. (1994), *Jesus in Contemporary Scholarship*, Valley Forge, Pennsylvania, Trinity Press International.

Bultmann, R. (1957), *History and Eschatology*, Edinburgh, Edinburgh University Press.

Bultmann, R. (1964), New Testament and mythology, in H.W. Bartsch (ed.), *Kerygma and Myth: a theological debate*, volume 1, (ET by R.H. Fuller), London, SPCK, pp 1-44.

Caird, G.B. (1980), *The Language and Imagery of the Bible*, London, Duckworth.

Chadwick, O. (1970), *The Victorian Church*, volume 2, London, A. and C. Black.

Childs, B.S. (1974), *Exodus: a commentary*, London, SCM.

Clements, R.E. (1983), *A Century of Old Testament Study*, Cambridge, Lutterworth.

Coggins, R.J. and Houlden, J.L. (eds) (1990), *A Dictionary of Biblical Interpretation*, London, SCM.

Cragg, K. (1981), According to the scriptures, in M. Wadsworth (ed.), *Ways of Reading the Bible*, Brighton, Harvester. pp 23-36.

Cully, I.V. (1995), *The Bible in Christian Education*, Minneapolis, Minnesota, Fortress.

Davidson, R. and Leaney, A.R.C. (1970), *Biblical Criticism*, Harmondsworth, Penguin.

Davies, W.D. (1949), *Paul and Rabbinic Judaism*, London, SPCK.

Dewey, J. (1903), Religious education as conditioned by modern psychology and pedagogy, reprinted in *Religious Education*, 69, 1974, pp 5-11.

Dunn, J.D.G. (1977), *Unity and Diversity in the New Testament: an inquiry into the character of earliest Christianity*, London, SCM.

Ebeling, G. (1960), The meaning of 'biblical theology', in L. Hodgson *et al.*, *On the Authority of the Bible*, London, SPCK, pp 49-67.

Eichrodt, W. (1961, 1967), *Theology of the Old Testament*, 2 volumes (ET by J.A. Baker), London, SCM.

Evans, C. (1971), *Is 'Holy Scripture' Christian? and other questions*, London, SCM.

Farley, E. and Hodgson, P.C. (1983), Scripture and tradition, in P.C. Hodgson and R.H. King (eds), *Christian Theology: an introduction to its traditions and tasks*, London, SPCK, pp 35-61.

Furnish, D.J. (1975), *Exploring the Bible with Children*, Nashville, Abingdon.

Gadamer, H.-G., (1982), *Truth and Method* (ET by G. Barden and J. Cumming), New York, Crossroad,

Gunneweg, A.H.J. (1978), *Understanding the Old Testament* (ET by J. Bowden), London, SCM.

Hanson, R.P.C. (1983), Tradition, in A. Richardson and J. Bowden (eds), *A New Dictionary of Christian Theology*, London, SCM, pp 574-576.

Hooker, M. (1975), In his own image?, in M. Hooker and C. Hickling (eds), *What about the New Testament?* London, SCM, pp 28-44.

Hooker, M. and C. Hickling, (eds) (1975), *What about the New Testament?* London, SCM.

Hull, J. (1992), The bible in the secular classroom: an approach through the experience of loss, in J. Astley and D. Day (eds), *The Contours of Christian Education*, Great Wakering, McCrimmons, pp 197-215.

Kelsey, D. (1968), Appeals to scripture in theology, *Journal of Religion*, 48, 1-21.

Kelsey, D.H. (ed.) (1975), *The Uses of Scripture in Recent Theology*, London, SCM.

Kümmel, W.G. (1973), *The New Testament: the history of the investigation of its problems* (ET by S.M. Gilmour and H.C. Kee), London, SCM.

Lampe, G.W.H. (1963), The bible since the rise of critical study, in D.E. Nineham, (ed.), *The Church's Use of the Bible: past and present*, London, SPCK, pp 125-144.

Morgan, R. (1973), *The Nature of New Testament Theology*, London, SCM.

Morgan, R. with Barton, J. (1988), *Biblical Interpretation*, Oxford, Oxford University Press.

Neill, S. and Wright, T. (1988), *The Interpretation of the New Testament 1861-1986*, Oxford, Oxford University Press.

Nineham, D. (1976), *The Use and Abuse of the Bible: a study of the Bible in an age of rapid cultural change*, London, SPCK.

Riches, J.K. (1993), *A Century of New Testament Study*, Cambridge, Lutterworth.

Rogerson, J. (ed.) (1983), *Beginning Old Testament Study*, London, SPCK.

Rohde, J. (1968), *Rediscovering the Teaching of the Evangelists* (ET by D.M. Barton), London, SCM.

Sanders, E.P. (1977), *Paul and Palestinian Judaism*, London, SCM.

Smart, N. (1973), *The Phenomenon of Religion*, London, Macmillan.

Soulen, R.N. (1977), *Handbook of Biblical Criticism*, Guildford, Lutterworth.

Styler, G.M. (1966[2]), Excursus IV: the priority of Mark, in C.F.D. Moule, *The Birth of the New Testament*, London, A. and C. Black, pp 223-232.

Styler, G.M. (1982[3]), Excursus IV: the priority of Mark, in C.F.D. Moule, *The Birth of the New Testament*, London, A. and C. Black, pp 285-316.

von Rad, G. (1962, 1965), *Old Testament Theology* (ET by D.M.G. Stalker), London, SCM.

Wiles, M. (1975), The uses of 'Holy Scripture', in M. Hooker and C. Hickling (eds), *What about the New Testament?* London, SCM, pp 155-164.

Teaching about the Bible

Unit B

Children's understanding of texts

Revd Dr William K. Kay

Trinity College

Carmarthen

Contents

Introduction

Aims

After working through this unit you should be able to understand:

- how speaking and reading are related;
- how children comprehend texts;
- the strengths and weaknesses of Goldman's investigations in children's understanding of the bible;
- how to select a suitable religious text for use with children.

Overview

We begin with a comparison between speaking and reading. Though both concern words and meanings, they take place in distinct contexts. From there we consider narrative, the telling of stories, and step into the world of literary theory to help put narrative into a large intellectual perspective. This leads us to narrative in religious education and to the role of metaphorical comprehension (which has been extensively studied) and to parables as a special form of narrative. We conclude by looking at the work of Ronald Goldman, the critiques of this work, and the lessons that can be drawn from it. Periodically we look at the possible future direction of theory and research.

B1 Speaking and reading

Children emerge into the world of spoken words when they are born. After a year they are beginning to speak for themselves and typically to use around two or three words. Within the next 12 months, the child experiences a language explosion and increases his or her vocabulary to over 250 words (Lovell, 1967, p 219). The bulk of early vocabulary is made up of labels for things and people (Bancroft, 1995, p 63) but its usage is extended by intonation and gesture that enable the child to express needs, wishes and intentions.

Understanding of speech and production of speech take place within a social context. Studies of conversations between parents and children find that there are lots of clues and cues for children to fasten on to: the simple conventions of taking turns to speak, of holding and showing, of offering and taking an object and of pointing help the child make sense of what is happening. The same is true if the child's life follows a regular routine where the same words are said about the same things at the same time of the day. In this environment of objects, people, activities and words, the child may learn to think about language. Mismatches become the substance of jokes. The child puts a plate on its head and says with great laughter, 'hat'. The joke shows the child knows the difference between a name and a function (cf. Horgan, 1981, p 218).

Reading is a different kind of activity. Its stages are reasonably well demarcated and the methods by which children come to recognise words have been exhaustively researched (Crystal, 1987). Reading is not, in the same sense as speech, a social activity. It does not take place as a form of communication between two people. The clues and cues for written words are pictures and their connection with words is irregular. In simple texts for children learning to read the picture is *of* an object. A is for Apple, B is for Boat, but then pictures become more complicated in their denotation. There are two people performing an action - kicking a ball, say - and the words on the facing page may describe the action in various ways. They are 'playing' or 'playing football' or 'enjoying themselves' and so on. The child must learn a complex series of conventions. The pictures are not necessarily about the meaning of individual words, but about the meaning of the narrative. Crystal (1987, p 179) puts it this way:

> Speech is time-bound, dynamic, transient - part of an interaction in which, typically, both participants are present, and the speaker has a specific addressee (or group of addressees) in mind. Writing is space-bound, static, permanent - the result of a situation in which, typically, the producer is distant from the recipient.

Crystal (1987) contrasts speech and writing in the six following ways:

- writing allows repeated reading and close analysis in a fashion impossible with speech;
- units of writing are laid out in an intricately structured way with sentences and paragraphs;
- written language displays unique features, for instance, punctuation and capitalisation;
- writing may include vocabulary items that are rarely or never spoken (for instance, legal terms or mathematical symbols);
- speech may exclude vocabulary items (for instance, slang and obscenities) that are rarely written;
- writing generally tends to be more formal than speech.

Attempts to produce the patterns of normal children's speech produce sentences like the following from William Golding, *Lord of the Flies*:

> These two - they're twins, Sam 'n Eric. Which is Eric --? You? No -- you're Sam.

Paradoxically, sentences like this may be more difficult for children to read and understand than less convincing approximations of spontaneous utterance. The same is true of regional accents. For example, in *Major Barbara* Shaw writes in Cockney:

> Aw knaow you. Youre the one that took away maw girl. Youre the one that set er agen me

In *Stalky and Co* Kipling gives a Devonshire accent:

> 'Do 'ee lov' me, Mary?'

> 'Iss--fai! Talled 'ee zo since yeou was zo high!' the damsel replied.

The first kind of reading children in the primary phase of education tackle almost invariably involves standard English. Only much later, in the secondary phase, and often only among brighter children, will there be an appreciation of the possibilities of using phonetic spelling to reproduce accents, sounds or speech rhythms.

> John pulled the trigger and there was an enormous BAAANG.

> Later, John was called in to see the headteacher who shook his head and said, 'Tsk, tsk, tsk, that was a very stupid thing to do.'

Finally, as a further refinement, there is the creation of a whole historical context by the use of ancient technical vocabulary. The following illustration comes from C.S. Forester, *Hornblower and the Crisis*.

> A glance towards the brig set the other two swinging round to look as well.

> 'Still headreaching on us, blast her!' said Baddlestone.

> 'Weathering on us too.'

Activity B1

Ask a child aged about seven or eight years old to tell you: (a) a well-known story and (b) what he or she did today. Tape record both accounts and then transcribe what the child has said as accurately as you can including all the mispronunciations, hesitations, asides, gestures and inflections.

Compare the two pieces of writing. Is there any difference in the vocabulary the child uses? For instance is there a special 'story' vocabulary ('Once upon a time...')? Is the structure of the two pieces of writing similar? Does the child start at the beginning and work through the events to a conclusion, or are there digressions and time shifts in one and not the other?

Comment on activity B1

The results of this activity will depend on the child you have chosen. A child who spends time with books will probably have picked up some of the conventions of story telling. The giant was very fierce, the princess was very beautiful, and it all happened long, long ago. The child who spends more time with television than books may be inclined to mimic cartoon noises and expressions and so to provide a kind of soundtrack for the story. The sequence of events may be imagined visually and described. In this case literary conventions may be absent.

For most children, it is a great deal easier to tell a story that begins at the beginning and runs forward to the end without any attempt to consider a parallel set of events ('While this was happening over here, that was happening over there...') that eventually intercuts with the main narrative.

The account of the child's day is likely to mix thoughts, reactions and events. There may be backtracking as an event reminds the child of an earlier thought and there may be snippets of conversation embedded within the account.

You will probably be able to detect structural differences between the story and the account of the day. This leads us to consider in more detail, the child's understanding of text and the relation between text and life.

B2 Narrative

We have so far considered reading in relation to speech and the broad contexts in which both occur. We could now consider how children learn particular words and sentence constructions and their appreciation of metaphor, but we defer this till later in this unit because we wish to link metaphorical comprehension with understanding of parables.

Our concern in this section is with *narrative*, with the stories children hear, read and remember. The simplest stories for children offer a sequence of events. One thing happens after another, and there is no attempt to show how the things are related. Here is a typical re-telling of *Jack and the Beanstalk*:

> Once upon a time there lived a lazy boy called Jack who was little help to his hard-working and widowed mother. One day his mother said to him, 'Jack, we have no money left. You must go to the market to sell our cow. Get as a good a price as you can and bring me back the money. Don't fail me.' Jack promised his mother that he would be responsible and wise and so he went off to market.

When he arrived, he met a vendor who told him that he had some magic beans that would bring him good luck. Jack forgot his mother's words and exchanged the cow for the beans.

He returned home and his mother scolded him. 'You useless boy, Jack, what have you done? We will not have enough to eat.' She tearfully threw the beans into the garden and sent Jack to bed without any tea.

That night the beans began to grow and in the morning there was a huge beanstalk in the garden reaching up to the clouds. Before his mother could stop him, Jack began to climb to the top and there, to his amazement, he found a palace and, in the palace, the hungry giant who had killed his father. With the help of a fairy he managed to rob the giant of a giant hen that laid golden eggs, a self-playing harp and a bag of diamonds. He escaped down the beanstalk with the giant chasing him. On reaching the bottom, he quickly cut the beanstalk down with an axe and so the giant fell to the ground and was killed.

When we begin to analyse this story, we can identify aspects of it that are not obvious to children. The story is a piece of folk lore based on a world-wide *myth*. There are elements in it that are magical: the beans, the fairy, the giant, the castle in the clouds. There are also elements in it that are *realistic*: the poor widow, the lazy son, the con man at the market and the mother's reaction to her son's return with a few worthless beans in exchange for a cow. If we ask about the *psychology* of the story, we conclude that it is intended to appeal to lazy teenagers and bereaved mothers. The son turns out all right in the end. He may be fooled at the market, but he outwits the giant. He eventually solves all his own and his mother's economic problems. The hen will lay golden eggs for ever and provide a permanent source of income. The diamonds give the family an immediate injection of capital and the music from the harp will soothe their hearts and minds in the absence of Jack's father. If we ask about the *symbolism* of the story, we may see the beans as representative of generation, of new life, of Jack's adolescent potency which are received in exchange for the loss of the cow, the mother's symbol of milk and fertility. As the older generation loses its reproductive ability, the younger generation comes to the fore. In another way, the giant may be representative of Jack's father whom Jack in an Oedipal and Freudian way removes.

The plot of the story, its satisfying shape, is dependent on two surprises. What will happen to Jack at the market? What will happen to Jack in the castle in the clouds? These two questions generate curiosity that drive the reader or listener forward.

If we stand back from the story and ask whether its intention is religious or moral, we find little to support this view. There is no lesson to learn from the scene at the market. The story does not teach that selling precious cows cheaply is a good thing to do. Nor does the story suggest that Jack deserved to defeat the giant. Jack is helped by the fairy, by good luck, and by the con man who happened to do him a good turn. If there is a moral, it is that good luck may strike the undeserving poor. The story, instead, is about the fulfilment of unlikely wishes. Everything ends happily because of the fairy in the clouds, but fairies in clouds are not a permanent part of everyday life; they give help and then disappear. The meaning of the story, if it has a meaning, lies in the fortuitous improvement in Jack's character: lazy and foolish children may turn out to be valuable in the end.

Literary theory

Historically, the meanings of stories have been accessed by reference to the intention of its author. Stories were seen as expressions of the author's feelings conveyed according to the literary forms available and to have been written with particular intentions in mind. Readers responded to these intentions privately and sensitively in the act of reading. The trouble with this approach was that the author's intentions are unknowable. The author may be long dead or, if alive, uncertain exactly what intentions were uppermost in his or her mind at the time of writing. Thus the focus of textual interpretation was shifted to the interplay of elements within the text itself. Comparisons between one part of the text and another and between structure and content were the essence of reading for meaning.

The downplaying of authorial intention, and therefore of subjectivism, and the emphasis on structure and 'inter-textuality' was expected to lead to an almost scientific objectivity. The structure of a story was fixed in a system that had an almost mathematical universality. French intellectuals of the 1960s were particularly keen on structuralism. In *Jack and the Beanstalk* we see a structure of 'departure' (Jack to the market or up the beanstalk) and of the 'testing' of the hero (in the market, where he fails; in the castle, where he succeeds). Thiselton (1992), in a book of more than 700 pages, explains the twists and turns of cultural history at this point. Structuralism, after enjoying a period of ascendancy, was suddenly overthrown by its critics.

Structuralism came to be seen as concerned with 'nothing other than the conventions of reading' (Thiselton, 1992, p 495). What counts as a structural system is at least partly determined by socially driven reading conventions. Systems are really socio-cultural frames and, if this is so, then societies fix how texts will be understood. Structuralism was therefore replaced by post-structuralism, and this throws the weight of interpretation back onto the individual reader. But the post-structuralist reader is not so much a solitary individual as the carrier of 'the conventions, cultural codes, and historically-conditioned expectations which constitute the reading-community as a socio-cultural phenomenon' (Thiselton, 1992, p 496). Post-structuralist readers leave behind private and sensitive feelings about a text since these can only have value as examples of social processes.

The next stages in the development of theory occurred when 'reader-response theories' came to prominence. Reader-response theories call attention to the active role of communities of readers who construct the text's meaning. Marshall (1995, pp 79-80) discusses how the Christian community might be seen as an ideal interpretative community. This may lead us almost in a full circle because the Christian community is defined by its canon, by its authoritative acceptance of particular (biblical) texts, and by the interpretations of those texts that have long been accepted as normative. These interpretations, expressed in the creeds and liturgies of the church, distinguish between symbolic and historical events and are seen to be grounded in the work of the Holy Spirit. Once again, the individual's response is important, though not in the way that it used to be; now the reader is a representative of a community, of a form of life, rather than of a common humanity shared by all readers and all writers.

This may seem a long way from children's understanding of texts, but it is designed to show where the following simple questions might lead:

- how do children understand stories?
- are children's understandings of stories right?

We conclude this section by itemising the three keys to understanding outlined above:

- authorial intention;
- narrative structure;
- personal response shaped by community.

Next, we consider National Curriculum aims in English (DFE, 1995), to see what it is teachers of English are working towards in their engagement with texts. At Key Stage 2 pupil's reading should include texts:

- with more complex narrative structures and sustained ideas;
- that include figurative language, both in poetry and prose;
- with a variety of structural and organisational features.

And, as one of their key skills,

> Pupils should be taught to consider in detail the quality and depth of what they read. They should be encouraged to respond imaginatively to plot, character, ideas, vocabulary and organisation of language in literature. They should be taught to use inference and deduction. Pupils should be taught to evaluate the texts they read.

The National Curriculum in English presumes that pupils will begin to read more widely and to *respond imaginatively* to features of what they read. This does not rule out a consideration of authorial intention or of structure, but the emphasis here is on the characters in a story and the ideas they hold. There is little consideration of symbolism or alternative interpretations. Indeed, these skills are specifically reserved for Key Stages 3 and 4, when pupils are to be taught to 'extract meaning beyond the literal' (DFE, 1995, p 21). Thus, the National Curriculum encourages a personal response to texts at Key Stage 2 but a search for meaning and interpretation in the Secondary phase in Key Stage 3 and above.

Activity B2

Here is the story of Cinderella:

A beautiful young woman named Cinderella lived in the home of her wicked step mother. The step mother had two ugly daughters who treated Cinderella unkindly. One day an invitation to a dance came, but the stepsisters said Cinderella must not go. Instead the two ugly sisters bullied Cinderella to make lovely clothes for them. They dressed up and went to the dance. They thought the handsome prince would fall in love with them.

As she sat sad and alone by the dying embers of the fire, Cinderella was visited by her fairy godmother. Magically, the fairy godmother transformed Cinderella's ragged clothes into a magnificent gown. Her mice became horses and an old pumpkin became a stately coach. Cinderella went to the dance, but on one condition. She must return home before the clock struck midnight. At midnight the magic would stop working. At midnight her clothes would once again turn to rags.

At the dance the handsome prince fell in love with Cinderella. He danced and danced with her. Then Cinderella noticed it was nearly midnight. She rushed out of the prince's arms and down the steps of the palace. There, in her hurry, she left behind one of her glass slippers.

The prince said he wanted to marry the girl the slipper fitted. He searched the kingdom for her. One day a royal servant came to Cinderella's door. He let the ugly sisters try on the slipper, but their feet were much too big. Then the servant called Cinderella. Her foot was found to fit the tiny slipper exactly. So she married the prince and escaped from her unkind stepfamily to happiness.

- What do you think the story means?
- Tell the story to a child (or children) under the age of 12 and ask what it means.

Comment on activity B2

You may have decided that the author's intention (Charles Perrault, 1628-1703, who retold the tale from French popular tradition) is unknown and unknowable.

You may have considered the structure of the story: exploitation of the innocent is solved by marriage. This is the prime meaning of the story. You may also take the view that the story speaks about the role of women in society: they cannot be economically independent and must marry men who will enrich them. You may compare the real father of Cinderella, who is clearly ineffectual because he allows her to be bullied by her stepsisters, with the determination and discernment of the handsome prince who manages to find Cinderella after she disappears from the dance. You may consider that the fairy godmother is symbolic of Cinderella's real, and presumably dead, mother who has been displaced by the scheming stepmother. You may notice that the story is not primarily about character - there are no tests Cinderella must pass to prove her virtue (though she works hard) - but about love kindled on the basis of beauty.

The secondary meaning of the story might be that fathers are weak and easily deceived by stepmothers but that lovers are strong and not easily deceived by stepsisters.

These meanings are partly based on the story's structure and partly on a personal response based on a membership of a modern community sensitive to the historically disadvantaged role of women and the traditional provisions of marriage.

A Key Stage 2 child's response to the story of Cinderella may be full of personal likes and dislikes and be clouded by an inappropriate scientific realism ('I don't believe in fairy godmothers. How could a mouse become a horse? When did you ever see a glass shoe?') that fails to take note of the conventions that make fairy stories what they are.

B3 Narrative in religious education

In April 1981 Jack Priestley published 'Religious story and the literary imagination' in the *British Journal of Religious Education*. In it he argued that, since the work of Goldman (surveyed later in this unit), bible stories have been dropped from the religious education curriculum and been replaced by all kinds of other stories of only tangential relevance to religious education. Why, he asks, can the bible not be treated as literature? If it is treated in this way, it merits inclusion within religious syllabuses. He goes on to point out that it is generally agreed that stories 'have a universal appeal and power to communicate' and that to deny the many bible stories a place in education is to 'deprive' RE teachers of their traditional material.

In the summer of 1982 the entire issue of the *British Journal of Religious Education* was devoted to religious education through story. In his editorial John Hull declared, 'story-telling, one of the oldest arts of the religious educator, is being re-born'. This was followed by an article by David Ford on narrative in theology that drew out the kinds of narratives available to the modern thinker. At one level is the big, overarching story like that of Marxism or evolution, which gives an account of the whole world and its origins and destiny. At the next level is the 'middle distance' narrative that embraces everything from personal relationships to national histories. This is the narrative of academic history, novels, myths and parables. It is here that most religious stories live. And then there is the level of personal narrative that addresses the inner self with all its workings and psychological and spiritual domains.

Within religious education the value of story is to be found in its ability to address the human condition by rendering 'the subconscious part of our experience overt' and by providing, through narrative flow, 'indications of the meaning and purpose of life' (Greenwood, 1982). Similarly in the same journal, Brenda Watson (1982) quotes McDermott-Shideler who asserts:

> It is the sovereign task of fairy tales, myths and legends in literature... to cast the spell which will fuse all the parts of man into an integrated being.

And, in her own words, she suggests that,

> good stories act like scaffolding in a child's mind in which the truth will grow up firmly until it is strong enough to stand on its own.

A similar point is made by Sullivan (1982) who contends that stories 'structure our experience' and that the images provided by story, because they are concrete and particular, are much easier to grasp than abstract and general truths.

These points are implied and added to by Chris Arthur's (1988) article, also published in the *British Journal of Religious Education*. Arthur argues that stories 'facilitate empathy' by helping us to stand in someone else's shoes or, more formally, to enter their thought-world. Thus stories fulfil, or help to fulfil, some of the aims of many religious education syllabuses. They also have a 'unique cognitive potential' because they can teach us what we could hardly learn in any other way. They make real to us, and articulate, truths that we have only half grasped. And, as an extension of this point, the story can approach the unsayable, that which is beyond words, much more nearly than any other form of written communication. Since 'claims of ineffability, of the *impossibility* of description, litter religious literature' (original italics) story is particularly well placed to explore the issues these claims raise.

In 1996 Cooling (cf. also Nichols, 1996) argued that narrative theology - the kind outlined by Ford above - offers one way of reconciling the educational and religious aspects of religious education. The Christian narrative, held and expressed in the biblical accounts, presents a world-view about what is the case, an explanation of the way things are, and, as such, it challenges other world-views. When pupils interact with the Christian narrative 'there is essentially a collision between two ways of understanding human experience'. Pupils may find the Christian account so compelling that they accept it. But this is not the point of the process. Pupils may also accept one of the insights of the Christian narrative and gain a greater understanding of themselves without becoming Christians. They may come to appreciate the value of forgiveness or of the environment and to splice this into their non-Christian self-identity. So narrative theology is the location and natural means by which the Christian community understands itself - thus contributing to the religious element of religious education and, at the same time, it presents an unthreatening way of gaining insight into religion that can be incorporated into an existing and personal world view - thus contributing to the educational element of religious education.

Activity B3

Think about religious stories you have heard or read. How would you classify them? Does your classification affect how you might expect to use such stories in the classroom?

Comment on activity B3

You might have thought of using a classification system derived from the reasons given by the writers in the *British Journal of Religious Education* and Cooling. This classification would ask about each story whether it:

- has a universal appeal and power to communicate;
- renders the subconscious part of our experience overt;
- might act like scaffolding in a child's mind;
- might facilitate empathy;
- teaches what cannot be taught in any other way;
- makes the unsayable easier to grasp;
- contains specific religious insights.

You may have grouped the criteria in various ways. For instance, you might think that the second and fourth criteria are humanistic and expressive, that the third, fifth and sixth are educational, that the seventh is specifically religious and that the first is general and, if anything, educational.

Alternatively, you may have ignored the reasons given by the writers in the section above and developed your own classification system based on the distinction between fact and fiction and their subdivisions. Under 'fact' we might have news stories, personal histories, for instance, and under 'fiction', we might have science fiction, romantic fiction, and so on. In terms of religious stories you might include 'personal accounts of religious experience' under facts and myths under fiction.

Your own classification of stories will probably lead you to decide which ones are appropriate for various age ranges of children and for the kind of religious education you are going to offer. It would be too complicated to say exactly how this might be done without knowing which system you have come up with.

B4 Readability

Considerable work has been done on the readability of texts (Gilliland, 1972; Lunzer and Gardner, 1979). This work has analysed text according to such components as: sentence length, word length, abstractness of words, passive or active sentences. One of the best known indices was developed by Flesch (1948) who recommended these steps[1]:

- select samples of 100 words from a text;
- calculate the number of syllables used per 100 words (word length);
- calculate the average number of words per sentence (sentence length);
- and then work out the following equation:
  reading ease = 206.835 - (0.846 x word length) - (1.015 x sentence length).

This produces a figure between 0 (zero) and 100. Standard writing averages approximately at 60 to 70. The higher the score, the greater the number of people who can easily understand the document.

Harrison (1979, p 107) converts American grades to age levels. A Flesch score of 90-100 would give an age level of 10, 80-90 an age level of 11, 70-80 an age level of 12, 60-70 an age level of 13 or 14. By adding 5 to the grade level an age level is reached.

---

[1]The Gunning (1952) 'Fog' Index is calculated by working out average sentence length and the percentage of words with more than three syllabuses and then adding these two figures together and multiplying them by 0.4. This figures gives a grade level, but the basis of the calculation is similar to the Flesch index. The main advantage of the Fog index is that it is easier to work out without the use of a computer.

Using a computer generated version of the formulae, we find the story of *Cinderella* told in activity B2 has a Flesch reading ease score of 76 and a Flesch-Kincaid grade level of 5. Similarly, the story of *Jack in the Beanstalk* has a Flesch reading ease score of 85 and a Flesch-Kincaid grade level of 5. By contrast the section above on Literary Theory from 'Historically, the...' down to the paragraph ending '... and all writers' has a reading ease score of 46 and a grade level of 11; the words and sentences are longer and there are more passive sentences.

B5 Metaphor comprehension

Normal language uses words in different senses. One of the most common devices that is found in speech is the metaphor. It is arguable that metaphoric language is the basis for much of our understanding of the world. In other words it is difficult to grasp and unify our experiences without the use of metaphor since metaphor is precisely the transfer of a word from a domain where it has a literal meaning into one where its meaning is figurative, or non-literal.

Consider the following two examples:

- The spring sun wakens the autumn seeds;
- on Saturday night he fell in love and walked home on air.

Here the word 'waken' is metaphorical. The autumn seeds are not literally woken up as if they were people getting out of bed. Yet the resemblance between the coming to life of the seeds in their flower beds at the onset of the warmer weather in spring and the act of jumping out of bed at the start of a new day is easy to see. Similarly, young men do not literally walk on air, even when they fall in love, but the commonality between the emotional high of being in love and the unreal springiness of walking on something as insubstantial as air makes the metaphor work.

The two metaphors are slightly different in that the first really makes two comparisons: the sun is like a person because it actively wakes up the 'sleeping' seeds, and the seeds are also like people because they fall asleep and wake up again after the 'night' of winter. The basis for the comparison lies in the fact that when people wake up they move, and get up, and when seeds begin to grow they also change shape (move) and send up shoots (get up). The second metaphor does not depend on similarity of observable actions but on the similarity between an imaginary physical state and the psychological state of being in love. For this reason, the second turns out to be harder for children to understand than the first (Winner, Rosenstiel and Gardner, 1976), a result supported by Billow's (1975) work that showed how children as young as five were able to understand some similarity metaphors intuitively.

Considerable investigation into children's understanding of metaphors has been carried out (see Hyde, 1990, appendix h). This investigation has been focused in the field of language development as a whole and in the field of religion. Language development, especially in its connection with Piagetian models of intellectual operations, is a rich source of insight into the growing minds of children. In the field of religion, metaphor is central to the expression of many ideas and it has been argued that religion *must* make use of metaphors since it addresses truths and beings whose functions transcend normal categories (Ramsey, 1957; Evans, 1986). To take one example, the Holy Spirit is, in the New Testament, compared with the wind which blows mysteriously and invisibly and yet with an obvious effect *and is also* capable of speaking inwardly to Christians (see John 3.8 and Acts 10.19). Clearly the Holy Spirit is being portrayed as being like the wind (mysterious and invisible) and as having personality (being able to speak). These two functions, co-existing in a single entity, can hardly be expressed without extensive use of metaphor.

Many of these issues have been addressed in a series of papers by McGrady (1987, 1994a, 1994b). He accepts the terminology of metaphors adopted by Richards (1936). One term of the metaphor is the 'tenor' and the other is the 'vehicle' and they are drawn from different domains. The basis of the comparison is the 'ground'. Thus the metaphoric statement 'God is my rock' (Psalm 18.2), has 'God' as the tenor and 'rock' as the vehicle and the implied ground is the 'immutability', 'reliability', and 'indestructibility' of each.

The metaphor works because a word originating in one domain is used in another domain and attributes belonging to its use in the native domain are displaced to the vehicle domain. The point to notice, however, is that some attributes are not displaceable. For instance, rocks are often jagged and brown in colour, but these are not the attributes that are being displaced towards God in the example given above.

Children can misunderstand metaphors by failing to abstract displaceable attributes properly. McGrady explored children's handling of metaphors in six ways. These are:

- recognition;
- comprehension;
- production;
- extension[2];
- interrelation;
- evaluation[3].

[2]referred to as 'elaboration' in the 1994 papers.
[3]referred to as 'validation' in the 1994 papers.

We are concerned about the first two in this list. McGrady distinguishes between three levels of recognition. First, children appreciate there is a cognitive conflict resulting from a rejection of a literal interpretation; then, there is an awareness that an idea has been displaced from a native to a novel domain; and lastly that is a search for vehicle, tenor and ground of metaphor.

According to McGrady (1994a) comprehension is expressed in this way:

> Metaphorical comprehension requires the translation of the comparison that has been recognised. This involves the articulation of the relevant elements of the analogy by identification of the common attributes of the concept in both the 'native' and the 'displaced' contexts. These elements must be mapped in a way which permits of a plausible set of comparisons and which sustains metaphoric tension to prevent the establishment of identity relationships by controlling the transfer of the attributes of the native concept into the displaced state.

McGrady tested his ideas with a group of 58 pupils in their first, third and sixth years of secondary education. The pupils were given a test to discover their Piagetian level of operational thinking (which will be relevant later in this unit) and a test specifically devised by McGrady called the *Metaphor and Model Test of Religious Thinking* (MMTRT). Pupils were given:

- four common religious metaphors (e.g. Jesus is the Lamb of God);
- four probably unfamiliar religious metaphors (e.g. the potter and the clay of Jeremiah 18.6);
- two parabolic statements of Jesus (the camel and the eye of the needle and the parable of the treasure in the field - Matthew 13.44);
- parental metaphors of the divine (e.g. God as father and as a woman feeding her child);
- important religious questions (pupils were required to take the metaphors previously provided and elaborate on them in terms of their usefulness in approaching these questions).

Pupils were interviewed and typed transcripts were submitted to a panel of judges for scoring. Judges gave a mark of 0, 1 or 2 for each element of the test.

Taking all the pupils together, the mean score for recognition of metaphors was 1.47, which suggests that most pupils recognised most metaphors. The comprehension scores were lower. Here the mean ran at 1.01. McGrady was able to report that 'metaphorical recognition scores, as indicated by the MMTRT interviews, were high across the post-primary school grades and approached fluency by the 6th year' (6th year pupils were on average aged 16.74 years). Whereas 'metaphorical comprehension scores were lower than those for recognition but increased uniformly with successive grade level.

Partial metaphorical comprehension of a range of religious material was firmly established by third year' (3rd year pupils were on average aged 14.78 years).

These figures can be expressed in another way. Only 3.45% of the whole sample could provide a fluent translation of the metaphor of Jesus as 'the Lamb of God' and, initially surprisingly, unfamiliar metaphors were better understood. Thus a third of pupils (32.7%) fluently translated the metaphor of God as a potter moulding the clay: 10% of first years pupils, 30% of third year pupils and 61% of sixth year pupils being successful.

Variations in metaphor comprehension were found in the parabolic statements. While 84.5% were able to translate the camel going through the eye of the needle metaphor, only 44.8% were able to do the same with the metaphor of the treasure in the field.

Activity B4

How would you account for the different levels of difficulty in metaphor comprehension McGrady found?

Comment on activity B4

You might have thought that readability was a factor. Perhaps some of the metaphors were difficult to understand because the words in which they were expressed were more unusual or more abstract. This, however, should not be the main source of the differences since the metaphors were presented as short excerpts and not in long sentences.

A possible clue to the differences lies in the kinds of comparisons being made (cf. Winner, Rosenstiel and Gardner, 1976). Does this apply here? For instance are any of the comparisons mentioned by McGrady comparisons of appearance? The answer here would appear to be 'no'. For instance, the Lamb of God metaphor says nothing about the appearance of Jesus and the Eye of the Needle statement says nothing about the appearance of rich people. In each instance, the comparison is to do with ideas. The most reasonable explanation given for the differential comprehension rates between familiar and unfamiliar metaphors is that the latter are not overlaid by pre-digested theology. The Lamb of God metaphor depends on an understanding of the Jewish sacrificial system and the place of the Passover in the biblical history of redemption. The Lamb image, in other words, is not linked with farming so much as with a theological understanding about the place of animal sacrifice in the Mosaic covenant. If children lack this background understanding, then the metaphor becomes impenetrable. By contrast, the metaphor of the potter requires only a general idea of how potters work and how God might be expected to work.

A further set of difficulties may apply to the parabolic statements about riches. The 'eye of the needle' is a metaphor in itself (needles have holes for thread, not eyes to see)[4]. The treasure in a field metaphor is confused by the apparent dishonesty of the man who bought the field at less than its market price in order to obtain the hidden treasure.

B6 Parable comprehension

The understanding of parables is linked with the understanding of metaphors, though research has so far dealt with the two topics separately. McGrady extends his findings to draw out implications for understanding of parables and theological models. Murphy (1979), whose work we consider here, investigated children's understandings of parables without looking directly at metaphor, though he did take into account children's understanding of word meanings, their concept of historical time and their ability to order events sequentially in time. He interviewed 440 children in the age range from 6 to 11 years.

Murphy (1979, p 217) was able to use his findings to state:

> we would conclude by rejecting a simplistic model of religious thinking in children, which equates religious thinking with the ability to be able to apply certain stage related styles of thinking to religious stories... to assume that someone has reached a fully developed stage of religious thinking once they can understand a religious story at a non-literal abstract level, would seem to us to be a misrepresentation of the whole problem of investigating the way individuals think about religion.

This overall conclusion (to which we return in the final section of this unit) was supported by the section of his work that concentrated specifically on parables. Murphy reported these in 1977 on the responses of 200 children aged between 7 and 11 years. These children were taken from four schools, 50 from each school, and each was randomly selected after the exclusion of children deemed by the school to be in need of remedial education. One school was an independent boys' boarding school, one was a Catholic school and the other two drew their pupils almost entirely from a working class area. All the schools were situated in the east of Scotland.

The children were asked what a parable was and, if they did not know, were given an explanation and an example (the story of the boy who cried 'Wolf!').

---

[4]If it is argued that 'eye of the needle' is the name of a particular narrow gate in the wall of Jerusalem, then this requires specialist knowledge that children can hardly be expected to have.

After this the children were read four New Testament parables from a typed sheet which each child was able to follow from his or her own copy. After this each was asked a series of questions to see how well the parables had been understood. Then the child told the parable back to the experimenter. If at any stage the child seemed to have forgotten the main facts of the parable, it was repeated. By this means it was made clear that any differences in responses were not caused by failures of memory.

To test for the way responses were elicited some children were given a multiple choice questionnaire in place of a semi-structured interview, though the printed questions were the same as those in the interview and the multiple choice answers were the same as those that were most frequently given by children during interviews. The parables used were: The Rich Fool, The Good Samaritan, The Pharisee and the Tax Collector, The Sower, The Two Houses, and The Lost Sheep. The parables were told from Shirley Steen's (1973), *A Child's Bible*, but modernised versions of the first three parables were also used.

Children's responses to parables were graded on a three point scale by two independent judges:

- 1 = the child can only repeat facts or elements of the parable, and shows no more than literal appreciation of it;
- 2 = the child can make an application in a simple way that shows a movement in the direction of understanding the allegorical meaning of a parable;
- 3 = the child shows an understanding of the allegorical meaning of the parable.

On the basis of this analysis Murphy produced the following findings.

- Children move steadily to level 3 as they grow older. Bar charts show quite obviously that there is a progression from literal appreciation to non-literal appreciation.
- Children's performance varied between parables. For instance the same 100 children performed very much better on The Good Samaritan than on The Rich Fool. Thus, while 45% of 7 year olds, 85% of 8 year olds, 70% of 9 year olds, 90% of 10 year olds and 80% of 11 year olds understood The Good Samaritan at level 3, only 0% of 7 year olds, 15% of 8 year olds, 40% of 9 year olds, 35% of 10 year olds and 30% of 11 year olds understood The Rich Fool in this way.
- In some cases children's understanding could be improved by a modernised version, but a modernised version made no difference in the case of The Good Samaritan - probably because of the very good level of understanding already achieved.

- Children who completed the multiple choice questionnaire produced higher levels than those who were interviewed.
- The analysis suggested there was no difference between the children from the different schools.

Activity B5

What implications do you think these findings might have for religious education teaching in school?

Comment on activity B5

You may have been surprised at the difference between the levels of understanding of the various parables and at the effect modernisation has on understanding. One implication that stands out, therefore, is that the readability and modernity of the text is likely to have a measurable effect on children's ability to comprehend religious stories. Above and beyond this, however, is the finding that some stories are much easier to understand than others. This might seem an obvious finding, but what is not so obvious is the reason why this should be so. The Good Samaritan is a very well known story and it may be that children tend to understand it because they have heard it re-told and explained several times and it is their memory of these applications and re-tellings that Murphy's results show up. Murphy was aware of this possibility but pointed out that there was no way he could avoid it. Nevertheless, the use of parables with children as young as seven years of age is legitimated by these results. Such children are capable of appreciating a non-literal sense to stories. By the time children reach the age of eight it seems that nearly eight out of ten of those above the remedial cut-off point can make the extrapolation from a literal account to a non-literal meaning.

Murphy's careful procedure and his setting of levels suggests that children pass through an initial process where they simply know the events of the story and their sequence. This level or stage seems to be an essential prerequisite for more mature understanding. The teaching of parables and religious stories may, then, proceed through an initial stage where children are not expected to go beyond the literal meaning. In other words, it may be a perfectly adequate educational aim to ask young children to hear and repeat the events of a story which they will later be able to endow with greater significance. All of the parables Murphy used contain what appear to be simple factual accounts of events: they make no reference to magic or fantasy and this makes them easier to understand at the literal level.

You could also argue that only parables that make sense at this literal level are suitable for religious teaching to young children. Religious stories of myth and legend, for example stories about giants, dragons and genies, are much more complicated because they have to be understood as dealing with imaginary events and then interpreted with reference to abstract truths. There are two translations to make in the child's mind. So, if the story of Adam and Eve and the speaking serpent is understood as a myth, it has first to be non-literalised (Adam = men in general; Eve = women in general; the serpent = evil) and then the non-literal version has to be given a wider meaning.

Research has not so far looked at the common features of parables that children find easy to understand and those they find difficult to understand. Nor has it broadened its scope to include questions to children of various cultural backgrounds or to include parables from non-Christian religious traditions.

Finally, Murphy's finding that the children in four socially distinct schools were indistinguishable suggests that social class and academic differences are not crucial to children's appreciation of parables. His finding that understanding of The Good Samaritan did not improve even when a modern version was given suggests that there is an age-related ceiling to children's ability to comprehend.

B7 Comprehension of the bible

Murphy's work was carried out in partial reaction against the influential studies of Ronald Goldman. Goldman's work had been carried out in the early 1960s and published in 1964 and 1965. Its conclusions, if they can be briefly summarised, were that young children cannot understand the bible because the bible contains non-literal, abstract truths and concepts that are beyond the grasp of children who think at the Piagetian level of concrete operations.

We have considered Piaget's account of mental development in units B and C of the module *Spiritual and Moral Development*, and you should turn to these units for a fuller account of the background to Goldman's work. Briefly, the Piagetian model is characterised by dividing children's mental development during their school years into three main stages. At the intuitive stage children are dependent on the perceptual features of a situation, and are often unable to co-ordinate them, and so fail to use logic effectively. At the stage of concrete operations, children are able to make mental representations of physical actions. Thinking is mentally rehearsing actions that manipulate objects. At the stage of formal operations (which, for the brighter children, occurs at the beginning of secondary education) children are able to manipulate abstractions.

What you will have noticed in this unit is that, while McGrady broadly accepts the Piagetian model, Murphy regards it as too simple and insufficient to be able to encompass all that religious thinking involves. Goldman, by contrast, *depends on* the Piagetian model.

Goldman interviewed 200 British pupils between the ages of 6 and 17 years (15-17 year olds were treated as one group). Ten boys and ten girls, selected according to systematic sampling techniques, were interviewed at each age level. All the pupils came from maintained schools. Children from Roman Catholic and Jewish homes and 'of foreign extraction' were excluded. The sample method ensured that children from the full ability range at each age level were represented.

The bible stories concerning Moses and the burning bush, the Israelite crossing of the Red Sea and Jesus' temptations in the wilderness were presented to the pupils through a tape recording. Each pupil was then asked a series of questions. Of the total of 22 questions on the biblical passages, answers on five were categorised according to the Piagetian stage of development. On the basis of pupils' answers to these five questions Goldman (1964, p 62) concluded:

> An analysis of results when scored on the three major stages of thinking... outlined above, substantiates very clearly the view put forward by Piaget that there is a continuum of thinking that follows an 'operational' sequence. When applied to thinking about religion, in the bible stories chosen, this threefold sequence is very evident.

Much of Goldman's book is taken up with quotations from his interviews with pupils. A six year old thinks Moses had to take off his shoes at the burning bush because the ground had holes in it. God had to take his shoes off as well and so Moses followed suit. The child thinks 'holy' means full of holes (Goldman, 1964, p 122). A nine year old thinks the Israelites are allowed to escape through the Red Sea because 'they hadn't got no guns' (Goldman, 1964, p 147). A seven year old girl thinks that not living by bread alone means that 'you should eat something else with it - butter'. An eight year old thinks that Jesus did not turn stones to bread 'because the devil didn't say please' (Goldman, 1964, p 167).

On the basis of his analysis Goldman (1964, p 225) argued that:

> the more we know of children's thinking, the more we can see that not only concepts but the level of formal operations (or propositional thinking) demanded by the Parables of Jesus make them, on the whole, unsuitable for children.

He concludes that 'the recommendation may have to be faced that very little biblical material is suitable for children before Secondary schooling'.

Comment on Goldman's work

Both at the time (Fleming, 1966; Howkins, 1966) and later (Murphy, 1978; Francis, 1979; Slee 1992; Kay, 1996) extensive criticisms have been made of Goldman's research and of the implications he drew from it. Some of Murphy's criticisms have already been outlined. The other writers criticised Goldman's confusion of theological and Piagetian criteria, his scoring system, his failure to distinguish religious thinking from thinking about religion, his insensitivity to literary genres and the theoretical difficulty, not to say impossibility, of applying Piagetian theory to textual interpretation. Although Hyde (1990) is generally favourable to Goldman, none of the criticisms mentioned above has been fully answered. Even McGrady (1996, p 99), who is basically positive about Goldman's work, comments:

> The model adopted by Goldman (1962) equating the development of religious thinking through the stages of logical operations can now be recognised as being over-stated; rather than talking of stages of religious development, it is more accurate to refer to the effect of the underlying stages of operational development upon religious thinking skills.

What none of the writers above has explored in any detail is the contrast between children's understanding of parables and their understanding of historical accounts containing miracles. These two kinds of writing are very different. Parables are self-contained stories of everyday events designed to convey at least one, and sometimes several, meanings. Historical accounts are always part of a longer story that is designed to convey a meaning to which short extracts may contribute little.

In addition historical narratives are themselves a genre that may be perplexing to children because of their failure to appreciate how the world has changed between the past and the present. Historical extracts containing miracles (Moses and the burning bush and the Red Sea crossing) are more complex still. Here a problem arises not only over the invisible (to children) wider context of the account but also over the moral role of miracle as well as its causation. There seems to be no justification for Goldman's conclusion that, because children have difficulty in understanding historical accounts containing miracles, they will have a corresponding difficulty in understanding parables.

Activity B6

Read back over this unit. How does children's understanding of non-religious stories throw light on their understanding of religious stories? What kind of religious texts do you think children aged 7 to 11 could be expected to understand?

Comment on activity B6

We began this unit with the entrance by children into the world of words and differentiated between the learning of spoken language and written language. We have considered children's reading of secular and religious texts and their ability to move from literal to non-literal meanings. In the process we have looked at metaphor as the miniature building block by which literal meanings become non-literal. We have seen evidence from Murphy's work that a literal understanding of a story may be a necessary prerequisite for a later non-literal understanding. We have also considered how readability may be measured and what its relevance is to children's understanding of texts.

You may have thought that, if children can understand fairy stories and folk tales, they can also come to understand religious texts. You may have deduced that, if National Curriculum English teaching, is expected to draw children into analysing the meaning of stories, it should not be too hard for similar work to be done on stories within religious traditions. You may have felt that there is a lack of clarity about how religious texts and stories should be used with young children, partly because religion is covered by Agreed Syllabuses rather than National Curriculum guidelines and partly because little research and thought has been systematically given to the matter.

You may have decided that children should be able to understand texts that:

- fulfil appropriate Flesch readability criteria;
- are self-contained (like parables or folk tales);
- function meaningfully at a literal level;
- contain metaphors based on comparisons of appearance.

In addition, you may take the view that religious metaphors *can* be understood (cf. McGrady's findings about Jeremiah and the potter) and that stories that concern behaviour within the experience of children (e.g. being kind or unkind as in The Good Samaritan) are also perfectly comprehensible. You may also have come to the view that children can understand fairy stories and folk tales because they intuitively learn to accept the conventions built into these stories (fairy godmothers are good; giants are generally bad; witches are bad; magic is effective but has certain limitations). If this is so, you may take the view that children can learn the conventions of religious stories, and therefore can understand them.

Readers

L.J. Francis, W.K. Kay and W.S. Campbell (eds) (1996), *Research in Religious Education*, Leominster, Gracewing, chapters 1-7.

Bibliography

Arthur, C.J. (1988), Some arguments for the use of stories in religious education, *British Journal of Religious Education*, 10, 122-127.

Bancroft, D. (1995), Language development, in C. Lee and P.D. Gupta (eds), *Children's Cognitive and Language Development*, Oxford, Blackwell in association with the Open University Press, pp 45-75.

Billow, R.M. (1975), A cognitive developmental study of metaphor comprehension, *Developmental Psychology*, 11, 415-423.

Cooling, T. (1996), Education is the point of RE - not religion? Theological perspectives on the SCAA model syllabuses, in J. Astley and L.J. Francis (eds), *Christian Theology and Religious Education: connections and contradictions*, London, SPCK, pp 165-183.

Crystal, D. (1987), *The Cambridge Encyclopedia of Language*, Cambridge, Cambridge University Press.

DFE (1995), *English in the National Curriculum*, London, HMSO.

Evans, G.R. (1986), Patristic and medieval theology, in P. Avis (ed.), *The Science of Theology*, Basingstoke, Marshall Pickering, pp 3-103.

Fleming, C.M. (1966), Research evidence and Christian education, *Learning for Living*, 6 (1), 10-12.

Flesch, R.F. (1948), A new readability yardstick, *Journal of Applied Psychology*, 32, 221-233.

Ford, D. (1982), Narrative in theology, *British Journal of Religious Education*, 4, 115-119.

Francis, L.J. (1979), Research into the development of religious thinking, *Educational Studies*, 5, 109-115.

Gilliland, J. (1972), *Readability*, London, University of London Press.

Goldman, R.J. (1962), Some aspects of religious thinking in childhood and adolescence, unpublished PhD dissertation, University of Birmingham.

Goldman, R.J. (1964), *Religious Thinking from Childhood to Adolescence*, London, Routledge and Kegan Paul.

Goldman, R.J. (1965), *Readiness for Religion*, London, Routledge and Kegan Paul.

Greenwood, D. (1982), Psychology and the use of stories in religious education, *British Journal of Religious Education*, 4, 120-123, 149.

Gunning, R. (1952), *The Technique of Clear Writing*, New York, McGraw Hill.

Harrison, C. (1979), Assessing the readability of school texts, in E. Lunzer and K. Gardner (eds), *The Effective Use of Reading*, London, Heinemann Educational Books for the Schools Council, pp 72-107.

Horgan, D. (1981), Learning to tell jokes: a case study of metalinguistic abilities, *Journal of Child Language*, 8, 217-224.

Howkins, K.G. (1966), *Religious Thinking and Religious Education: a critique of the research and conclusion of Dr R. Goldman*, London, Tyndale Press.

Hyde, K.E. (1990), *Religion in Childhood and Adolescence*, Birmingham, Alabama, Religious Education Press.

Kay, W.K. (1996), Bringing child psychology to religious curricula: the cautionary tale of Goldman and Piaget, *Educational Review*, 48, 205-215.

Lovell, K. (1967), *Educational Psychology and Children*, London, University of London Press.

Lunzer, E. and Gardner, K. (eds) (1979), *The Effective Use of Reading*, London, Heinemann Educational Books for the Schools Council.

McGrady, A.G. (1987), A metaphor and model paradigm of religious thinking, *British Journal of Religious Education*, 9, 84-94.

McGrady, A.G. (1994a), Metaphorical and operational aspects of religious thinking: research with Irish Catholic pupils (part 1), *British Journal of Religious Education*, 16, 148-163.

McGrady, A.G. (1994b), Metaphorical and operational aspects of religious thinking: research with Irish Catholic pupils (part 2), *British Journal of Religious Education*, 17, 56-62.

McGrady, A.G. (1996), Measuring religious thinking using Piagetian operational paradigms, in L.J. Francis, W.K. Kay and W.S. Campbell (eds), *Research in Religious Education*, Leominster, Gracewing, pp 97-112.

Marshall, D.G. (1995), Reading and interpretative communities, in D. Barratt, R. Pooley and L. Ryken (eds), *The Discerning Reader: Christian perspectives on literature and theory*, Leicester, Apollos, pp 69-84.

Murphy, R.J.L. (1977), Does children's understanding of parables develop in stages? *British Journal of Religious Education*, 16, 168-172.

Murphy, R.J.L. (1978), A new approach to the study of the development of religious thinking in children, *Educational Studies*, 4, 19-22.

Murphy, R.J.L. (1979), An investigation into some aspects of the development of religious thinking in children aged between six and eleven years, unpublished PhD dissertation, University of St Andrews.

Nichols, K. (1996), Imagination and tradition in religion and education, in J. Astley and L.J. Francis (eds), *Christian Theology and Religious Education: connections and contradictions*, London, SPCK, pp 184-197.

Priestley, J.G. (1981), Religious story and the literary imagination, *British Journal of Religious Education*, 4, 417-424.

Ramsey, I.T. (1957), *Religious Language*, London, SCM.

Richards, I.A. (1936), *The Philosophy of Rhetoric*, Oxford, Oxford University Press.

Slee, N.M. (1992), Cognitive developmental studies of religious thinking: a survey and discussion with special reference to post-Goldman research in the Kingdom, in J.W. Fowler, K.E. Nipkow and F. Schweitzer (eds), *Stages of Faith and Religious Development: implications for church, education and society*, London, SCM, pp 130-146.

Steen, A. (1973), *A Child's Bible*, London, Pan Books.

Sullivan, J. (1982), Stories of commitment, *British Journal of Religious Education*, 4, 129-131, 167.

Thiselton, A.C. (1992), *New Horizons in Hermeneutics*, London, Harper Collins.

Watson, B. (1982), The imagination, human development, and the importance of the story, *British Journal of Religious Education*, 4, 124-128.

Winner, E., Rosenstiel, A.K. and Gardner, H. (1976), The development of metaphoric understanding, *Developmental Psychology*, 12, 289-297.

Teaching about the Bible

Unit C

Teaching the bible

Revd Dr William K. Kay

Trinity College

Carmarthen

Contents

Introduction

Aims

After working through this unit you should be able to understand:

- the context of bible teaching in schools;
- how the bible might be taught in primary religious education;
- how the bible might be taught in cross-curricular themes in primary schools;
- how the bible might be taught in secondary religious education;
- how the bible might be taught in GCSE courses.

Overview

After looking at the broad context of bible teaching in schools, this module focuses on the narrower context of the classroom. First it considers bible teaching in school assemblies and then it examines three modern Agreed Syllabuses to see how bible teaching might be carried out under their auspices. It looks at a lesson outline on a biblical passage to see whether it would be suitable for all three syllabuses. After this it considers the application of the skills fostered by National Curriculum English to bible passages and a similar application of National Curriculum history skills in a cross curricular theme.

C1 Context of bible teaching in schools

The immediate context of school is part of a larger context defined by the legal framework that controls the school curriculum. This larger context, which is bedded within British culture as a whole, is made up of three strands: the first is the law defined by statute and made by parliament (see unit A of the module *Philosophy of Religious Education*); the second derives from the national bodies (particularly the QCA) under the control of the Secretary of State which monitor and adjust National Curriculum subjects; the third concerns syllabuses drawn up locally by SACREs according to guidelines laid down by parliament.

The majority of the school curriculum (ten subjects in England and 11 in Wales) has been structured by attainment targets appropriate to each Key Stage. Modern Agreed Syllabuses for religious education normally follow this pattern. This is helpful to OFSTED and denominational inspectors and beneficial to teachers in their preparation and planning of work. In this respect religious education is treated like National Curriculum subjects: teacher knowledge, the standard of teaching, schemes of work, reporting to parents and resources are all open to the inspectorial gaze. Where religious education is different is that it is usually thought to contribute to the spiritual, social, moral and cultural dimension of the curriculum.

As we shall see, teaching about and from the bible is included in many Agreed Syllabuses, though the parameters of this teaching are determined by the attainment targets the syllabus sets and its overall structure. For closer examination during this unit we have selected three modern Agreed Syllabuses. Nottingham has rural and urban areas and is situated towards the north of England. Wolverhampton represents the less prosperous ethnically mixed urban midlands and Essex is both rural and urban and in the heart of the prosperous south east.

These three syllabuses all include Genesis 1 at Key Stage 2, but their aims, structures and assumptions are detectably different and might influence the way this text was presented in the classroom. Nottingham has a comparative element, Wolverhampton has an ecological thrust and Essex is somewhere in the middle. Having said this, good bible teaching at either primary or secondary level should be recognisable as such in any part of Britain, and the examples given later in this unit ought to be widely applicable.

The larger context that bounds the legal framework is British culture as a whole. Copley (1997) has described the development of religious education since 1944. He sets this development against the background of social changes in Britain and is able to build a case showing that, whatever the legal stipulations that governed religious education, the actual practice of the subject in schools was influenced by the general apathy towards religion shown by most British voters and therefore most local authorities. The law tended to be ignored. Very few parents in the 1970s knew of their legal right to withdraw children from school worship and few, if any, bothered to challenge a system that failed to deliver the daily collective morning worship that was then statutorily required. Enthusiastic or religiously motivated parliamentarians might provide a legal platform from which Christianity could be provided, but teachers tended to disregard this and nobody seemed to mind. In Copley's view both the provisions of the 1944 Education Act and those of the 1988 Education Reform Act were remarkable for their bias towards Christianity and the slackness within which this bias was implemented.

Activity C1

As an imaginative exercise briefly consider how the context of schooling influences what goes on inside a campus. Consider first the influence of the school community on its sporting provision. Then consider the influence of the wider society on the clothes children wear, the fashions they follow and the moral standards they accept. Is society likely to influence biblical and moral teaching in school?

Comment on activity C1

This activity is designed to point up the influence of factors outside the school on what goes on inside it. The sporting provision of a school is influenced by what is available in the neighbourhood. There may be a large swimming pool nearby or a badminton or squash court popular with parents and accessible to children. There may be a sports centre that makes its facilities available to local schools at discounted rates. There may be plenty of green spaces for field games, or there may be little except asphalt and a few battered netball hoops. You may have thought of other valid connections which illustrate how sport is community-dependant.

The influence of television and fashion on children is remarkable. A new toy becomes a craze and children fight over it in the playground, swap it, collect it, boast about it and then, quite suddenly, move on to something else. The same phenomenon is observable with clothes, jewellery, footwear, face painting, music and food. This underlines the fact that the school is open to its social context. In the same inescapable way it is reasonable to suppose that the teaching of the bible is affected, as Copley argues, by the treatment received by religion in society as a whole.

Having said this, there is certainly a connection between legality and morality in the sense that most British people appear to accept that what is legal must also be moral (Devlin, 1968). Where the law is changed in a liberal direction, morality tends to follow suit. Conversely, where moral opinion favours a liberalisation of law, this usually follows. Insofar as the teaching of the bible is concerned, Copley's argument suggests that, if the legal situation were turned round and parents of pupils had to opt in to assembly and religious education rather than having to opt out, there would be a great deal less biblical teaching in schools than at present.

C2 Bible in the primary school

Children may be introduced to the bible within three general contexts in school. These are the school assembly, the religious education lesson and the cross-curricular theme (which may be part of the social, moral, spiritual and cultural dimension of education). First, however, we consider preliminary matters that often trouble teachers. Most of these issues are discussed in more detail by Cooling, Walker and Goodwin (1993a).

Preliminary matters

Until recently little attention was given to the background of bible stories that were used in primary classrooms. For example, customs of New Testament times that might illuminate the meaning of a story were often ignored. Similarly, the chronology of the bible, where a thousand years separates King David from Jesus, was often insufficiently understood. Bible stories were either seen simply as good stories which floated in the timeless zone of religious literature or as convenient pegs on which to hang a moral illustration. Their religious meaning and the distinction between historical narrative, parable, epistle, psalm and law were rarely given prominence. These deficiencies are beginning to be addressed by the modern generation of Agreed Syllabuses, but teachers who have not received in-service or initial training in religion may continue to need help from specialists at school or county level.

More insidiously teachers may continue to lack confidence in their approach to the bible because they have been told that the bible is too difficult for children to cope with and, indeed, that 'the bible is not a children's book'. This worry, which has been partially confronted in the previous unit, stems from the work of the late Ronald Goldman. It gives rise to the anxiety that children who meet the bible will, in later life, be unable to shake off their childish misconceptions about God or theology in general.

This worry, however, largely melts away when it is examined closely. Clearly, the bible is *not* a children's book, but then much of what children read in classical literature may not be written primarily for them. Is Dickens' *Christmas Carol* really for children? And, in a parallel way, much of what children either see on television or engage with in other areas of the curriculum - for example in the realm of science - is not *for* children in any specialist way. It exists and children understand it using the concepts available to them and, in later life, come to understand it better or differently. The same may be said of the bible, especially if children are taught in such a way that what they learn relates to their own experience. Indeed, it is the reference to children's own experience which is the key to good teaching, as the examples given later will show.

Miracles are also problematic for teachers. Young children have difficulty distinguishing reality from fantasy, and miracle stories can seem to them to belong to the realm of make-believe. To ignore miracles, though, would be to remove many traditional biblical passages from consideration within the primary school. In addition, non-Christian religions also contain accounts of miraculous events. It would seem strange to include these in a primary school curriculum but to leave out Christian miracles. One solution to this problem is to tell children that they are going to hear a story that is important for Christians and, if asked whether it really happened, to explain that some people think it did and others think it did not. Such a solution can also be extended to the bigger questions about the truth of religion as a whole though, as we shall point out in relation to teaching the bible in the secondary school, there are further lines of argumentation to explore here.

Religiously informed teachers may be disconcerted about the treatment of the Old Testament as a Christian book. There is no easy way round this problem. For two thousand years Christians have built their faith on the assumption that the New Testament fulfils the Old. It makes little sense to pretend otherwise. Any presentation of the New Testament which neglects its Old Testament background can hardly be properly Christian. A similar problem will arise for the Islamic teacher because, for him or her, Abraham (in the Old Testament) and Jesus (in the New Testament) are really speaking about the faith of Islam.

What the primary school teacher is likely to do, and to do instinctively in many cases, is to concentrate on the themes and passages that Christianity, Judaism and Islam interpret similarly. For instance, Genesis 1 is seen by all these faiths as an account of creation that says nothing divisive about the relationship between them. Having said this, it has to be recognised that religions do not agree with each other and that any attempt to brush aside differences will result in distortions. Eventually, though not in the primary school, the teacher is probably going to end up saying that while a particular biblical passage is interpreted is this way by religion A, it is interpreted in that way by religion B.

Bible and school assembly

The first educational context where children may meet the bible may be the school assembly. There is a great variety within this context. The school may be large or small, urban or rural, multi-cultural or mono-cultural, church-related or not, headed by Christian staff, agnostics, atheists or members of non-Christian faith communities.

At one extreme the bible may be read from more or less every day and visible to the children as a large book which staff appear to treat as authoritative. At the other extreme, the bible may be vaguely and disparagingly referred to at Christmas or Easter and never shown to pupils. Within these extremes various tensions may arise either as different takers of assembly treat the bible in obviously diverse ways or as the bible in assembly seems to be quite a different book from the bible in the classroom.

As long ago as the mid-1970s Hull (1975) argued that there was an incompatibility between the faith-based use of the bible as a religious text in assembly and the reason-based use of the bible as an object of study in the classroom. When Hull first wrote his target was school assembly itself rather than the bible as used in assembly. More recent developments as a result of legislation and government guidelines (e.g. Circular 10/94) have made arrangements for school assembly more flexible and, to many minds, less contentious[1]. Furthermore, in the primary school, this tension may be eased for two reasons: first, because the kind of critical investigation that is likely to be carried out into the biblical text by Key Stage 1 and 2 children is minimal and, second, because the bible in assembly is frequently used to make a moral point rather than a theological or metaphysical one.

The ideal is surely that the bible's use in assembly leads smoothly and naturally into its exploration within the classroom. Assembly can function as a lead lesson and be educationally valid. This is what is implied in the little regarded drafting of the 1988 Education Reform Act which placed collective worship under the general heading of 'religious education' (see Education Reform Act section 6 and 6.3). In other words, worship was seen as facilitating rather than inhibiting religious education. Even if assembly is not, or ceases for practical reasons to be, worship in any full-bloodied confessional way, it can, nevertheless, be a time for reflection and stillness and provide an opportunity for silent prayer. Within this setting the bible may have the role of a stimulus - as poetry also does - and there need be no conflict with its classroom role. The following extract from an OFSTED report of a country school in Nottinghamshire shows how the connection between religious education and assembly can work in practice:

> Religious education reflects the intentions of the Local Education Authority's Agreed Syllabus and a policy document outlines the aims of the subject. Achievements at both Key Stages are satisfactory and there are examples of good work throughout the school. Religious education both in classes and during assemblies contribute significantly to the spiritual and moral education of the pupils.
>
> There is allocated time for religious education in every class, and at Key Stage 2 year groups plan collaboratively, sometimes bringing pupils together for a key talk or video. Year group assemblies occasionally follow the same themes

---

[1] McCreery (1993), on the basis of the study of three schools, commends the development of a 'whole school policy' to ensure that what is offered to pupils in assembly has a clear structure and purpose within the life of a school. She foresees the content of assembly as being negotiated by interested parties - teachers, parents, governors.

as outlined in the guidelines and this means that key ideas are effectively reinforced in the classroom.

Cooling (1990) provides a series of largely bible-based assemblies for primary schools. Most of these involve a short opening activity that concretises the assembly's theme, a bible story, a comment, something to think about and a prayer. For instance, 'Friends in need' is introduced by the idea of writing secret messages and asking children how they can be passed on. The bible story is an extract from the adventures of David and Jonathan, the comment points out that Jonathan helped David at a time of great trial and danger, the thinking point is a poem on friendship and the prayer asks that we should be helpful to friends and not let them down.

This simple pattern is applicable over a variety of themes, many of which appear within Agreed Syllabuses. For instance 'Friends in need' is placed within the theme of *Friends*; other themes include *Me* and *Forgiveness*. More specifically religious themes are built around the festivals connected with harvest and Christmas.

If infants are taken separately for assemblies, then the Teddy Horsley stories (e.g. Francis and Slee, 1996), which make biblical themes comprehensible to small children, would be suitable.

Bible and primary religious education

To anchor this discussion in practicality, the three modern Agreed Syllabuses mentioned earlier are compared for their treatment of the bible.

The Nottingham Agreed Syllabus (1979) suggests the following learning experiences at Key Stage 1 under attainment target 1 (learning about religions).

- Read and listen to stories about people who have followed Jesus, e.g. the disciples.
- Look at and handle carefully some special bibles, e.g. a family bible.
- find out why the bible is special to Christians.
- Read some well-loved stories from the bible, e.g. the birth of Jesus.
- Listen and respond to stories about the birth of Jesus.

Under attainment target 2 (learning from religion) the Nottingham syllabus adds the following learning experience.

- Talk about how the Christmas stories relate to experiences and feelings in their own lives, e.g. the birth of a baby, venerability[2], being loved and protected, giving and receiving.

---

[2] This appears to be a misprint for 'vulnerability'.

The Nottingham Agreed Syllabus suggests the following learning experiences at Key Stage 2 under attainment target 1 (learning from religions).

- Read Genesis 1-2, and illustrate the days of Creation.
- Identify beliefs about God in the Creation story.
- Place the life of Jesus in a historical context.
- Talk about, and discuss, the meaning of stories that Jesus told, and stories about his life, e.g. the Lost Son, the Good Samaritan, the Widow's Mite, and Zacchaeus.
- Compare different translations of short bible passages.

Under attainment target 2 (learning from religion) the Nottingham Agreed Syllabus adds the following learning experience.

- Consider the experiences and feelings which give rise to questions about meaning and purpose.
- Consider feelings of being lost and found, and talk about feelings of being accepted.
- Compare the experiences of people in biblical stories with their own experiences and feelings, e.g. how Jesus felt when he was abandoned by his friends in the Garden of Gethsemane.
- Read passages in the bible that give guidance on issues such as jealousy, friendship and honesty, and discuss the message of these passages in relation to their own experiences.

The Essex Agreed Syllabus (1997) is too extensive and complex to reproduce in detail here. In essence it breaks down religious material into seven categories: the self and being human, relationships and community, the natural world and the universe, spiritual experience, morality and ethics, questions and beliefs, language and expression and then provides a leading Christian idea under each category and illustrates this from biblical passages. For example at Key Stage 1, under the first category, the Christian idea is 'God loves and cares for each of us' and this is illustrated by 'Gospel stories indicating individual worth' and the birth narratives of Christ are mentioned here as well as Jesus blessing children (Mark 10.13-16), Zacchaeus (Luke 19.1-10), the lost sheep (Luke 15.4-6) and the lost son (Luke 15.11-32).

At Key Stage 2, the same categories are used, but the notions of implicit and explicit religion are introduced as a further refinement. The implicit material is a development of the seven categories listed in the previous paragraph. The explicit material is divided more theologically. The Christian content, for example, is placed under the headings: God and sacred writings, community and worship, festivals, Jesus and his followers. Bible passages are suggested in respect of God and sacred writings (Genesis 1) and Jesus and his followers, including Jesus' life and teaching (Matthew 22.37-39), the Christian view of

Jesus (John 10.11; 6.35; 4.14 and 8.12) and the concern for the poor expressed in the Sermon on the Mount (Matthew 5-7).

The Wolverhampton Agreed Syllabus (1996) has similarities in structure to the Essex syllabus. It also speaks of 'learning about religion (and life issues)' and 'learning from religion (and life issues)'. In addition there are six 'area themes' around which the content of the syllabus is based. These are: creation and the natural world, community and relationships, worship, tradition, occasions and celebrations and symbolism. At Key Stage 1 the first theme specifies creation stories from Genesis and other cultures. The tradition theme suggests stories of Jesus and stories Jesus told. The symbolism theme suggests parables like the Good Shepherd.

At Key Stage 2 creation stories again come under the first theme and further bible stories from the parables and miracles of Jesus come within the tradition theme. There is also reference to Jesus himself, Peter, Paul and key Old Testament figures. There are no other obvious references to the text of the bible at these two levels.

In commenting on these Agreed Syllabuses and suggesting how they might impact bible teaching in primary classrooms, there is one important preliminary point to make. This is that the bible itself is an object of study and explanation at an early stage in some syllabuses. For example, under Key Stage 2 for Essex, there is a section on 'the nature of the bible' (p 46) which is broken down into the headings:

- the bible is a special book for the Christian faith;
- the bible includes many books;
- most biblical material was handed down orally before being written down;
- the bible contains many different types of writing;
- the bible can be interpreted in different ways.

This section must be sharply distinguished from the Key Stage 1 work specified in the Wolverhampton syllabus on 'rituals associated with holy books' and with the Key Stage 1 learning experiences in the Nottinghamshire syllabus letting children 'look at, and handle carefully, some special bibles, e.g. a family bible'. Essex is concerned with the nature of the bible as a text; Wolverhampton and Nottingham about its status as a religious object.

The teacher in an Essex school has far more opportunity to lay the foundation for perceptive questions about the bible that arise in secondary schools. Why did God command *this* then and *that* now? And the Essex teacher has more opportunity to consider the historical nature of the biblical text, the way it was added to over the years until the canon was closed, and its relationship to the communities (the church and Israel) which defined it and were defined by it. In short, the Essex syllabus paradoxically suggests a less authoritarian text which is, at the same time, more authoritative in the lives of believers.

Teaching Genesis 1

So far as bible teaching is concerned all three syllabuses recommend or stipulate Genesis 1 as a passage primary children should consider at Key Stage 2. We consider two ways of teaching this text.

The first way of teaching Genesis 1 comes from a lesson from a *Resource Bank* of photocopiable sheets by Cooling, Walker and Goodwin (1993b). These sheets make use of the 'cracking RE' concept explained by Cooling (1994b). This concept is a method for exploring Christian beliefs that relies on finding a:

• clear and simple focus of the beliefs; and a
• way of relating the focus to pupil experience.

Once understood the method can be applied to almost any Christian belief. The trick is to find an appropriate link between the focus and the experience of the child. As Cooling points out, what is important is that the focus arises from the theology of any narrative under consideration. Discussing Noah's flood simply because it fits a topic on animals will not do (p 15).

Resource Bank provides teachers' notes and a lesson outline of Genesis 1.1 to 2.4. Teachers are given theological help by an explanation that the biblical presentation of God is as a being who is involved with humanity and involved with the world. Yet it is pointed out that Christians differ over how the Genesis story is to be interpreted, though they agree that it shows the world was deliberately created and purposeful and bears its creator's stamp. Human beings are separate from animals and in God's 'image', a term that suggests either a capacity for relationships or for moral choices. Pupils are introduced to the idea of God as creator by looking at things children have made or hand-crafted objects and then by discussing the idea of providing for people. The lesson culminates in a one page summary in simple language of the Genesis passage itself. The passage is suitable for reading aloud to children. Pupils can follow this up by making a picture that uses animal, vegetable and mineral elements.

The crucial question is whether any major alterations would be needed to make this lesson outline on Genesis fit the three Agreed Syllabuses under consideration.

The introductory pupil activity seems eminently suited to all three syllabuses. It bridges the gap between the experience of children and the main concept contained in the text. The discussion might be steered in different directions by a teacher to make the link between this part of the syllabus and what was going to be taught next. For example the Wolverhampton syllabus is more inclined to mix religions together than the others. Creation stories are here used to illustrate a general religious belief in God as creator rather than a specific belief belonging to one religion. Nottingham, though it does not rule out thematic teaching, is concerned that the Christian ideas of God as being 'sustaining, loving, just, saving' are known and understood (p 46) whereas the Islamic creation stories are intended to show 'God has no partners' and 'cannot be compared to anything else' (p 54).

The follow-up activity is also well suited to the topic because it flows straight from one of the main ideas of the text. In practice, aims of learning *about* religion, which are present to a greater or lesser extent in all three syllabuses, should allow bible teaching to occur without the need to put a 'spin' on the text. Learning *from* religion ought also to be unhindered since the syllabuses do not prescribe what it is that children are expected to learn - to do so would be educationally highly questionable.

The second way of teaching Genesis 1 comes by transferring the skills that might be used in English lessons to biblical texts. We have already referred to this possibility in the previous unit. Under the heading of 'key skills' the National Curriculum stipulates that children should be encouraged to respond imaginatively to the 'plot, characters, ideas, vocabulary and organisation of language in literature'. Of course, not all children will be equal in their ability to cope with the full range of reading skills. This is recognised by the six attainment targets set out to quantify pupils' progress. The six attainment targets at Key Stage 2 may be summarised as (DfE, 1995a):

- recognising familiar words in simple texts; expressing responses of like and dislike to poems, stories and non-fiction (level 1);
- reading simple texts, stories or poems, fiction or non-fiction, and understanding them generally accurately; being able to express opinions about them (level 2);
- reading a range of texts fluently and accurately; showing understanding of the main points of a text and expressing preferences (level 3);
- responding to a range of texts; pupils can show understanding of significant ideas, themes, events and characters and begin to use inference and deduction (level 4);
- showing understanding of a range of texts; pupils can select essential points and use inference and deduction where appropriate; pupils can select key features, themes and characters and select sentences to support their views (level 5);

- reading and discussing a range of texts; pupils can identify different layers of meaning and comment on their significance and effect; they can give personal responses to literary texts and refer to aspects of language, structure and themes to justify their views (level 6).

If the government literacy drive is successful then 80 per cent of children should reach level four by the end of Key Stage 2. The majority of children, then, ought to be able to address a wide range of texts and understand their main ideas. If there are characters in the text, they should appreciate this. If there are ideas in the text, they should be able to comprehend them. The more able children should begin to make deductions from a text. At all levels children should be able to respond to a text, whether by expressing like or dislike, or in more complex ways taking into account a variety of linguistic, ideational and inferential features.

For the teacher the questions are, 'how to teach so that those features of a text identified by the National Curriculum are appreciated?' and 'how can I make children aware that a text has a complicated life, that it is something needing a response?'

Teachers in primary schools are equipped with numerous methods for taking a text to children[3]. Some of these methods are better at conveying plot and narrative and others are more suited to drawing attention to structure and implication. For example, if teachers want to convey narrative to young children they can use a story book with big pictures and gather the class in a circle on the mat. The class faces the teacher and the teacher turns the book towards the children and reads the text upside down aloud. As the story progresses the teacher turns the pages displaying fresh pictures.

This method can be varied to allow character to be appreciated by reading the story with different voices (the sulky threatening voice of the grumpy giant, the sibilance of deceitful snake, the sing-song whiney voice of the spoilt child) and by exaggerating their traits.

Older children can work through a story together by using a class set of reading books and reading aloud in turns. Provided the children are at roughly the same level this works well. Discussion before or afterwards can pick up less obvious parts of the narrative and help children to look for multiple meanings or structural patterns.

A variation of these methods makes use of a tape recorded 'talking book'. Such a resource can be used with younger or older children. As they follow the words in their own copies, they can learn how to pronounce and read new

---

[3] The *Blueprints English Key Stage 2 Copymasters* by J Fitzsimmons and R Whiteford (Cheltenham, Stanley Thornes, 1992) suggest ways of developing reading, writing, speaking and listening skills in line with National Curriculum attainment targets. Many of the ideas in Blueprints could be transferred to the teaching of biblical texts.

words. If the 'talking book' is skilfully produced characterisation will be evident, and there may be a soundtrack of background noises that will appeal to children's imaginations. Again, discussion can help children to find subtleties they would miss by themselves.

The third way of teaching Genesis 1 involves telling the story to the class using visual aids. Once the story has been told, the children can then be asked to turn to a written version and to answer questions on it. The advantage of this method is that it can avoid the need for a formal discussion since the telling of the story, if it is done vigorously, will imply the points that the discussion might make. The written version, too, is easier to understand since its basics have already been conveyed through extempore narration[4].

Alternatively the teacher can introduce the story and explain its main structural features and then ask the children to read it to themselves or in groups. This method presumes that children have basic reading skills and only need help to reach the higher attainment targets.

Responses to the story, however it is presented, can be written, spoken, drawn or acted. Children can be asked to involve themselves with the *emotions* of the text (write a letter to the girl in this story and say how you felt when the horse died), in its *moral choices* (do you think the king did the right thing when he sent the soldier to prison?), in its *historical setting* (why couldn't the people in those days defend themselves against wild animals?), in its *realism* (could a peach really grow that big?) or its *multiple meanings* (why is it always winter when the witch rules?).

Activity C2

Plan a lesson on the story of Zacchaeus for a class of seven year olds in an inner city area. Include an opening activity or set of discussion points, a method of conveying the narrative to the children and a follow up activity

Comment on activity C2

There are many approaches you could take to this task. For instance, you might decide that the story of Zacchaeus would best be understood by these inner city children if you stress first of all the *money-grabbing* and nasty character of Zacchaeus. He was a tax collector and tax collectors in those days made their living by collecting more than their entitlement and keeping it instead of sending it on to the Romans. Tax collectors were seen as working

---

[4] I used to introduce *Macbeth* to a GCSE group by telling them the story of the play before they got to grips with Shakespeare's English.

for the enemy, for the Romans, who occupied Judea at the time. The Jewish people hated tax collectors and the Romans despised them. They were in the middle of two peoples, belonging properly to neither. Children in an inner city area may be aware of gangs, of belonging and not-belonging and the idea of being someone in between two groups might be familiar.

In addition Zacchaeus was a small man and perhaps he had been picked on when he was younger and *bullied*. This might explain his mean character in later life. He wanted to get his own back on the Jewish people. He was also one of the chief tax collectors. He was probably a *proud* man, one who was used to bossing people about.

Your opening activity might begin to sketch in the historical and psychological backgrounds. The historical background has to be explained. It could be illustrated by imaginary examples (how would we feel if we were ruled by a foreign power which had defeated our army?), but these may be confusing to children. The psychological background is much nearer to home. Children know what it is to be small, and they know what it is to have seen small children bullied by bigger children. A set of drawings could show small people being disadvantaged by big people. Children could then complete these drawings showing what they think the small people will do if they keep being treated like this.

The story of Zacchaeus could be conveyed by any of the methods mentioned above. Since these are seven year olds and in an inner city area, it would probably be best for the teacher to tell the story with an illustrated book. If the story has a picture of Zacchaeus climbing the tree and then coming down to Jesus, the idea of climbing can be associated with pride and the idea of coming down with humbling. So the psychology of the story can be symbolised visually. Alternatively and in addition, the pictures may show Zacchaeus as not being part of the crowd when he runs ahead to climb the tree but, after meeting Jesus, being surrounded by people as he gives money away. The themes of not belonging and belonging are thus also represented visually.

Your follow up activity could concentrate on the effect that Jesus had on Zacchaeus' life. Either in discussion or as a piece of written work children could write what they think Jesus said to Zacchaeus that made him give away so much money. Alternatively discussion and written work might explore why Zacchaeus wanted to see Jesus and how Zacchaeus afterwards changed the way he lived.

Bible and cross-curricular themes

OFSTED reports contain a section on the 'spiritual, moral, cultural and social development' of pupils. This extract is taken from an OFSTED report on a Nottinghamshire primary school.

> The development of moral and spiritual awareness is supported by daily assemblies and acts of worship. Themes such as 'friends and neighbours' are laid down in the guidance for collective worship and are used effectively for whole school, year group, Key Stage and 'presentation' assemblies in which pupils participate enthusiastically.

Cultural development is often placed at the door of history, geography, art or music and social development often belongs either to the range of opportunities pupils are given for out-of-school activities where they may learn tolerance and co-operation or the merit system that rewards good behaviour.

The bible is likely to be used in assembly and so its role will extend not only to religious education but more broadly to the cross curricular dimension presupposed by spiritual, moral and cultural development.

As Wright (1994) points out the National Curriculum history document specifically mentions the need to look at the church in medieval society (Key Stage 2), the beliefs of Anglo-Saxons and Vikings (Key Stage 2), religion in the Roman Empire (Key Stage 3) and the holocaust (Key Stage 4)[5]. At primary level the linkage between Christianity and British history is well explored by Cooling (1994a), whose materials could be used for the religious component in a topic, for stand-alone religious education or for history lessons or assemblies. Many of the lesson outlines she proposes have a biblical passage at their heart. For instance, a section on 'Roman Christian Faith and Worship' gives background information on the coming of Christianity to Britain and the eucharistic pattern that was adopted. The 'kiss of fellowship' with which these Christians greeted one another was adapted from the greeting that would customarily be given in Roman society by family members. The implication was that the church, rich or poor, slave or free, was composed of people who were together in one big family. This notion is supported by biblical passages (Colossians 3.11 and Galatians 3.28).

The National Curriculum attainment targets for history, like those for English paraphrased earlier, contain ideas and skills that would be applicable to the study of biblical texts. To take one example, pupils at level 3 should be able to show an understanding of chronology, of the division of the past into periods of time, of dates and terms and begin to appreciate a few reasons for the main events and changes (DfE, 1995a, p 82). Certainly the long historical sections of the Old Testament need to be placed into chronological order and

---

[5] We have not included a separate section on cross curricular themes at secondary level since they are touched on here.

the distinction between the different periods (nomadic Abraham, city-dwelling Solomon) explained and understood. The dangers of invasion and predation that faced the Israelites in the period of the Judges, for example, are similar to those which faced the British when they were being harried by the Vikings.

Lessons could be constructed that treated suitable biblical passages as historical documents. The skills of history could be applied to the content of religious education. In short, cross curricular themes could utilise the rich resources of the bible.

Finally, bible teaching in primary schools, following a good syllabus or scheme of work, will demonstrate continuity and progression. This means that the teacher will ensure that there is a co-ordination between what children learn at the beginning of their primary education, what they learn in the middle and what they learn at the end. Planning will ensure that the same story is not endlessly repeated and that, if it is repeated, different aspects of it will be emphasised. More than this, planning will ensure that what has been learnt earlier will be of use later. Agreed Syllabuses ought to have been constructed with these principles in mind but, even if this is not always obviously the case, the schemes of work teachers devise for their own schools should select a path through optional material within syllabuses that allows for continuity and progression within the overall needs of their children.

C3 Bible in the secondary school

Again, we anchor the discussion in the three Agreed Syllabuses we have used earlier. As might be expected they diverge more at secondary level than at primary level. The biblical content is less prevalent and the world religions content more likely to occupy classroom time. Nevertheless all the syllabuses provide opportunities for bible teaching though all of them note that GCSE syllabuses are likely to come into play for pupils who opt for religious education at Key Stage 4.

Essex, while continuing its seven categories of implicit material, specifies that pupils should engage with the nature of God and evidence for God when they deal with the Christian tradition. They should also concentrate on Jesus and the key events in his life as presented in the gospels. The divinity and humanity of Christ as seen through his birth and baptism, teaching, miracles, relationships with others and suffering, death and resurrection are included. Clearly there is enormous scope here for bible teaching.

Nottingham, again, makes use of the learning from and learning about aims in religious education. In its Christian content, it suggests pupils might look at how God is portrayed in art, at 'the meaning of key words such as incarnation and redemption' and 'study examples of creeds, writings, hymns and songs which illustrate key Christian beliefs'. They should also 'deepen their understanding of the Easter story through art, music and drama' and 'consider how the Early Church's understanding of Jesus is reflected in the different gospel writings'.

Wolverhampton at secondary level also gives scope for bible teaching, though the examples within the syllabus and the thematic structuring of material make this less likely to be distinct and free-standing. Pupils are expected to work on creation and the natural world under the headings 'awe and delight' and 'sin and salvation' which might be exemplified by Genesis 3. Under the 'occasions and celebrations' area theme pupils will look at Christmas (incarnation) and rites which mark the journey of faith (baptism, confirmation, ordination and circumcision). Under the unfortunately titled area theme of 'symbols' pupils are asked to look at meanings and values and to consider 'how the cross represents the importance of the death and resurrection of Jesus and beliefs about him and these events for Christians'. Key Stage 4 uses the same area themes but specifies very little explicitly religious material.

Preliminary matters

The county's Agreed Syllabus will define what sort of religious education, and what sort of engagement with the bible, the majority of primary children have undertaken. But, where a secondary school is supplied by some feeder schools that are church-related and others that are not, a variety of syllabuses will have been in operation. Consequently, it is unsafe for the year 7 religious education teacher to assume that all children have arrived at secondary school with similar levels of bible knowledge.

Similarly, the religious background of pupils is likely to have a discernible effect on pupils as they reach secondary age. Some will have been regular church-goers for most of their lives. They will have heard the bible read in church, listened to sermons or Sunday school stories and be familiar with much basic content. The majority, by contrast, will have little bible knowledge and assume that all religious books are either fundamentally the same or equally 'disproved' by science (Francis and Kay, 1995; Kay and Francis, 1996).

In theory the secondary religious education teacher is a specialist, with specialist training and knowledge. He or she should feel confident about using the bible in a classroom, though this is not always the case and anecdotal evidence suggests that teachers vary enormously in this respect. One of the purposes of this unit, therefore, is to build the confidence of teachers in the possibility that the bible may be taught by educationally valid means and be understandable to pupils.

Cross curricular teaching of the bible can occur in humanities courses, PSE courses and other generalised or thematised areas of the curriculum. Wright (1994) calls attention to the need for the teaching of the bible in such courses to arise out of the 'inner logic' of the syllabus rather than to be tacked on as an educational or administrative afterthought. The danger here is that the distinctiveness of bible teaching and, more widely, religious education is lost in the subjects with which it is being associated.

Bible and school assembly

The systematic information available in the public domain about assemblies in secondary schools is remarkably poor. Orchard (1993) summarised HMI reports in the period immediately following the 1988 Education Reform Act and noted frequent reference to school assembly. 'The reports often comment on pupil participation as a yardstick of effectiveness of the worship. There is also some observation of content... on the balance between religious and moral input.' However, Orchard does not attempt to systematise this information, presumably because it does not merit such treatment. Specific reference to the bible is not made.

Individual OFSTED reports may also comment on the conduct of assembly but there is little composite evidence available from which a *national* picture may be drawn. OFSTED reports suggest that where the bible is used in assembly it appears to be in the more traditional grammar schools or the more prestigious grant maintained schools, though often this amounts only to the reading of the text without comment. Souper and Kay (1982) collected evidence showing that the bible was the third most used book in secondary school assemblies in Hampshire. And O'Keeffe (1986) drawing on a sample of 28 secondary schools found only four were likely to be devotional, a further two to be religious and five to be a platform for social and moral issues. Whether the bible was used in these assemblies was unclear, though, where it was used, the Qur'an and other religious texts might also be read on other occasions.

Activity C3

What problems do you see with the use of the bible in secondary school assemblies? Are there ways round these problems?

Comment on activity C3

Two recent books on assemblies (Webster, 1995; Wright, 1995b) deal with the current legal framework which, it is clear, certainly does not forbid, and in many respects, through the requirement for Christian worship, encourages the use of the bible in assembly. Practical problems arise in trying to answer the two questions 'what is worship in a maintained school?' and 'how can it be properly developed?'

A *traditional* Christian model of worship might be said to cause the following problems with the bible:

- it encourages a non-critical approach to the bible that is inappropriate for schools;
- it encourages preaching in assembly which staff and pupils may find offensive;
- it is distant from the life-world of pupils and does not speak to their concerns;
- it is difficult to provide in the absence of staff who are committed Christians;
- if it is provided by those who are not committed Christians, the result will inevitably be boring to pupils;
- the many staff who take assembly will, if they use the bible, be uncoordinated in their approach and in the texts they use.

The reality of these problems cannot be glibly dismissed. Nevertheless, they may be partly resolved by a school policy on collective worship, by putting one or more members of staff in charge of assembly, by the use of local clergy who come in on a regular basis, by attention to the matter of assembly in initial and in-service teacher training and by involving the pupils themselves in the presentation of biblical materials in religious education lessons or lunchtime activities.

Less traditional models of worship may avoid some of these problems at the expense of creating others. Whichever model is used, however, it is important to allow pupils time for personal, private and silent reflection to whatever is presented to them from the biblical text. In this way worship, as a free and spontaneous response to God, is possible.

Bible and secondary religious education

A large-scale empirical project carried out by Smith (1998) on 13 year old pupils in 22 secondary schools in the counties of Northampton, Cambridge and Buckingham found that just over a quarter (27.5%) had never used a bible in secondary religious education. Just over a third (37.3%) had used a bible sometimes and only 13.1% used a bible often. If these figures are generalised to the remainder of England and Wales - and the demographic features of the areas would make this reasonable - it could be said that nearly three quarters of pupils use the bible at some point early in their secondary religious education. There is enormous scope, then, for thoughtful and lively teaching from and about the bible.

The three Agreed Syllabuses examined earlier all provide opportunities for teaching about aspects of the life of Christ, and this is also an important element in most GCSE religious education syllabuses. There is no consensus about the principles that inform current projects on teaching the bible. For example, the Biblos Project has sponsored *Splashes of God-light* (Copley, Bowness, Savini and Lane, 1997) which contains bible stories retold by a miscellaneous group of people who are practising members of the Christian and Jewish faith communities. The stories are designed for all-age audiences though Key Stage 2 and Key Stage 3 are particularly in mind, and writers selected their own passages. The result gives us incidents and teachings from the New Testament: the Canaanite woman (Matthew 15.21), the striking dumb of Zechariah (Luke 1.5-25), the prodigal son (Luke 15.11-32), walking on the water (Matthew 14.13-33), the woman who washed Jesus' feet (Luke 7.36-50) and the boyhood of Jesus (Luke 2.41-52). Each story is retold in a way that would make sense if it were read aloud to pupils or if they read it for themselves. At the same time each story attracts a comment from the teller explaining its significance and appeal.

Wright (1995a) shows both how the bible itself may be introduced to Key Stage 3 and Key Stage 4 and how the major events in the life of Christ may be approached. He uses a double page with colour photographs, line drawings, quotations, a summary and a 'Brain Engage' section asking pupils to think about the contents and ideas of the section. The bible is compared with a guide through a maze, has become a best seller containing God's message to humanity and is a book of several different types of writing (parable, history, proverbs, songs, laws) that can be interpreted in different ways to speak to us today. Wright's section on Jesus has pages on a real touch-and-go rescue in the mountains (to introduce the idea of Jesus as Saviour), on the miracle of birth (to link with the miraculousness of Jesus' birth), photographs from the film *Jesus of Nazareth* (to illustrate baptism, temptation and triumphal entry to Jerusalem), a poster advertising a computer game (to introduce the idea of a super hero) and icons (to show Jesus as representing the human face of God).

Cooling (1997) introduces a textbook designed to help secondary pupils learn 'about the Bible and why it is important for Christians and our culture'. She draws out a series of syllabus links to: revelation, sources of belief, sacred texts, the impact of the bible on culture and gospel narratives. Each double page contains a series of lively pictures interspersed with chunks of text and questions or discussion starters, summaries, glossaries, cartoons, comic strip characters and photos of young people with whom pupils can identify. While there are no sections specifically on the life of Jesus, the events of Jesus' life are presented as part of the panorama of history that the bible supplies. Jesus is seen as the fulfilment of Old Testament prophecies and the church as the body designed to further the continuation of his mission.

As with teaching of the bible at primary level, the possibilities opened to religious education by National Curriculum English are inviting. At Key Stage 3 and Key Stage 4 (DFE, 1995b, p21) pupils are expected to have read from a variety of genres and should be taught key skills to:

- extract meaning beyond the literal;
- analyse and discuss alternative explanations, unfamiliar vocabulary and hidden meanings;
- analyse and engage with ideas, themes and language in fiction, non-fiction, drama and poetry;
- reflect on the writer's presentation of ideas... the overall impact of a text;
- appreciate the significance of texts whose language and ideas have been influential, e.g. the *Authorised Version of the Bible*.

English teachers have an armoury of weapons at their disposal for the presentation of the texts to secondary pupils. They can alternate creative writing and literary appreciation so that each reinforces the other. For instance, children are asked to write a poem and then to read a poem of acknowledged excellence. As the merits of the example are drawn out by discussion and explanation children come to see how their own work can be improved. As they wrestle with the demands of writing a poem, they more fully appreciate the challenge of the blank piece of paper which faces every creative writer. They may begin to feel, but perhaps not to express, the conflict between the endless possibilities of creativity and the demands of a disciplined form.

Similarly, teachers can alternate between dramatic and verbal media and so draw attention to what can be better shown and what can be better said. Any piece of drama exists both as a written text and as a multi-interpreted and repeatedly enacted performance. As pupils write and act, act and write, their imaginations are engaged and their interests are (theoretically!) aroused.

A variation of this process is found in the use of visual media. At its worst, pupils are merely asked to draw a bible story. At its best, the art of the past, or the contemporary line drawings of pupils can bring a biblical text to life. At a less grandiose level, religious education teachers will know what it is to ask pupils to retell a parable using a cartoon strip. In this way, pupils are bound to recount the narrative and to select important incidents in it.

Yet, as English teachers know, the religious educator should not be afraid of simply reading (either round the class or in groups) the text of the bible and then discussing its meaning. At some point, particularly with pupils starting on secondary school examination work, the bare text without adornment must be enough to excite their intellectual faculties. Anyone who has visited a Jewish school in the UK (where the text is usually studied in Hebrew) will know that pupils are capable of sustained engagement with the lexical, syntactical, structural, semantic and theological features of the bible (Kay, 1989).

A parallel can be drawn between teaching theology and grammar. The National Association for the Teaching of English (1997) points out that grammar can be taught 'as an object in its own right' or through 'experiential learning, embedded in pupils' own contexts'. These options, though, are best thought of as ends of a continuum and teachers can move backwards and forwards across it. Grammar teaching is designed to help pupils become effective communicators and to enable them to analyse language. This, the Association argues, can only be done by 'systematic setting of learning objectives'. Similarly, theology can be taught as an object in its own right (God is love, forgiveness for sin is essential) and as implied by our treatment of other people in the contexts of daily life. And, just as grammar cannot be taught without reference to texts that exemplify it, so Christian theology cannot be taught without addressing the biblical texts that are its earliest expression and foundation.

Activity C4

How would you begin to teach the life of Christ to a year 7 class (aged 11-12) in a large urban secondary school with a mixed catchment area? The school has a mixed ability policy in years 7-9.

Comment on activity C4

It is usually best to assume that some children know almost nothing about the life of Christ and have never opened a bible.

One option the teacher has is simply to tell the story of the life of Christ in 20 minutes. The advantage of this is that, if the teacher is capable of holding the attention of the class, information can be conveyed quickly, adapted to the needs of a particular group, illustrated by pictures or drawings and then discussed in small groups or reproduced by pupils in the form of a piece of writing. Moreover the teacher, by this means, is capable of giving an *overview* of the life of Christ so that the parables and miracles and events of Christ's death and resurrection can be placed in a coherent sequence. Once this sequence is established in the minds of pupils parables and miracles can be fitted in to it in subsequent lessons.

Another option is to *build up* the life of Christ through its incidents and components. Lessons can be devoted to the historical background, to the birth of Jesus, to the ministry of John the Baptist, to the call of the disciples, to the early ministry in Galilee, to the miracles and parables, to the conflict with religious authorities in Jerusalem, to the events of Holy Week and to the resurrection. This series of lessons can then be summarised with an overview which puts all the pieces together into an organised whole.

Once the general approach has been decided, then the teacher has to decide how to deliver it. One factor often omitted from planning is the need to keep lessons fresh by varying the method of presentation from week to week. So a week that contains a simple telling of the story by the teacher might be followed by a week that makes use of reading from a modern translation of the bible and this might be followed by a film strip that re-tells a parable in a modern way. If the method is varied, pupils are less likely to complain of boredom. Similarly, if pupils are asked to do different things to express or assimilate what they have learnt, they will also be less likely to feel that there is a sameness to all religious education lessons.

The particular challenges offered by a mixed ability class are met by using methods of presentation of the account of Christ's life which are, as far as possible, suitable to everyone. In their own work, however, the ability range of the class will be most evident. Able pupils will produce beautifully spelled and grammatical written work. Less able pupils will be much weaker here - though in discussion they may be perceptive.

GCSE

Most examination syllabuses are designed to provide pupils with options about which religion they study and how closely it is linked to the modern world. For example, the Welsh Joint Education Committee (WJEC) offers *either* Jesus and the Foundation of Christianity *or* Christian Life and Contemporary Society *or* Christian Life and Worship *or* Sikhism (or Hinduism, Buddhism, Judaism or Islam) in Contemporary Society. Pupils must choose any two options. They therefore have a wider choice of Christianity than of other faiths, and their Christianity can either focus on the New Testament, as in option 1, or on contemporary manifestations and issues. If they select option 1, then they study specified biblical passages relating to the birth, ministry and passion of Jesus. If they select other Christian options they will also, by implication, look at biblical passages, though these are not specified so closely. Similar patterns of choices are found in the syllabuses drawn up by the Southern Examining Group (SEG), the Midland Examining Group (MEG), the Northern Ireland Council for the Curriculum, Examinations and Assessment (CCEA) and the Northern Examinations and Assessment Board (NEAB).

The nature of syllabuses is to concentrate on the content to be covered by pupils and to let teachers decide how that content should be delivered. But teachers are steered to the extent that assessment objectives in syllabuses draw attention to the need to produce:

- evidence and arguments to support and evaluate points of view (NEAB);
- reasoned argument based on evidence collected (SEG).

Where biblical texts are set for study, pupils must, presumably, use them as evidence for conclusions relating to beliefs and opinions. Teaching methods therefore are almost bound to lead pupils to a scrutiny of the structure and meaning of the biblical text.

Textbooks dealing with the teaching of the bible at GCSE level vary in their sophistication and accessibility. *Jesus and the Gospels* (de Lacey and Turner, 1983) is part of a series on the whole bible and provides historical and geographical information at a level suitable for pupils, photographs and explanatory comments on short pieces of biblical text. There are extra boxed paragraphs on specialist features headed, for instance, 'what is a parable?' or 'the prayers of Jesus'. *Luke: a gospel for today* (Smith and Raeper, 1989) breaks the gospel into 59 units, each of which is designed for only one lesson. This allows the teacher to work over a two year course and cover the whole gospel comfortably. Graphics, illustrations, headings and follow-up ideas lighten the presentation -which is basically that of a simplified commentary.

Heavier and more church-based is *Christianity for GCSE* (Minney, 1989). This deals with festivals, worship, rites of passage, Christian beliefs and Christianity in a non-Christian world. Again, pictures and diagrams lighten the appearance of each page. The bible, as a subject for pupils to learn about, is not given a section of its own but is used as a resource in many of the pupil activities.

Activity C5

Plan in outline that part of a programme of study which deals with the bible. Write the material either for years 7-11 in a secondary school or for the top end of a junior schools (years 4-6). Show how the programme differentiates between pupils of different ages, abilities and backgrounds and progresses from what is learnt at the start to what is learnt later.

Comment on activity C5

Unless the school is voluntary aided, the programme of study will have to conform to the requirements of the Agreed Syllabus applicable to the school. The approach outlined below is one that is feasible in a variety of contexts.

In starting to produce an outline of a programme of study, we have only given general principles and suggested the way they might work. In order to allow for differentiation in each topic, learning activities must be worked out so that less and more able children will find appropriate degrees of difficulty. In order to allow for progression, there must be a logical order to the content of the topics studied and the nature of the learning tasks given.

We therefore suggest that children start with stories from the bible, move on to an historical or thematic framework and then go from there to a discussion of the way the framework has been put together. This might sound complicated and suitable only for more able or older children. An alternative development would be to move from stories to contemporary situations and the interests of children.

Stories are the most accessible type of literature and may be arranged to suit the interests either of junior or secondary school children. For example, key stories such as Joseph and his brothers, David as king, Jesus and his followers or Paul and the early church could all feature. Parables function as stories and so should be included at this stage of the programme. Differentiation may be achieved by arranging for the delivery of stories according to different methods so that older and more able children approach the narration by a more demanding process. Many of these teaching methods are discussed earlier in this unit.

The investigation of the historical or thematic framework is more difficult to pin down. An historical framework might involve the events by which the Hebrew people were unified and came to their settlement in the land or the chronology of the New Testament or the translations and versions of the bible. A thematic framework would have to be selected to illustrate ideas that were suitable to children (right and wrong; people who wrote the bible; finding and following God; God and the natural world; war and peace) which allowed the biblical material to be arranged in sequences that allowed for differentiation and progression. Scholars have questioned the authenticity and historicity of many bible stories, of course, but the technicalities of critical debate need not prevent children from hearing bible stories in the first place.

Readers

L.J. Francis, W.K. Kay and W.S. Campbell (eds) (1996), *Research in Religious Education*, Leominster, Gracewing.

Bibliography

Cooling, M. (1990), *Assemblies for Primary Schools*, Exeter, Religious and Moral Education Press.

Cooling, M. (1994a), *Faith in History*, Guildford, Eagle.

Cooling, M. (1997), *Best Seller*, London, Bible Society.

Cooling, M., Walker, D. and Goodwin, M (1993a), *Resource Bank 1*, Swindon, British and Foreign Bible Society.

Cooling, M., Walker, D. and Goodwin, M (1993b), *Resource Bank 3*, Swindon, British and Foreign Bible Society.

Cooling, T. (1994b), *Concept Cracking: exploring Christian beliefs in school*, Stapleford, Stapleford Project Books/Association of Christian Teachers.

Copley, T. (1997), *Teaching Religion: fifty years of religious education in England and Wales*, Exeter, University of Exeter Press.

Copley, T., Bowness, C., Savini, H. and Lane, S. (eds) (1997), *Splashes of God-light*, London, Bible Society.

de Lacey, D.R. and Turner, M.M.B. (1983), *Jesus and the Gospels*, Cheltenham, Hulton Educational Publications.

Devlin, P (1968), *The Enforcement of Morals*, Oxford, Oxford University Press.

DfE (1995a), *Key Stages 1 and 2 of the National Curriculum*, London, HMSO.

DfE (1995b), *English in the National Curriculum*, London, HMSO.

Francis, L.J. and Kay, W.K. (1995), *Teenage Religion and Values*, Leominster, Gracewing.

Francis, L.J. and Slee, N.M. (1996), *Water*, Birmingham, National Christian Education Council. See also *The Picnic, The Windy Day* in the same series.

Gilliland, J. (1972), *Readability*, London, University of London Press.

Hull, J.M. (1975), *School Worship: an obituary*, London, SCM.

Kay, W.K. (1989), Pupils of the Promised Land, *Times Educational Supplement*, 22 December.

Kay, W.K. and Francis, L.J. (1996), *Drift from the Churches*, Cardiff, University of Wales Press.

Lunzer, E. and Gardner, K. (eds) (1979), *The Effective Use of Reading*, London, Heinemann Education Books.

McCreery, E. (1993), Developing a whole school policy for collective worship, *British Journal of Religious Education*, 16, 1, 14-20.

Minney, R. (1989), *Christianity for GCSE*, Oxford, Basil Blackwell.

National Association for the Teaching of English (1997), *Position Paper no 1: Grammar*, Sheffield, NATE.

O'Keeffe, B. (1986), *Faith, Culture and the Dual System: a comparative study of church and county schools*, Lewes, The Falmer Press.

Orchard, S. (1993), A further analysis of HMI reports on Religious Education: 1989-91, *British Journal of Religious Education*, 16, 1, 21-27.

Smith, L. (1998), *What does RE achieve? an investigation of secondary school pupils' experience of RE and their attitudes to religion*, Unpublished PhD dissertation, University of Wales.

Smith, L. and Raeper, W. (1989), *Luke: a gospel for today*, Oxford, Lion.

Souper, P.C. and Kay, W.K. (1982), *The School Assembly in Hampshire*, Southampton, University of Southampton.

Webster, D. (1995), *Collective Worship in Schools: contemporary approaches*, Cleethorpes, Kenelm Press.

Wright, C. (1994), Cross-curricular links, in J King (eds), *Teaching RE in Secondary Schools*, Eastbourne, Monarch Publications, pp 75-82.

Wright, C. (1995a), *Key Christian Beliefs: faith for living*, Oxford, Lion.

Wright, C. (1995b), *Delivering Collective Worship: a guide for schools*, Bury St Edmunds, Courseware Publications,

Spiritual and Moral Development

Spiritual and Moral Development

Unit A

The basic curriculum and spirituality

Clive Erricker

Chichester Institute of Higher Education

Chichester

and

Jane Erricker

King Alfred's College

Winchester

Contents

Introduction

Aims

After working through this unit you should be able to:

- analyse what is meant by spiritual development in an educational context;
- interpret and critique approaches to spiritual development;
- consider the implementation of spiritual development in the basic curriculum.

Overview

This unit introduces you to current government directives and guidelines and discusses the initiatives of the School Curriculum and Assessment Authority (SCAA, now QCA). In doing so it necessarily examines the relationship between spirituality and theology, and does so by giving examples from recent research. After this the unit goes on to examine the relationship between selected curriculum areas and the development of spirituality.

A1 What is spirituality?

The question of what we mean by the word 'spiritual' and what it means to live with the concept of spirituality has exercised the minds of many thinkers over the centuries, now no less than at other times. This may seem surprising given the common perception of the present as secular and materialistic. Right now we are charged with the task of introducing children in school to this concept, within the context of their everyday lives. In order to do this, to plan spirituality into the curriculum, we must first come to some kind of common understanding of what spirituality is.

We all have our own concept, and the quotes below offer two. The first outlines Rizzuto's (1979) original reworking of Freud's hostility to religion. Spirituality occurs in the 'transitional space' each of us needs for play, for creativity. The second outlines Macquarrie's (1972) notion of spirituality which owes something to his Christianising of the philosophy of existentialism.

> Freud considers God and religion a wishful childish illusion. He wrote asking mankind to renounce it. I must disagree. Reality and illusion are not contradictory terms. Psychic reality - whose depth Freud so brilliantly unveiled - cannot occur without that specifically human transitional space for play and illusion.... Asking a mature, functioning individual to renounce his

God would be like asking Freud to renounce his own creation, psychoanalysis, and the 'illusory' promise of what scientific knowledge can do. This is, in fact, the point. Men cannot be men without illusions. The type of illusion we select - science, religion, or something else - reveals our personal history - the transitional space each of us has created between his objects and himself to find a 'resting place' to live in.

Fundamentally spirituality has to do with becoming a person in the fullest sense... this dynamic form... can be described as a capacity for going out of oneself and beyond oneself; or again, as the capacity for transcending oneself.... It is this openness, freedom, creativity, this capacity for going beyond any given state in which he finds himself, that makes possible self-consciousness and self-criticism, understanding, responsibility, the pursuit of knowledge, the sense of beauty, the quest of the good, the formation of community, the outreach of love and whatever else belongs to the amazing richness of what we call 'the life of the spirit'.

The notion of 'spirituality' relates traditionally to the lived experience of religion - not as something exclusive and feeding on itself, but as something evolved by faith in its engagement with the world. It is not the same as knowing about dogma, doctrine or church history, though knowledge has something to do with it. It is not even the same as personal devotional experience, though attention to a personal or subjective element brings us perhaps nearer to the target. As traditionally understood, spirituality seems primarily to represent an achieved state of all gathered knowledge and experience within the religious life. It has corporate as well as individual manifestation - displaying (from one case to another) distinctive qualities of sensibility in form, style and tone. Its appreciation calls for an approach very close to the way we appreciate art - demanding, for example, some sensitivity to the founding tradition, and a willing attention to its distinctive 'voice' (Starkings, 1993).

Webster's approach in chapter 14.1 of the Reader edited by Francis and Thatcher (1990) speaks of the need for education to gain a vision, engage with mystery and re-think its understanding of knowledge. He uses examples to illustrate what this would mean, taken from life-stories, plays, literature and religious teachings. One thread that runs through Webster's approach is that we need to reflect on our own experience in order to engage with the spiritual or 'a more profound reality'.

A2 The law, government directives and guidelines

Jack Priestley (1996) noted in his Hockerill Address of 1996 that the key moment in the use of 'spiritual' in modern educational usage was its appearance in the 1944 Education Act preceding 'moral, mental and physical' in the first sentence of the preamble. He also remarks that it owes its presence to 'a simple piece of archiepiscopal jiggery-pokery' (p 2). He explains this by going on to relate that the author of that part of the preamble was Canon J. Hall, Chief Officer of the National Society, who was chosen for the post by William Temple to gain 'the confidence of local authorities, directors of education and the teachers in their organisations' in order to look for a coming together of church and state schools. When Hall was asked why he had used the word spiritual rather than religious he replied 'Because it was much broader' explaining that 'if we had used the word religious they would all have started arguing about it' (p 8).

Ironically, and by contrast, Priestley also relates how, in 1977, the word was almost lost when the DES published its list of relevant areas of experience in *Curriculum 11-16*, when one view offered was that 'Spiritual is a meaningless adjective for the atheist and of dubious use to the agnostic' (p 2). He also states that such views often flew in the face of, or were simply ignorant of, relevant educational research, such as that published by David Hay, at Nottingham University, during that period. This we shall see is not an uncommon phenomenon.

The most significant points to note about Priestley's observations are how:

- the notions of spiritual and religious are overlapping but distinct;
- contentious the word spiritual is in modern society;
- the notion of the spiritual has a particularly ambivalent place in the idea of a curriculum.

These will be re-occurring themes in this unit.

The 1988 Education Reform Act and Circulars 3/89; 1/94

The 1988 Education Reform Act ensured that the place of spiritual development retained, and perhaps re-asserted, its presence without gaining any greater curriculum prominence. In the context of 'the government's commitment to strengthening the position of religious education and collective worship in schools' Circular 3/89 stated that religious education, religious worship, and the National Curriculum should secure that the curriculum of each maintained school is balanced and broadly based and:

- promotes the spiritual, moral, cultural, mental and physical development of pupils at the school and of the society;
- prepares such pupils for the opportunities, responsibilities and experiences of adult life.

In Circular 1/94 a further comment (paragraph 1, p 9) stated that:

The Government is concerned that insufficient attention has been paid explicitly to the spiritual, moral and cultural aspects of pupils' development and would encourage schools to address how the curriculum and other activities might best contribute to this crucial dimension of education.

As supportive as these comments were in respect of addressing the spiritual in education, criticism of what might be realised in practice was forthcoming. For example see unit C of the module *Church Schools: history and philosophy* in volume 1 of *Religion in Education*, in which lack of reference to the Transcendent, or God, was identified and a lack of reference to theological principles was commented on, so presenting spirituality in a humanistic form under the guise of neutrality.

Equally it can be claimed that, given the Circulars' reference to spiritual development being included in collective worship, there was an ambiguity as to whether a suggestion of Christian nurture was implied. At the same time no specific examples of how it should be included in curriculum subjects other than religious education were provided. In effect there was a governmental charge to deliver spirituality across the curriculum (and beyond it) but insufficient guidance. The result was a confusion, a vacuum, which, subsequently, OFSTED was required to resolve.

Activity A1

Using two separate sheets of A4 paper, write 'religion' and 'spirituality' in the middle of each. Now brainstorm the words you associate with each. Reflect on your observations and write a commentary as to how far the concepts are similar and different in your view. Add your reflections on how far the development of spirituality could be encompassed in the teaching of religion.

Identify ten ways in which spirituality could be addressed in the curriculum and beyond which would be consistent with an overall approach to the concept. Elaborate on the points you have made by identifying how they would represent a consistent approach to spiritual development and to what extent they could be incorporated within the guidelines offered by the DES circulars.

Comment on activity A1

Your commentary should indicate how far the two terms 'religion' and 'spirituality' are interchangeable or distinct. It should also indicate to what extent each term is concerned with personal, social, institutional and political life. You need to indicate to what extent these factors influence your view of the relationship between spirituality and religion.

Your reflections should build on the above in determining whether spirituality is intimately connected with the teaching of religion or a subject that needs to be addressed independently. This will be influenced by whether you think there is such a thing as 'non-religious spirituality'.

Your ten points and your commentary on them should address consistency on the following issues:

- whether spirituality encompasses distinctive Christian beliefs;
- whether spirituality encompasses the beliefs of other religious traditions;
- whether spirituality can be addressed effectively across the curriculum;
- whether spirituality is nurturing in a faith or broad and inclusivist;
- whether, if it is the latter, it is implicitly secularist;
- in what ways the DES guidelines prove to be problematic or inconsistent.

We will deal with some of these points, either directly or by implication, in the rest of this unit.

OFSTED guidance on inspection

The difficulty for OFSTED was that they are not a policy-making body. Thus the following OFSTED (1995, p 8) definition from *Framework for the Inspection of Schools* can be subjected to the same criticisms as those made previously.

> Spiritual development relates to that aspect of inner life through which pupils acquire insights into their personal existence which are of enduring worth. It is characterised by reflection, the attribution of meaning to experience, valuing a non-material dimension to life and intimations of enduring reality. 'Spiritual' is not synonymous with 'religious'; all areas of the curriculum may contribute to spiritual development .

The commentary on this definition emphasised that:

- spiritual development is not another name for religious education;
- it is a responsibility of the whole school;
- it is important to emphasise its uniqueness to each individual;
- it encompasses a unique relationship between the inner self or soul, the heart (i.e. feelings and emotions) and the mind;
- a key concept might be confidence in one's own identity;
- it concentrates on the process of exploration.

It should also be borne in mind that it is the school that is inspected, not the pupils. With this in mind the *Framework* document identifies how the range and quality of the provision designed to encourage such development might operate through:

- the values and attitudes the school upholds and fosters;
- the contribution made by the whole curriculum, religious education, acts of collective worship and other assemblies;
- extra curricular activity, together with the general ethos and climate of the school. (p 12)

One of the obvious difficulties that this movement toward inspection created was identifying the criteria and context in which development could be assessed. Schools with a religious foundation could have recourse to theological principles and community practices relating to values, attitudes and ethos, but OFSTED was at pains to make clear that this was not expected in maintained schools generally. One reason given for this was that it might result in the confessional teaching of religious education, 'which legislation since 1944 has been at pains to avoid' (p 15).

As a result the OFSTED *Framework* could be said to be just the opposite, a lack of a framework, because it could supply no generally acceptable criteria or context. The result is a stress throughout on the importance of the development of the individual and the uniqueness of what is meant by spirituality to each individual (p 10).

This has attracted criticism from different quarters. Thatcher in unit C of the module *Church Schools: history and philosophy* in volume 1 of *Religion in Education* comments that, 'The OFSTED approach to spiritual development is gripped by the notion of individuality and the problem of the individual's reflexive relationship to herself... there is a complete lack in Government literature of any mention of neighbour love, or (to use an equally biblical word) justice.'

This criticism exposes how individualistically oriented notions of spirituality fail to address values, common notions of human responsibility and the creation of a just society. A further criticism, by Andrew Wright (1997) draws on Alasdair MacIntyre and Paul Ricouer in stating:

> The story of my life is always embedded in the story of those communities from which I derive my identity. I am born with a past; and to try to cut myself off from that past, in the individualistic mode, is to deform my present relationships. The possession of an historical identity and the possession of a social identity coincide.

Wright goes on to point out that it is necessary to understand spirituality in terms of national identity, which must begin with 'recognising and nurturing children into the specific spiritual tradition they bring with them to the classroom' (p16). In contrast he suggests that a 'spiritual education that seeks to dislocate itself from any specific tradition' will end up 'indoctrinating children into the spiritual tradition of romanticism' (p 17) which he identifies with the teachings of Rousseau and those of progressive child-centred educators.

Both the above criticisms point to a nurturing by default into an inadequate form of spiritual development precisely because no one has any real responsibility for the educational and social implications that attach to spiritual development in schools. Whilst Thatcher (1997) criticises lack of attention to Christian theology, Wright identifies the lack of any hermeneutical underpinning in policy-making.

Partly in response to these sorts of criticisms OFSTED actually ends its *Framework* document with four questions, raised as 'Points To Consider', which are reproduced below in abbreviated form. It is, perhaps, evidence that OFSTED itself was unsure of the workableness of its own approach.

- Is the attempt to define spiritual development to take account of those with a non-religious perspective and by those with religious beliefs reasonable?
- Are there some aspects of spiritual development which are the prerogative of religious education and others that are a whole school responsibility?
- To what extent is it possible to gain *evidence* of spiritual development? For example: does the school have ideals related to the concept of spiritual development and a strategy to promote their effect on pupils?
- Does the teaching of other subjects in the curriculum relate to the promotion of this whole view of spirituality?

A3 SCAA and spiritual and moral development

The School Curriculum Assessment Authority was set up under the Conservative government soon after the 1988 Education Reform Act. It took the place of the National Curriculum Council and as one of its initiatives republished the NCC's *Spiritual and Moral Development: a discussion paper* (1993) in 1995 as a basis for its major conference day on *Education for Adult Life: spiritual and moral aspects of the curriculum* on 15 January 1996. Following this a National Forum was established on the subject, which resulted in the publication *Education for Adult Life: the spiritual and moral development of young people* (SCAA *Discussion Papers: No. 6*) in July 1996, and *Findings of the consultation on Values in Education and the Community*, published in November/December 1996. This section is concerned with the work of the SCAA as presented in its conferences and publications on spiritual and moral development and values.

The initiatives of the SCAA have been important because they have raised the profile of spirituality, linked to morality and values, in education. The approach pursued has been one of consensus, drawing together informed opinion across different groups in society: education, youth work, industry and employment, faith communities, parenting and government. Its agenda was outlined by its chief executive, Dr Nicholas Tate, as follows.

> The issues we are here to discuss are not just ones for schools. Moral and spiritual education in schools is only possible if the society which maintains these schools is clear about its ends... As the statutory custodian of the school curriculum, the School Curriculum Assessment Authority is perhaps uniquely placed to initiate a national debate on these issues. But we hope to do more than just that. Our objective today is to come up with an agenda for action.

Dr Tate then identified reasons for the present moral and spiritual malaise.

> What has done most to undermine our surviving moral language has been the spread of an all pervasive relativism... By relativism I mean the view that morality is largely a matter of taste and opinion, that there is no such thing as moral error, and that there is no point therefore in searching for the truth about moral matters or in arguing and reasoning about it.

He identifies one of the predominant reasons for the spread of moral relativism as the decline of religious faith.

> As the Archbishop of Canterbury has recently said, people ever since the Enlightenment 'have been living off the legacy of a deep residual belief in God. But as people move further away from that, they find it more and more difficult to give a substantial basis for why they should be good.' This is one reason why religious education must continue to be a vital part of every child's curriculum... It is also a reason why children's development is so important, as the origin of the will to do what is right.

He also suggests that in personal and social education

> we need to review dispassionately the emphasis it often gives to the promotion of pupils' self-esteem... Is it too heretical a thought that it is possible to place too much emphasis on self-esteem (a peculiarly late twentieth century occupation) and too little on some of the traditional moral qualities?

Activity A2

 You will observe from the above quotes that Nicholas Tate is concerned with the moral attitudes of society, the role of the spiritual in relation to the moral, the function of religious education and personal and social education in schools in relation to these issues, and the importance of the relationship between education and society. Construct a response to the points he makes, based on your own teaching experience and further reading done in this module, as to the assumptions he makes and the value of his approach to spiritual and moral education. Take into account the relationship he identifies between spiritual and moral development and the role he assigns to the spiritual.

Comment on activity A2

In his speech it is clear that Nicholas Tate assumes a predominant emphasis on morality over against spiritual development. One of the issues that arises from this is the relationship between the two. Is spiritual development the handmaiden of moral education? If so, how, in practice, are the two to be related? Also, can we really arrive at an understanding of spiritual development without recourse to a specific doctrinal understanding embedded in a religious tradition? Your response in the task should have addressed these issues as well as interrogating his assumption that there is moral decline in society caused by prevailing relativism. Bear these questions in mind as we move on to the next topic.

Definitions

Below are lists taken from SCAA *Discussion Paper 3* illustrating what spiritual and moral development might include. The first list concerns the steps to spiritual development in an educational context:

- recognising the existence of others as independent from oneself;
- becoming aware of and reflecting on experience;
- questioning and exploring the meaning of experience;
- understanding and evaluating a range of possible responses and interpretations;
- developing personal views and insights;
- applying the insights gained with increasing degrees of perception to one's own life.

These steps operate within consideration of aspects of spiritual development such as:

- beliefs;
- a sense of awe, wonder and mystery;
- experiencing feelings of transcendence;
- search for meaning and purpose;
- self-knowledge;
- relationships;
- creativity;
- feelings and emotions.

The elements of moral development include:

- the will to behave morally;
- knowledge of the codes and conventions of conduct agreed by society;

- knowledge and understanding of the criteria put forward as a basis for making responsible judgements on moral issues;
- the ability to make judgements on moral issues.

One of the criticisms of the SCAA approach is that it has no theological basis and thus ignores the very foundations on which spiritual development has to be based. How can you carry out spiritual education if you have no identifiable ends to which it leads? (see Thatcher, 1996) Indeed Thatcher is one of the most persistent and prominent critics of the SCAA approach from this point of view. Thatcher (1990) argues that 'one of the most important tasks for the theologian is to draw attention to the climate of unbelief within which the religious educator operates' (p 274). This he parallels with Alasdair MacIntyre's charge of emotivism, 'the doctrine that "all evaluative judgements and more specifically all moral judgements are nothing but expressions of preference, expressions of attitude or feeling, insofar as they are moral or evaluative in character"' (p 274). Thatcher arrives at the conclusion that what, in the moral case, can be identified as the need for contemporary society to recover a sense of virtue, in the theological case amounts to a need to recover religious truth (p 275).

Thatcher's argument proceeds from a critique of the phenomenological approach to religious education which, he claims, reveals the problems that arise from taking up a relativistic position that is supposedly value free. On the contrary, he observes, it operates on the assumption that 'in treating religions as equal or religion as a universal feature of existence, the stipulation that no religion is absolute is as absolute as the stipulation that any one religion is absolute' (p 279). The consequence of this is that securing religious commitment ceases to be an aspect of religious education. This relativism then becomes problematic when addressing spiritual development since no faith stance, and in particular none based on the distinctiveness of Christian commitment, can operate as the basis of spiritual development within the SCAA model of consensus, which suffers from the same flawed premises derived from the climate of unbelief within which it operates. Thus, despite an apparent consonance of view with the remarks of Nicholas Tate, Thatcher identifies the reasons why the statements in the SCAA document are at variance with Tate's comments and why SCAA cannot deliver the goods!

The above critique provides the basis of a further criticism, that the points identified above are so vague as simply to be obvious, therefore offering no guidance or direction. Moreover there is no obvious connection between spiritual and moral development that can again be identified because of a lack of a distinctive faith stance within which they can both operate.

Coming at the problem from a different perspective, Dennis Starkings (1993) argues the case for a broader definition than Thatcher. But does it overcome Thatcher's objections to SCAA? Does it offer a more workable approach?

Starkings is concerned with the problematic divide between the religious and the secular in the definitions to be applied to spirituality and he sees the arts as a mediating instrument. He poses the problem of how to take an overall view of spirituality whist maintaining the distinctiveness of (for example) Christian spirituality. He suggests that 'while the religious kinds of spirituality find their focus and authentication in the distinctive experience of worship, secular spirituality is authenticated in a progressive integration of life's experience' and yet that 'the religious and the secular are related to each other through the contemporary experience of living across essentially distinguishable frameworks of meaning' (p 9). Starking's position is that:

> the challenge for anyone who wishes to form a view of the nature of spirituality that is sufficient for the comprehensive purposes of a national education system is... to draw such a map of spirituality's overall landscape as may relate spirituality's distinctively religious forms to its broader and secular manifestations (p 10).

Starkings charts the steps toward this relationship by identifying Christian faith as an experience of moving toward God through the disclosures of revelation. Revelation is to be grappled with in the movement from unknowing to knowing. This he understands as worship, in its broadest sense. Starkings wishes to retain the distinctiveness of the religious path but assert the authenticity of the secular with reference to the spiritual value of music, ballet, painting or drama. He suggests that through these and other human activities we reach out towards some wisdom, some humanity, some integration of our life's experience (p 14). Thus both the religious and the secular use of the term refer to moving beyond the purely material and in neither case can spiritual development be gained solely on the basis of confessional attachment. The important issue is to sustain the dynamics of the religious and secular options whilst discarding neither.

In SCAA *Discussion Paper 6, Education for Adult life: the spiritual and moral development of young people* we are provided with a summary report of SCAA's consultations. We read that:

- spirituality was generally viewed as enriching individuals in their understanding of, and ability to relate to others and society as a whole (p 6);
- the spirituality of young people can be developed in many ways: for example, by religion, thinking, prayer, meditation or ritual (p 7);
- providing regular times of stillness and quiet and contemplation are central to spiritual development (p 12);
- schools should evaluate the process and its effects upon pupils (p 12).

The discussion paper makes the point that spiritual and moral development should extend across religious education and the statutory curriculum and beyond into collective worship, economic and political education, citizenship education, school and community partnerships, the ethos of the whole school, and be addressed in the school policy document. In the summary of key points the paper first identifies that 'there is cause for concern about spiritual and moral values and the current state of society' (p 5).

It is clear from the above that the process of consultation followed by SCAA has resulted, on the one hand, in the collection of a broad range of views on the nature of spirituality and the means of fostering spiritual development in the curriculum. On the other hand, the SCAA approach firmly weds the purpose of spiritual development to a moral end, arresting a state of moral decline. To what extent can this marriage be justified? Ought it to be annulled on the basis of having no theological authority? Is it workable in an educational context?

A4 Spirituality and theology

As we have witnessed in the previous chapters identifying approaches to spiritual development raises fundamental questions as to what we are educating for. The primary task is to distinguish whether the concept of spirituality belongs within a particular theology of education, within a broader religious context, or can be located within an even wider framework that includes the secular. This unit and the one that follows addresses these issues in relation to the work of scholars and researchers in the field.

We can start on this odyssey with Derek Webster's observation that 'most of all at this time education "needs a vision"'. Here he quotes from Giroux's Theory and Resistance in Education (Webster, 1990, p 363). Webster's concern is to pay attention to the integrity of young people and seek ways of 'awakening to the sublime' (p 363). Webster's starting points are to recognise that the concept of the spiritual is both unique for each individual and yet universal (p 357). In education he insists that the whole process of teaching and learning is grounded in mystery and that this can be identified in such basic curriculum activities as number work, using a microscope and reflecting on biological maturation. In each case we are pursuing that which lies beyond the human grasp and points to a more profound reality, which some religious believers might want to call 'the work and the way of God' (p 358).

Webster is also concerned that the dark side of human experience is included in this approach: 'negation, emptiness, disgrace, deprivation, hurt, sin, bitterness or death' (p 360). Modern literature and the experiences of pupils illustrate the significance and weight of these issues and the need to address them. Webster's analysis is pupil centred, broad and inclusivist, and allows for an openness of outcome. The question can be raised as to whether it does justice to the committed teacher or child in terms of the development of faith.

Others take the need to address this issue further. Elmer J. Thiessen (1990, pp 83-92) arguing for a distinctively Christian curriculum, maintains that:

> there must be a unique content to Christian education in all areas of study. Christian presuppositions do provide an interpretative framework for all forms of knowledge. Christian education, if it is truly Christian, will be radically different from secular education even in subjects like mathematics and physics.

Thiessen's view presumes the need for a theology of education that would determine what spiritual development would mean. Whilst appearing to give greater clarity to the debate, raising the question of a need for a theology of education results in a detailed examination of what the term would mean.

John Hull (1990) observes, in the context of arguing that it is of itself difficult to know what theology is, that it is not legitimate to establish a view of education based exclusively on theology. This would mean that only theists or believers could take part in education and that the integrity of theology in education would itself be undermined. Rather a theology of education must serve as a legitimate but not necessary source of understanding. To extrapolate from Hull's analysis we may say that, in relation to spirituality, a theological position can be rightfully posited but it cannot be seen as the sole basis of spiritual development or act as its sole condition in theory or practice. Hull identifies areas of education in which a theology of education, or theologies, must engage in debate (Hull, 1990, pp 14-19) not attempt to establish a hegemony. Spirituality can be considered as one of these areas.

Activity A3

Read both the chapters by Thiessen and Hull and identify the main strengths of the two arguments as they apply to your school curriculum. Can the disparity of opinion between Thiessen and Hull be resolved?

Comment on activity A3

Points you should have addressed in your answer include:

Hull's chapter is a detailed and theoretical piece of writing about theology and education. It analyses what might be expected in both disciplines and then systematically tries to discover how they interact. Hull is concerned to show that the 'theology of education' is justified 'as a branch of educational study' because the study of what theologians have said is a perfectly reasonable activity. Doing theology, however, he takes to be relevant to those who are religious and wish to 'articulate their religious consciousness' and *this* activity is properly confined to theological colleges and the like rather than to secular institutions like universities. The theology of education, however, belongs within the discipline of education and has similarities with other disciplines that contribute to education like the philosophy of education, the sociology of education and so on.

Thiessen argues that Christian presuppositions provide an interpretative framework for all forms of knowledge and that Christian education will be very different from secular education even in respect of the most neutral kinds of subject like mathematics. In other words there *is* a relationship between religion and other forms of knowledge. This is partly because all the forms of knowledge are inter-related and it makes sense to say that religion is therefore connected with all the others. The nub of the issue is that forms of knowledge are *not* autonomous as is sometimes insisted.

The strengths of the two positions, then, lies in what they seek to do: Hull wishes to show how education in general may relate to religion in general and Thiessen wishes to show how Christianity in particular (though the argument does not rule out religion in general) may be used as the basis for the construction of a curriculum. Hull shows how religious consciousness (and by implication the religious consciousness of Christians) might be articulated within an educational context. Thiessen shows how Christian knowledge might have an influence on all other kinds of knowledge. The two positions, then, have similarities. Hull speaks of consciousness and disciplines; Thiessen speaks of beliefs and forms of knowledge.

Theology and curriculum

Astley (1990, pp 264-265) approaches the problem from a different angle. Whilst speaking more generally about theology and curriculum selection he observes that criteria of selection, theologically and educationally, are never neutral because they take account of what is considered to be true and of value. Therefore, just as selectivity within what is to be taught concerning Christianity, religion and in the curriculum generally will be determined on this basis, so, we may presume, selectivity in spirituality will be subject to the same criteria, that is, we cannot construct an approach to spiritual development that is theologically and educationally neutral (pp 268ff). Astley's point in relation to religious education can be applied to the way in which we conceive of spiritual development, in that Christian spirituality cannot just be included, in some descriptive sense, in what we offer to children. This, in itself, would be a value judgement as to the relativity with which we recognise claims to 'spiritual truth'. Rather, we have to be quite clear as to the basis for which we devise a notion of spiritual development in schools and how this takes account of the truth claims of those who occupy differing theological positions, Christian, religious or otherwise. In this respect Astley is presenting a position that sits alongside that of Thatcher, who warns us of the danger of a 'climate of unbelief' which was referred to in the last chapter.

One way forward in this central debate over truth and belief is to focus on the process of moving toward truth rather than simply possessing it. In this context belief or faith can be understood as directing forces or vehicles that carry us forward. Thus Martin (1990) argues for a commitment to questions rather than answers which is 'holistic and inclusive as well as critical' (p 176). Here Martin is presenting a case for a distinctively theological approach to higher education in church colleges, but the implications of this argument are relevant to the notion of spirituality and spiritual development in schools and especially church schools. Drawing on Paolo Freire (1972) he sees this leading to a new praxis which makes sense to both Christians and non-Christians in re-defining the response to social need (p 177).

Martin's approach is significant because he wishes to address the question of Christian mission in an educational context and yet not separate it off from the concerns of non-Christians. Thus he is drawn to accenting the centrality of values and social action. In this he quotes Jenkins (1985).

> Nothing is certain, but everything is possible. Such a constructive and committed openness is the basic condition of freedom and love (p 175).

Hull (1996), equally, recognises the same issues. By speaking of education for Christian-ness, which he distinguishes from Christendom, identified with the church, and Christianity, identified with a particular religion, he sees the mission of Christians as concerned with the suffering of the world. According to Hull, 'human suffering arouses the compassion of God and is the focus of the ministry of Jesus, who lays down his life for the world' (p 14). Furthermore, since such compassion is the work of the Spirit, God acting in his role as the one who inspires and dwells in creation, such activity cannot be circumscribed by confining it to the church (p 14). By positing three successive ages, of the Father, the Son, and now, of the Spirit, Hull asserts that we can know the Father and Son through the Spirit, and that such knowledge of God is not restricted to Christians (p 15). By positing an inclusivist view of the knowledge of God through the work of the Spirit, which can be witnessed 'wherever men and women follow paths of reconciliation' (p 16), Hull eliminates the traditional distinction between the Christian Church and the world by asserting that works of justice and freedom are everywhere inspired by the same Spirit, who is God over all (p 16). He concludes that such a Christian education:

> will enrich the experience of children with poetry and music, artwork and dance, knowing that all these, whether in the church or outside it, are the works of the Spirit of God if they contribute to justice, peace and the integrity of creation (p 16).

Activity A4

By reflecting on the reading you have done in this section and the tasks you have completed, consider how far and in what respects theology is integral to the development of children's spirituality.

Comment on activity A4

Your response should have taken account of the following issues.

- What exactly constitutes a Christian theological perspective within the curriculum of state schools?
- How far can this perspective be said to be explicit or implicit, i.e. to what extent does it involve encountering Christian doctrine over and above Christian values?
- To what extent is it necessary to explore notions of social justice as an integral element of spirituality?
- What constitutes the difference between 'Christian-ness', 'Christendom' and 'Christianity' and how plausible is this distinction?
- To what extent, if at all, does taking up either an explicit or implicit Christian position denigrate, or implicitly devalue, the positions of other religious and non-religious positions on spirituality?

A5 Recent research in spirituality

This section presents different approaches to researching spirituality in children's development and therefore different approaches to its inclusion in the curriculum. It includes reference to the work of Robert Coles and David Hay. The following section turns attention to the Children and Worldviews Project. Here we are concerned with research and writing on children's spirituality that is not grounded in theology. For some, being loosed from the embrace of theology has allowed spirituality to escape an old captivity; for others it has meant spirituality losing its maternal soul.

Recent research in the spirituality of children has taken a variety of forms. The extracts included have been chosen to represent differing approaches, though they are not intended to be either entirely representative of a genre or the only approaches possible. Each is informed by a particular understanding of what spirituality is, and by a particular approach to the undertaking of research itself.

Robert Coles

Coles' work is best typified in his book *The Spiritual Life of Children* (1990). In this he remarks how he came to be inspired to carry out research into children's lives by witnessing the racial riots and their effect on children in New Orleans in 1960. At that point he turned from his training as a psychoanalyst to become a 'field worker' talking with children going through their everyday lives 'amid substantial social and emotional stress'. His work on children's spirituality was a project begun in 1985 spanning the Americas, Europe, the Middle East and Africa and covering conversations with children of various faith backgrounds and others belonging to no faith community. Significant in his choice of approach was a movement away from the Freudian psychoanalysis of his training. He moved instead toward the view that the construction of religious ideas was a valuable aspect of people's identity and that children themselves already evidenced this original and creative activity rather than simply being the receptors of adult ideas. Influenced by the writings of Dr Ana-Maria Rizzuto and her view that 'it is in the nature of human beings, from early childhood until the last breath, to sift and sort and to play, first with toys and games and teddy bears and animals, then with ideas and words and images and sounds and notions' (p 6), he understood this activity as deriving from 'our predicament as human beings, young or old - and the way our minds deal with that predicament, from the earliest years to the final breath' (p 7).

Coles' approach can be characterised by the following distinctive characteristics. It is:

- qualitative, being conducted through semi-structured interviews with individuals and groups;
- anti-reductionist, by not imposing a pre-established theoretical framework on the interpretation of findings;
- non-judgemental, in that it does not subject respondents' views to a rational or systematic scrutiny.

As an example of Coles' research consider the following extract from an interview with a Hopi Indian girl.

When I went to Hopi homes there was no sudden miracle [Coles had failed to successfully interview the Hopi children in school]. But without question the work I did with those children really began only during those home visits ...they gave me some memorable thoughts that crossed their minds, so memorable that now I recall those children when I find myself saying that I began then to have some fairly solid notions about the spiritual life of children.

Here, for example, is what I eventually heard from a ten-year-old Hopi girl I'd known for almost two years. 'The sky watches us and listens to us. It talks to us and listens to us. It talks to us and hopes we are ready to talk back. The sky is where the God of the Anglos lives (white Americans), a teacher told us. She asked where our God lives. I said, "I don't know." I was telling the truth! Our God is the sky, and lives wherever the sky is. Our God is the sun and the moon, too; and our God is our (the Hopi) people, if we remember to stay here (on the consecrated land). This is where we're supposed to be, and if we leave, we lose God.'

Did she explain the above to the teacher?

'No.'

'Why?'

'Because she thinks that God is a person. If I'd told her, she'd give us that smile.'

'What smile?'

'The smile that says to us, "You kids are cute, but you're dumb; you're different - and you're all wrong!"'

It is instructive to read Coles' (1990, pp 342-343) own commentary on the approach and methodology of his research, in contrast to that of others. In his notes on method he writes as follows.

I have no quarrel with the notion of 'faith development' (see James Fowler, *Stages of Faith*, San Francisco, Harper and Row, 1981) nor with efforts to learn, through cognitive analysis, how our reasoning life connects with our religious or spiritual life. I can only repeat... that my work is contextual, that it aims to learn from children as they go about their lives: in the home, the playground, the classroom, the Hebrew school or Sunday school.

I am obviously less interested in analysing the structure of the thought of children... than in rendering for others what I have regarded as highlights in what I have been privileged to hear them say.

David Hay

David Hay's research, both with adults and children, is influenced by the previous studies of Alasdair Hardy (1966, 1979) and his hypothesis as to the biological origin of religious awareness which Hay regards as a broadly based, plausible and testable conjecture about spirituality. Hay (see Hay, Nye and Murphy, 1996, p 61) also favours Hardy's approach because 'it implies that there is in every child a spiritual potentiality no matter what the child's cultural context may be'.   Thus, in a manner akin to that of Karl Rahner (1974) in *Theological Investigations*, Hay conceives of an innate spiritual capacity in childhood which may focus in particular ways and take different and changing forms as the child's other capacities develop, but is not dependent on religious nurture or religious language *per se*.   Given this, research into children's spirituality must move beyond pre-occupation with 'God-talk' and a concern with religious constructs and concepts toward a 'focus on the perceptions, awareness and response of children to those ordinary activities which can act as what Peter Berger (1967) calls "signals of transcendence"' (Hay, Nye and Murphy, 1996, p 62).

Below is an extract from Hay's work illustrating its purpose and method, taken from Hay and Nye (1996).

> We have been working with children aged six and ten years in Nottingham and Birmingham and have had to consider how spirituality might be given expression at the fringes of its traditional vehicle in European culture, the language of Christian theology...   Where the language and institutions of formal religion are absent or unconvincing for many people, we had to try to identify the areas of children's language and behaviour where the 'sparks of spirituality' may be found.
>
> For this purpose we needed to create a hypothetical map as a kind of template to guide our conversations with children.   We examined the converging evidence of writers on spirituality and on child psychology, as well as our own experience of talking with children in the pilot stage of the project.   As a result we proposed a set of three inter-related themes or categories of spiritual sensitivity (Nye and Hay, 1996) which were basic enough to allow expression within or outside the familiar (usually religious) languages of spirituality.   The intention is to make possible the identification of spirituality in a wider and more abstract context than has been achieved elsewhere.   We will thus be able to move beyond an understanding of children's spirituality based on 'knowledge' towards a more general psychological domain of spirituality as a basic form of knowing, available to us all as part of our biological inheritance.

A table of categories of spiritual sensitivity

Awareness Sensing: Or, being aware of one's awareness.   In particular this can mean an awareness of the *here and now*, instead of letting the mind wander into the past and future, something which characterises much of adult life.   Margaret Donaldson (1992) calls this the 'point mode', the most basic mode of the mind's operation and, as such, present in even the youngest child. Religious interest in the point mode spreads across all cultures and expresses itself in the practice of meditation and contemplative prayer.

Another way of considering heightened awareness is through Alfred Schutz's (1964) metaphor of tuning.   Tuning for Schutz is the kind of awareness which can arise in aesthetic experience, for example when listening to music.   Feeling 'at one' with nature, which is a commonly reported context for adult recollection of childhood spiritual experience, might be an illustration of this type of awareness.

Csikszentmihalyi (1988) looks particularly at the experience of *flow*. This refers to the liberating sense of one's activity managing itself, or being managed by some outside influence, so that a task which previously seemed complex and demanding transforms into a single flow. It has been suggested that the spiritual exercises of St Ignatius are a formal attempt to generate flow. For the child who is almost daily mastering new skills, the experience of flow is potentially very familiar, given the ability to reflect upon or become self-conscious of this awareness.

Mystery-Sensing: Mystery here refers to our experience of realities that are *in principle* incomprehensible. Rudolf Otto (1950) identifies two sides to our experience of mystery, fascination or *wonder*, and fear or awe. Awareness of things beyond one's current understanding is very familiar in childhood. It is important that in the process of education a recognition of mystery is matured rather than dismissed as infantile thinking.

Mundane experience is transcended through imagery and metaphor in the deployment of *imagination*. Probing mystery requires the imagination to conceive what is beyond the known and what is 'obvious'. Studies of children's ability to enter into fantasy show they have a powerful capacity for (and enjoyment of) letting go of material reality, or using it in a new way to discover meanings and values in response to their experience, especially experience for which their language is inadequate (Hammond, *et al.*, 1990). Imagination is of course central to religious activity through the metaphors, symbols, stories and liturgies which respond to the otherwise unrepresentable experience of the sacred.

Value-Sensing: The term 'value-sensing' in relation to feeling was coined by Margaret Donaldson (1992). She states that the degree of affect is a measure of value, reflecting a stance towards what is felt to matter. It is because the matter of spirituality is of central existential importance that it is associated with strong feeling. Indeed the emotions associated with such value-sensing are commonly reported as profound. Hence we have adopted the terms *delight* and *despair* in reference to them, intending to convey something of the intensity of the emotions associated with spiritual awareness. It is a commonplace of our experience of children that they are, at least if their upbringing is adequate, easily in touch with the intense awareness that generates delight or despair.

Earlier we mentioned our expectation that we would discover further categories of experience related to spirituality as the research progressed. It is here that we wish to insert the category of *relationship* which has surfaced repeatedly in conversations with children as a sensitivity or awareness characteristic of the spiritual. Though we overlooked it originally, its appearance is hardly surprising since our general characterisation of spirituality is that it is about our relationship both with the self and holistically with all that is not ourselves... Religious ideas that spring to mind as being linked with this include Martin Buber's emphasis on 'I and Thou' (Buber, 1970) and John Cumpsty's more recent theory of religion as 'belonging' (Cumpsty, 1991).

Meaning is our final subcategory. This has been a guiding category for several researchers into the nature of religion from a predominantly cognitive perspective, including James Fowler (1981) on faith as a meaningful personal framework, and Daniel Batson's (Batson, Schoenrade and Ventis, 1993) emphasis on the spiritual quest as a search for ultimate meaning. 'Meaning' is certainly of central importance in relation to children's spirituality. At the same time we criticise the proponents of a purely cognitive approach for their tendency to ignore the existential basis for the creation of religious meaning. Questions of meaning which are essentially spiritual are raised by young children: Who am I? Where do I belong? What is my purpose? To whom or what am I connected or responsible? We suggest that these more cognitive signs of spiritual activity are in many cases the secondary products of spiritual stirrings found in awareness-, mystery- and value-sensing.

Hay's approach can be identified by the following distinctive characteristics.

- He believes spirituality is innate, biological and concerned with the sense of mystery.
- Spirituality cannot be regarded as purely cognitive and therefore absent if not learnt through nurture and knowledge.
- The process of spiritual development relies on reflection on experience which can be typologically represented according to specific categories.
- Children's spirituality can be both advanced and retarded by education and schooling.
- Religious literacy and spiritual development are entirely distinct operations, thus the former is not a mark of the latter.

A6 Children and Worldviews Project

This section deals with a small part of the Children and Worldviews Project through which we investigated the way in which children learn. This research stems from a belief that the way in which children learn cannot be separated from who they are and the experiences that have shaped that identity. The experiences, and their interpretation by the child, form the vehicle by which all subsequent experiences (including formal learning experiences) are moulded and readjusted in order that the child can make sense of them. This selective patterning of experiences and reflections, forms the child's world-view - the window through which he or she looks out on the world and that protects his or her being.

The process approach to education (Blenkin and Kelly, 1987) advocates a view of knowledge that is essentially tentative and suggests that the essence of education is the facilitation of the development of skills and not the transfer of a traditionally agreed body of knowledge which may not endure. The transfer theory of knowledge makes exactly that assumption: that knowledge is something unchangeable and unchanging and that the job of the teacher is to transfer this knowledge from his or her mind to that of the learner. The assumption is also made that the knowledge is transferred in its pure form, untainted by its passage through the teacher's mind and its reception in the learner's.

This obviously cannot be the case. Each person must re-interpret and adjust the knowledge as it passes into his or her sphere of perception. If we ignore this then we make dangerous assumptions about the nature of what is taught and what is learned. The personal construct theory of learning suggested by Kelly (1986) takes this into consideration, holding that an individual invariably approaches any situation in life with a personal theory of explanation. Thus the acquisition of a new concept by a learner involves the interpretation of that new concept within the existing framework. The framework is altered by the appearance of the new idea and the whole process is repeated until the learner is comfortable with his or her understanding. Knowledge is therefore context-dependent.

The personal construct theory and the related process approach to education both see learning as beginning with existing knowledge, and therefore the interpretative framework, of the learner. If the teacher wishes to start where the learner is, then some idea of the learner's existing knowledge is required. In a classroom situation this is taken to mean that which has been previously taught. But as we have seen, this does not take into consideration the adjustment of these taught ideas by the frameworks of the learners. If these ideas, either taught or caught, are ones which deal with existential issues, then we may be said to be considering children's spirituality.

We wish to access these frameworks, to gain some understanding of the way in which children attempt to understand and come to terms with these important existential issues. After looking at the information provided by conversations with children we developed the idea that the way to access children's understanding is to look at the metaphors that they use when talking about these important issues. According to Cooper (1986):

> Metaphor's essential role is a cognitive one, sustained by our need to explain and understand through comparison.

We thought that they would use metaphors from their existing experiences and understanding and that this would help us to access their frame of reference. We do not expect their frames of reference always to appear the same. The child in the classroom being 'good' may see himself very differently from that same child in the playpark being a 'hero' to his gang. He is operating in a different situation and occupying a different role and we would expect him to use different metaphors.

Methodology

Quantitative research tends to rely heavily on a hypothetico-deductive, scientific paradigm with an emphasis on the verification of an already established theory. Such research requires a hypothesis that can be tested and data that can be quantified and possibly subjected to statistical analysis. Variables need to be manipulated and controlled. There is a need to have controls for the sake of comparison and to feel that the sample is chosen to cover as much of the range as possible. The method must be seen as rigorous, heading towards a definite 'proof' that can then be applied generally.

We were concerned that this methodology was not appropriate for our research and we adopted a qualitative approach. The lack of a tight idea of a testable hypothesis or question to answer means that the theory is 'grounded' in the data collected. The notion of 'grounded theory' was put forward by Glaser and Strauss (1967). Thus we went into this research with the idea that we should allow the children to speak to us in as natural and unstructured a way as possible and that these data should allow us to construct theory.

The data were collected by unstructured interviews among Key Stage 2 children in four schools: one inner city and one multi-ethnic school in Southampton, a Catholic school in Southampton and a multi-ethnic school in Hounslow. Children were interviewed in small groups, usually of four or five children, or in pairs, and the conversations were tape-recorded.

The distinctive characteristics of the Children and Worldviews Project's approach are to:

- work from an open-ended account of children's recollection of their experiences;
- concentrate on significant experiences in children's lives, often involving death and loss;
- identify children's use of metaphor and narrative as the way in which they convey meaning and world-construction;
- utilise no pre-constructed paradigm of spirituality.

Example

Here is an example of the narrative of one child from three successive interviews:

> I think that in heaven you can ride a white pony and have marshmallows. Before my Nan died she told me lots of things because she knew she was going to die and she told me about all the things she was going to do and she said she was going to send me a postcard. Before she went she gave me a piece of paper and stuck a photograph on it. I've still got it.

She said she would be happy and she wanted me to be happy when she died. On that day she got a picture of her and all the family, stuck it on a postcard and wrote on the back, 'I'll see you in your heart.' Now she's always with me. Now I talk to her all the time. I talk to her when I'm lonely. When I've argued with my friends I go and sit on the wall and think about her and talk to her. When I get fed up I sit there and talk to her about my friends. She tells me that she's riding on things. She says she's having a really nice time. She says she's going to ring me up. She says things in my head, she rings up my brain and talks to me. When she went up in heaven she took one of her special secrets. She took it with her and she can just ring me up, it's clever. This special secret makes her able to do that.

I keep on wanting to tell people things but they don't understand. I know everyone's in heaven who has died. Grandma tells me. She works in a cleaners. She washes all the clouds in heaven. She's got lots and lots of friends in heaven. She hopes we'll stay alive a long time but she wants me to go up there to see her. I'd like to go and see her but if you go up there you've got to stay there. You can't go unless you've died. Heaven is high, high in the sky, it's higher than space.

I've never worried about these things. I just keep it in my heart. It's not a problem. It makes me quite sad they [people] don't believe. But when God talks to them they will know. We are very, very lucky that just some people care in this world. Like me and my friends and everybody in this school, I hope, we care, we keep this planet going. I think heaven is part of this planet.

My Nan was burnt when she died, cremated. I think that's better than worms coming into your coffin.

Activity A5

Analyse the above narrative. Indicate what concepts the child utilises to make sense of her experience. Indicate what relationships she relies upon and how she is facilitated by these relationships in making sense of the experience. Identify the understanding and use made of story and ritual by the child. Identify the use made of imagery familiar to the child in constructing a picture of her grandmother's life beyond death. Conclude with an assessment of the value of this child's account of her reflections in developing her spirituality.

Comment on activity A5

Your analysis should have taken account of the following points.

- The child utilises the information conveyed to her in the context of her relationship with her grandmother (Nan) as an authority figure.
- The concepts of heaven, heart, caring, God, death and planet are woven together to construct a framework of meaning derived from this relationship.

- The notion of communicating beyond death is primarily derived from the 'teachings' offered by her grandmother and involves the use of imagery, ritual and 'doctrine' in the construction of values. Here we are referring to the postcard, the sitting on the wall and the special secret.

- The child's expression of meaning is couched in metaphorical language: 'I'll see you in my heart' and 'she rings up my brain'.

- This construction of meaning is used by the child at times when she seeks to cope with sadness and make sense of the relationship between her sense of community and its relationship with the world and God.

- The child uses the familiar images related to her age, interests and childhood culture (marshmallows and white ponies), plus her experience of everyday activity (cleaners) to envisage a heavenly existence.

- Her constructs can be compared to those that operate within religious communities at a popular level and may have similar functional qualities in enabling and developing spirituality.

Activity A6 (optional)

Determine to what extent any of these approaches, proposed by Robert Coles, David Hay and the Children and Worldviews Project can be valuable in furthering children's spirituality and in what respect. Indicate to what extent any of these approaches can be aligned with theological approaches or with Government and SCAA initiatives relating to spiritual development.

Comment on activity A6

At this stage a number of fundamental issues should be addressed in your answer. Here are some examples.

- Is the development of children's spirituality fundamentally different from that of adult spirituality?

- Is the development of spirituality dependent on acknowledging the distinctive truth of a particular theology?

- Can we proceed by simply acknowledging areas of agreement as 'lowest common denominators' which can serve moral development regardless of faith adherence?

- To what extent must the process of spiritual development be led by building on and facilitating the child's perspective?

- To what extent does spiritual development rely on introducing the child to other ways of 'seeing the world'?

A7 Spirituality and the curriculum

Science and religion

In considering these two important divisions within western culture we may note religion and science tend to derive their authority from different sources. One way of viewing this is to see religion and science as different methods of investigation and interpretation which, within popular culture, lead to the knowledge derived from each being granted unequal status. As a consequence of this, but partly as a result of the different methods employed in each, religion and science have different ideas about the nature of truth: scientific truth is more related to empirical tests and religious truth is more personal, more like the truth that is found in the truthfulness and trustworthiness of a person. Inevitably, then, the two realms tend to have a different understanding of human history and human progress.

Ever since the Enlightenment, a commonly held view has been that there is a conflict between science and religion. This view has been challenged recently but still remains fairly deeply embedded in the consciousness of most people.

The Enlightenment was a period in the eighteenth century in Europe and America, when philosophers and writers felt that they were emerging from an age of ignorance into one characterised by reason and science. By the use of reason, unending progress would be made possible, in science, technology and in the area of morality. The period was one of great optimism and one where old ideas were open to challenge by observation, experience and reason. This empirical approach had been given credence by the scientific discoveries of the sixteenth and seventeenth century, such as the astronomy of Copernicus and Galileo, and the discovery of gravity by Isaac Newton. It was hoped and expected (and still is today in many ways) that the use of empirical data and reason would allow humanity to discover all the laws controlling and defining the natural world, and therefore to produce a utopian society in the future. From this basis scientific method developed, which is the way in which a scientist investigates and makes sense of the natural world.

Poole (1990, p 368) considers how science and religion may seem to misunderstand each other and how this apparent misunderstanding is reflected in the views and ideas of pupils. There is a:

> 'tap root' misunderstanding... which, for historical reasons, has become firmly ingrained at every level of our culture... (this) is the failure to differentiate between the distinct logic and concepts of science and of religion, a failure which may result in the mistaken assumption that science is the final arbiter of truth in matters of religion.

Poole describes the philosophical system, logical positivism, which, with its verification principle, is seen to underpin scientific thinking. The verification principle says that meaning can only be granted to statements that can be verified by sense data. Since statements about God cannot be verified in this way, they are relegated to the category of meaningless talk. However, scientific language, concepts and logic are not by nature superior to the language, concepts and logic of religion and ethics. In other words scientific language is not a 'metalanguage' above all other kinds of languages and against which they judge. One reason for this, of course, is that the verification principle cannot itself be verified by the sense data by which it insists on judging all other statements.

Historically, one of the issues over which religion and science came into conflict was the origin of the universe, and in particular the origins of man himself. The argument is seen to be one between the biblical account in Genesis of the creation of the universe and everything in it, including human beings, by God in seven days, and the scientific accounts. The scientific account has changed over the course of this century as more and more information has been gathered by sophisticated techniques and instruments and the most widely accepted theories are now the Big Bang Theory for the origin of the universe, and evolution as the means by which *homo sapiens* has developed from the first stirrings of life on this planet. Various theories have also been put forward for the way in which life first started from a non-living primeval 'soup'. It is around these two issues that the most heated arguments have centred.

Geography and religion

Geography, like other curriculum subjects and especially the humanities, constantly wrestles with questions of approach and method in determining its identity and purpose. Although there is a tendency to differentiate between 'human geography' and 'natural geography', at the heart of the subject is a concern with the relationship between human activity and the earth's resources. As Michael Bradshaw (1990, p 378) explains:

> Geographers try to explain how human activities give rise to distinctive patterns in the use of the earth's surface.... It also involves an understanding of the operation of the natural world, and of human activities which interact with that world - geographers are concerned with both environmental and social issues.

Bradshaw points out that systems of explanation provided by geographers are based on particular philosophies. Such philosophies provide metanarratives that necessarily take account of political and ideological and, sometimes, theological explanations covering economics and social systems. Intrinsically therefore, they frame the discipline of geography in a system of values. Bradshaw believes the view that the Capitalist system is based on the accumulation of wealth by a few people, emphasises the role of the individual and may link itself to Christian ideals by employing the Protestant work ethic as a justification for its aims. The Marxist critique emphasises the oppression of workers and the importance of state control to ensure equality. Its Socialist equivalents in Capitalist countries emphasise the poverty and injustice that free market economics fosters. In Bradshaw's Christian view he cites the importance of 'God-people revelation and relationships' which ground progress in relationships with God and other human beings. 'Sin' is understood as emphasising the individual without consideration for the requirements of God or the well-being of others. At the same time any attempt to establish a wholly secular alternative to capitalist ideology inevitably neglects the Christian perspective. It is necessary to free the Christian faith from the notion that it is a wholly personal perspective on life and recognise its public significance in order to challenge capitalist and Marxist systems. Thus, by engaging with major human dilemmas that fall within the context of geography from a Christian viewpoint, the significance of a theological perspective can be recognised. Ecological issues and those of poverty and social injustice are clear examples. One of the most important issues raised by Bradshaw's account is the political nature of geography. Most teachers attempt to teach the subject in a 'neutral' fashion. The implication of Bradshaw's argument is that this is both impossible and inappropriate.

Activity A7

It is probably a good time now for you to try to articulate your own views on these issues. They are discussed in many different books, and you are advised to read widely, since not only are various sciences involved (astronomy, physics, geology, botany, zoology, chemistry) but also various religious and religio-scientific views.

Comment on activity A7

You might have come to conclusions along the following lines. They are listed by Jennifer Trusted (1994) in her book *Physics and Metaphysics*.

- There is no longer confidence that scientific enquiry can lead to a definitive and true account of the world.

- It has come to be appreciated that any explanation must depend on metaphysical presuppositions which are to be accepted as the ones most appropriate for the solving of current problems rather than being seen as ultimate truths.
- Although science is seen as a secular activity, it is now acknowledged that the natural world, not only living things but also inanimate objects, cannot be adequately described, let alone explained, purely in terms of human sense experiences.

Of course, you may think Trusted is, in practice, wrong and that we do have enormous confidence in science, especially technology as an off-shoot of science, since we use it every day, expect it to make our lives easier and marvel at its power and progress. On the other hand, you may take a more suspicious view of science – its pollution and potential for mass destruction – and consider that the love affair of human beings with science has gone on long enough. As teachers, the question is how we should add to our science teaching to help children deal with this ambiguity. In the second of the above beliefs Trusted states that any metaphysical explanation should also be regarded as tentative, that is, there are and can be no ultimate truths and in the third she indicates that there is some other aspect of the world that must be taken into consideration. This appears to be the spiritual dimension.

When we say we do, or do not, believe in absolute truths we enter all kinds of complicated philosophical areas. We need to define what we mean by absolute truth (do we mean something that is always and under all circumstances true?) and, if we do mean that, then don't we believe that the laws of physics are always true *even in those situations (like black holes and at the beginning of time)* when physics is pushed to extremes? And, if we believe that, paradoxically, the laws of physics are true, even in extreme situations, then we have absolute truths. On the other hand, we may think that, since the laws of physics are subject to revision in the light of new experimentation and theory, they cannot be absolute. But perhaps we have to distinguish between absolute truths and permanent truths or between absolute truths held provisionally and provisional truths held absolutely?

Your response to the issues raised by geography should explain clearly how approaching geography from these different points of view alters the understanding of the subject and involves different understandings of the nature and place of human spirituality within the subject. It should also have indicated how far it is possible to maintain a synthesis between the approaches and to what extent it is necessary to identify any of these approaches as unacceptable as a basis on which to construct the curriculum.

Readers

You will find a discussion of spirituality in section 14 of L.J. Francis and A. Thatcher (eds) (1990), *Christian Perspectives for Education*, Leominster, Gracewing.

Bibliography

Astley, J. (1990), Theology and curriculum selection, in L.J. Francis and A. Thatcher (eds), *Christian Perspectives for Education*, Leominster, Gracewing, pp 265-272.

Astley J. and Francis L.J. (1996), *Christian Theology and Religious Education: connections and contradictions*, London, SPCK.

Batson D., Schoenrade, P. and Ventis, L.W. (1993), *Religion and the Individual: a social psychological perspective*, New York, Oxford University Press.

Berger, P. (1967), *A Rumor of Angels*, London, Penguin.

Best, R. (ed.) (1996), *Education, Spirituality and the Whole Child*, London, Cassell.

Blenkin, G. and Kelly, A.V. (1987), *The Primary Curriculum: a process approach to curriculum planning*, London, Harper and Row.

Bradshaw, M. (1990), The Christian and geographical explanation, in L.J. Francis and A. Thatcher (eds), *Christian Perspectives for Education*, Leominster, Gracewing, pp 376-382.

Buber, M. (1970), *I and Thou* (W. Kaufmann trans.), New York, Scribners.

Coles, R. (1990), *The Spiritual Life of Children*, Glasgow, HarperCollins.

Cooper, D. (1986), *Metaphor*, London, Basil Blackwell.

Csikszentmihalyi, I.S. (1988), *Optimal Experience: psychological studies in the flow of consciousness*, Cambridge, Cambridge University Press.

Cumpsty, J. (1991), *Religion as Belonging: a general theory of religion*, London, University Press of America.

DFEE, *Circulars 3/89 and 1/94*, London, HMSO.

Donaldson, M. (1992), *Human Minds*, London, Penguin.

Erricker, C., Erricker, J., Ota, C., Sullivan, D. and Fletcher, M. (1997), *The Education of the Whole Child*, London, Cassell.

Fowler, J.W. (1981), *Stages of Faith*, New York, Harper and Row.

Fox, M. (1991), *Creation Spirituality*, London, HarperCollins.

Freire, P. (1972), *Pedagogy of the Oppressed*, Harmondsworth, Penguin.

Glaser, B.D. and Strauss, A.K. (1967), *The Discovery of Grounded Theory*, Chicago, Aldine.

Hammond, J., Hay, D., Moxon, J., Netto, B., Raban, K., Straughier, G. and Williams, C. (1990), *New Methods in RE Teaching*, Harlow, Oliver and Boyd.

Hardy, A. (1966), *The Divine Flame: an essay toward a natural history of religion*, London, Collins.

Hardy, A. (1979), *The Spiritual Nature of Man*, Oxford, Clarendon Press.

Hardy, A. (1991), *The Spiritual Nature of Man*, Oxford, Alister Hardy Research Centre.

Hay, D. (1982), *Exploring Inner Space*, London, Mowbray.

Hay, D. and Nye, R. (1996), Investigating children's spirituality: the need for a fruitful hypothesis, *International Journal of Children's Spirituality*, 1 (1), 6-16.

Hay, D., Nye, R. and Murphy, R.J.L. (1996), Thinking about childhood spirituality: review of current research and current directions, in L.J. Francis, W.K. Kay and W.S. Campbell (eds), *Research in Religious Education*, Leominster, Gracewing, pp 47-71.

Hull, J.M. (1990), What is theology of education?, in L.J. Francis and A. Thatcher (eds), *Christian Perspectives for Education*, Leominster, Gracewing, pp 2-19.

Hull, J.M. (1996), The Holy Trinity and the educational mission of the Church, *Viewpoints*, September, 14-16.

Jenkins, D. (1985), *The God of Freedom and the God of Love*, London, Hibbert Trust.

Kelly. A.V. (1986), *Knowledge and Curriculum Planning*, London, Harper and Row.

MacIntyre, A. (1985), *After Virtue: a study in moral theory*, London, Duckworth.

Macquarrie, J. (1972), *Paths in Spirituality*, London, SCM.

Martin, I.S. (1990), The future of church colleges: standing for something, in L.J. Francis and A. Thatcher (eds), *Christian Perspectives for Education*, Leominster, Gracewing, pp 174-178.

Nye, R. and Hay, D. (1996), Identifying children's spirituality: how do you start without a starting point? *British Journal of Religious Education*, 18, 144-154.

OFSTED (1994), *Framework for the Inspection of Schools*, London, HMSO.

Otto, R. (1923), *The Idea of the Holy*, Oxford, Oxford University Press.

Poole, M.W. (1990), Science and religion in the classroom, in L.J. Francis and A. Thatcher (eds), *Christian Perspectives for Education*, Leominster, Gracewing, pp 365-375.

Priestley, J. (1996), *Spirituality in the Curriculum*, Frinton, Hockerill Educational Foundation.

Rahner, K. (1974), The experience of God today, in *Theological Investigations 11*, London, Darton, Longman and Todd.

Ricouer, P. (1977), *The Rule of Metaphor: multi-disciplinary studies in the creation of meaning in language*, Evanston, Northwestern University Press.

Ricouer, P. (1984), *Time and Narrative*, Chicago, University of Chicago Press.

Rizzuto, A. (1979), *Birth of the Living God*, Chicago, Chicago University Press.

Robinson, E. (1977), *The Original Vision: a study of the religious experience of childhood*, Oxford, Alister Hardy Research Centre.

SCAA (1995) *Discussion Paper 3*, London, School Curriculum and Assessment Authority.

SCAA (1996), *Discussion Paper 6*, London, School Curriculum and Assessment Authority.

SCAA (1996), *Findings of the Consultation on Values in Education and the Community*, London, School Curriculum and Assessment Authority.

Schutz, A. (1964), Making music together: a study in social relationship, in A. Broderson (ed.), *Collected Papers 11: studies in social theory*, The Hague, Martinus Nijhoff, pp 135-158.

Starkings, D. (ed.) (1993), *Religion and the Arts in Education: Dimensions of Spirituality*, Sevenoaks, Hodder and Stoughton.

Thatcher, A. (1990), The recovery of Christian education, in L.J. Francis and A. Thatcher (eds), *Christian Perspectives for Education*, Leominster, Gracewing.

Thatcher, A. (1996), Policing the sublime: a wholly (holy?) ironic approach to the spiritual development of children, in J. Astley and L.J. Francis (eds), *Christian Theology and Religious Education: connections and contradictions*, London, SPCK, pp 117-139.

Thatcher, A. (1997), Theology of education and church schools, in W.K. Kay and L.J. Francis (eds), *Religion in Education (1)*, Leominster, Gracewing, pp 61-99.

Thiessen, E.J. (1990), A defense of a distinctively Christian curriculum, in L.J. Francis and A. Thatcher (eds), *Christian Perspectives for Education*, Leominster, Gracewing, pp 273-281.

Tilby, A. (1993), *Science and the Soul*, London, SPCK.

Trusted, J. (1994), *Physics and Metaphysics*, London, Routledge.

Webster, D (1990), A spiritual dimension for education? in L.J. Francis and A. Thatcher (eds), *Christian Perspectives for Education*, Leominster, Gracewing, pp 356-364.

Wright, A. (1997), Embodied spirituality: the place of culture and tradition in contemporary educational discourse on spirituality, *International Journal of Children's Spirituality*, 1 (2), 8-20.

Spiritual and Moral Development

Unit B

Piaget and Fowler

Revd Professor Jeff Astley

North of England Institute for Christian Education

Durham

and

Revd Dr William K. Kay

Trinity College

Carmarthen

Contents

Introduction

Aims

After working through this unit you should be able to:

- understand Piaget's model of mental development in outline;
- understand Fowler's theory of faith development in outline;
- understand the relationship of faith development to spiritual development.

Overview

This unit introduces you first to the developmental theory of Piaget before considering in detail the faith development theory of Fowler. In many respects Fowler builds on Piaget's theory, though he takes it in a direction that Piaget himself never explored. The first part of this unit, on Piaget, was written by William K. Kay and the second, on Fowler, by Jeff Astley.

B1 Development

The concept of *development* is a matter of discussion. For example, Moran (1991, p 150-151) says that:

> development means that there is direction but not a point of termination... developmental theories presume that the movement is from good to better... everyone is in favour of development... the modern idea of development began as a protest against a closed world.

Moreover, the stimulus for this development, whether it is intellectual, moral, spiritual or whatever, may be from sources external to the individual or from some unfolding of the individual's internal resources, or both. The disputed points, however, concern exactly how this improvement should be described or measured (who says improvement has taken place?) and the extent to which external and internal factors are implicated in the developmental process. Would spiritual development take place, for instance, simply as a result of a child's growing older?

This question helps clarify the concept of development. Growth and development do not necessarily take place together. Whereas growth simply refers to increase in size or quantity, development implies something else. A factory making cars can grow (it can make more cars per day or add further buildings to its site), but the factory develops if there are *structural changes* within the business. Usually the structural changes are intended to facilitate the increase in size but, in principle, the two concepts are distinct.

Spiritual and moral development fit the basic concept identified by this analysis. They are both thought of as improvements to spiritual and moral life that are brought about by underlying changes to the cognitive structures the individual characteristically applies to spiritual and moral experiences. In other words, it is assumed that without cognitive change, there is no spiritual and moral development. For this reason, this unit begins with an outline of the theory of cognitive development proposed by the Swiss psychologist Jean Piaget (1896-1980). Nearly all the writers considered in this module take Piaget as their starting point.

B2 Cognitive development: Piaget's theory

Piaget's theory of cognitive development arises from his philosophical concerns about the growth of knowledge, and in particular from his answer to the problem of the emergence of necessary knowledge from all the fluctuating and random circumstances of each person's life (Smith, 1993). The paradigm of necessary knowledge is found in mathematics: all mature rational beings agree that $12 - 7 = 5$, and that this must be so, given the meaning of the numbers in the equation. Similarly, for example, all mature rational beings agree that, if all men are mortal and if Socrates was a man, he must have been mortal. Despite changing historical and cultural circumstances over many thousands of years, necessary truths have remained unaltered. Piaget wanted to know how children's minds developed so that they appreciated what it is about some kinds of knowledge that makes it necessary.

Piaget's interests led him to observe children from the earliest years of life till their mid-teens. His initial training and interest were in the field of biology. From biology, he derived the idea of the interaction between an organism and its environment. By adding biology to philosophy and logic, he derived the idea that there was a correlation between the internal changes within human beings, especially those within their minds, and the structure of knowledge (Piaget, 1971). One writer depicted Piaget as 'biologising' Kant (Phillips, 1982, p 420) because, in Kant, there is a similar correlation between the internal structurings of the mind and the external world on which the mind acts.

So far as the external world was concerned, Piaget was a realist (Vuyk, 1981, p 49; Piaget, 1972); that is, he accepted the reality of the world as something objective and 'out there'. So far as his epistemology, or theory of knowledge was concerned, he was a 'constructivist', someone who believed that knowledge is constructed within the mind. He rejected simple empiricism, where the mind reads facts from the book of nature without error, but equally he rejected simple rationalism, where the mind constructs necessary truths without reference to the world. On the contrary, the interaction between world and mind is vital, and appears in various ways within his theory. The necessity for interaction can be illustrated by considering extreme hypothetical situations where:

- the organism changes and its environment remains the same or;
- the organism undergoes no change and its environment constantly alters.

In the first case the organism's changes would result entirely from the unfolding of its genetic programme. The programme ensures that cells divide and specialise and that they are grouped together in larger and larger co-ordinated physical structures that are the basis for differentiation. Under a microscope it is possible to see the very first cells of a human being that divide looking identical to each other. Gradually, as time progresses, cells take on specialist functions (bones, skin or blood) and are organised hierarchically, that is, so that some cells, for example brain cells, begin to control the movement of others, for example muscle cells.

Piaget extends this view of development to the growing mind so that, according to this conceptualisation, the mind makes differentiations using mental structures which are hierarchically arranged according to their complexity and generality. By this definition, development remains distinct from growth and mental development is parallel to physical development.

But if the environment remained exactly the same throughout the organism's development, the organism could not act upon the environment in any way. Development would be independent of environment which, in the case of human beings, is clearly not so. To take one illustration: the linguistic environment of a child determines the language he or she will learn to understand and speak in later life.

In the second case the organism would neither develop nor learn from the environment, where learning is defined as the extension of existing mental structures to new content (Fincham, 1982, p 379). Eventually the unchanging organism, unable to foresee or avoid threats from the environment, would be obliterated. Only when the organism interacts with the environment can they co-exist. Thus the Piagetian notion that human beings acquire knowledge partly or largely by interacting with their environments makes sense and, in Piaget's view, begins in babyhood.

In performing actions on the environment, the young human being builds up a repertoire of *schemata*. This is a technical term that has slightly different meanings at different stages of life. Among children of school age it usually refers to an action which has been internalised and so becomes a mental construct. It is these which are the structures within the mind and by which differentiation takes place. Each schema is gradually generalised and may be applied more and more widely.

Each schema may be developed by the processes of *accommodation* by which it adjusts to new situations; but situations themselves may be adjusted to existing schemata by the process of *assimilation*. In Piaget's words, 'accommodation is determined by the object, whereas assimilation is determined by the subject' (Bringuier, 1980, p 43). These two technical terms are originally biological and apply much more extensively than to mental development. For example, a plant may accommodate to changes in the position of the sun by turning its flower to the correct position in the sky. A flower may also assimilate by taking nutrients from the soil that is part of its environment. Piaget, by using these technical terms for mental development, has placed it within the range of natural processes common to all living things.

Equilibration, a third technical term, holds accommodation and assimilation in balance, though where this can not be achieved, cognitive growth is stimulated (Flavell, 1963). The notion of equilibrium is complex because it takes several forms. The simplest kind occurs where a person encounters an object which is hard to classify according to existing schemata. A child who knows about oranges may cope with pears quite easily but have difficulty in classifying pineapples. A more complicated kind of disequilibrium takes place when internal cognitive systems do not match. An example given by Ginsburg and Opper (1988, p 223) occurs when children have more advanced ways of dealing with numbers than they do with lengths. Thirdly, disequilibrium may occur when children cannot integrate cognitive subsystems with their overall cognitive system.

The schemata available to children of school age are general. For example, Piaget talks of a 'looking schema' which describes a searching motion with the eyes. Far more important in the relationship between the child and the environment is the capacity to predict the results of specific actions on the environment. This takes place as the child engages in *operations*. These are internalised or imagined actions which may be reversed. The child can imagine pouring water from a jug into a glass and reversing this action by pouring it back again. Operational thinking at a concrete level deals with the moving about of physical objects, often in a trial-and-error way. From about the age of seven onwards the child makes use of concrete operational thinking and is designated as being at the concrete operational *stage*.

Although the notion of stage has been revised, it is important to grasp the general idea. The child, aged between about 7 and 11, who thinks in a concrete operational way is able to classify objects on the basis of their appearance and to subdivide classes of objects. If the class of boats contains the class of canoes and the class of yachts and the class of boats which are neither canoes nor yachts, the child is able to understand that the class of canoes equals the class of boats minus the class of yachts and the class of boats which are neither canoes nor yachts. Or, expressed more simply, where B = boats; C = canoes; Y = yachts; O = boats which are neither canoes nor yachts:

$$B = C + Y + O \text{ therefore } C = B - Y - O.$$

This sort of logic can also work with simple relations: A is bigger than B and B is bigger than C so A is bigger than C, but this is really another way of expressing the logic of classes because B and C may be thought of as subclasses of A.

Also at the concrete operational stage the child understands conservation. There are various kinds of conservation, and the activity below will ask you to test two of them out. The basic concept of conservation is that something remains unaltered in an essential respect despite changes in physical appearance. This is illustrated by using a piece of plasticene which is elongated or flattened. The young child, who does not understand conservation, often thinks that substance, weight and volume have been altered by changing the plasticene's shape. At about the age of 6 or 7 the child is able to understand conservation of quantity or substance. About two years later, the child is able to achieve conservation of weight, followed, at the end of the concrete stage, by conservation of volume.

Activity B1

Conservation of number is illustrated by lining up two rows of sweets.

Step 1: Put two rows of sweets out in front of a child of five.

    □ □ □ □ □ □ □

    □ □ □ □ □ □ □

Now ask, 'Is the number the same in both rows?'

Step 2: Spread out the second row of sweets, making sure that the child watches what you are doing.

    □ □ □ □ □ □ □

□ □   □   □   □   □   □

Now ask, 'Is the number the same in both rows?'

Conservation of substance is illustrated by putting two exactly equal amounts of plasticene in front of a five year old child. In step 1 the child is asked whether the two balls have the same amount of plasticene or a different amount. Then, as step 2, and in front of the child, one of the balls is flattened so that it is spread out on the table as a thin circle. Now the child is asked the same question as before.

What do these experiments show you?

Comment on activity B1

Although the tasks may seem simple to an adult, it is surprising to find that most children aged about 5 years old fail to appreciate that the number of sweets and the quantity of plasticene remains the same after its transformation. At about the age of 7 years, the child understands what has happened. The child capable of operational thinking is able to reverse the transformation to check that no change in number or quantity has occurred.

This simple experiment with children illustrates the Piagetian method: it involves talking to children, trying to understand what and how they think and, on the basis of this, to see how they construct the world. It also shows how the Piagetian theory, simple though the experiments are, addresses fundamental issues relating to the conditions, limits and construction of human knowledge.

Formal operational thinking

At the beginning of secondary education, at about the age of 12, the child is expected to enter the stage of formal operational thinking. There are two main differences here. First, formal operational thinking is *formal* in the sense that it deals with the shape of logical arguments expressed in propositions. It can see that the problem of finding the tallest in this sentence, 'John is taller than Fred and Fred is shorter than Peter', is the same as finding the fairest in this sentence, 'Mary is fairer than Ann and Ann is darker than Mandy'. Concrete operational thinking deals with objects. Formal operational thinking deals with truth values. This allows the logic used in concrete operational thinking, the logic of classes and relations, to be replaced by propositional logic. Second, the formal operational thinker is freed from the immediate situation to consider a wide range of possibilities, and it is the consideration of what might be rather than what is which explains adolescent predilection for idealism (Flavell, 1963, p 205).

Propositional logic is expressed by the connections between propositions. Take the propositions 'it is raining' and 'I shall put up an umbrella'. When we try to work out the relationship between raining and whether or not the umbrella is up, we notice that each proposition can exist in two forms (raining or not raining and putting up an umbrella or not putting up an umbrella). Connections between propositions can also exist in two forms, conjunction ('and', that is, both are jointly true) and disjunction ('or', that is, one is true).

If, for convenience, we call these possibilities the letters A, B, C and D, then A means 'it is raining and I shall put up an umbrella', B means 'it is raining and I shall not put up an umbrella', C means 'it is not raining and I shall put up an umbrella' and D means 'it is not raining and I shall not put up an umbrella'. A + B means either 'it is raining and I shall put up an umbrella *or* it is raining and I shall not put up an umbrella'. Both conditions could be true. Altogether there are sixteen possible combinations of A, B, C and D, including that none of them is true and that all of them are true[1].

The concrete operational child does not put all the combinations of variables into any particular system. He or she typically focuses on only one variable. The formal operational adolescent, however, appreciates that several variables may be relevant to a particular problem and can appreciate how they might combine and all the possible combinations that might occur. The evidence for this change is given by a series of classic Piagetian experiments. One involves a pendulum whose weight, length, and force of push can be varied. The adolescent is asked to work out the factors that influence the period of the pendulum's swing. The formal operational thinker can test systematically by holding the variables constant and varying one at a time. In another experiment with five liquids which have to be mixed in a particular way to obtain a particular colour, the formal thinker is able to work systematically through the possibilities until arriving at the answer. He or she 'undertakes the co-ordination of concrete groups into a single system (of the second degree) because it deals with possible combinations and no longer with objects directly' (Inhelder and Piaget, 1958, p 292).

The change to formal operational thinking is as a result of a series of transformations which take place on the structures of concrete operations. Concrete operational thinking is the necessary foundation for formal operational thinking and, for this reason, the sequence of mental stages cannot be varied. Each stage is characterised by a corresponding set of structures, but the structures of formal operational thinking are the most complete. This is shown by a special set of transformations that permits the thinker to return to an original starting point.

This set of transformations makes use of four operations. These are the I (or *identity*) operation which changes nothing in any proposition. If the I operation is performed on A ('it is raining and I shall put up an umbrella') nothing alters. The N (or *negation*) operation changes everything in the

---

[1]They are 0, A, B, C, D, A + B, A + C, A + D, B + C, B + D, C + D, A + B + C, A + B + D, A + C + D, B + C + D, A + B + C + D.

proposition on which it bears. Thus if N is applied to A it becomes 'it is not raining or I shall not put up an umbrella'. The R (or *reciprocal*) operation changes assertions and negations but leaves conjunctions and disjunctions unchanged. So R applied to 'it is not raining and I shall not put up an umbrella' becomes 'it is raining and I shall put up an umbrella'. The C (or *correlative*) operation changes conjunctions and disjunctions but leaves assertions and negations untouched. So R applied to 'it is raining and I shall put up an umbrella' becomes 'it is raining or I shall put up an umbrella'. In short, I = NRC, IRC = N, CR = N, NR = C and so on (Inhelder and Piaget, 1958, pp 293-333).

Needless to say there have been criticisms of Piaget's work. It has been argued that he neglects language and the role of training, that his experiments do not show what he claims for them, that stages are less coherent than the theory demands and that some of the failures of children to perform Piagetian tasks, like those given in activity B1, are due to lapses of memory or failure to understand what is expected of them rather than to level of mental development. These criticisms are discussed in unit B of the module *Teaching about the Bible* and by Kay (1996) and Kay, Francis and Gibson (1996). The debate is detailed and technical but many of the criticisms are relevant to an appreciation of Fowler's work on faith development which, though independent, is distinctly Piagetian in orientation.

B3 Faith development I: faith and its aspects

The phrase 'faith development' has been adopted by the practical theologian and psychologist of religion, James W. Fowler who, with his colleagues at Harvard and Emory Universities in the States, has applied it to a particular theory and set of research findings[2].

According to Fowler's usage, the term 'faith' designates the almost universal human activity of creating or finding meaning, and of knowing, valuing and relating to that which is taken to be meaningful, in commitment and trust. This is a very broad understanding of what might be termed *human faith*, a phenomenon that is not necessarily religious, for we all 'believe in' something or someone - whether objects, people, ideas or values. For Fowler, *religious* faith differs from other forms of faith primarily in having specifically religious objects or contents. These are labelled religious 'centres of value' and 'images of power' in which we believe, and religious 'master stories' by which we live

---

[2] Some short sections of the material on Fowler are from earlier publications by Astley, and are reproduced here with permission.

our lives (Fowler, 1981, pp 276-277)[3]. Faith, according to Fowler and Keen (1978, p 25), is understood as:

> the composing or interpreting of an ultimate environment *and* as a way-of-being-in-relation to it. [It] must be seen as a central aspect of a person's life orientation. Faith is a primary motivating power in the journey of the self. It plays a central role in shaping the responses a person will make in and against the force-field of his or her life. Faith, then, is a core element in one's character or personality.

In Fowler's view of faith, we are in relation both 'vertically' and 'horizontally', for faith is our relationship both to the perceived conditions of our existence and to our companions-in-faith. So we compose our image of our *ultimate environment* - that which we take to be of ultimate concern - through our commitment to certain centres of value and power 'in interaction with communities of cointerpreters and co-commitants' (Fowler, 1979, p 329). As social beings our faith is a social faith. This is a feature of Fowler's theory that is often ignored by those who castigate him for offering only an individualistic account of meaning-making.

This account of the nature of faith may be traced to several theological sources, including H. Richard Niebuhr and W. Cantwell Smith (Fowler, 1974)[4]. Fowler draws particularly on Niebuhr's accounts of (i) the triadic relationship between the individual, society and our perception of transcendent value (as shared centres of value), and (ii) the distinction between the 'polytheism' of those who believe in a range of values and the 'radical monotheism' of those who give their devotion to a single, properly transcendent, centre of value and power (Fowler, 1981, pp 19-23). Cantwell Smith provided Fowler with an analysis of the original meaning of *belief* that comes close to the sense of 'giving one's heart' and 'pledging one's allegiance'. These activities of trust and loyalty are just the elements that Fowler wishes to incorporate in his own concept of faith, alongside the more cognitive dimensions that determine its structure (Fowler, 1981, pp 9-15).

Aspects of faith

Fowler's account of faith concentrates on various structures of knowing, valuing and meaning-making that he describes as 'windows into faith'. This is a useful metaphor, if only because it draws our attention to the fact that faith is

---

[3] The *ultimate* status and *cosmic* scope ('breadth', 'depth') of such faith objects is often said to be what enables us to distinguish religious faith from other forms of faith. This distinction would probably be treated by Fowler as a function of the 'cosmic status' of the contents or objects of religious faith.

[4] See H.R. Niebuhr, *Radical Monotheism and Western Culture* (New York, Harper, 1943) and J. Fowler, *To See the Kingdom: the theological vision of H. Richard Niebuhr* (Nashville, Tennessee, Abingdon, 1974), especially chapter 5; W.C. Smith, *The Meaning and End of Religion* (New York, Macmillan, 1963), chapters 6 and 7 and *Faith and Belief* (Princeton, New Jersey, Princeton University Press, 1979), chapter 1.

here being 'observed' from a limited number of perspectives. It allows us the freedom to say that there may be more to faith than can be spotted through these particular windows.

The aspects of faith analysed by Fowler largely comprise cognitive skills and competences, although a number also 'represent psychosocial as well as cognitive content' in focusing on relationships and the nature of the self (Moseley, Jarvis and Fowler, 1986, p 55). Some aspects are therefore more 'affective' (related to feeling) than others. As we have already noted, then, what Fowler sometimes calls 'faith-knowing' has its affective side too; faith is a holistic concept involving the whole person - feeling and volition included. Fowler is interested in the development of this whole complex of 'structures or patterns of thinking, valuing, committing and believing' that make up a person's faithing (Fowler 1976, p 200). ('Faithing' is perhaps a proper word to coin in this context, for the logic of faith is that of a verb rather than a noun; it is an activity, something we *do*.)

Fowler's seven aspects of faith are as follows:

- Aspect A *form of logic:* the way we think and reason.
- Aspect B *perspective taking:* our ability to adopt another person's perspective and see ourselves in relation to others.
- Aspect C *form of moral judgement:* the way in which we think about moral issues and make moral decisions.
- Aspect D *social awareness:* how and where we set the limits to our own 'community of faith', and how we regard those who are outside it.
- Aspect E *relation to authority:* where and how we select authorities for our lives and faith, and the way in which we relate to them.
- Aspect F *form of world coherence:* our way of holding things together and forming a single, workable 'world-view' that makes sense to us.
- Aspect G *symbolic function:* our way of understanding and responding to symbolic objects and language.

Activity B2

Please take the opportunity at this point to read the account of these faith aspects from the *Manual for Faith Development Research*. This material is reproduced in the Astley and Francis (1992) reader, *Christian Perspectives on Faith Development*, pp 41-45. Please note that it is the form (*how* people believe) not the content (*what* they believe) in which Fowler is interested. How acceptable is all this to you as an account of faith? As you read, reflect on the way you expect these aspects of the form of faith might change as people develop

Comment on activity B2

For Fowler, 'faith' essentially has to do with 'the making, maintenance, and transformation of human meaning' (Fowler, 1980, p 53). It is a disposition, a stance, 'a way of moving into and giving form and coherence to life' (Fowler and Keen, 1978, p 24). One might argue that there is more to faith than this, in that in order to be called 'faith' at all this meaning-making stance should have a particular (religious) content. But Fowler offers an analysis of human faith, and concentrates in his account on the form of faith. The description of these aspects of the form of faith ought to be neutral with regard to the actual contents of what we know, value and take seriously - in a word, 'believe in'.

You may not be happy with the distinction between form and content, and you have probably noted that it is difficult to talk about form without talking about content. But perhaps you can see the point of the distinction - and the value of a more general (and not specifically religious) interpretation of faith? Fowler's account of faith may indeed be incomplete, and perhaps unbalanced, as far as you are concerned. But does it still have value?

Questions that people raise about these aspects include, 'Is this all there is to faith? What dimensions do you think are missing? Is the account too dominated by the cognitive dimension ('faith knowing')? Is there enough room for the affective dimension (faith as attitude and feeling), and indeed the action dimension (faith as trust-in-action)?' All these are valid questions. They are raised in the critically evaluative papers in the reader (Astley and Francis, 1992, sections 2-4). we shall explore some of them further below.

I also asked you to think about the possible ways in which these faith-aspects may change as people develop. Your comments can now be tested against Fowler's own views in our next section. But before moving on to that, perhaps I might raise another question. In what sense is Fowler's work on faith development a study of 'spiritual development'?

Activity B3

Look back at the quotations about spirituality at the beginning of unit A, and your own responses to them. Does Fowler's account of faith fall under the heading of 'spirituality' according to these measures? According to Gordon Wakefield (1983), 'the word 'spirituality' has come much into vogue to describe those attitudes, beliefs, practices which animate people's lives and help them to reach out towards super-sensible realities'. How far does Fowler's notion of 'faith' capture these elements?

Comment on activity B3

It would appear that Fowler's faith development theory offers us an account of the changes in the *form* of the believing, trusting and loving which 'animate people's lives', and the *ways in which* they 'reach out' to what is ultimate for them. But he says less than many would hope about the *content* of this faith. May we say, then, that Fowler maps the form rather than the content of *human spirituality*?

B4 Faith development II: faith and its stages

Developmental change, which is largely driven by internal factors, is to be distinguished from *learning*, which is defined as a change brought about by experience. The two are closely related, however, for two reasons. First, the precise nature of the learning that results from experience is dependent on the developmental stage of the learner. Thus, for example, at one stage the concept of God is likely to be treated concretely and its language literally if the learner's cognitive powers are not such as to encourage the use of metaphor or reasoning about things that are not direct objects of experience. Second, stage change may itself be accelerated or retarded by the provision of different learning (life) experiences. In cognitive developmental theory, as was noted above (sections B1 and B2), development is not a simple maturation or unfolding process, but a *restructuring* that takes place in reciprocal interaction with the educational environment. Fowler's faith development scheme falls mainly within this tradition.

What's in a stage?

In his account of the development of the *form* (the aspects) of faith, Fowler claims that up to six styles of human faith may be discerned, which together constitute a hierarchical and invariant sequence of stages through which people move, at least to some extent. To claim that the sequence is *hierarchical* is to assert that each stage builds on the previous stage. The faith contents from the earlier stage are carried over and reworked by the different structures of the new stage of faith. To claim that the sequence is *invariant* is to assert that the stages always follow one another in a specific order; no one can 'skip' a stage in development. The assumption is also made that people do not 'slip back', i.e. that there is no stage regression. However, this does not mean that a person at one stage cannot revert occasionally to using the structures of an earlier stage, for in a sense they are still available to us - as is 'the child within'.

And in order to give an account of cases of senility or psychological trauma, we have to acknowledge that the more sophisticated cognitive structures can break down, with a consequent regression to more infantile ways of thinking. This will also be true of faithing.

The notion of the stage is drawn from Piagetian theory, as utilised by Kohlberg (see above sections B1 and B2, and unit C). For Fowler, a cognitive stage is 'an integrated set of operational structures that constitute the thought processes of a person at a given time' (Fowler, 1981, p 49). Faith stages are very similar, although the processes involve more than cognition. Each stage represents a situation of *equilibrium*. This is essentially a balanced relationship between the person and her world, in which she can 'assimilate' what is to be known and related to into the structures of her knowing and valuing. When some challenge or new experience arises that cannot be incorporated into a person's structures of faithing, those structures may be changed - or, to put it differently, new structures may be created - as the person 'accommodates' or adapts her patterns of thinking, relating or valuing to take account of the novelty (see above section B2). A faith stage may also be thought of as an equilibrium that may be upset as one or another aspect develops further, and the person moves through a period of *transition* to the next stage. At each stage, as we shall see, people 'faith' rather differently.

Activity B4

In the Reader *Christian Perspectives on Faith Development* you will find a number of accounts of Fowler's faith stages. My own summary is on pp xx-xxii. Fowler's most succinct summary is given on pp 16-18. Please read both of these now, just to give you a taste of this development scheme. This is an important first task in getting a taste of, and possibly for, faith development theory. If you are uneasy about the general scheme, try to get clear in your own mind where the problems lie. Does anything in these accounts 'chime in' with your experience of what you recall of your own, or other people's development? Does your own experience raise any question marks against this account of the development of faith? Make a note of your first reactions.

We are now ready to immerse ourselves more fully in the faith development scheme. Please now read the more extended accounts provided by Fowler and his associates, with a particular eye on the initial comments you made about the stages. Read pp 45-57 (reprinted from the official *Manual for Faith Development Research*), pp 332-336 (from an early essay by Fowler) and pp 372-383 (from one of Fowler's later works). As you reflect on the new summaries below, try to relate them to these fuller accounts from the reader.

Comment on activity B4

We do not give a comment on this activity because you are simply asked to reflect and read at this point. If, for some reason, you do not have access to the Reader or the Fowler manual, the summary of his position given below is adequate for many purposes.

Stages of faith

Stage 0

Up to about four years old we are in the pre-stage of *'primal faith'*. Obviously, Fowler has not done interviews with this age group, but it is of some importance to his developmental scheme as it is a time for laying the foundations of faith. Fowler himself acknowledges an intellectual debt to the neo-Freudian Erik Erikson, who described the first task of the ego at this stage as 'the firm establishment of enduring patterns for the solution of the nuclear conflict of basic trust versus basic mistrust in pure existence'. This is dependent, Erikson claims, on the quality of the maternal relationship, and forms the basis for the child's developing sense of identity.

The responsibility of *parents* at this stage is a major one. They must be able 'to represent to the child a deep, an almost somatic conviction that there is a meaning to what they are doing'. Interestingly, Erikson argues that the parental faith that supports this emerging trust has as its institutional safeguard - at least in principle - organised religion; and 'many who are proud to be without religion' - or rather 'vital faith' - have children who 'cannot afford their being without it' (Erikson, 1977, pp 223-225). Fowler himself writes of the way we are nursed into 'our first *pre-images* of God', mediated through 'recognising eyes and confirming smiles' (Fowler, 1981, p 121).

We may perhaps fill out a picture of this stage with some reflections from other sources. The sociologist Peter Berger offers an account of a child wakening in the night and being comforted by her mother with actions and words that imply 'a statement about reality as such': 'Don't be afraid - everything is in order, everything is all right' (Berger, 1970, pp 72-73). Basic trust would appear to have such *cosmic*, in the end perhaps *theological*, implications[5]. According to Donald Evans, *basic trust* is 'an inner stance which one brings to each situation... an initial openness to whatever is life-affirming in nature and other people and oneself' (Evans, 1979, p 2). Its main elements are outlined below (Evans, 1979, pp 19-20). You may care to reflect on the value

---

[5] On the theological implications of basic trust, cf. also Hans Küng, *Does God Exist?* (New York, Random House, 1981), pp 442-477 and *passim*. See also Evans (1979, pp 172-184).

of this analysis of the developing trust of the very young child, and also on Evans' claim that basic trust is the foundational 'attitude-virtue' that underlies both religion and morality[6]. The components are:

- *assurance* that the essentials for life are already being given to us: the means to satisfy our needs and the presence of the Loving Other reassuring us that we are accepted as we are, that life has meaning and that we can depend on ultimate reality;
- *receptivity*, as a grateful acknowledgement and enjoyment of what is provided in life;
- *fidelity*, in the sense of a recognition and faithful commitment to the source of the essentials of life;
- *hope* that even *in extremis* renewal and sustaining love will continue;
- *passion*, in the sense of allowing oneself to feel and express one's most profound and intense emotions.

Stage 1

Fowler's first true faith development stage is the stage of *'intuitive-projective faith'*. At this stage the subject perceives reality as a scrap-book of impressions. The world is not yet ordered, with things and experiences consistently related together. The child's 'reality' is constructed by an impressionistic projection of his own perceptions and imaginings, uncontrolled by logical thought, for his thinking at this stage is 'preoperational', intuitive and episodic.

The particular importance of this faith stage is that it is a time when long-lasting images are laid down that, while they provide the raw material for our rather chaotic, imaginative construction of reality at Stage 1, will also serve us in our more sophisticated and self-aware reflections later in life. Symbols are viewed 'magically' at this stage: they are what they represent. As with Pre-stage 0, this is a stage of *egocentrism*, in which the child lacks the ability to adopt another's perspective in any depth. Moral judgements are based on the child's observation of rewards and punishments, without reference to intention; authority figures are big adults. Stage 1 is usually entered into about age three or four, and left between the ages of seven and eight.

Stage 2

Later, at this stage of *'mythic-literal faith'*, our ability to think more logically and causally, and to unify our experience will help us to order reality. From about age seven onwards, we are more able and willing to separate fact from fantasy, and more successful at entering into the perspectives of others. The

---

[6] According to Evans, the other 'attitude-virtues' that form an integral part of human fulfilment and a goal of human life are: humility, self-acceptance, responsibility, self-commitment, friendliness, concern and contemplation. They develop over a person's life-span, building on the foundation of basic trust laid down in our early years.

form of thinking at this stage is one of concrete operations. It is a time of 'narrative faith', when life and meaning are particularly captured in concrete stories (which now become very important to us). Children at this stage are intensely affiliative and therefore very willing to join clubs at school or church.

Our moral thinking now does pay attention to motive, but is largely based on an ethic of 'you scratch my back and I'll scratch yours'. Symbols are often treated in a rather wooden, one-dimensional and literal fashion. The bounds of social awareness have by now extended beyond the family, to include others who are 'like us'. The age range for this stage is approximately from six or seven through to eleven or twelve, but many adults are to be found who have stayed at this stage.

Stage 3

By Stage 3, the stage of *'synthetic-conventional faith'*, abstract thinking has fully developed and there is a new capacity for mutual, interpersonal perspective-taking ('I see you seeing me: I see the me I think you see...' Fowler, 1987, p 64). This stage is entered into usually at about eleven years of age. Relationships are now all-important to me; my friends are very significant. So I am now most likely to swim with the 'faith current', to *conform* to what 'they say'[7].

My meaning-making is therefore largely at second hand, derived in bits-and-pieces from the world-views of others, including my parents and teachers but also (particularly) my peer group. I put my faith together ('synthesise' it) from these disparate elements. But as yet I know not what I do in my faithing; this is a stage of *tacit* meaning-making, in that I unreflectively accept the views of others and am not usually aware that I am doing so (or even that I *have* a view). I have not yet started truly to think for myself. 'In this stage one is embedded in his or her outlook' (Fowler and Osmer, 1985, p 184). This stage is often marked by a naïve moral relativism, an ethic of 'living up to expectations' or a 'law and order' morality. Many leave Stage 3 at about seventeen or eighteen, but large numbers of people stay at this stage for the rest of their lives.

At Stage 1 children tend to *image God* in terms of impersonal images such as the air or the sun. At Stage 2 they are most likely to adopt anthropomorphic imagery for God. But at Stage 3 this has been transcended in favour of a more sophisticated picture of a God of whom we must speak in analogies and metaphors, with a particular emphasis on the personal qualities of the deity - as friend, comforter or guide (Fowler and Keen, 1978, p 64).

---

[7] This aspect of the stage is well captured in the phrase, 'the tyranny of the "they"'. S. Parks, *The Critical Years: the young adult search for a faith to live by* (San Francisco, Harper and Row, 1986), p 76.

Stage 4

The development to a more autonomous, self-reflective, *critical* faith can be a traumatic transition and may take several years. Many make this transition in late adolescence, others in mid-life. Perhaps a quarter of all adults never make it at all. As I move to this stage of *'individuative-reflective faith'* I step out of my faith current and away from the faith crowd to choose a world-view for myself. The move from Stage 3 to Stage 4 inevitably involves a psychological 'leaving home', a withdrawal to a vantage point from which I feel that I can make my own decisions, a 'critical distancing from one's previous... value system' (Fowler, 1981, p 179). I now know where I am and why. What I believe is now at last what *I* believe; I have chosen to be here. This is the first stage at which my world-view is held *explicitly*, and in a self-aware fashion relying on my own authority for my own beliefs and values. That is why I need to be clear about things, to have a coherent and consistent - and tidy - faith. I am therefore tempted to 'close' or resolve difficult issues, sometimes rather too early. There is at this stage a new ('third person') skill of perspective-taking, and morality is increasingly a matter of adopting a principle of justice, although a person's class or group bias often restricts the employment of universal moral principles.

Stage 5

Some adults will later change further as they enter the mid-life Stage 5 of *'conjunctive faith'*. Stage 4 was intensely concerned with independence and autonomy, conceptual clarity, doctrinal orthodoxy and the demythologising of symbols. I have described it elsewhere as an *Either/Or* faith (Astley, 1991, p 27). Stage 5 is more open ('porous and permeable': Fowler, 1986a, p 30), and more responsive to others and their world-views. It is less tidy than, but represents a re-working of, Stage 4 faith.

Compared with Stage 4, the person at this stage is more realistic and humble in her cognitions and affections, recognising in particular the *interdependent* nature of her life. She is more able to cope with tensions, and more responsive to paradox and the value of symbolism. If Stage 4 is the stage of narrow 'Enlightenment rationality', marked by a sometimes arid over-intellectualism and lust to explain, Fowler suggests that Stage 5 may reflect a move to a more open, 'post-Enlightenment' approach to meaning and truth (Fowler, 1988). It seeks *understanding* more than *explanation*, and is less defensive of its own world-view. Fowler describes those who are at this stage, which is rare before the age of 30 and characterises less than 15% of the adult population, as knowing 'the sacrament of defeat and the reality of irrevocable commitments and acts' (Fowler, 1980, p 73). Moral thinking is now fully based on universal moral principles. Symbols have regained their power, as we are freed from the compulsion to explain them.

Fowler claims that Stage 5 is marked by a new style of thinking: a dialectical or dialogical knowing, which is able to see many sides of an issue at the same time. We are content to dwell in our own world of meaning at this stage, but we now know that it is inevitably only a partial and relative apprehension of reality (Fowler, 1981, p 198). Thus Stage 5 is an 'inclusive', *Both/And* type of faith (Astley, 1991, p 30). Those who are at this stage are not easily accommodated in churches or families that are unable to understand those who reject the rather rigid demands for conceptual clarity and the resolution of intellectual and moral tensions, that characterise Stage 4.

Stage 6

Very few people reach Stage 6's *universalising faith*[8], an all-encompassing, selfless, passionate but detached style of relating to the whole of reality and all other people. In many ways Stage 6 is a theoretical extrapolation from Stage 5, and Fowler appeals to 'contemporary saints' such as Martin Luther King and Mother Teresa as exemplars of it (Fowler 1981, chapter 21).

B5 Faith development III: criticisms

Activity B5

Perhaps you would like to make your own short list of criticisms at this point. Where do you now think 'the shoe pinches' for faith development theory and research? Having done that, it would be worthwhile to read Fowler's 'Foreword' to the reader (Astley and Francis, 1992, pp ix-xv). Has he addressed any of your criticisms? Has he adequately answered them? Has he raised any further queries in your mind?

Comment on activity B5

A more detailed set of criticisms, and some responses to them, are provided in section 2 of the Reader. You may care to look at some of them now, in particular Sharon Parks' essay 'Faith development in a changing world' (Astley and Francis, 1992, chapter 2.4). Students who have access to the *Research in Religious Education* Reader will also find Nicola Slee's review useful (Slee, 1996). In this section I shall pick up only a few of these critical issues.

---

[8] Only 0.3% of Fowler's research sample (one male over the age of 61) was identified as being at this stage.

Conceptual and theological criticisms

Much of the theological criticism of Fowler's position focuses on his *understanding of faith*. In particular, some theologians complain that by concentrating firmly on the human side of faith, Fowler makes faith a human act of constructing meaning, rather than a divine gift (Avery, 1990, p 127), and allows more effectiveness to fallen human nature in relating to the divine than many Protestants would allow (Osmer, 1990, pp 139-144). Nevertheless, Fowler's theological critics often admit that he has given a plausible account of the process of sanctification and growth in discipleship, if not of the faith relationship itself.

Fowler's own comments on this are available in the Reader, *Christian Perspectives on Faith Development* (see Astley and Francis, 1992, pp xiii-xiv). We should note that Fowler describes faith development as part of God's providential creative care: the work of *'ordinary grace'* built into our human nature. But he also allows for interventions of 'extraordinary grace' (Fowler, 1981, p 303), or at least of a working partnership (synergy) between human nature and the divine Spirit (Fowler, 1984, p 74). Perhaps faith development is not as predictable and inevitable as it might appear.

Another criticism that is often made is that an account of faith that is to be of use to religion should not be defined so formally. Fowler understands *religious faith* as human faith with religious content (including religious 'master stories'). This may be acceptable, but it leaves us with a definition of faith so broad that on it 'idolatry is a form of faith' (Dykstra, 1986, p 56), and that seems distinctly odd to many theological commentators. But having said this, there is a respectably orthodox understanding that, as Martin Luther put it, 'whatever... thy heart clings to... and relies upon, that is properly thy god'.

Activity B6

Look up Philippians 3.19 and 1 Corinthians 8.5. Can you distinguish here:

- a (general) faith that trusts in our 'god', in the sense of whatever concerns us greatly, whatever we truly value;
- a (specifically religious) faith in the true God, who is the only appropriate object of worship?

Comment on activity B6

This distinction can certainly be drawn in scripture, and in religion generally. Otherwise Paul is implying that 'the enemies of Christ' worship some Great

Stomach-in-the-Sky! Misplaced worship, which is a matter of giving worth where it is not due, is at the heart of the notion of a 'false religion'.

A further theological point relates to *conversion*. For Fowler, conversion is a change in the contents of faith - a matter of believing in different things (Fowler, 1981, p 281; 1984, p 95). Others, however, have identified transition from one stage to another as itself a sort of conversion. We might think of this as a 'conversion' in the form of faith, a structural change that is a type of identity-formation in which someone discovers who she really is. This sort of conversion unifies and integrates the self, particularly in adolescence and middle-age. V. Bailey Gillespie has called it religious-identity-conversion[9]. When form-change and content-change go together (and Fowler recognises that either may precipitate the other: see Fowler, 1981, pp 285-286), we may indeed have 'a re-orientation of a person's entire life' (Astley, 1996, p 17).

A more general point that is often raised about Fowler's account is whether it is properly a neutral *descriptive* account of how people do develop, or a *prescriptive*, 'normative' account of how they ought to develop. Although Fowler insists that people can be mystically alive, spiritual saints etc. at most stages, and that each stage is appropriate for the person who has equilibrated at it, yet later stages are presented as 'more adequate', if not as 'better' (cf. Moseley, Jarvis and Fowler, 1986, p 178). This is especially true of Stage 6. Much has been written on this thorny issue, but you may care to read the brief comments on it in the Reader by myself (p xx) and Fowler (pp xi-xii). See also Astley, (1991, pp 40-43).

Empirical and psychological criticisms

Fowler's research is based on lengthy (up to three hours) semi-structured interviews, of which many hundreds have now taken place. The Life Tapestry Exercise (see Astley, 1991, pp 92-97) precedes the interview. Accounts of the interviews and the questions used may be found on pp 32-41 of the Reader. Probe questions are used to elicit further comments and explanations. The interview is taped and transcribed, and then analysed by a trained and experienced person who reads and re-reads the script and assesses the interviewee's comments in terms of both the *Aspects of Faith* they reflect, and the *Stage of Faith* that each comment reveals with regard to this aspect. A number of passages in a transcript will be relevant to each faith aspect. Each is coded (e.g. as Stage 3 or Stage 4, with '3.5' indicating a midway response).

---

[9] V.B. Gillespie, *Religious Conversion and Personal Identity* (Birmingham, Alabama, Religious Education Press, 1979), p 126; cf. W. Conn, *Christian Conversion: a developmental interpretation of autonomy and surrender* (New York, Paulist, 1986), pp 31, 208-210.

All these coded figures are then averaged out, and the averages for each of the seven aspects averaged again to give the final stage score[10].

Many criticisms have been made of Fowler's methodology. However, Nelson and Aleshire (1986) broadly endorsed it after a careful study, despite some unease in a number of areas[11]. They commented that:

- Fowler, quite properly, treats his data very tentatively;
- the research is adequate 'for the proposal of a theory, if not for its confirmation (although to some extent this theory can be disconfirmed)';
- 'his research methods are, by and large, quite consistent with his structuralist approach'.

While commenting wryly that 'at each point of his research Fowler has opted for the difficult', they note that 'the best evaluation of empirical research... is more empirical research'[12], and conclude with this question: 'Does the developmental journey Fowler traces "ring true" with people who take seriously their constructions of meaning, values, relationships and centres of power?' (Nelson and Aleshire, 1986, p 200). You must make your own assessment of this criterion and its applicability to Fowler's work.

The most careful empirical study of faith development theory was undertaken through interviews of Jewish 'nontheists' by John Snarey. Among other things he discerned no statistically significant difference between the scores of men and women, but found that faith development was significantly and positively correlated with education and 'work complexity'. Snarey (1991, p 301) also noted that:

> The nontheists' scores compared very favorably with similarly aged or older Protestant, Catholic, Jewish, and other theistic religious groups. It appears that Fowler's model and measure is able to capture the thinking of persons whose religious orientation and background is quite different from those of his original sample. In this study, that is, the faith of non-Christians was not undervalued by Fowler's model.

More significantly, the entire study provided evidence in support of a number of hypotheses.

---

[10] By convention, final scores are related to stages as in this example: 2.70 to 3.29 - Stage 3; 3.30 to 3.69 - Transitional; 3.70 to 4.29 - Stage 4; etc. Some doubt may be cast on the averaging out procedures and the conventional allocation of results to stages.

[11] Their criticisms include (i) the fact that the sample is not necessarily a representative one (but it is a fairly broad one), (ii) doubts about the bias of the interviewers (an inevitable criticism of all interview work), (iii) the generality and abstraction of the constructs being measured (which makes it difficult to point to precise evidence of their existence), (iv) the wide-ranging nature of the hypothesis, e.g. that faith is a human universal (but every part of the theory is not dependent on such large-scale claims), (v) the uncertain meaning of some of the terms used in the questions (something which can be clarified during the interview), (vi) the limitations of single interviews by relatively untrained interviewers to provide psychoanalytic data (but this does not invalidate the whole work), (vii) the complexity of the problem of scoring and interpreting the interview results (admitted, but the complexity is inevitable), and (viii) the large number of unproven assumptions involved (but all research takes some assumptions on trust). You should compare the earlier critical comments by Nelson in Astley and Francis (1992, pp 65-67).

[12] The recent English study by the Faith Development Research Group (M. Smith, *Ways of Faith*, forthcoming) involved over 52 interviews, including eight subjects who were interviewed again after a period of between 3 and 5 years. The distribution of stages by age broadly corresponds with Fowler's data, and the longitudinal studies revealed clear evidence of some individuals moving from one ('earlier') stage to another.

- Stages of faith development are not reducible to or solely determined by stages of moral development.
- Stages of faith development are structural wholes.
- Variations in level of faith development significantly predict relevant outcomes (e.g. consequences or characteristics defined by psychological, sociological and religious criteria).
- Stages of faith development are cross-culturally universal.

Snarey (1991, p 279) concluded that his findings 'provide tentative support for the legitimacy of Fowler's model and indicate that the degree of construct validity is adequate for research purposes'.

Cognitive developmentalism revisited

Fowler's theory is particularly vulnerable in its reliance on work in cognitive developmental psychology. Three of Fowler's faith aspects (form of logic, social perspective-taking and form of moral judgement) adopt a Piagetian perspective, the latter two being mediated through the researches of Robert Selman on social perspective-taking and Lawrence Kohlberg on justice reasoning[13]. What are the problems here, and do they undermine Fowler's work?

Critics of Piaget have produced research findings that appear to show that young children are more capable of complex logical and moral thinking than Piaget's findings revealed, and more able to empathise with another's emotions and adopt their perspective (see, e.g., Borke, 1971; Donaldson, 1978; Dunn, 1988). A distinction is often made in the literature between the possession of a logical ability and the deployment of it. Piaget, unfortunately, 'did not seem to accept that it is possible to be illogical sometimes and yet to be able in principle to make the necessary logical moves' (Bryant, 1984, p 257). Divergent claims have also been made about children's ability to understand and use metaphors. Broadly speaking this increases with maturity (Winner, Rosenstiel and Gardiner, 1976), but children as young as four can distinguish metaphorical from literal statements in certain circumstances (Vosniadu and Ortony, 1983). Some have argued that educational intervention can increase a child's performance beyond what appears to be her developmental stage, and that children often adopt the *adult's* restricted understandings and assumptions about the child's capabilities (see, e.g., Davies, 1984; Wood, 1988). Thus Olivera Petrovich's interviews with three- and four-year-olds revealed very few who naturally thought of the creator anthropomorphically (i.e. in the form of a

---

[13] See R.L. Selman, *The Growth of Interpersonal Understanding* (New York, Academic Press, 1980). For references to and criticisms of Kohlberg see unit C of this module and also S. and C. Modgil (eds), *Lawrence Kohlberg: consensus and controversy* (Lewes, Falmer, 1985), and Munsey (1980), which contains an essay by Fowler.

man), but if she introduced the word 'God' early in the discussion the majority identified God with a man. She concluded that this inadequate concept of God had been learned or deduced from the comments made to the children, and was not the result of the children's limited reasoning powers (Petrovich, 1989; cf. Watson, 1993, chapter 5 and Petrovich, 1988).

Some of this material is to be found in Heywood (1986, reprinted in the Astley and Francis Reader), who accuses Fowler of being far too uncritical of Piaget's work. There is no doubt that this is a serious criticism. However, a developmental scheme may perhaps be traced that relates more to how people usually think than to how they *can* think. In the view of some researchers, what changes is not so much the child's logical abilities as her ways of using these abilities. Meadows (1987, pp 29-30) writes as follows:

> It seems likely that, as far as the school years are concerned, the difference between younger and older children will turn out to be that the former can do what the latter can; but only sometimes, only under favourable conditions, only with help, only without distractions, only up to a point, without so much efficiency, without so much self-control, without so much awareness of the implications, without so much certainty.

However, in a very thorough survey of such criticisms, Kenneth Hyde recently concluded both that 'there is good reason for the continued use of a Piagetian model for the study of religious thinking but with qualifications', and even that 'the overall description of religious thinking set out by Goldman remains the best guide so far available' (Hyde, 1990: Appendices F and G)[14]. But the *qualifications* acknowledged here are important and might lead to a blurring of sharp distinctions between forms of (and perhaps 'stages' of) thinking, and a recognition that performance depends not only on cognitive competence but also on the specific content of the task being undertaken. Nevertheless, to quote Hyde again, 'there are fundamentally different ways of thinking that are characteristic of different periods of mental development' (Hyde, 1990, p 374), and these show themselves in children's thinking about religion.

Introducing the name of Goldman here is perhaps misleading. Fowler does not advocate - as Goldman did - keeping children away from *biblical stories*, even though young children often do not have the intellectual ability and sophistication to understand these stories on a more abstract theological level. Rather, the stories should be told, with the proviso that they are told in an open, not a closed way, so that the child can grow up with them and through them - rather than rejecting them as 'magic' or as 'fairy tales' in later years.

---

[14] For Goldman's work, see unit B of the module *Teaching About the Bible*. The most recent research into religious thinking derives from Fritz Oser, who proposes another hierarchical sequence of six stages of 'religious judgement' (theological thought), based on interview studies. It is claimed that the relationship between God and humankind is perceived differently at different stages. The details of this work are not easily summarised; readers will need to sample it for themselves (see Oser and Gmunder, 1991).

Fowler's own *interview method* has been criticised as an inadequate base for discovering cognitive change, especially in children. In response one may argue that the faith development interview should allow ample time for people to reveal the way they think, and that it is from their comments taken across the whole interview that the researcher infers their cognitive performance (unlike Piaget, Fowler uses no concrete experimental situations). But it should be admitted that the method and the questions are likely to be much more effective in discovering this aspect of an adult's faith than it is in the case of a child. With young children the problem of interpreting what the child really intends to say is also much more pronounced. Great interviewing skill is needed here, the *Manual's* bald questions are insufficient for this task.

Piaget is often criticised for neglecting *social influences* and the effects of interpersonal relationships on an individual's development, but Fowler cannot be accused of the same failings for the interview schedule picks up these elements rather well.

There are two other broad areas in which *Fowler claims to go beyond the work of Piaget and Kohlberg*, recognising as he does some 'serious limitations' in the structural-developmental perspective (and the need to incorporate imagination into knowledge here: Fowler, 1981, pp 103-105).

Fowler's use of a very different developmentalist, the neo-Freudian psychologist *Erik Erikson* (Fowler, 1981, chapter 11; 1984, chapter 2), shows his concern for a psychoanalytic perspective on the development of the self which goes beyond what cognitive developmentalism provides. This focus on the development of the self leads him to draw also on the work of *Robert Kegan* (e.g. in Fowler, 1987). Kegan argues that the Piagetian paradigm needs to be integrated into a wider framework of a 'process' or 'motion' of the self that has both social and affective dimensions. This 'underlying logic' of the developing self (developing through stages of 'incorporative self', 'impulsive self', 'imperial' self', 'interpersonal self', 'institutional self' and 'inter-individual self') is said to take account of the structural developmental stages of Piaget, Kohlberg and Fowler[15].

Other evidence for a transcending of the limitations of structuralism includes Fowler's account of a stage of *'dialectical thinking'* at Stage 5, which takes us beyond Piaget's last stage of formal operations. More generally, Fowler treats Piaget's objective, impersonal sort of knowing ('a logic of rational certainty') as part of a more complex, comprehensive, inclusive and primitive 'logic of conviction'. (Clearly, Fowler is using the term 'logic' as a metaphor here: Fowler, 1981, p 103). For Fowler, the logic of conviction is the form knowing

---

[15] See R. Kegan, There the Dance is: religious dimensions of a developing framework, in J. W. Fowler and A. Vergote (eds), *Toward Moral and Religious Maturity* (Morristown, New Jersey, Silver Burdett, 1980) and R. Kegan, *The Evolving Self* (Cambridge, Massachusetts, Harvard University Press, 1982). Fowler claims that Kegan's six stages correspond with his own faith development Stages 0 to 5.

takes in faith (Fowler, 1981, pp 101-103; 1986a, pp 23, 33). It is like the trunk of a tree 'nurtured by roots of experience, intuition, feeling, imagination and judgement', while Piagetian reasoning is one of its principal branches - emerging 'as a narrowing and specialisation of this broader knowing and reasoning' (Fowler, 1986b, pp 286-287). Thus the logic of rational certainty, which leads to self-critical, objective knowing, is to be found *within* this more comprehensive process of the logic of conviction (which includes the other aspects of faith). This is another way of saying that the *rationality* of Piaget and Kohlberg forms a part of the more passionate, committed, self-involving, imaginative and holistic mode of *faith-knowing*. 'Reasoning in faith' involves a balanced interaction between the two ways of structuring knowledge (Fowler, 1981, p 103). According to Moseley (1991, p 165), Fowler has thus 'recast the concept of structure so that it can accommodate the moral and religious factors that comprise the domain of faith'. Moseley's article is reprinted in the Reader; see also Heywood's article in the Reader, especially pp 158-160. Both scholars are critical of the way Fowler attempts to go beyond the restrictive cognitive focus he has inherited from Piaget. For Moseley, the issue is partly related to the significance of dialectic - 'dialectical psychology does not entertain a closed system of stages' (p 169); for Heywood, the problem is more fundamental - 'the logic of conviction, in Fowler's sense, bears no relation to the achievement of rational certainty' (p 159).

Readers

J. Astley and L.J. Francis (eds) (1992), *Christian Perspectives on Faith Development*, Leominster, Gracewing. This Reader is devoted to the work of James Fowler and gives much useful information on the subject.

Bibliography

Astley, J. (1991), *How Faith Grows*, London, National Society and Church House Publishing.

Astley, J. (1996), Adolescent faith and conversion, *Journal of Beliefs and Values*, 17 (2), 16-18.

Astley, J. and Francis, L.J. (eds) (1992), *Christian Perspectives on Faith Development*, Leominster, Gracewing.

Avery, W.O. (1990), A Lutheran Examines James W. Fowler, in J. Astley and L.J. Francis (eds) (1992), *Christian Perspectives on Faith Development*, Leominster, Gracewing, pp 122-134.

Berger, P.L. (1970), *A Rumour of Angels*, Harmondsworth, Penguin.

Borke, H. (1971), Interpersonal perception of young children: egocentrism or empathy?, *Developmental Psychology*, 5, 263-269.

Bringuier, J-C. (1980), *Conversations with Jean Piaget*, Chicago, University of Chicago Press.

Bryant, P.E. (1984), Piaget, teachers and psychologists, *Oxford Review of Education*, 10, 251-259.

Davies, B. (1984), Children through their own eyes, *Oxford Review of Education*, 10, 275-292.

Donaldson, M. (1978), *Children's Minds*, London, Fontana.

Dunn, J. (1988), *The Beginnings of Social Understanding*, Oxford, Blackwell.

Dykstra, C. (1986), What is Faith? An experiment in the hypothetical mode, in C. Dykstra and S. Parks, (eds) (1986), *Faith Development and Fowler*, Birmingham, Alabama, Religious Education Press, pp 45-64.

Dykstra, C. and Parks, S. (eds) (1986), *Faith Development and Fowler*, Birmingham, Alabama, Religious Education Press.

Erikson, E. (1977), *Childhood and Society*, London, Granada.

Evans, D. (1979), *Struggle and Fulfilment*, Cleveland, Collins.

Fincham, F. (1982), Piaget's theory and the learning disabled: a critical analysis, in S. Modgil and C. Modgil (eds), *Jean Piaget: consensus and controversy*, New York, Holt, Rinehart and Winston, pp 369-390.

Flavell, J.H. (1963), *The Developmental Psychology of Jean Piaget*, London, D Van Nostrand Company Inc.

Fowler, J.W. (1974), Faith, liberation and human development, *The Foundation* (Atlanta, Gammon Theological Seminary), 79, 1-35.

Fowler, J.W. (1976), Faith development theory and the aims of religious socialization, in G. Durka and J. Smith (eds), *Emerging Issues in Religious Education*, New York, Paulist, pp 187-208.

Fowler, J.W. (1979), Perspectives on the family from the standpoint of faith development theory, in J Astley and L.J. Francis (eds) (1992), *Christian Perspectives on Faith Development*, Leominster, Gracewing, pp 320-344.

Fowler, J.W. (1980), Faith and the structuring of meaning, in J. Fowler and A. Vergote (eds), *Toward Moral and Religious Maturity*, Morristown, New Jersey, Silver Burdett, pp 51-85.

Fowler, J.W. (1981), *Stages of Faith: the psychology of human development and the quest for meaning*, San Francisco, Harper and Row.

Fowler, J.W. (1984), *Becoming Adult, Becoming Christian*, San Francisco, Harper and Row.

Fowler, J.W. (1986a), Faith and the structuring of meaning, in C. Dykstra, and S. Parks, (eds) (1986), *Faith Development and Fowler*, Birmingham, Alabama, Religious Education Press, pp 15-42.

Fowler, J.W. (1986b), Dialogue towards a future in faith development studies, in C. Dykstra, and S. Parks, (eds) (1986), *Faith Development and Fowler*, Birmingham, Alabama, Religious Education Press, pp 275-301.

Fowler, J.W. (1987), *Faith Development and Pastoral Care*, Philadelphia, Fortress.

Fowler, J.W. (1988), The Enlightenment and faith development theory, in J Astley and L.J. Francis (eds) (1992), *Christian Perspectives on Faith Development*, Leominster, Gracewing, pp 15-28.

Fowler, J.W. and Keen, S. (1978, 1985), *Life Maps: conversations on the journey of faith*, ed. J. Berryman, Minneapolis, Minnesota, Winston Press; Waco, Texas, Word Books.

Fowler, J.W. and Osmer, R. (1985), Childhood and adolescence: a faith development perspective, in R.J.Wicks, R.D. Parsons and D.E. Capps (eds), *Clinical Handbook of Pastoral Counseling*, New York, Paulist, pp 171-212.

Ginsburg, H. and Opper, S (1988), *Piaget's Theory of Intellectual Development*, Englewood Cliffs, Prentice Hall.

Heywood, D. (1986), Piaget and faith development: a true marriage of minds?, in J Astley and L.J. Francis (eds) (1992), *Christian Perspectives on Faith Development*, Leominster, Gracewing, pp 153-162.

Hyde, K.E. (1990), *Religion in Childhood and Adolescence*, Birmingham, Alabama, Religious Education Press.

Inhelder B. and Piaget, J. (1958), *The Growth of Logical Thinking from Childhood to Adolescence*, London, Routledge and Kegan Paul.

Kay, W.K. (1996), Piaget: revisions and innovations, *Spectrum*, 28, 153-164.

Kay, W.K., Francis, L.J. and Gibson, H.M. (1996), Attitude toward Christianity and the transition to formal operational thinking, *British Journal of Religious Education*, 19, 45-55.

Meadows, S. (1987), Piaget's contribution to understanding cognitive development, in K. Richardson and S. Sheldon (eds), *Cognitive Development to Adolescence*, Hove, Erlbaum, pp 19-31.

Moran, G. (1991), Alternative developmental images, in J.W. Fowler, K.E. Nipkow and F. Schweitzer (eds), *Stages of Faith and Religious Development*, London, SCM, pp 149-161.

Moseley, R.M. (1991), Forms of logic in faith development theory, in J. Astley and L.J. Francis (eds) (1992), *Christian Perspectives on Faith Development*, Leominster, Gracewing, pp 163-172.

Moseley, R.M., Jarvis, D. and Fowler, J.W. (1986), *Manual for Faith Development Research*, Atlanta, Georgia, Center for Faith Development.

Munsey, B. (ed.) (1980), *Moral Development, Moral Education and Kohlberg*, Birmingham, Alabama, Religious Education Press.

Nelson, C.E. and Aleshire, D. (1986), Research in Faith Development, in C. Dykstra, and S. Parks, (eds) (1986), *Faith Development and Fowler*, Birmingham, Alabama, Religious Education Press, pp 180-201.

Oser, F. and Gmunder, P. (1991), *Religious Judgement*, Birmingham, Alabama, Religious Education Press.

Osmer, R.R. (1990), James W. Fowler and the Reformed tradition: an exercise in theological reflection in religious education, in J. Astley and L.J. Francis (eds) (1992), *Christian Perspectives on Faith Development*, Leominster, Gracewing, pp 135-150.

Petrovich, O. (1988), Re-review: Ronald Goldman's *Religious Thinking from Childhood to Adolescence*, *Modern Churchman*, 30 (2), 44-49.

Petrovich, O. (1989), An examination of Piaget's theory of childhood artificialism, unpublished DPhil dissertation, University of Oxford.

Phillips, D. (1982), Perspectives on Piaget as philosopher: the tough, tender-minded syndrome, in S Modgil and C Modgil (eds), *Jean Piaget: consensus and controversy*, New York, Holt, Rinehart and Winston, pp 13-29.

Piaget, J. (1971), *Biology and Knowledge*, London, The University Press.

Piaget J. (1972), *Insights and Illusions of Philosophy*, London, Routledge and Kegan Paul.

Slee, N.M. (1996), Further on from Fowler: post-Fowler faith development research, in L.J. Francis, W.K. Kay and W.S. Campbell (eds), *Research in Religious Education*, Leominster, Gracewing; pp 73-96.

Smith, L. (1993), *Necessary Knowledge: Piagetian perspectives on constructivism*, Hove, Lawrence Erlbaum Associates

Snarey, J. (1991), Faith development, moral development, and nontheistic Judaism: a construct validity study, in W.M. Kurtines and J.L. Gewirtz (eds), *Handbook of Moral Behavior and Development. Volume 2: Research*, Hillsdale, New Jersey, Erlbaum, pp 279-305.

Vosniadu, S. and Ortony, A. (1983), The emergence of literal-metaphorical-anomalous distinction in young children, *Child Development*, 54, 154-161.

Vuyk, R. (1981), *Overview and Critique of Piaget's Genetic Epistemology 1965-1980* (vol. 1), London, Academic Press.

Wakefield, G.S. (ed.) (1983), *A Dictionary of Christian Spirituality*, London, SCM, p 361.

Watson, B. (1993), *The Effective Teaching of Religious Education*, London, Longman.

Winner, E., Rosenstiel, A.K. and Gardner, H. (1976), The development of metaphoric understanding, *Developmental Psychology*, 12, 289-297.

Wood, D. (1988), *How Children Think and Learn*, Oxford, Blackwell.

Spiritual and Moral Development

Unit C

Piaget, Kohlberg and Gilligan

Revd Dr William K. Kay

Trinity College

Carmarthen

Contents

Introduction

Aims

After working through this unit you should be able to:

- understand Piaget's contribution to moral development;
- understand Kohlberg's extension of Piaget's theory;
- understand Gilligan's critique and extension of Kohlberg's work.

Overview

In this unit you will read about Piaget's pioneering work on moral development and be encouraged to conduct brief experiments along the lines he used. You will then read about Kohlberg's elaboration and extension of Piaget's work, especially in its relation to moral development and moral education. Finally this unit takes you into Gilligan's critiques of Kohlberg and, by implication, Piaget. Lastly the unit considers classroom approaches and techniques in the field of moral education.

C1 Piaget on moral development

Piaget carried out his work on moral development early in life, but he conducted this research within the broad outlines of his theory of mental development. According to Piaget, the young child thinks and acts morally within the confines of concrete operational thinking. The older child begins to call on the resources of formal operational thinking. The young child, as a consequence of the limitations of concrete operational thinking, sees situations largely from his or her point of view and finds difficulty in considering alternative viewpoints. The older child is less egocentric and more able to co-operate with others.

As a prelude to his enquiry Piaget wanted to investigate how children understood rules that had no connection with adults. He chose the rules of the game of marbles. We consider first his method and then the findings and their interpretation. After this we turn to the most substantial part of the enquiry. Here children were told a series of stories and asked about them. Again, we consider first the method and then the findings and their interpretation.

Playing marbles

Method

About twenty boys aged between 4 and 12 or 13 were questioned. In the first part of the enquiry the researcher says, 'Here are some marbles. You must show me how to play. When I was little I used to play a lot, but now I've quite forgotten how to.' The researcher plays with the child, sometimes making deliberate mistakes so that the child explains points of procedure, and enters into the spirit of the game.

In the second part of the enquiry, the researcher begins by asking the child if a new rule could be invented and, if the child agrees to this, the researcher asks whether the new rule is a 'fair' or a 'real' rule 'like all the others'. Following this, questions are asked about whether people have always played marbles in the way the child has explained and what the origin of the rules was.

Interpretation

Four stages are found:

- *Individual rules* where the young child plays aimlessly and without consistency;
- *Egocentric rules* where the child imitates the play of older children and plays alone or in company with others but not against them; everyone can win at once. No attempt is made to codify the rules or uniformly apply them to the group;
- *Co-operation* appears about the age of seven or eight. Players try to win and concern themselves with the question of mutual control and consistency though often, despite playing together, the children give different and contradictory accounts of the rules they are playing to;
- *Codification of the rules* appears about the age of 11 or 12. Every detail of the game is fixed and known by all the players.

Piaget's interpretation of his findings runs to about 30 pages and leads him to conclude that, because the young child lives in a world where rules are imposed by adults, the rules of marbles are like the rules that govern the physical regularities of life. Piaget (1932, p 47) wrote as follows.

> From its earliest months the child is therefore bathed in an atmosphere of rules, so that the task of discerning what comes from itself in the rites that it respects and what results from the pressure of things or the constraint of the social environment is one of extreme difficulty.

The child's consciousness of rules, insofar as it has one, is conditioned by its moral life as a whole. This changes at the next stage.

At the egocentric stage, at around the age of seven, the child 'regards the rules of the game as sacred and untouchable... and claims that any modifications, even if accepted by general opinion, would be wrong' (p 50). This kind of fixed regard for the rules co-exists with consciousness of adult constraint (Piaget, 1932, p 57). So, while the child regards the rules as fixed and imposed by a higher authority (parents? God?), the purpose of the rules as a means of ensuring co-operation and fairness is not understood.

Only at the final stage, when children act out of mutual respect for each other, are the rules seen to be modifiable by general consent. At this point the rules are interpreted as being rational and changes in them may occur as children learn to make their own decisions. It is important to notice the overall shape of the course of moral thinking, as displayed by this analysis of the rules of marbles. Children progress from *heteronomy* (where rules are imposed by others for their own reasons) and constraint to *autonomy* (where rules are made or chosen rationally and individually) and freedom.

Stories about causing damage

Method

Children between six and ten years were told three pairs of stories. Each pair contrasted children who caused damage, in the first case while trying to do good and in the second while playing or being naughty. We reproduce the two shortest:

> A. There was once a little girl called Marie. She wanted to give her mother a nice surprise, and cut out a piece of sewing for her. But she didn't know how to use the scissors properly and cut a big hole in her dress.

> B. A little girl called Margaret went and took her mother's scissors one day that her mother was out. She played with them for a bit. Then as she didn't know how to use them properly she made a little hole in her dress.

About each pair of stories two questions were asked, 'Are these children equally guilty?' and 'Which of the two is the naughtiest, and why?' An extended conversation with the researcher may then follow.

Interpretation

Piaget (1932, p 106) is clear young children are generally 'moral realists', that is, they

> regard duty and the value attaching to it as self-subsistent and independent of the mind, as imposing itself regardless of the circumstances in which the individual may find himself.

The moral realist believes duty is imposed - often by other people and objectively demands the letter rather than the spirit of the law.

Children's answers to the stories show that between seven and ten there is a mixed set of responses: some regard the child who did the most damage as being naughtier irrespective of its good motives, and others take motive into account and judge accordingly. After the age of ten, subjective responsibility (that is, including consideration of motive) is always a factor.

Stories about lying

Method

As a next step in the investigation children were asked three further questions.

- What is a lie?
- Who is responsible for the lie?
- Who is responsible for the material consequences of the lie?

These questions were probed by reference to intention. Although there was evidence that children could distinguish between intentional acts and involuntary mistakes, they tended to classify both kinds of false statement as lies. Four pairs of stories were used to extend the analysis. The first two are:

> A. A little boy goes for a walk in the street and meets a big dog who frightens him very much. So then he goes home and tells his mother he has seen a dog that was as big as a cow. [The child's gender is changed when the story is told to a girl.]

> B. A child comes home from school and tells his mother that the teacher had given him good marks, but it was not true; the teacher had given him no marks at all, either good or bad. Then his mother was very pleased and rewarded him. [The child's gender is changed when the story is told to a girl.]

Interpretation

Piaget expected, on the basis of objective responsibility and moral realism, that the more a statement departed from the truth, the more it would seem to the child to be a lie. This is what was found. There were complications in the interpretation because children had to make distinctions between statements and the stories relating to the statements. Some children (aged about six) judged the naughtiness of a lie by the degree of its incredibility to adults. In this case, the lie about the dog as a big as a cow was more serious than the lie about the good marks.

When Piaget's researchers looked to see whether the child in the story's intention was taken into account in the moral judgements of the children they questioned, they found that it was not.

How, then, do children move from moral realism to judge conduct by intention? In essence, Piaget (1932, p 164) concluded that unilateral respect (when the young child respects the adult for being an adult) was replaced by, or became less important than, mutual respect, when children relate to each other as peers or to adults on an equal footing. In the first stage the lie is wrong because it is an object of punishment. In the second stage a lie becomes something wrong in itself and would remain wrong even if the punishment were removed. Finally, in the stage of mutual respect, the lie is wrong because it is in conflict with mutual trust and affection. The three stages unfold between the ages of about 7 and 11 and correspond with the gradual transition from concrete operational thinking to formal operations.

Stories about justice

Method

Seven stories were told to about 100 children aged between six and 12 years. The children were interviewed on the basis of the stories. One of the shortest stories was:

> A boy has broken a toy belonging to his little brother. What should be done? Should he (1) give the little fellow one of his own toys? (2) pay for having it mended? (3) not be allowed to play with any of his own toys for a whole week?

The children were then asked, 'Are the punishments given to children always very fair, or are some fairer than others?' Then a selection of the stories was told (the children were not told all the stories since this would have been too many for them to cope with) and a set of possible punishments for the character in the story was offered. Once the child had chosen the fairest, care was taken to ask why it was the fairest.

Five further sets of stories were told to children. The first dealt with collective responsibility, the second with immanent justice (bad things happening by accident to people who do wrong) and the third with a conflict between retributive and distributive justice. A story used in this set was simply, 'A mother had two little girls, one obedient, the other disobedient. The mother liked the obedient one best and gave her the biggest piece of cake. What do you think of that?' The last two sets concerned equality and authority and justice between children.

Interpretation

Piaget argued that every action that is judged guilty by a social group is so judged because it is a violation of the rules of that group and breaks the group's social bonds.   The first kind of punishment to be expected was *expiatory*, that is, intended to bring home to the wrongdoer his or her guilt. This sort of punishment would be effective in the measure that it expressed the anger of the social group.   It would, however, be arbitrary in the sense that no connection between punishment and crime would be made.

A second kind of punishment, called a *punishment of reciprocity*, would go hand in hand with co-operation and rules of equality. This sort of punishment occurs when the wrongdoer willingly accepts the rules of the group and is conscious of having broken them.   There is no need for painful coercion but only for the group to register the consequences of breaching its agreed norms. According to Piaget (1932, p 199f) there may be:

- temporary or permanent exclusion from the group;
- a punishment that appeals only to the immediate consequences of the wrongful act (having no bread for dinner because you have refused to go and fetch some when there was not enough in the house - which is the situation in one of the longer stories);
- deprivation of the thing that was misused (taking a book away from a child who damaged it);
- simple reciprocity (where the child who has broken a toy has one of his broken);
- restitutive punishment (where the child must replace the stolen or broken object);
- censure only to make the wrongdoer realise that he or she has broken the social bond.

The findings confirmed the trend for children to begin with expiatory punishment and to move on from there to punishments based on reciprocity. The younger children prefer the most severe punishments to emphasise the necessity of punishment - they always think in terms of expiation - whereas the older ones are more inclined to justify punishments by their preventative value and by explanations.   The younger children's thinking is influenced by heteronomy and imposed duty; the older children's thinking is influenced by co-operation and an ethic of autonomy.

After analysing results from all these stories, Piaget concluded that there are three great periods in the development of the child's sense of justice.   In the years:

- up to 7 and 8 justice is subordinated to adult authority without regard to reasons for this; cheating is wrong because teacher says so; lying is wrong because parents say so; rules are absolute and apply in all circumstances regardless of intention or any other factor; intellectually the child is functioning in a pre-operational way; morally this is the stage of *heteronomy*;

- between 8 and 11 there is progressive sense of social equality, though obedience to authority takes precedence over justice; there is some shift away from a purely egotistical position and the beginnings of an internalisation of rules and an understanding of motive; intellectually the child is functioning at the concrete operational stage; morally this is the stage of *socionomy*;

- from the age of 11 or 12 onwards, the basis of social equality leads to a willingness to take personal circumstances and motives into account in distributive and retributive justice; causing accidental damage is not as wrong as causing deliberate damage; moral rules are examined rationally and may be changed; punishment should fit the crime instead of being an automatic response to breaking rules; intellectually the child is beginning to function at the formal operational stage; morally this is the stage of *autonomy*.

In summary, the ethics of authority, which is obedience to duty imposed by adults, leads in the domain of justice to an identification of justice with established rules or laws and to an acceptance of expiatory punishment. The ethics of mutual respect, which places a premium on what is good, leads in the domain of justice to a view of social equality that is expressed by fair distribution and co-operation.

Activity C1

With the help of no more than ten children between 7 and 11 years carry out your own replication of Piaget's work. *Either* take one or two of the stories that he told and ask the questions he used *or* use the example of the marbles game. If marbles are not popular with your children you may, if you wish, select any other game you see children playing which you think they have not been taught by adults. Notice that the method is sufficiently flexible to allow you to ask extra and subsidiary questions to try to discover the concepts behind children's opinions and judgements.

Make notes of what the children say in answer to your questions and try to find out whether their responses match the pattern discovered by Piaget. You will, of course, find a fuller account of the studies in Piaget's own book on moral judgement, but the information given here is enough for a small-scale study that will enable you to get a feel for moral development as it appears from a Piagetian perspective.

When you have carried out your study, jot down what you have learnt, what your main difficulties were and what other topics connected with moral development you would like to find out about.

Comment on activity C1

Naturally, your findings will depend on which stories you have decided to use or whether you have investigated the marbles game or another game. This is not a full-blown research project and you may feel that you have not been given enough information to do the work properly in the methods sections above (though Piaget's own account does not give much more information than we have given here). Yet, previous researchers attempting replications have discovered that Piaget's findings are remarkably robust and translate not only to other cultures but do indeed show the sort of, at first sight, inexplicable results he records.

If you have used the moral stories, you may have been surprised, unless you work with primary school children, at the ideas children entertain about right and wrong and justice and injustice. Your difficulties may have arisen in knowing how to categorise children's answers and whether or not what they say supports the developmental scheme you were expecting to find. This has been one of the main criticisms of Piaget's work in the past, though it has usually been made by those who come from a 'hard science' background.

The deficiencies in the Piagetian account are often thought to cluster round the gap between children's moral judgements and their moral behaviour; to include the lack of attention to moral feelings; to cover the concentration on justice rather than less lofty moral problems.

C2 Kohlberg on moral reasoning

Lawrence Kohlberg (1927-87) admired Piaget's *Moral Judgement of the Child* and used it as the starting point for his own description of moral development. He wanted to put the assessment of moral development onto a secure statistical and objective basis and so developed a rating system that was later turned into a test. The test was placed firmly in the world of cognitive development and, over twenty-five years, Kohlberg collected data, analysed it, revised his scoring system and the descriptions of moral development derived from it until he reached the final version of his six stage theory[1].

---

[1] Kohlberg's original sample consisted of 72 males aged 10, 13 and 16 from the Chicago area whom he tested every two to five years for the next 30 years.

This theory posited a universal account of the development of moral reasoning which was independent of culture or gender. The theory was not concerned with the content of morality but with the reasons given by people to justify their moral decisions. The theory did not try to describe what was immoral or moral or what particular social groups would regard as right or wrong. The point of the theory was, following Piaget, to see how moral reasoning took place and what sort of reasons were offered for moral decisions.

The data were collected by presenting participants with a series of moral dilemmas. Each dilemma contrasted laws, social rules or moral principles with basic human needs. Participants had to decide whether to uphold or reject the laws, rules and principles and to give reasons for their choice. The well-known Heinz dilemma used by Kohlberg illustrates the problem:

> In a civilised country a woman was dying from cancer. One drug might save her life, a form of chemotherapy that had been discovered by a firm in the town where she lived. The firm was charging £1000, ten times what it cost to make, even allowing for research costs. The dying woman's husband, Heinz, went to everyone he knew to borrow the money, but he could only get together about half the price. He told the firm that his wife was dying and asked them to sell it to him more cheaply or to let him pay later. But the firm said 'No'. The husband became desperate and broke into the firm's premises to steal the drug for his wife.

We have here a conflict between stealing and saving life. Has Heinz done right or wrong? What reasons would you give for your answer? You might like to ask yourself what you would answer before looking at the stages Kohlberg describes. What kind of Kohlbergian moral level are you operating at?

The theory presumes that what drives moral development is cognitive development rather than social relationships. The theory also presumes that people must pass in strict sequence through the stages in their journey of moral development. It is not possible, in other words, to jump from Stage 1 to Stage 3 without going through Stage 2. This is because the higher stages depend on the lower stages and incorporate their features. The stages are described as follows, illustrated by possible answers to the Heinz dilemma.

Level 1 Pre-conventional morality

Stage 1 is characterised by avoiding pain and punishment: doing the right thing is decided in terms of obedience to external moral authority.

- Heinz will get into trouble if he lets his wife die.
- Heinz should not steal because he will go to prison.

Stage 2 is characterised by maximising pleasure or benefit, minimising pain or negative consequences.

- If Heinz got caught, he could return the drug and, after a short sentence, would get home and his wife would be alive.
- If Heinz was sent to prison, his wife would probably die before he got home and so it would not be worthwhile.

Level 2 Conventional morality

Stage 3 is characterised by the good boy: behaviour is aimed at conforming to the group and group solidarity determines what is good or bad.

- No one will think that Heinz is bad if he steals the drug but they will if he lets his wife die.
- Everyone will think Heinz is a criminal if he steals.

Stage 4 is characterised by law and order: it is important to obey rules and laws and it is right to feel guilty if others are harmed.

- Heinz will not have done his duty to his wife if he fails to do his utmost to save her.
- Heinz may not know he is doing wrong, but he will always be ashamed of having been dishonest and of having broken the law.

Level 3 Post-conventional morality

Stage 5 is characterised by contract: this has legal overtones. There is an awareness of the relativism of moral opinions but a willingness to accept law while seeking to change it where it is disagreeable. In the personal realm, free agreement and promises create a sense of obligation.

- Heinz would lose the respect of other people by not stealing and by letting his wife die.
- Heinz would lose respect for himself by being carried away by emotion and forgetting long-term consequences.

Stage 6 is characterised by universal ethical principles: action is determined by fairness and concern for maintaining one's own freely worked out rational moral principles; the individual here is autonomous and operates according to a code that transcends local laws and customs.

- If Heinz let his wife die, he would have betrayed his own moral principles about respecting life and these principles supersede those of respect for profit.
- If Heinz stole he would have betrayed his respect for the labour and property of fellow human beings.

Activity C2

Tell the Heinz story to ten people ranging in age from ten years old to middle age. Ask each person whether Heinz has done right or wrong and explore the issues in a series of questions. If possible tape record the conversations. Each conversation need take no longer than 15 minutes. Then try to analyse the answers according to Kohlberg's scheme.

You will not be able to score the answers properly without the manual and your impressions, using the stage descriptions and examples given above, will only give you a rough idea of the way the system works. But your understanding of the stages will be improved by this exercise and it will prepare you for the next section of this unit.

Comment on activity C2

As with the Piagetian task, you may have found it difficult to decide which moral stage people are functioning at. This is especially the case where you are dealing with differences in age, education, articulation and even sub-culture. You may therefore have found that it is difficult to be precise about stages and that such stages as you think you have found are soft at the edges. If you have found this, then you are aligning yourself with general critics of stage developmentalists who wonder whether soft stages are too elusive to be useful and hard stages are too precise to be realistic.

You may have noticed that males and females tend to approach moral problems from separate standpoints and, if you have, then you will be ready to look at Gilligan's critique of Kohlberg.

On the other hand, it may be that you can see the logic of the progression through the stages and your only difficulty may have been in deciding whether your questions put ideas into the heads of your sample and pushed some of their replies up to the next stage. If this is so, you will have stumbled into the area which Kohlberg worked in during the latter part of his life - the problem of lifting young people to a more sophisticated level of moral reasoning.

C3 Developments in Kohlberg's theory

Because he was a campaigner and a reformer as well as a theoretician, Kohlberg was keen to apply his theory to disadvantaged social groups. He embarked on a pilot project with prisoners to try to raise their thinking to Stage 4 by means of discussions and moral dilemmas. The method for trying to raise levels of thinking grew straight from Piaget's theory which, as you have seen, contended that an imposed morality of constraint changes to a freely chosen morality of moral principles through a change from subservience to adults to co-operation with a peer group.

Stage 2 thinking is egotistical. The Stage 2 thinker is only concerned with his or her own advantage or pleasure. Most prisoners work at Stage 2. Stage 4 thinking is much more concerned for others, much less egotistical and takes into account rules and laws as a fair means of regulating behaviour. A prisoner moving from Stage 2 to Stage 4 has made the transition from being an habitual law-breaker to being convinced of the value of law-abiding. Kohlberg knew that if his project worked, he had found a key to great social advance. Prisoners would be reformed in prison, not simply punished, and would therefore not re-offend on release. Huge amounts of public money would be saved and the reformed prisoners would be ready to become settled and productive citizens.

Kohlberg's results were promising but not widely taken up[2]. More recently Taylor and Walker (1997) have reported on a study of 101 institutionalised young offenders in Canada that made use of Kohlberg's ideas but varied two factors in the research design. First, three institutions were selected and the 'moral climate' of each was assessed. Moral climate is understood in the light of the discussion taking place in them about the real moral problems inmates face. This feature is taken directly from Kohlberg: he substituted real-life situations for hypothetical moral dilemmas when he worked with offenders because he came to realise that, unless he did so, he failed to connect with the moral worlds of those he was trying to help.

One of the institutions in Taylor and Walker's study had engaged in community discussions for approximately two years, another for three months prior to the onset of the study and the third held no such meetings, though in other respects it was the same as the other two.

Second, Taylor and Walker noticed that prisoners vary enormously in the prestige they have within the institution. The source of the prestige is often physical strength, but it may be based on other means of manipulation and influence. Whatever its source, however, both prisoners and warders know which prisoners have high status and which are at the bottom of the ladder. Taylor and Walker hypothesised that high status prisoners would stand in the same relation to low status prisoners as adults did to children in the classic Piagetian account of moral development. Therefore a high status prisoner functioning at a higher moral stage than a low status prisoner was much more

---

[2] Though three schools in Germany participated in a Just Community project in 1987 in which Kohlberg was involved (Oser, 1996). The project was similar to the American scheme, but better prepared.

likely to help the low status prisoner to advance than when the situation was reversed.

They arranged for pairs (dyads) of prisoners to spend time together discussing moral problems and they predicted changes set out as follows:

Type	Other	Target	Change
1	High status higher/same stage	low status lower/same stage	yes
2	high status low stage	low status high stage	no
3	low status higher/same stage	high status lower/same stage	no
4	low status low stage	high status high stage	no
5	high status higher/same stage	high status lower/same stage	yes
6	high status low stage	high status high stage	no
7	low status higher/same stage	low status lower/same stage	yes
8	low status low stage	low status high stage	no

The results were in line with expectations. The offenders paired with a higher status person who also operated at a higher level of moral reasoning were significantly more likely to move up themselves.

The study also allowed comparisons to be made between the institutions and their distinct moral climates. Would offenders living in a moral climate that facilitated discussion and co-operation be more likely to function at a higher moral stage than those where the moral climate was more restricted? Here the findings were not exactly in line with expectations because, although no direct connection was found between moral reasoning and moral climate, a connection *was* found between moral climate and moral behaviour.

This finding is interesting and important and it raises two other issues. First, the line of enquiry explored in this unit so far has followed the development of moral reasoning, not moral behaviour, but, according to Kohlberg, moral climate is one important element in the linkage between reasoning and behaviour. This makes good sense. A highly moral person in an immoral environment cannot entirely avoid its effects. Anyone who wishes to improve moral behaviour, therefore, needs to improve both moral reasoning and moral climate - a finding most school teachers would intuitively understand. Second, the social environment is made up of norms of behaviour some of which are moral and some of which are non-moral and it is often difficult to distinguish the two. In the institutions for young offenders, for example, drug taking was not seen as a moral issue. It was part of the general culture of institutional and adolescent life. While adults and prison officers might easily draw moral distinctions relating to drug-taking, inmates found this confusing.

Oser (1996) describes studies by Nunner-Winkler and Sodian (1988) that explored moral emotion. How do children think people feel after stealing? More generally, a question might be asked about the motivation to perform moral actions. Oser suggests that it will be important to test the moral emotions surrounding actions carried out at each of the six stages. He suggests that at Stage 2, people feel shame if they are punished for wrongdoing and indignation if someone else is punished for wrongdoing. The shame and the indignation are two sides of a coin and are the emotions corresponding to being wrong oneself and seeing others do wrong. So far this piece of research has not been done.

It is reasonable to suppose that moral reasoning would be influenced by empathy, by the ability to feel what others are feeling. Empathy and sympathy are connected, though sympathy is associated with co-suffering while empathy is broader and associated with all kinds of emotions. This ability to discern and enter the feelings of others is likely to sensitise moral judgements. Kay and Francis (1996) reviewed research on this area and found that empathy tends to decline in the school years. Young children are much more able to enter into other people's feelings than older ones, though what is odd about this finding is that young children lack the mental capacity to see things from the viewpoints of other people. Thus, while mental development would point in the direction of increased empathy, actual research points in the direction of an increased 'hardening' among young people. This puzzle is solved when it is related to religious disposition and attitude. Kay and Francis report that, where young people entertain a positive attitude toward Christianity, their empathy increases with age. It appears that a positive attitude to Christianity prevents the 'hardening' taking place and so allows the capacity for empathy to grow in step with cognitive growth.

Kohlberg's description of moral development, heavily reliant as it is on cognitive development, has thus been taken forward in these two ways, in some instances by Kohlberg himself [3]:

- the environment of the moral agent has been brought more fully into view;
- the inner emotional life of the agent has been assessed.

Yet, these developments seemed inadequate to Carol Gilligan to whose critique we now turn.

C4 Carol Gilligan on women's moral reasoning

Carol Gilligan was an associate of Kohlberg at Harvard and published at least one piece of work with him. Her own independent research has led her to believe that the trajectory of women's moral development is different from that of men and that, to the extent that Piaget and Kohlberg make masculine assumptions, they are in need of correction. In essence, she believes that, whereas men operate with an 'ethic of justice' women operate with an 'ethic of care'. This has implications for the way Kohlberg's theory is scored for women since their life experiences of relationships and relatedness can cause them to appear to regress, to go backwards, from a higher to a lower moral stage rather than to move steadily from lower to higher. What can happen is that women tend to see the moral dilemmas presented by Kohlberg's test in terms of people who are likely to have more choices than Kohlberg gives them. In other words, women often refuse the either/or nature of the dilemma by looking for a third possibility.

Gilligan's investigations covered three separate studies. The *college student study* explored experiences of moral conflict in the early adult years by interviewing 25 students, selected at random from a group who had chosen as undergraduates to take a course on moral and political choice.

The *abortion decision study* considered the 'role of conflict in development' in the lives of 29 women, ranging from 15 to 33 years of age, of diverse ethnic backgrounds and social class, some of whom were married and others single, who were considering abortion. Of the 29 women referred, complete interview data were available from 21. These 21 were interviewed while considering their options and then a year after their decision.

The *rights and responsibilities study* involved a 'sample of males and females matched for age, intelligence, education, occupation and social class at

---

[3] We have not considered the construction of pencil and paper tests (rather than interviews) that have been derived from Kohlberg's theory. These tests offer a simple and quick way of assessing moral development. They include the Sociomoral Reflection Objective Measure (SROM) (Gibbs *et al*, 1984) and the Defining Issues Tests (DIT) (Rest, 1979; 1986).

nine points in the life cycle: ages 6-9, 11, 15, 19, 22, 25-27, 35, 45 and 60'. Eight males and females at each point were interviewed, making a total of 144 in all. Data were collected on 'conceptions of self and morality, experiences of moral conflict and choice, and judgements of hypothetical moral dilemmas' (Gilligan, 1982, p 3).

Gilligan began by reviewing the emergence of the self in Freudian theory. She pointed out that Freud thought the superego or conscience is ill-developed in women because, in men, it is an outcome of the boy's love for his mother and fear of his father. Freud concluded that women 'show less sense of justice than men, that they are less ready to submit to the great exigencies of life, that they are more often influenced in their judgements by feelings of affection or hostility' (quoted by Gilligan, 1982, p 7). Moreover, the sense of identity developed by boys is generated by their understanding that they are different from their mothers. In girls, by contrast, sense of identity begins by a feeling that they are the same as their mothers. Male development entails 'more emphatic individuation and more defensive firming of the ego boundaries'. Female development entails a sense of empathic tie.

Turning to Piaget's work Gilligan notices that Piaget found girls have a more 'pragmatic' attitude to rules than boys and 'regard a rule as good as long as the game repaid it' (Gilligan, 1982, p 10, quoting Piaget). Girls' games are typically co-operative and occur in smaller and more intimate groups. Boys' games are competitive and they learn to deal with disputes in a forthright manner by reference to well-understood rules and procedures. Consequently girls and boys arrive at puberty with 'different interpersonal orientation and with a different range of social experiences' (Gilligan, 1982, p 11).

Continued development during the life cycle sees men as defining themselves through competitive achievement and women as defining themselves through intimacy and relationships. This divergence of male and female paths has implications for the proper description of moral development. Whereas the Piaget/Kohlberg model assumes that people progress towards separation, autonomy and rights, women place a value on attachment and interdependence that runs counter to this goal. The mature woman is not prepared to conform to the male ideal and, to this extent, the model of moral developments that we have so far considered, and the stages of development delineated by Kohlberg, are in need of revision. That, at any rate, is Gilligan's contention.

The responses of boys and girls and men and women to the Heinz dilemma illustrate the point at issue. Jake, a bright 11 year old boy, gives an answer that scores between Stages 3 and 4. Jake thinks Heinz should steal the drug and justifies his choice:

> For one thing, a human life is worth more than money, and if the druggist only makes £500, he is still going to live, but if Heinz doesn't steal the drug, his wife is going to die (*Why is life worth more than money?*) Because the druggist can get a thousand pounds later from rich people with cancer, but Heinz can't get his wife again. (*Why not?*) Because people are all different and so you couldn't get Heinz's wife again.

Jake is able to differentiate morality and law and to see that laws can be mistaken and, in this, he is on the road to the 'principled conception of justice that Kohlberg equates with moral maturity' (Gilligan, 1982, p 27).

Amy, a similarly bright 11 year old, approaches the problem very differently. Asked if Heinz should steal the drug, she replies by saying:

> Well, I don't think so. I think there might be other ways beside stealing it, like if he could borrow the money or make a loan or something, but he really shouldn't steal the drug - but his wife shouldn't die either.

So, although her answer seems evasive, she is looking for a solution that solves Heinz's problem without breaking his relationship with his wife or with the law. When she is asked why Heinz should not steal the drug, she 'considers neither property nor law but rather the effect that theft could have on the relationship between Heinz and his wife'. Later she is confident that 'if Heinz and the druggist had talked it out long enough, they could reach something besides stealing'. Her instincts are to see the problem as a set of interpersonal relationships that will allow a negotiated settlement.

In Kohlberg's terms Amy is operating at Stages 2 and 3, a full stage below Jake, but Gilligan argues that other aspects of Amy's life show her to be mature. Amy is able to understand the nature of choice in a sophisticated way, realising that, where two possibilities exist, it is impossible to know what would have happened if the other choice had been made after the point of decision. 'There's really no way around it because there's no way you can do both at once, so you've got to decide.' Her understanding of morality arises from 'the recognition of relationship [and] her belief in communication as the mode of conflict resolution' (Gilligan, 1982, p 30).

Activity C3

Pause and think about Gilligan's engagement with the work of Kohlberg and Piaget. What additional factors does she bring into play which have been ignored by Kohlberg and Piaget? Do you think these factors are relevant? What are the strengths and weaknesses of her approach as it has been explained so far?

Comment on activity C3

First and foremost Gilligan takes personality theory into account. We have quoted from her review of Freud, but she also draws Erickson (1965) into her discussion. Her foray into Freudian theory is relevant to her concentration on the self since it is the balance between the interests of the self and of others that is at the heart of much morality. Clearly, then the formation of the self and its definition in relation to, and in contradistinction from, others is extremely relevant to morality. The strengths of her approach are that she widens the theoretical basis for moral development. But the weakness of her approach is that it fails to engage with a model of cognitive development. Moral judgement, because it is a cognitive activity, must reflect the general cognitive capacities and processes of the individual. Gilligan has little to say on this matter and she neither approves nor criticises Piaget's work. Consequently, her view of moral judgement is anchored in life experiences rather than in cognition.

Women's stages of moral development

The data from the abortion decision study were analysed by Gilligan to show the factors women took into account when weighing up the pros and cons of having an abortion or having a baby. She interpreted the women as, at first, focusing on a care for the self to ensure survival. The woman's top priority must be to survive emotionally and physically. This narrow focus gave way to a transitional phase in which this judgement was thought to be selfish and wrong. A third stage followed where 'a new understanding of the self' was articulated 'by the concept of responsibility' (Gilligan, 1982, p 74). At this point good behaviour, morally good activity, is equated with caring for others. This stage is that of self-sacrifice, of living for others. But further transformation takes place when the woman appreciates she has also to care for herself: self and others must be kept in balance. The tension between selfishness and responsibility is dissolved by a new appreciation of the way others are interconnected with the self. The ethic of care, for self and others, is gradually extended until it becomes a principle of judgement that affirms all kinds of care and condemns all kinds of exploitation.

We may present this sequence in a simplified form:

- care of the self ensuring survival is the main principle to determine what is right;
- care of the self is wrong; it is literally selfish;
- care for others responsibly ensuring their well-being is the main principle to determine what is right;

- simultaneous care of others and self is possible and is the main principle to determine what is right and may be extended universally.

These stages are illustrated by the way the abortion decision is analysed. At the first stage, women typically centre the decision on themselves. 'The concern is pragmatic and the issue is survival' (Gilligan, 1982, p 75). This way of thinking is carried over into comment on the Heinz dilemma. Betty, aged 16 says:

> I think survival is one of the first things in life that people fight for. I think it is the most important thing, more important than stealing. Stealing might be wrong, but if you have to steal to survive yourself or even kill, that is what you should do.

Josie, a 17 year old, 'started feeling really good about being pregnant... I was looking at it from my own sort of selfish needs, because I was lonely...' yet she comes to change her mind. 'I wasn't looking at the realistic side, at the responsibility I would have to take on. I came to this decision that I was going to have an abortion because I realised how much responsibility goes with having a child.' The tension between 'feeling good' and 'responsibility' marks the transition to the next stage.

This is seen more clearly in the explanation Denise, a 25 year old, gives for her decision. Denise wished to maintain her relationship with her boyfriend and knew that a baby would jeopardise this relationship. She wanted to have the baby but she also wanted to continue the relationship, so either choice could have been construed as being selfish. Eventually, she decided to sacrifice her own needs to those of her lover even though, of course, this entailed aborting the baby and sacrificing the care she would have given as a mother. Denise interprets her decision as a caring decision though subsequent anger with her boyfriend erupted in accusations that he is responsible for the child's death.

Janet, a 24 year old married Catholic, becomes pregnant two months after the birth of her first child. Janet thinks of her decision in terms of responsibilities to others since she has been advised on medical grounds not to have another child and a second child would put emotional and financial pressure on the family. There is another reason, too. Janet, as a Catholic, believes that abortions are wrong but she also recognises that she might be thought to be immoral if, for the sake of her moral beliefs, she harms three other people: her husband, her first child and herself. Gilligan sees Janet as struggling with the issues of goodness and truth. Goodness demands that she should act morally; truth demands that she should face her own feelings honestly. Goodness belongs to the ethics of self-sacrifice; truth belongs to the ethics of the co-care for self and others.

Gilligan (1982, p 105) concludes her analysis by summarising the developmental sequence she believes her data reveal:

The sequence of women's moral judgement proceeds from an initial concern with survival to a focus on goodness and finally to a reflective understanding of care as the most adequate guide to the resolution of conflicts in human relationships. The abortion study demonstrates the centrality of the concepts of responsibility and care in women's constructions of the moral domain, the close tie in women's thinking between conceptions of self and morality, and ultimately the need for an expanded developmental theory that includes, rather than rules out from consideration, the differences in the feminine voice.

C5 Critiques and developments of Gilligan

Gilligan's theory has been enthusiastically taken up and inspired a series of studies testing or extending it. Her original book has been reprinted at least thirty-three times. Nevertheless, her work has been criticised from several angles. Kerber, Greeno, Maccoby, Luria, Stack (1986), in a paper to which Gilligan herself had a right of reply, pointed out that there is no male equivalent to the abortion dilemma. For this reason it is particularly unsuited to pointing up differences between men and women. Ideally men and women would respond to exactly the same dilemma, as they do with the Heinz dilemma, and then their responses should be compared. As it is, the abortion dilemma, posed as it was to young women undergoing counselling at a clinic, operates unlike the hypothetical dilemmas posed by Kohlberg. It is a real dilemma, one that must be decided upon and one that can be revisited after the decision has been made. Moreover, the very fact that the young women in the study attended this clinic, shows that they were disposed to undergo an abortion. We do not learn, for example, either how different was the reasoning of women who decided to have an abortion from those who decided not to have an abortion or how the women visiting the clinic might be different from women who, even after becoming pregnant unintentionally or stressfully, nevertheless carried their child through to birth without going so far as to seek abortion counselling.

A more blunt and aggressive critique of Gilligan has been mounted by Pollitt (1992) who points out women in many situations are concerned with issues of justice, sometimes on political and economic platforms and sometimes within the family.

These criticisms do not undermine the subtle and creative analysis Gilligan made of her data, but they do suggest that her thesis that men and women's moral development is distinct has methodological weaknesses. This is certainly the view of Greeno and Maccoby (1986) who looked again at Gilligan's primary data and found that the rate of progress from Kohlbergian Level 3 to Level 4 could be explained by the educational grades of respondents. Educationally more advanced women were more likely to function at

Kohlberg's Level 4. Thus the issue could be interpreted to be one of education rather than of gender.

In addition, as Colby and Damon (1983) have shown, Kohlberg has revised his scoring system to include care and responsibility at each level. It would be incorrect, then, to see Kohlberg as *only* propagating or testing for an ethic of justice.

Developments of Gilligan's work include the enquiries pursued by Belenky, Clinch, Goldberger and Tarule (1986). These concluded that women's intellectual growth passes typically through five stages. The first level is that of *silence* where women 'experience themselves as mindless and voiceless and subject to the whims of external authority'. There follows a level of *received knowledge*, a 'perspective from which women conceive themselves as capable of receiving knowledge' from authorities and reproducing it. Following this is *subjective knowledge* which is a 'perspective from which truth and knowledge are conceived of as personal, private, and subjectively known or intuited'. After this is *procedural knowledge* where women 'are interested in learning and applying objective procedures for obtaining and communicating knowledge'. Lastly *constructive knowledge* allows women to 'view all knowledge as contextual' and to become creators of knowledge themselves and to 'value both subjective and objective strategies for knowing'.

The moral strategies followed by women, and outlined by Gilligan, fit the stages proposed by Belenky *et al*. Received knowledge is compatible with the moral stage where women think care of the self is wrong and, indeed, where care for others becomes the guiding principle. The reason for this is that received knowledge is conformist knowledge, knowledge that is socially imparted and connected with stereotypical behavioural norms. Such norms stress the caring, mothering role of women. Subjective knowledge, by definition, concerns the inner thoughts and feelings of the knower. This level is compatible with Gilligan's emphasis on truth, on 'what is right for me' and paves the way for insights of contextual knowledge where care of the self and of others co-exist.

Activity C4

What is your evaluation of the validity of the criticism raised against Gilligan's work? Does her position undermine or support the view that we should expect to find moral development take place in human beings?

Comment on activity C4

The criticisms of Gilligan's work fall into two main categories. There are those which suggest that she has failed to prove her case that male and female moral development are different. And there are those which deal the perceived methodological weaknesses of her work.

Taking the first category, it is clear that the lack of a comparable male equivalent of the abortion dilemma *does* undermine a strict comparison between males and females. Suggestions that males be questioned on their unwillingness to accept conscription to the army are not very helpful here. More to the point might be questions to potential fathers about the possible abortion of their children. Parallel studies could then examine male and female attitudes to the abortion of the same child. However, even this does not really solve the problem of equivalence. What is needed is a series of studies or moral dilemmas and life situations involving men and women and an attempt to interpret the data both according to the Kohlbergian scheme and according to Gilligan's scheme. It would then be necessary to see which of the two schemes provided the most satisfactory account of the dilemmas posed. It is possible, for example, that men might also show a developmental sequence similar to that found in women. If this were so, then it might be that moral development was not influence so much by cognitive structures as by the masculinity and femininity of the individual. Females who showed signs of masculinity and males who showed signs of femininity might show similar developmental patterns. All this, however, is speculative because the necessary empirical work has not yet been carried out.

Taking the second category, methodological weaknesses in Gilligan's work can be overcome. For instance the use of a larger sample and a statistical control of the educational level of subjects within the study could easily rule out differences in moral development caused by educational sophistication. The other criticisms can also be surmounted, for example by providing other dilemmas in addition to the abortion one posed by Gilligan.

Her findings support the notion that moral development takes place in human beings since she observes a *sequence* of explanations for moral judgements. The judgements, in other words, do not appear in an arbitrary order.

C6 Classroom approaches to moral education

The production of classroom materials relevant to moral education and building on Piaget, Kohlberg and Gilligan has been limited. This is partly because it is argued by Piaget and Kohlberg that moral development takes place through cognitive development and social relationships. Cognitive development can be stimulated but not taught. Social relationships can be discussed and the framework for their formation can be put in place but, again, they cannot be forced into a particular shape. They must develop spontaneously.

Having said this, experiments have been conducted in which ethical programmes have been taught, sometimes on their own and at other times mixed in with other subjects. Dehaan *et al* (1997) report on an a set of teaching strategies used with fifty-four 15-18 year olds that produced advances in moral reasoning.

With younger children the approach frequently favoured is one that helps them see situations from other people's point of view. This can be achieved by stories, role play and cartoons which are followed up by suitable questions. What did *this* character think about *that* character? How did this person *feel* when another person did that? How would *you* feel if someone treated you this way? The approach was pioneered by the 'In other people's shoes' *Lifeline* programme of McPhail, Ungoed-Thomas and Chapman (1972).

A modern variant of this approach is found in the helpful material prepared by Rowe and Newton (1994, p 137). One story they use tells how a young girl was wrongly accused of stealing. She was shunned by her classmates, told off by her teachers, ashamed of what her parents would say. And then, quite by chance, the real thief was discovered. The story carries an emotional punch and illustrates the pain that stealing can cause.

An approach pioneered by Wilson, Williams and Sugarman (1967) started by analysing the intellectual and emotional components of a moral decision-making. This approach is not developmental and, when it is used to generate ideas for the classroom, broadly follows the outlines that might be derived straight from Piaget and Kohlberg. For example, Wilson suggests that young people need a secure sense of group identity, an understanding of the merits of co-operation against competition, appreciation of rule-governed behaviour, some degree of self-government, and so on.

Activity C5

How would you promote moral development in school? Consider in detail what needs to be done to enhance the moral reasoning and moral behaviour of children.

Comment on activity C5

You may have divided your answer into two sections. One may deal with the environment of the school, the classroom, the relationships between pupils and teachers as they make decisions and the other may deal with more formal instruction or teaching in the classroom.

If Piaget and Kohlberg are correct, the moral development of children passes through a phase where rules are imposed by adults to a phase where rules are freely accepted, may be modified and are understood by everyone. The first phase is not essentially one where equal relationships take place. The second is, and the equal relationships are necessary for the emergence of reciprocity - the realisation that we have obligations to each other. Consequently, you may have argued that structural changes within the management of the classroom or within the school are necessary to allow children to begin to participate equally with teachers in decisions about what ought to be done in specified areas of school life.

You may have thought of ways that cognitive development might be stimulated (perhaps by asking children to think about forming rules, by considering moral dilemmas or by initiating teaching into the causes or consequences of behaviour) and you may also have worked out how empathy might be encouraged (by role play, for instance). If you are concerned also with moral behaviour as well as moral reasoning, then you might have considered character development, perhaps through team activities like games or by setting selected physical challenges to help build up the confidence of children in their own abilities. In any event you may have tried to include the notion of 'responsibility' in your thinking since, without this, children disown their own actions.

If you have followed up the reference to Rowe and Newton (1994), you will have seen the ring-back folder of ideas for primary schools, the outcome of a project sponsored by the Home Office. The materials are designed for teachers with 'responsibility for citizenship, PSE, and spiritual and moral development'. Role play and pictures help children to appreciate the feelings of others and the reasons for rules in any society. One exercise asks children how they would organise themselves if they were shipwrecked on a desert island. They have to work out what sort of rules everyone could agree to.

Readers

You will find helpful sections in J. Astley and L.J. Francis (eds) (1992), *Christian Perspectives on Faith Development*, Leominster, Gracewing.

Bibliography

Astley, J. and L.J. Francis (eds) (1992), *Christian Perspectives on Faith Development*, Leominster, Gracewing.

Belenky, M.F., Clinch, B.M., Goldberger, N.R. and Tarule, J.M. (1986), *Women's Ways of Knowing: the development of self, voice, and mind*, New York, Basic Books.

Colby, A. and Damon, W. (1983), Listening to a different voice: a review of Gilligan's In a Different Voice, *Merrill-Palmer Quarterly*, 29, 473-481.

Cowan, C.P. and Cowan, P.A. (1992), *When Partners become Parents: the big life change for couples*, New York, Basic Books.

DeHaan, R., Hanford, R., Kinlaw, K., Philler, D. and Snarey, J. (1997), Promoting ethical reasoning, affect and behaviour among high school students: an evaluation of three teaching strategies, *Journal of Moral Education*, 26, 5-20.

Erickson, E.H. (1965), *Childhood and Society*, Harmondsworth, Penguin.

Gibbs, J.C., Arnold, K., Morgan R., Schwartz, E., Gavaghan, M. and Tappan M. (1984), Construction and validation of a multiple-choice measure of moral reasoning, *Child Development*, 55, 527-536.

Gilligan, C. (1982), *In a Different Voice: psychological theory and women's development*, London, Harvard University Press.

Greeno C. and Maccoby, E. (1986), How different is the different voice? *Signs*, 11, 310-316.

Kay, W.K. and Francis L.J. (1996), *Drift from the Churches: attitude toward Christianity during childhood and adolescence*, Cardiff, University of Wales Press.

Kerber, L.K., Greeno, C.G., Maccoby, E.E., Luria, Z., Stack C.B. and Gilligan C., (1986), On 'In a Different Voice': an interdisciplinary forum, *Journal of Women and Culture*, 11, 304-333.

Kohlberg, L. (1987), *Child Psychology and Childhood Education: a cognitive developmental view*, New York, Longman.

McPhail, P., Ungoed-Thomas, J.R. and Chapman, H. (1972), *Moral Education in the Secondary School*, London, Longman Group.

Nunner-Winkler, G. and Sodian B. (1988), Children's understanding of moral emotions, *Child Development*, 52, 1323-1338.

Oser, F.K. (1996), Kohlberg's dormant ghosts, *Journal of Moral Education*, 25, 253-275.

Piaget, J. (1932), *The Moral Judgement of the Child* (first English edition published by Routledge and Kegan in 1932), Harmondsworth, Penguin.

Pollitt, K (1992), Marooned on Gilligan island: are women really superior to men? *The Nation*, 255, 799-807.

Rest, J.R. (1979), *Development in Judging Moral Issues*, Minneapolis, University of Minnesota Press.

Rest, J.R. (1984), The major components of morality, in W. Kurtines and J. Gewirtz (eds), *Mortality, Moral Behaviour, and Moral Development*, New York, John Wiley.

Rest, J.R. (1986), *DIT Manual: manual for Defining Issues Test* (third edition), Minneapolis, Minnesota, University of Minnesota Centre for the Study of Ethical Development.

Rowe, D. and Newton, J. (eds) (1994), *You, Me, Us!* London, Citizenship Foundation.

Taylor J.H. and Walker L.J. (1997), Moral climate and the development of moral reasoning: the effects of dyadic discussions between young offenders, *Journal of Moral Education*, 26, 21-43.

Wilson, J. Williams, N. and Sugarman, B. (1967), *Introduction to Moral Education*, Harmondsworth, Penguin.

Christian Values and the Curriculum

Christian Values and the Curriculum

Unit A

Models of the curriculum

Revd Dr William K. Kay

Trinity College

Carmarthen

Contents

Introduction

Aims

After working through this unit you should be able to:

- understand what a curriculum is;
- understand theories of curriculum development;
- understand how a curriculum is organised and controlled;
- evaluate the effect of assessment on curriculum;
- place the National Curriculum in the context of earlier aims.

Overview

This unit will introduce you to the wider perspectives and issues related to curriculum theory. In other words, it will provide you with a background against which to view the National Curriculum in England and Wales. It will therefore provide you with concepts and tools by which the National Curriculum may be understood and evaluated. It will also suggest to you the role of assessment in curriculum development and how local areas and individual schools may deliver the National Curriculum in different ways. The second part of the unit will give a brief overview of the National Curriculum itself and explain its general features.

A1 Preliminary issues

In essence a curriculum is a graduated course of study. It is graduated in the sense that it is arranged according to a plan or underlying theory to enable certain things to be learnt - or, as it is more usually expressed, for certain 'learning outcomes' to be achieved. This definition does not specify exactly what kind of learning is to take place. For example, is the learning related to facts, concepts, attitudes, skills, evaluations or experiences and, if so, how are these to be related to each other? For instance, should learners acquire skills so that they may evaluate facts? Or should learners acquire concepts so that they interpret experience in the light of certain attitudes? Or is there some other permutation that is best? And, then, who should decide which facts or attitudes or skills should be acquired by the learner? Is this a task for parents, teachers, children, the government or, in some sense, society in general?

To illustrate the questions about curriculum content and society, we consider Benjamin's (1939) famous satire, *The Sabre-tooth Curriculum*. He envisages an ancient society where food was obtained by grabbing fish from the river, where horses were clubbed to provide skins for shelter and where sabre-toothed tigers were scared away by fire. Children were taught fish-grabbing, horse-clubbing and tiger-scaring. The tribe prospered. Then, after many years, the climate changed. The river became dark and fish became impossible to catch, the horses moved away from their previous habitat because it had become swampy and tigers succumbed to pneumonia and died. Moreover, where once the tigers had been the chief danger to people, bears that were unafraid of fire moved in. The tribe declined.

A few radical and quick-thinking members of the tribe learnt the art of making nets to catch fish, the technique of snaring antelopes and the trick of digging holes to trap bears. They came to the elders and asked if the curriculum could be changed. The elders smiled indulgently and explained that this could not be done. 'We teach fish-grabbing', they explained, 'because it is a generalisable skill. We teach horse-clubbing to build up your physical strength. We teach tiger-scaring to give you a concept of noble courage.' The radicals were disappointed, but they persisted. 'Surely', they pleaded, 'you recognise that times have changed.' The elders looked severely at the radicals. 'Of course we recognise that times have changed, but don't you know that the essence of a true education is its timelessness? The sabre-tooth curriculum is one of the eternal verities and cannot be altered.'

A second illustration comes from the teaching of geography in 19th century England. This is relevant to the questions about method, attitude and purpose. Marsden (1989) outlines the kind of curriculum used. In addition to the rote learning of the 'capes and bays' round Britain's coastline a catechetical method of teaching might be employed. Here is an actual example of a passage designed to explain William Penn's founding of the colony of Pennsylvania, taken from *Educational Record*, 1911, p 257:

- Q. How did he get the land?
- A. Bought it off the Indians.
- Q. Did all do so who founded colonies?
- A. No
- Q. Who did not?
- A. The Spaniards.
- Q. How did they obtain them?
- A. By force of arms.
- Q. Was this right?
- A. No.
- Q. How do we know it was not right?

- A. Because Christ would not even let Peter defend him, but made him put up his sword.

Tate's (1860) text comparing England and Spain reinforces the anti-Spanish, anti-papist stereotype using a basic comparative method:

England	Spain
The climate is damp and changeable	The climate is generally warm and salubrious
The religion is Protestant	The religion is Roman
The workshop of the world...	Cannot supply its own people with manufactured goods...
Possesses the most perfect political institutions...	A prey to civil discords...
It colonies flourish in every part of the globe...	Its colonies are dismembered and enfeebled...

Activity A1

What lessons do you think *The Sabre-tooth Curriculum* is intended to teach you about the relationship between curriculum and society?

Comment on the issues raised by the extracts from the nineteenth century geography curriculum given above.

Comment on activity A1

The Sabre-tooth Curriculum is clearly intended to show how society and curriculum are connected and that, where a curriculum serves the needs of a society, people will thrive and prosper. Where the contrary occurs, and the curriculum becomes an end in itself, something that is fixed and idealised as belonging to a philosophical realm or to a golden era, society flounders. Castle (1961) makes the same point in a less colourful way in respect of the ancient Spartans who, because of their inflexible educational system, were much less successful than their rivals, the Athenians.

You may have thought the nineteenth century extracts raised a series of issues. The catechetical method suggests that there is only one answer to every question and that each question is completely answered by a few words. Did Penn give the Indians fair value for money? If the biblical text about Peter not defending himself is applicable in this situation, is it also applicable in time of war? These are matters ignored by the catechetical method.

What this method and the comparison method both suggest is that no research needs to be done and that children have no need to look at the evidence for moral or political judgements implicit in their school texts. The extracts seem to be intended to promote patriotism (Britain is best) and rest on the selection of authoritative 'facts'. Yet who selects these 'facts' and decides they belong together? If we know that national character was a fundamental element in the content of geography (Marsden, 1989), then the reason for the juxtaposition of climate and English superiority is clarified. The 'facts' are put together on the basis of a theory about the effect of climate on character.

A2 Organisation of the curriculum

In a classic text on the curriculum, Tyler (1949) asks 'How can learning experiences be organised for effective instruction?' He speaks of 'learning experiences' and he does so to keep the conditions of learning as wide as possible. He does not wish to tie himself down to particular kinds of learning by particular kinds of method; he wants to consider the curriculum in an abstract and general way. He also recognises that the 'elements' of a curriculum that will be organised vary. In general these elements must be organised so as to allow continuity, sequence and integration.

- Continuity is ensured by making the 'major curriculum elements' recur in a suitably modified form as the learner moves through the curriculum; in Tyler's terms this is a 'vertical' process because learners move 'up' the curriculum from younger to older grades (Tyler, 1949, p 84).
- Sequence ensures that each successive element builds on the preceding one.
- Integration refers to 'horizontal' relationships in the curriculum and ensures that the student gets 'a unified view' (p 85).

Much of this is uncontroversial. What is more difficult to obtain agreement upon is the notion of the curriculum's *elements*. We turn to six ways the curriculum might be deconstructed into its constituent parts.

Phenix and realms of meaning

Phenix (1964) argued that it is essential for the curriculum to be held together by a single philosophical idea and he believed he had found this idea in the capacity of human beings to grasp meanings. 'Distinctively', he wrote, 'human existence consists in a pattern of meanings' (Phenix, 1964). These realms or patterns of meaning were to be found in six areas:

- symbolics - communication (languages, mathematics and art);
- empirics - scientific truth (physical and social sciences);
- aesthetics - beauty (literature, art and music);
- synnoetics - relationships (literature, philosophy, history, psychology and theology);
- ethics - codes of behaviour (philosophy and theology);
- synoptics - integration (philosophy, religion and history).

Symbolics includes gesture and ritual as well as the signs and symbols of words, letters of the alphabet and so on and is the most basic realm because it must be used to express meaning in all the other realms. Empirics and aesthetics are straightforward, but synnoetics is said to include 'personal knowledge' derived from human relationships and spoken of by Martin Buber (1970) as the 'I-Thou' relation.

The realm of synoptics is said to combine empirical, aesthetic and synnoetic meanings into coherent wholes. The realms form a hierarchy, therefore, with symbolics at the bottom as the most basic and necessary and synoptics at the top as the most comprehensive and inclusive.

When he applied his analysis of meaning to the curriculum Phenix believed that 'every student at every stage of his learning career should receive some instruction in all six of the realms of meaning'[1] (Phenix, 1964; quoted in Golby, Greenwald and West 1975, p 169). However, he also believed that the hierarchy of the realms implied an age-related progression: language teaching was to be emphasised in the early years of schooling, and synoptics in the later years. Yet the actual content of teaching should, in Phenix's view, draw from 'disciplined fields of enquiry', that is, from academic disciplines that are recognised, though not necessarily from traditional fields, and this allowed him to argue that his approach would lead to a modern curriculum.

Hirst and forms of knowledge

The concept of a 'disciplined field' resonates in Britain with the work of Hirst and Peters (1970) and Hirst (1974). These writers proposed seven or eight 'forms of knowledge'. Hirst (1974) gives:

- mathematics;
- the physical sciences;
- knowledge of persons;
- literature;
- the fine arts;

---

[1] Like most writers at this time Phenix uses the masculine to include the feminine. 'His learning career...' might equally well be 'her learning career...'.

- morals;
- religion;
- philosophy.

It is not clear in this analysis, however, whether the fine arts and literature belong as one form. In his explanation of these forms Hirst examines and then dismisses the notion that the mind is like a room into which different kinds of furniture may be placed. The mathematical form and the moral form, for example, are not to be thought of as being a matter of mental furniture. It is not the case that the mind is an unchanging room that must be filled or emptied with different kinds of furniture depending on whether someone is doing mathematics or morals. Rather, the mind is thought of as being constituted by reason and reason is expressed in different forms. The development of mind is marked by progressive differentiation in human consciousness into the seven or eight cognitive structures that characterise the forms. Rather than being a room of unchanging shape the mind is constantly changing its structure so as to operate in different knowledge forms.

How are the forms to be separated from each other? Here the answer Hirst gives is that each has its own concepts that relate together into distinctive networks. We cannot speak of magnetic fields being angry or actions being coloured because magnetic fields belong in one form and anger belongs in another. The concept of a magnetic field fits very well with those of electricity or forces and the concept of anger fits well into morals or religion. Similarly, judgements using concepts are validated by appropriate means. We validate moral judgements one way and mathematical theorems another. So the forms of knowledge are distinguished by their concepts and the particular criteria of truth or validity associated with them. Underlying them all is reason itself and it is this which binds everything together.

Activity A2

> What problems do you see with constructing a curriculum from Phenix's realms of meaning? How useful and convincing do you find Hirst's description of forms of knowledge?

Comment on activity A2

Phenix assumes we all know what meaning is. He does not, for instance, ask how meaning is conceived. For instance, the meaning of a name has a one-to-one correspondence with the thing named but the meaning of a preposition (like 'on' or 'after') cannot be captured in this way. Nor does Phenix attempt to distinguish between meaning and significance. It was certainly significant that flowers were piled outside Buckingham Palace when Princess Diana died. But what did it mean? Was it an expression of bereavement, an act of sympathy for her sons, a sign of support for the Royal Family, or a kind of prayer?

Perhaps even more problematic is Phenix's insistence that the content of the curriculum is made up of disciplined fields of enquiry. How are these to be cast into his realms of meaning? In other words how are the fields to be presented and packaged into the realms that he advocates? More sharply, we may ask whether it matters if the fields *are* packaged in this way since anything that is understood is also imbued with meaning. In this respect meaning is unavoidable and does not need to be superimposed on an existing field.

Hirst's forms of knowledge are far more systematically and rigorously advocated than Phenix's realms of meaning. To this extent they are more solid and more useful. It is true they are likely to be used to support a traditional curriculum, especially as the forms he delineates are very close to established disciplines. Moreover, Hirst's view of interdisciplinary enquiry is that it amounts to a second order activity, an activity that does not generate new knowledge but that focuses existing forms on new areas of study. Interdisciplinary enquiry therefore, in his view, is reducible to the original forms of knowledge. You might, then, find Hirst's forms useful in justifying traditional curricula but less useful in stimulating innovation.

Difficulties with Hirst's forms, however, arise on two counts. First, it is not clear that some concepts belong only in one form. Take the concept of 'right'. We might say in the moral form that an action was right and in the philosophical form that human beings have a particular civil right. We might say, in a discussion of literature, that a particular word was just right. There is a sense in which we are using different meanings of the word 'right' in all these contexts. Yet there is also a sense in which there is an underlying conceptual similarity: right speaks of appropriateness and legitimacy. Second, it is not clear how the criteria for the application of concepts are to be formulated and agreed upon or why, if all these forms of knowledge are expressions of reason, the criteria should not be the same. You will find further criticisms of Hirst's forms in Pring (1976).

Psychology

A psychological organisation of the curriculum starts from the learner. It argues that the human mind naturally develops along particular lines or that human learning follows certain mental laws and that what is taught should be sensitive to these considerations.

Piagetian psychology offers an account that was highly influential among teachers in the 1960s (Plowden Report, 1967, p 522). Piaget understood mental development to take place by interaction with the environment and that this development was bound to an invariant sequence of mental stages that were initially derived from actions. This had two consequences. First, young children should be provided with an environment where they might play in a fashion that would encourage intellectual progress. Water and sand, weight, shapes, colours, counters, balances and swings can all be used to learn important operational truths. Second, the trajectory of intellectual development is to be seen in a pathway from actions (or operations) performed on physical objects (e.g. lining up two sets of counters and comparing them) to operations performed on operations (e.g. algebraic transformations of mathematical equations). This being so, it is in keeping with mental development to reserve abstract ideas, and systematic thinking about them, to the secondary curriculum. The organisation of the curriculum, regardless of whether it is conceived of as being composed of realms of meaning or forms of knowledge or some other categorisation, should reflect the discovered changes contained in this general account of mental development.

Another kind of organisation is implied by the behavioural psychology of Skinner (1950). Here the learning is conceptualised primarily as changes of behaviour as a consequence of rewards (reinforcements) and punishments. In this kind of psychology learning is thought to follow laws built round these concepts. Applied to programmed learning this approach results in:

• programmed text books;
• computer assisted instruction;
• teaching machines.

These have in common sets of small steps for learners to work through at their own pace. The learner is given a question and then asked for an answer before the correct one is given. The correct answer acts as a reinforcement and allows the learner to pass on to the next stage. It also ensures there is active participation in the learning process. Alternatively, if the material is conducive to it, software or video demonstrations can be given and learners can work through suitable exercises. The material itself can be arranged in a *linear* or a *branching* fashion.

The *linear* programme takes learners in a strict sequence beginning with what is simple and passing logically to what is complex. In mathematics, which offers the most obvious material that is suitable for this treatment, children might learn first the concept of number, then addition, then subtraction, then multiplication and then division. Learners must pass from A to B and then on to C. The *branching* programme deals in bigger chunks of information rather than short, simple questions and answers and allows a variety of different routes to be taken. Learners may pass from A to C and then go to X and Y. Equally, they may go from A to B and then to D.

There is also a further psychologically based concept for ordering the curriculum that has been derived from the work of Jerome Bruner (1960; 1972). This produces a *spiral* curriculum where the principal organising ideas are continually presented to the learner but at a level of understanding and complexity that is suitable for his or her stage of development. We might illustrate this idea by teaching children about Christmas. At the first visit to the idea, we would present the scene in the stable with the shepherds and kings. At the second stage, we might compare the birth narratives in Matthew's and Luke's gospels and show how the traditional picture, given in the first stage, is a conflation of two rather different events. The third stage might deal with the theologically advanced idea of 'incarnation' and therefore of the 'pre-existence' of Christ.

The psychological basis for ordering the curriculum is helpful, but it rarely stands on its own. It supplements or underpins other considerations. One more radical and pervasive basis that functions similarly is found within epistemological theory.

Epistemological theory

Epistemology is concerned with the grounds and limits of knowledge. It is also a part of larger philosophical trends.

Gough (1989) and Doll (1989) discuss the issues. Gough begins by arguing that there is a need to unite the knowledge claims of science, philosophy, psychology and religion into one overarching whole. He believes that this whole can be found in a new synthesis of ecological consciousness, feminism, transmaterialist spirituality, cultural pluralism, political decentralisation and human-scale technology. He instances what he takes to be the typical complaints against conventional school curricula. They are 'impractical', 'compartmentalised' and 'superficial'. A new paradigm is needed. The Newtonian universe of an objective observer looking at a mechanical universe needs to be replaced by one where observer and world are more intimately connected. The Newtonian certainties of empirical studies are disregarded in favour of the holistic, more ecopolitical approach where the only certainty is that everything is connected with everything else. Gough commends a return to the sensory and a retreat from the analytic and conceptual. Consequently the curriculum needs to strengthen the differentiation of sensory awareness while, at the same time, generalising conceptual understanding towards the whole. Teachers need to 'share and do' rather than 'showing and telling'.

Gough's curriculum is shaped towards a large and unchallengeable concept of ecology. In this respect it is *not* organised, but in another sense the organisation comes from the value of protecting and sustaining biodiversity. He summarises differences in a table:

Aspect	Traditional	Ecopolitical
Learning contexts	Age-grading, class timetable	Community settings
View of knowledge	Socially structured (theoretic, technical)	Individually structured (practical, personal)
Learning materials	Textbooks and standardised procedures	Reality-centred project
Learning activities	Paying attention, rote learning, memorising	Discrimination, searching, creating

A complementary account is given by Doll (1989) as he discusses the foundations of a post-modern curriculum. He also begins with a long historical overview stretching back to Isaac Newton. The Newtonian worldview became the dominant modern paradigm for the western scientific and intellectual thought. Yet, with the revolution engendered by Albert Einstein's theory of relativity[2], the physics[3] of Niels Bohr and the uncertainty principle[4] of Werner Heisenberg, the Newtonian world falls to pieces. Strict mechanical causation cannot be maintained. Probabilities replace certainties. Phenomena (like light) appear to exist in contradictory forms. Nature can no longer be seen as a closed system, fully predictable and completely understood; instead, the value of open systems comes to the fore. In an open system structures are unstable or dissipate and, instead of reaching an equilibrium or a place of stasis, systems alter their character. Water evaporates and takes on the properties of vapour. Transformation rather than incremental change characterises our world.

These broad and general considerations are set by Doll against the model of the curriculum used by Tyler where the ends are pre-set and objectives are developed in line with those ends. Tyler offers a closed not an open system view of the curriculum. Skinner, too, accords with this mentality. He

---

[2] Events happening in one frame of reference will not be simultaneous in all frames of reference. Identical twins, one on the earth and the other in an accelerating rocket in space, will age at different speeds.
[3] Bohr believed that reality is paradoxical. Concepts grounded in facts divide into mutually exclusive groups.
[4] It is impossible to predict the values of certain pairs of physical magnitudes - for instance, if one predicts the momentum of a particle, then its position is indeterminate. Uncertainty is built into the process of measurement.

'represents the twentieth century, modern view towards change: committed to it within certain well-defined parameters, but fearful of it less change break those parameters'. The post-modern approach, espoused by Doll, must 'break away from the modernist framework' and should study contemporary developments in biology, chemistry, cognition, literary theory, mathematics and theology. In these fields new models 'are emerging which pay attention to such issues as disequilibrium, internal structuration, pathways of development and transformative reorganisation'. Indeed Piaget is called into the picture here since he recognised many of these points: cognitive disequilibrium is what leads to learning and, eventually, to the transformation of mental structures that usher in a new mental stage. In Doll's view, therefore, 'lesson plans would be designed to provide just enough disequilibrium that students would develop their own alternatives and insights'. Learning is to become a by-product of enquiry and not a direct and exclusive goal. Mutual enquiry by pupils and teachers rather than the 'transmission of knowledge or specific behaviours is the general framework in which this relationship would be placed'. The curriculum itself is to be a 'mutifaceted matrix' rather than a 'linear trajectory'.

Activity A3

Is Gough's account persuasive? Could it be applied within the school system in England and Wales? Do you think Doll overstates his case in respect of the likely implications of post-modernism on the school curriculum?

Comment on activity A3

Gough's account appears to overstate the weaknesses of the traditional approach. It is inaccurate to say that traditional curricula depend on rote learning and memorisation. Certainly in Britain it would be difficult to find a school that embraced this kind of teaching. And the same may be said with regard to the co-ordination of learning. There is very considerable relationship with the community, especially in rural British primary schools. And, in respect of learning materials, it is simplistic to argue that the ecopolitical model supports 'reality-centred' projects since this begs a question about the nature of reality. Moreover, Gough's desire to move the curriculum from a conceptual to a sensory base appears to remove mathematics and engineering at a stroke, and probably a great deal of history as well. Where Gough is more convincing is in his account of the nature of the cultural forces at work in the late twentieth century - transmaterial spirituality, feminism, subjectivity, and so on. These forces are changing the climate of academic study and have had subtle effects on the status accorded to scientific objectivity and even to rationality itself.

The school system in England and Wales is already responsive to cultural shifts in the value of different kinds of knowledge. There certainly *could* be changes to the National Curriculum along lines that Gough envisages though it is unlikely that a responsible government, keen to ensure basic skills of literacy and numeracy are in place, would accept his whole package.

Doll's analysis of the emphases and strengths of post-modernism would probably be generally accepted. It is interesting also because it attempts to align the analysis of post-modernism with Piaget's insights into the process of learning through disequilibriation. In practice it is hard to believe that a clearly structured and designed curriculum like that of the British National Curriculum would be replaced by a multifaceted learning matrix without any linear dimension. To do so would be to go from one extreme to another. For this reason it seems probable that the post-modern effect embraced and advocated by Doll is more likely to be seen in higher and further education than in the primary or secondary school. Doll's case for change has therefore to be balanced against social factors relevant to the control of education.

Assessment

Murphy and Torrance (1988) have already indicated that much educational reform in Britain during the period of the 1990s Conservative government was assessment-driven. This implies that the subjects taught within the curriculum are partially shaped and presented in a form that is suitable for assessment. Assessment becomes a tool for organising the curriculum: only that which can be assessed is taught and that which is most readily assessed is most prominently taught. This consequence is observed by Hill (1997) and leads him to subtitle his article, 'the tail that wags the dog?' Citing the situation in Western Australia he points out that the syllabuses submitted for approval there are technically required to specify 'cognitive, affective and psychomotor' objectives, but, since affective gains are hard to measure, these are omitted. In practice syllabuses only deal with cognitive and psychomotor objectives.

At another level the organisation of the curriculum is determined by the needs of assessment through the terminology of 'aims' and 'objectives'. *Aims* are normally thought to be general and unmeasurable intentions; *objectives* are precise and measurable. Thus, while an aim might be 'to help a child converse in French', an objective might be 'to teach a vocabulary list' or the 'tense formation of common reflexive verbs'. The curriculum is organised by the translation of aims into objectives and of objectives into learning experiences or schemes of work. Organisation, though, by whatever means, implies control. To this issue we now turn.

A3 Control of the curriculum

We examine the historical situation in England and Wales where the curriculum has been successively controlled by the examinations system in conjunction with the universities, by teachers and local authorities with the support of the Schools Council and national projects, by local consortia (in the special case of religious education) and most recently by central government.

Examinations system and universities

The Secondary Schools Examination Council (SSEC) was formed in 1917. Through it, in the years that followed, British curricula were effectively controlled from the top down by the needs or specifications of university faculties. The expectations placed by universities on first year undergraduates strongly influenced the construction of syllabus for pupils aged between 16 and 18 years of age. Similarly, syllabuses for sixth formers (16-18 year olds) strongly influenced syllabus for pupils in the 14-16 age group (Curtis, 1961). Since the universities were respected institutions at the apex of the educational system, the curriculum was largely left by government in their hands. The SSEC was frequently populated by university teachers and so the mechanism of control needed no other formal structure. In 1946 the council was revised by the addition of subject panels whose job was to ensure parity across subjects, but this did not prevent the shadow of the universities falling across the secondary school curriculum.

Teachers and local authorities

The school leaving age was raised to fourteen years of age in 1918 and then to fifteen in 1947. In 1972 it was raised to sixteen.

To accommodate the fifteen year olds in the system the GCE (General Certificate of Education) examination was introduced in 1951 and its O (Ordinary) level was intended for the most able 20 per cent of the population. Without exception O levels were externally examined, that is, examined by boards which were independent of teachers and schools. During the 1950s roughly 80 per cent of the children left school without any indication of what they had achieved. In 1960 the Beloe Report recommended a new examination for candidates for whom O levels were inappropriate. These examinations, which later became CSEs (Certificate of Secondary Education), could be examined in three modes. Mode 1 followed the pattern of GCE and made the syllabus the responsibility of the boards (externally examined); mode 2 allowed the school to write a syllabus (externally examined) and mode 3 gave teachers of a particular school the responsibility of writing the syllabus *and* examining it, though the examination was supplemented by a process of external moderation to ensure comparability of standards (Lawson and Silver, 1973).

Mode 3 placed the responsibility for curriculum development firmly in the hands of teachers. It presumed their professional expertise and allowed them to draw on their day-to-day contact with pupils; it gave them opportunities to match the interests of pupils more closely with the subject matter of the syllabus.

Surprisingly, teachers often preferred to work with Mode 1 syllabuses, however. The effort of drawing up a new syllabus, having it accepted by the board, showing colleagues how to examine it and ensuring that books and equipment were compatible with it was considerable. What was to happen if an energetic member of staff, having established a Mode 3 syllabus, moved on to another school? Incoming teachers often preferred giving the responsibility for syllabus construction to boards. Nevertheless it is important to see the principle illustrated here. In the 1960s and 1970s teachers in England and Wales were deemed to be professionally competent both to develop a curriculum (for all but the more able pupils) and to examine it.

Meanwhile what of the government? Was it happy to let the curriculum and examinations pass into the control of teachers?

A cautious interest in the curriculum was shown by the government in the 1940s. A conversation between R.A. Butler, appointed to the Board of Education in 1941, and Winston Churchill, then Prime Minister, took place as reported by Butler (1973, p 91):

> I [Butler] said that I would like to influence what was taught in schools but that this was always frowned upon. Here he [Churchill] looked very earnest and commented, 'Of course not by instruction or order but by suggestion.'

It is clear that in this matter Churchill largely had his way. Eventually the huge 1944 Education Act steered through Parliament by Butler placed all curricular requirement for secondary schools on local education authorities and school governors (Section 23). And, as far as younger children were concerned, after 1926 there had in any case been no prescription of the curriculum at primary level at all (Gordon and Lawton, 1975, p 69). The general consensus against government intervention in the curriculum is expressed by Lord Hailsham, Minister of Education in 1957. According to Hailsham (1978, p 139), he said:

> I was convinced then, and I am convinced now, that any attempt by the State to control the intellectual content of education was incompatible with the preconceptions of a free society.

Edward Boyle, Minister of Education 1962-64, set up the Schools Council, an organisation with responsibility for the curriculum and its associated examinations. The Secondary Schools Examination Council was abolished. Half the funds for the new Schools Council were provided by local education authorities, and its numerous committees were dominated by teachers or teachers' organisations. In effect, the curriculum, so far as it was controlled, was in the hands of the increasingly autonomous examination boards and the teachers rather than universities or government. Even the Labour Party, which was then more inclined than the Conservatives to favour governmental control of the curriculum, took the view that this was right. Anthony Crosland, Labour Minister of Education 1965-67, said, according to Kogan (1971, p 173):

> teachers have a considerable amount of freedom in what and how they teach. I would have thought that in principle it was a good thing.

Of course what politicians *said* and what they *did* were not always in tune and there were arguments behind the scenes about the measure of control the Schools Council might have over the curriculum. In the end the terms of reference for the Council affirmed that it was not a controlling but a supporting and facilitating body (Reynolds and Skilbeck, 1976, p 105). School-based curriculum development became the ideal to which lip service was paid. In practice, however, teachers were either too busy or too uncertain of their responsibilities to invest huge amounts of time in developing new curricula. Consequently the expertise of teachers was supplemented by a series of high profile and well funded projects that concentrated on producing good quality classroom materials. Many of these projects emanated from the Schools Council.

The Humanities Project (MacDonald and Walker, 1976, p 81) associated with Stenhouse was a classic example. It featured stimulating discussion materials that were designed to be used by groups of pupils who would be chaired by the teacher acting as a strictly neutral arbiter. The process was criticised on various counts: the teacher could not and should not pretend to be neutral; uninformed discussion was no more than the 'sharing of ignorance'. More successful in many respects was the Science Teaching Project, which was funded by the Nuffield Foundation from 1961. Inventive and interesting schemes of science work were written (usually by teachers) and the materials were made available to schools at a reasonable price. This whole period of curriculum change has been called the 'research, development and diffusion' model by Beecher (1971). It relied on funding for research and development and then for heads of departments within schools to spend their budgets on the newly produced classroom materials. Diffusion was slightly haphazard but occurred through a network of support services and in-training initiatives (often run by Teachers' Centres or local education authority advisers).

Local consortia

The 1944 Education Act and the 1988 Education Reform Act put into statute the composition of the local committees that were to draw up 'Agreed Syllabuses' for religious education. Details of this are given in unit A of the module *Philosophy of Religious Education* (found in *Religion in Education 1*). Reference is made to them here since they show another way of controlling the committees. Since 1988 the committees are made up of representatives from:

• Christian and other religious denominations that in the opinion of the authority reflect the principal traditions of the area;
• the Church of England (except in Wales);
• such associations representing teachers as in the opinion of the authority ought to be represented;
• the authority itself.

All four groups must be in agreement with the syllabus they produce and this syllabus must be accepted by the Secretary of State for Education. In other words, the local consortia must produce a syllabus that conforms to the general guidelines laid down by central government. Thus, within a centrally stipulated framework, there is local flexibility.

This model for controlling religious education has not been applied to any other part of the curriculum, and is unlikely to be, but it does show that the issue of control is amenable to local democratic procedures. To this extent Agreed Syllabuses are an important example of the control mechanisms that *can* operate in an open society.

Central government

The control of the curriculum by central government after the passing of the 1988 Education Reform Act represented a dramatic shift in power within the educational system of England and Wales. According to the political accounts given by two of the main protagonists, Kenneth Baker (Baker, 1992) and Margaret Thatcher (Thatcher, 1993), their original intention was to specify a simple core of maths, science and English that would be taught to a high standard and be the entitlement of all children irrespective of where they lived.

The political debates of the 1970s and 1980s resulted in serious re-thinking about the curriculum and its assessment. It is impossible to summarise the twists and turns of these debates in a few sentences, but it is clear both ends of the political spectrum began to appreciate a need to ensure that education equipped pupils for employment. If industry and commerce complained that their yearly intake of trainees were ignorant of basic mathematics or incapable of written communication, blame was placed firmly on teachers and schools. It is usual to date the Labour Party's awareness of this problem from James Callaghan's speech at Ruskin College, Oxford, in 1976 (see also, Callaghan, 1987).

Conservative views were analysed by Ball (1990) and he identified both a *New Right* who wanted to safeguard the literary, historical and cultural achievements of Britain and the *Industrial Trainers* who wished to technologise the curriculum so that school leavers were fully adapted to the market place of post-school work. In a sense the eventual National Curriculum is to be seen as a compromise between these two sets of views.

In order to gain control of the curriculum Mrs Thatcher's government needed to dismantle the Schools Council and to set up alternative bodies to do its work while, at the same time, ensuring that neither teachers, teachers' organisations nor local education authority representatives could gain majorities on them.   The Schools Council was replaced in 1984 by the Schools Curriculum Development Committee (SCDC). The Secretary of State appointed members to the SCDC and so, at a stroke, he and his civil servants took charge of the curriculum.

It came as no surprise that ministerial control was written into statute in Section 14 of the 1988 Education Reform Act. A new body, the Schools Examination and Assessment Council (SEAC) was brought into existence by the Act and the minister was able to appoint all its members. By then the SCDC had been abolished. A National Curriculum Council (NCC) was also formed, again under the minister's control, but quite quickly SEAC and NCC were amalgamated into the School Curriculum and Assessment Authority (SCAA). In each instance the Secretary of State was able to appoint either all or a majority of members. By this means genuine power over the curriculum was removed from teachers, local authorities, examination boards or local consortia and given to the upper echelons of Whitehall.

Activity A4

Consider briefly the ways the curriculum has been controlled in England and Wales. What advantages and disadvantages are there in each case?

Comment on activity A4

Examination boards and universities have been strong on formal curricula and on ensuring traditional subjects have been preserved and suitably presented to more able pupils. They have been less good at initiating change and in taking note of the needs of the majority of pupils. In addition, and this is to make the previous point in a different way, they have been less responsive to the needs of society and of the market place.

Teachers have been good at identifying the learning capacities of less able pupils and at constructing syllabuses which are interesting to teach. Because many teachers have never worked in commerce or industry, they have not been as good at ensuring that what is taught will be of benefit to pupils in the labour market. In addition teachers have not always had time to keep up to date with the developments in their subject specialisms.

Local consortia provide a good democratic way of drawing up a syllabus, but they depend for their educational usefulness on the presence of teachers or educationalists on the working groups that draw up the syllabuses. In this respect the qualities of local consortia are similar to those provided by teachers. Moreover, the danger that local interests will eclipse national needs and standards has to be admitted and can only be avoided by nationally given guidelines.

The Schools' Council was a cumbersome and unsystematic mechanism for curriculum reform and it was never able to have its ideas and schemes universally accepted. Much of its work was original and valuable but there was little co-ordination between its separate projects and no obvious philosophy of education guiding the whole enterprise.

Central government holds all the cards. It can enforce its directives by legislation and encourage them by substantial funding. In the years of Conservative government its New Right and Industrial Trainers provided unifying themes within the curricula process. But it also tended to see education (Ball, 1997) in terms of an industrial machine producing a product whose quality needed to be ensured by regular inspection and whose headteachers operated as entrepreneurial managers competing for public funds. It envisaged education as important insofar as it contributed to national wealth-creation but it took little note of the experience and views of teachers or educationalists in the drawing up of its aims and attainment targets. Moreover, it tended to see education as a skills-based activity and this has the effect of devaluing more abstract or intuitive functions (like appreciating music or poetry).

On the positive side, however, a National Curriculum has a very distinct advantage for pupils who move schools between different parts of the country. There is now much greater similarity between schools and regions and pupil mobility is therefore much simpler and less risky. Equally, there is greater similarity between the subjects boys and girls study. Most noticeable, and most fundamental to the whole concept of the National Curriculum, is the notion of national standards: all pupils are, in theory, studying almost identically and can therefore be assessed and compared much more easily. The drive to raise national standards becomes a more manageable task, and is more urgently pursued in the light of the presumed correlation between national economic performance and the educational achievements of the workforce.

A4 The National Curriculum

In this section we consider the National Curriculum in outline and draw attention to some of its key features. These features are largely structural and pedagogic. However, while they are designed to ensure the balance and quality of each pupil's educational experience, they are also drawn up so as to be accessible to external inspection by OFSTED. A National Curriculum nationally inspected is designed to raise standards, but it does so by reducing the role of the teacher to a functionary, a foot soldier whose task is to carry out orders.

The National Curriculum offers ten subjects (in the secondary section - modern languages are not taught in primary schools), three of which are defined as *core* subjects and the remaining seven as only *foundation* subjects. In Wales, Welsh is also taught as a core foundation subject in schools where the medium of instruction is Welsh. In other Welsh schools where the medium of instruction is English, Welsh is one of the foundation subjects. The ten subjects (eleven in Wales) are supplemented by religious education which is said to be part of the *basic* curriculum.

There is little distinction in practice between the core and foundation subjects except for the time allocated to them and, since religious education is also stipulated by law, its resources too ought to be protected. Each subject is described by three terms. These are:

- programmes of study;
- attainment targets;
- levels of attainment.

The programmes of study are ways the attainment targets are to be reached. An example of a programme of study for Key Stage 2 mathematics states that pupils should be taught to:

- visualise and describe shapes and movements, developing precision in using related geometrical language;
- make 2-D and 3-D shapes and patterns with increasing accuracy, recognise their geometrical features and properties, and use these to classify shapes and solve problems;
- understand the congruence of simple shapes; recognise reflective symmetries of 2-D and 3D shapes, and rotational symmetries of 2-D shapes.

Attainment targets are precise statements indicating what each pupil should understand or be able to do. In mathematics at Key Stages 1 and 2 there are, for example, four targets and each one is related to several strands. For example attainment target 3 at level 5 in the 'Shape, Space and Measures' theme requires:

> When constructing models and when drawing or using shapes, pupils measure and draw angles to the nearest degree, and use language associated with angle. They identify all the symmetries of 2-D shapes. They know the rough metric equivalents of Imperial units still in daily use and convert one metric unit to another. They make sensible estimates of a range of measures in relation to everyday situations.

Each attainment target is itself divided into ten levels. Level 2 corresponds with what should be achieved by a child at the end of Key Stage 1 and level 10 corresponds with the last year of compulsory secondary education. Since the levels are used as a basis for assessing pupils, it is usual for children's progress to be registered by an attainment target score between one and ten. A very able child at the end of Key Stage 2 might reach level 6, two levels above the expected norm for that age group.

The precise nature of the attainment targets and the relationship between the targets and the programme of study is shown by comparing the two extracts above. Both are taken from *Key Stages 1 and 2 of the National Curriculum* (DfE, 1995). The extracts have been chosen from the same 'Shape, Space and Measures' strand.

As Moon (1994) had predicted the attainment targets at each level, while precise, were modified in 1995: the detail they previously imposed on teaching was almost impossibly restrictive. Where flexibility comes, however, is in the recognition that teachers can cover more than one attainment target at a time. This is especially so where themes (like health education, environmental education or citizenship) are introduced. Flexibility also occurs where skills cross subject boundaries. So, despite the organisation of the curriculum into separate subjects, there are unifying features in its presentation to pupils.

The vertical ordering of the National Curriculum is by four *Key Stages*:

- Key Stage 1: 5-7 year olds;
- Key Stage 2: 7-11 year olds;
- Key Stage 3: 11-14 year olds;
- Key Stage 4: 14-16 year olds.

The main years of education are numbered and correspond with age. Thus year 1 describes 6 year olds and year 11 sixteen year olds.

Within the classroom the National Curriculum brings a greater uniformity than existed previously into teaching at primary and secondary levels of education. Each scheme of work, and in theory each lesson, contributes to attainment targets and the recording of pupils' learning takes place not only during end-of-year examinations but also during the ordinary business of lessons. Technology, which previously was provided for children patchily, has now become part of their entitlement and is taught at secondary and primary level. Foreign languages are likewise an entitlement of the secondary curriculum.

The most contentious part of the National Curriculum, and the part which has attracted most criticism in the educational press, concerns assessment. Before considering this, it is worth noting, as Moon (1994, pp 31-32) does, that assessment may be *norm*-referenced or *criterion*-referenced. Norm-referencing relates pupil achievements to statistical indices (usually averages) and ensures that grades are distributed in roughly the same proportions year by year. Thus, for example, in a GCE examination, about ten per cent of candidates would be expected to attain a grade A, and so on. This system is essentially competitive and presumes the ability level of each cohort of students is the same year by year. There is no possibility that standards will appear to rise or, indeed, to fall, when this method is used since the percentages of pupils allocated to each grade remain inexorably the same. By contrast criterion-referencing operates much more like a driving test or a music examination. Here the performance of the candidate is measured against a fixed set of criteria and so the percentages of candidates reaching particular grades will almost be bound to fluctuate with each batch of candidates.

The National Curriculum makes use of criterion-referencing and by this means intends to identify shifts in standards. Clearly, however, criterion-referencing depends on precise criteria and equally precise evidence, derived from the pupils' work, that the criteria have been met. Obviously the criteria built into the National Curriculum are found in attainment targets which, because of the way they are constructed and used to guide classroom teaching, must be monitored by teachers rather than external assessors. This gives teachers the task of watching each child and trying to gauge whether he or she has fulfilled a particular target and, if so, what evidence can be produced to substantiate this claim. Needless to say, many teachers find that they are inundated with paperwork at this point. How else can they keep track of the attainments of thirty (or more) children in ten subjects? Moreover, what are they to do when pupils progress and then regress - learning something on Monday and forgetting it by Friday?

Perhaps because of the natural desire of teachers to support the learning of their children, there may also be a tendency to inflate children's educational attainments, a temptation that is all the greater when schools are rated on the performance of their pupils in published league tables. To cancel out this temptation, the government has introduced Standard Assessment Tasks (SATs). But SATs have had a chequered history. In the early 1990s, they were implemented as complex and time-consuming tasks which did, however, mirror children's learning while, at the same time, baffling the parents to whom reports were sent. When the tasks were simplified and reduced to 'pencil and paper' tests, they were seen to reflect learning less well and, in addition, to impose a huge administrative load on teachers while robbing them of valuable classroom time. In 1993 teachers and parents' associations expressed their anger at the wholesale and messy changes to which the education system had been subjected since 1988. SATs were simplified, the education system was promised a five year respite from change and large sums of money were spent on having SATs externally marked to relieve teachers of excessive burdens. In 1997, as evidence of the mounting pressures placed by central government on schools, huge numbers of teachers opted for early retirement and in the autumn of that year there were about 2000 vacancies in headships throughout England and Wales (BBC Radio 4 interview with Head Teacher's Association, 11 Sept 1997; *Times Educational Supplement*, pp 1, 5, 10-12, 5 Sept, 1997).

Activity A5

How might the National Curriculum be improved? Are there changes that could be made which would meet the government's objective of raising standards while making education relevant to social harmony and economic growth?

Comment on activity A5

The National Curriculum imposes an enormous workload on teachers, especially in small primary schools. This workload is made heavier by OFSTED inspections and the often uninformed interpretation of published league tables (cf. Murphy, 1996). The morale of teachers is affected by all this but, more than morale, it is arguable that efficiency is also reduced. By insisting, for example, that teachers produce detailed schemes of work to supplement programmes of study and by asking them to monitor the attainments of each child *without reducing class sizes*, the human resources of the system are threatened. It is arguable that the large sums of money spent on OFSTED inspections (£150 million per year according to Channel 4's *Dispatches*, 19 March 1998) would be better deployed in recruiting more teachers or providing better support for teachers who have to cope with children who have special educational needs (for example who have behavioural problems or conditions like Down's syndrome).

The OFSTED system, which is integral to the National Curriculum as it is presently conceived, largely ignores the 'value added' contribution of schools. One school might improve the performance of its pupils considerably but still reach lower absolute standards than another school whose pupils, on arrival, were much more advanced (see Strand, 1997). The school which improved the performance of pupils to a greater extent is still liable to a worse report than the other one. To the present writer it seems strange that OFSTED inspections and league tables are used since, essentially, they provide the same information.

The relationship between the National Curriculum itself and the conditions under which it is delivered, including the professional standing of teachers, is a delicate one. At present there is a contradiction between the lack of pedagogic initiative expected of the classroom teacher and the managerial initiative expected of headteachers. There is also a contradiction in the treatment of parents as 'customers' and the treatment of schools as 'service providers'. The school must respond to the requests of parents and the demands of government, but can often only do so by displeasing one party.

Many of these issues are controversial but it appears from OFSTED reports and league tables that the number of failing schools is very small. In other words, the places where improvements are desperately needed are in small well-defined areas of the education system. Most inspections and most league tables tell us very little we did not know already but at the cost of great effort, finance and stress. If, then, the system is to be improved it must be by concentrating resources and energy on the failing areas and supporting teachers elsewhere in the system.

Readers

You will find helpful reference to the curriculum in the two chapters in sections 10 and 14 of L.J. Francis and A. Thatcher (eds) (1990), *Christian Perspectives for Education*, Leominster, Gracewing.

Bibliography

Baker, K. (1992), An insider's notes on the curriculum, *Education Guardian*, 24 November.

Ball, S.J. (1990), *Politics and Policy Making in Education: explorations in policy sociology*, London, Routledge.

Ball, S.J. (1997), Policy sociology and critical social research: a personal review of recent education policy and policy research, *British Educational Research Journal*, 23, 257-274.

Beecher, A. (1971), The dissemination and implementation of educational innovation. Annual Meeting for the British Association of the Advancement of Science, Section L, September.

Benjamin, H. (1939), Foreword to J A Peddiwell, *The Sabre-tooth Curriculum*, New York, McGraw-Hill Book Company. This is reprinted in M. Golby, J. Greenwald and R. West (eds) (1975), *Curriculum Design*, London, Croom Helm in Association with the Open University Press.

Bruner, J.S. (1960), *The Process of Education*, Cambridge, Massachusetts, Harvard University Press.

Bruner, J.S. (1972), *The Relevance of Education*, London, George Allen and Unwin.

Buber, M. (1970), *I and Thou* (W. Kaufman trans), New York, Scribner.

Butler, R.A. (1973), *The Art of the Possible: the memoirs of Lord Butler*, Harmondsworth, Penguin.

Callaghan, J. (1987), *Time and Chance*, London, Collins.

Castle, E.B. (1961), *Ancient Education and Today*, Harmondsworth, Penguin.

Curtis, S.J. (1961), *History of Education in Great Britain*, London, University Tutorial Press.

DfE (1995), *Key Stages 1 and 2 of the National Curriculum*, London, HMSO.

Doll, W.E. (1989), Foundations for a post-modern curriculum, *Journal of Curriculum Studies*, 21, 243-253.

Golby, M., Greenwald, J. and West R. (eds) (1975), *Curriculum Design*, London, Croom Helm in Association with the Open University Press.

Gordon, P. and Lawton, D. (1978), *Curriculum Change in the Nineteenth and Twentieth Centuries*, London, Hodder and Stoughton.

Gough, N. (1989), From epistemology to ecopolitics: renewing a paradigm for curriculum, *Journal of Curriculum Studies*, 21, 225-241.

Hailsham, Lord, (1978), *The Door Wherein I Went*, Collins, Fount Paperbacks.

Hill, B.V. (1997), Evaluation and assessment: the tail that wags the dog? in J. Shortt and T. Cooling (eds), *Agenda for Educational Change*, Leicester, Apollos, pp 132-147.

Hirst, P.H. (1974), *Knowledge and the Curriculum*, London, Routledge and Kegan Paul.

Hirst, P.H. and Peters, R.S. (1970), *The Logic of Education*, London, Routledge and Kegan Paul.

Kogan, M. (1971), *The Politics of Education: Edward Boyle and Anthony Crosland*, Harmondsworth, Penguin.

Lawson, J. and Silver, H. (1973), *A Social History of Education in England*, London, Methuen and Co.

Marsden, W.E. (1989), 'All in a good cause': geography, history and the politicization of the curriculum in nineteenth and twentieth century England, *Journal of Curriculum Studies*, 21, 509-526.

MacDonald, B. and Walker, R. (1976), *Changing the Curriculum*, London, Open Books.

Moon, B. (1994), *A Guide to the National Curriculum*, Oxford, Oxford University Press.

Murphy, R.J.L. (1996), Like a bridge over troubled water: realising the potential of educational research, *British Education Research Journal*, 22, 3-15.

Murphy, R.J.L. and Torrance, H. (1988), *The Changing Face of Educational Assessment*, Milton Keynes, Open University Press.

Phenix, P.H. (1964), *Realms of Meaning*, New York, McGraw Hill.

Plowden Report (1967), *Children and their Primary Schools*, London, HMSO.

Pring, R. (1976), *Knowledge and Schooling*, London, Open Books.

Reynolds, J. and Skilbeck, M. (1976), *Culture and Classroom*, London, Open Books.

Skinner, B.F. (1950), Are theories of learning necessary? *Psychological Review*, 57, 193-216.

Strand, S. (1997), Pupil progress during key stage 1: a value added analysis of school effects, *British Educational Research Journal*, 23, 471-487.

Tate, T. (1860), *The Philosophy of Education: or the principles and practices of teaching*, London, Longman, Green, Longman and Roberts.

Thatcher, M. (1993), *The Downing Street Years*, London, HarperCollins.

Tyler, R.W. (1949), *Basic Principles of Curriculum and Instruction*, Chicago, University of Chicago Press.

Christian Values and the Curriculum

Unit B

Knowledge and values at school

Dr J. Mark Halstead

Rolle Faculty of Education

University of Plymouth

Contents

Introduction

Aims

By the end of the unit you should:

- have thought carefully about the nature of knowledge and values and about their place in schooling;
- understand the difference between objectivist and constructivist approaches to knowledge and between different kinds of values;
- be aware of the impact of pluralism on our understanding of knowledge and values, and of the thinking which lies behind current attempts to develop a framework of shared values to underpin the work of schools;
- have an understanding of the arguments put forward in support of different approaches to teaching knowledge and values in school.

Overview

There is a widely held view that schooling has two main functions: helping pupils to develop their knowledge and understanding of the world, and helping pupils to learn values. The influential sociologist Basil Bernstein, for example, draws attention to 'two distinct... complexes of behaviour which the school is transmitting to the pupil: that part concerned with character training and that part which is concerned with more formal learning' (Bernstein, 1977, p 38). The aim of this unit is to look more closely at these two broad aims or functions of education and to consider what they mean and what they entail. The unit is thus divided into two parts: Knowledge and Values.

The approach will be broadly philosophical, but in the sense of thinking clearly and rationally, analysing concepts and seeking justifications for opinions rather than simply taking them for granted or accepting them on authority. The approach adopted involves exploring different views and subjecting them to critical analysis, to see how well they stand up to close examination. Please note that nothing that I say will be uncontroversial, and you will need to acknowledge the possibility of alternative views being equally valid.

B1 Knowledge and education

'Knowledge' and 'education' are inextricably linked, for whatever else the concept of education includes, it involves the idea that those who are being educated are adding to their store of knowledge. It would not make much sense for someone to claim that he had been very well educated but did not know anything. In any case, even being aware of one's own ignorance is a kind of knowledge.

Sometimes knowledge is viewed almost as a commodity, with an existence that is fixed and independent of the knower. Mathematical knowledge in particular has until recently been viewed in this way - pre-existing, immediately recognisable as 'truth' once it is discovered, and thereafter capable of unproblematic transmission to others (Ernest, 1994, p 1). When the Prophet Muhammad, for example, famously said, 'Seek for knowledge, even as far as China', this may conjure up an image of a caravan of camels returning, laden with sackfuls of the precious nuggets. On this view, to acquire knowledge is to accumulate 'truths' about the world, and to be educated is to acquire as much knowledge as possible. The task of the teacher is thus to transmit knowledge to her pupils, to fill their empty minds with the precious commodity.

In part one I shall try to show why this unsophisticated account of what is involved in teaching is unsatisfactory, and most of our time will be taken up with a comparison between the educational implications of a much more sophisticated objectivist view of knowledge and those of the currently influential constructivist views. But first we need to note some of the complexities of the term knowledge itself.

Kinds of knowledge

It is clear that we use the word 'know' in different ways, and often we can only judge the precise meaning of the term from the context. Since epistemology (the study of knowledge) is an important branch of philosophy, it is not surprising that philosophers have tried to make clear distinctions between the different uses of the term. Let us look at some of these distinctions more closely.

Activity B1

Read the following pairs of statements carefully and try to work out the different ways the word 'know' is being used in each statement.

- a) I know how to swim.
  b) I know that all bachelors are unmarried.
- a) I know that David Hockney was born in Bradford.
  b) I know that David Hockney is a greater artist than Beryl Cook.

- a) I know that my teeth hurt when I eat ice-cream.
  b) I know that swimming is good for people's health.
- a) I know that sea covers a greater area of the earth's surface than land.
  b) I know that Chelsea won the FA cup in 1997.

Comment on activity B1

The first pair of statements draws attention to the difference between 'knowing how' (which is usually indicative of a skill) and 'knowing that' (which involves cognisance of a state of affairs in the world). While some skills (such as walking) appear to develop naturally, many skills develop only as the result of sustained practice, usually reinforced by learning and understanding. 'Knowing' in the propositional sense ('knowing that') is generally taken to involve (a) that one has a belief; (b) that the belief is true; and (c) that there is adequate evidence for it. The statement 'all bachelors are unmarried' is true by definition, but the truth of most knowledge claims is less certain, and often we do not even know what evidence would count as sufficient to establish the truth of a belief (see below).

The second set of knowledge claims raises issues of verification. The claim that David Hockney was born in Bradford is verifiable at a common-sense level by reference to an encyclopaedia, the claim made in the encyclopaedia is verifiable by reference to hospital records, and so on. The claim that David Hockney is a greater artist than Beryl Cook is not verifiable in the same way. We may want to say that the latter claim is a value judgement, and different people may have different understandings of what an artist is as well as different criteria by which they judge great art. Another way of expressing the difference between these two statements is to say that the first is an example of objective knowledge and the second an example of a subjective judgement. For knowledge to be objective, it has to be true or false independently of any person's feelings, attitudes or points of view. Subjective judgements, on the other hand, do not depend on simple facts to determine their truth or falsity, but are also influenced by the attitudes and values of whoever makes the judgement. However, it is by no means uncontroversial to claim that a statement such as 'David Hockney is a greater artist than Beryl Cook' is a subjective judgement. Some will wish to argue that the discussion of quality in art is a matter of objective judgement based on rational criteria. Others will claim that even if there are no objective criteria by which the matter can be decided, then the fact that most people hold the same opinion on a matter is sufficient to objectivise the judgement, so that it can be treated as if it were a matter of true belief, i.e. knowledge.

The third pair of statements draws attention to the difficulty of reaching agreement over what evidence is sufficient to establish the truth of a belief. In the first statement, can I be sure that my perception of pain is the same as yours? (Think of arguments that people have even about external things like the colour of objects, let alone internal things like pain.) Also, how much trust can we place in what our senses tell us? (Do not our senses tell us that the sun goes round the earth each day?) The second sentence expresses a belief for which there is limited scientific evidence available. Perhaps at an everyday level this limited scientific evidence is sufficient for us to make decisions about how to live our lives; but if we are to call this 'knowledge' at all, we have to hold it in a way that is open to challenge and change over time, for new knowledge may be developed which indicates that swimming is actually bad for your health. Our knowledge of healthy eating habits seems to follow this pattern of challenge and change very frequently at the present time.

The final pair of statements illustrates the difference between knowledge of a reality which is totally independent of human activity (except of course that it can only be *explained* through language, which is a human institution) and knowledge of a reality which is entirely socially constructed. Searle (1995, p 2) calls the former 'brute facts' and the latter 'institutional facts'. Institutional knowledge is objective in the sense that it is not a matter of personal preference or evaluation, though it depends on human institutions for its existence. Searle suggests, for example, that money, marriage, property and citizenship are all 'facts' (and implies that it is appropriate to teach them to children as such), yet they exist only because we believe them to exist. But can it be an objective fact that the piece of coloured paper in my pocket is money if it is at the same time true that something is money only because we believe it is money?

Approaches to teaching knowledge

In the light of the above discussion, we can turn again to the question of the link between knowledge and education. The 1988 Education Reform Act states that schools have a duty to promote the mental development of children, and it is clear that their mental development would be impoverished without the growth of knowledge. But as Pring (1976, p 23) points out, we must retain a 'generous definition of knowledge'. Our understanding of knowledge must not be confined to propositional knowledge ('knowledge that'), for pupils will not be able to judge the usefulness of such knowledge if they do not at the same time develop certain skills ('knowledge how'), including, for example, the ability to question, explain, understand concepts, verify, react, imagine, criticise, evaluate evidence, make judgements, and above all reason and come to justifiable conclusions. These skills presuppose certain qualities (or 'intellectual virtues') including openness of mind and the pursuit of truth, and one mark of these qualities is a willingness to recognise that new evidence may come into being which causes one to reassess one's existing knowledge.

The acquisition of knowledge in the context of the school is a social activity, in that it involves interaction with other minds (even 'discovery learning' usually turns out to be guided discovery), and involves the internalising of socially evolved modes of thinking and behaving. Whether or not we accept the claim that *all* knowledge is socially constructed (cf. Berger and Luckmann, 1967), it is clear that our understanding is shaped, legitimised and maintained by social institutions which may vary from one society to another. This leads Oakeshott (1967) and others to suggest that education is the initiation of a pupil into a tradition. But if this is so, can we still claim that the knowledge we are helping pupils to develop is in any way objective? In the next section we will explore an important and highly influential objectivist theory of knowledge and consider its educational implications, and then in section four we will examine a theory of knowledge which rejects objectivism.

B2 Objectivist view of knowledge

Paul Hirst's (1974) 'forms of knowledge' thesis has been enormously influential in curriculum planning and in thinking about education over the last thirty years, and has undoubtedly been an important influence on the structure of the National Curriculum and on current thinking about assessment, though, as will be noted in due course, Hirst himself has revised his thinking very significantly in recent years (see Hirst, 1993). The main points in the thesis are summarised here.

First, the development of a human person is the same as the development of mind (or consciousness). The mind has many dimensions to it, such as the cognitive and the affective, but the cognitive is fundamental to all the rest.

Second, concepts are central to cognitive development. The potential to conceptualise is innate, but the innate potential has to be structured by learning. Knowledge and understanding depend on the use of shared concepts, and this begins significantly with the use of public symbols (language); it is the fact that there is a word for a concept that makes sharing much more available and necessary. The child must learn to use the word 'dog', for example, exactly in the same situation that other people use it. Until public concepts are developed, the notion of truth is empty. But when the public concept is internalised, one can say, 'It is true that Fido is a dog.' The use of the symbol detaches the thought from the occurrence. Education is about pupils acquiring the public concepts that enable them to develop as rational persons, to make objective judgements and to search for truth.   An individual's capacity to pursue life according to rational principles thus depends on language, which is a social construction, and it is also through language that groups and communities can ensure that their social arrangements are rationally constructed.

Third, human knowledge can be differentiated into a number of forms that are distinguished by their particular concepts, their unique logical structure and the nature of their truth claims.   These forms of knowledge are, contingently: mathematics, the physical sciences, knowledge of persons, literature and the fine arts, morals, religion and philosophy.   The forms of knowledge attempt to map out distinctive sets of concepts.   The central concepts of one form seek to capture the things that are objectively the case in their own particular form, but are not relevant to those of another form; thus 'worship' makes little sense in a mathematical context and 'quadratic equations' have no meaning in the context of aesthetics.   The truth of 'worship' is judged differently from the truth of 'pain', the truth of 'altruism' or the truth of 'beauty'.   If children are to become fully rational autonomous individuals, they need to be provided with an education which introduces them to the concepts of each of the forms of knowledge.   In teaching them public concepts, we are initiating pupils into the achievements of humanity and facilitating the pursuit of further achievements.

Fourth, liberal education is thus defined in terms of initiation into the forms of knowledge (as characterised by their distinctive internal logical features).   Pupils must be initiated into each of the forms, but this does not mean that the curriculum must be directly structured around the forms.   Many other factors may influence the curriculum, and it is important that schools should develop courses where the forms of knowledge are related to what the pupils will actually experience in their lives, such as Health Education.   And of course other considerations, including psychological ones, will determine the most effective ways in which knowledge can be taught to children; the forms of knowledge thesis implies no preference for traditional teaching methods over child-centred approaches or discovery learning.   It is concerned with content, not method.   Initiation into the forms of knowledge is seen as the essential core of a wider education.   The wider education includes personal and social education, character development, skills needed for practical living, the education of the emotions and dispositions, but all of these are subservient to the main goal of education which is to develop knowledge and understanding so that children may grow into autonomous individuals capable of rational choice.

Fifth, even though concepts are socially constructed, this does not mean that all knowledge is relative.   It is true that some concepts are locked into the kind of social relations that we have, so that in some areas we inevitably confine the development of children, in the early stages of education at least, to knowledge of their own society and its values. In morality or aesthetics, for example, there may be many principles that are relative to a particular cultural group; if one changes the culture, new moral or aesthetic concepts will arise. But even in morality there may be certain principles (such as equality of treatment and respect for persons) which are the base of any moral structure. And in other forms of knowledge, it is nonsense to claim that all conceptual schemes are socially relative. There are fashions in scientific research, certainly, and what scientists choose to develop may be socially determined, but the essential nature of science is not. Concepts judged by the sense organs, for example, are universal.

This is a subtle and carefully thought out version of the objectivist view of knowledge. It avoids most of the criticisms that can be made of the unsophisticated objectivist view set out above in section two.

Activity B2

What criticisms can you put forward of this version of the objectivist view of knowledge and of its implications for education?

Comment on activity B2

There are several points you may have raised.

First, in the post-modern world we have seen a significant decline in authority, certainty and objectivity in the way we look at the world. The forms of knowledge thesis is itself a human construction and thus both subject to change over time and only one of a number of possible ways of categorising knowledge. Others include Searle's (1995) distinction between 'institutional facts' (which are dependent on human agreement) and 'brute facts' (which are independent of any human activity); White's (1973) distinction between those activities which cannot be understood without actually engaging in them (such as philosophy or art appreciation) and those that can; Phenix's (1964) distinction between six 'realms of meaning' (symbolics, empirics, aesthetics, synnoetics, ethics and synoptics); and Barrow's (1976) distinction between empirical and logical knowledge, between religious and scientific 'interpretative attitude' and between moral, aesthetic, religious and scientific awareness. Each of these ways of categorising knowledge offers useful insights, but none can claim the status of being the final authoritative statement on the matter.

Second, implicit in Hirst's theory is a dualism of mind and body and a tendency to overemphasise the cognitive dimension of learning at the expense of the affective and the psychomotor - or at least a tendency to overlook the direct interplay between these various dimensions. The education of emotions and dispositions is considered important primarily because it makes rational development easier, rather than because of the contribution it makes to leading a fulfilling life. The theory also pays inadequate attention to the part played by wants and desires in defining what a fulfilling life is.

Third, the criteria by which the seven forms of knowledge are distinguished are problematic. It is not clear, for example, why 'literature and the fine arts' are put together as one form of knowledge: does the concept of 'sonnet' have anything more to do with ballet than with mathematics? Does not mathematics play a large part in music? Is not all of 'literature and the fine arts' part of our 'knowledge of persons'? Is it possible to have 'religion' without 'morality'? As we become increasingly aware of the cultural diversity in the world, is it possible to find *any* concepts which *all* religions share (cf. Kleinig, 1982, chapter 12)? Does not 'religion' have important conceptual links with 'knowledge of persons' as well as 'morality'? Once the boundaries between the different forms merge, it can no longer be claimed that in order to be educated children need to be initiated into all seven forms.

Fourth, in any case, is it an adequate conceptualisation of education to describe it as initiation into the forms of knowledge? Does knowledge in fact have the kind of objective reality implicit in this conceptualisation? And does not this approach imply too passive a role for the pupil in the development of knowledge? We turn now to an approach which gives pupils a much more active role in the construction of knowledge.

B3 Constructivist views of knowledge

Although it is becoming increasingly common in educational circles to hear phrases like 'We aim for pupils to become constructors of their own knowledge', it is important to remember that constructivism is not itself an educational theory (though it may underpin particular approaches to teaching and learning), but an epistemology. It offers a psychological and philosophical explanation of what knowledge is and of the cognitive processes involved in the construction and development of knowledge. From a constructivist perspective, knowledge does not consist of a collection of fixed, objective 'truths' that are external to the knower, nor does learning consist of harvesting these 'truths' and making them one's own; on the contrary, knowledge is created or constructed by people through the interaction between their existing knowledge and the new situations, experiences or ideas they encounter, and learning is the outcome of this interaction. Knowledge on this account is personal and subjective, and learning is the tentative acceptance of the knowledge that has been constructed, tentative because one must recognise that the knowledge is always open to challenge and change.

What has been said so far is common to all constructivist thinking, but to proceed further is to run up against an increasing number of disagreements and differences of interpretation. A full exploration of the many nuances of interpretation is beyond the scope of this brief overview, but it is important to distinguish between two major strands in constructivist thought: individual (or 'developmental' or 'traditional') constructivism, and social (or 'sociocultural') constructivism.

Individual constructivism focuses on the individual as the meaning-maker, and claims that the individual responds to her interaction with the world on the basis of her own pre-existing concepts. This view is a development and adaptation of Piaget's (1977) observations of the developmental changes in the ways people process information. Piagetian constructivism is based on the idea that the developing human intelligence, like any other living organism, has to adapt to the conditions in which it exists. The outcome of this adaptation is the development of the individual's knowledge, and this development does not consist of the acquisition of isolated bits of learning but of a coherent map of the world, which learners have to make a constructive effort to piece together from their existing knowledge, their environment and their new experiences. For some, however, this approach is too individualistic and neglects to pay adequate attention to the social and cultural context of learning and meaning making.

Social constructivism is based on a Vygotskyan or social theory of mind (Vygotsky, 1978; Wertsch, 1985). Social constructivism places more emphasis on language and the social construction of knowledge and rejects the more individualistic orientation of Piagetian theory. For social constructivists, knowledge is constructed by the interaction of the individual with a social or cultural environment. Knowledge, therefore, has a social component and cannot be generated independently of its social context. Drawing on the developmental theories of Vygotsky (1962), social constructivism emphasises the fundamental role of language and social interaction in the process of learning. Learning on this view means developing the ability to participate increasingly adequately in socially structured and situated activities (John-Steiner and Mahn, 1996).

Both individual and social constructivism have important implications for education, for approaches to classroom practice, for understanding the role of the teacher and for defining and evaluating successful teaching.

Educational implications of constructivism

It is easy to see why there is a growing interest in and acceptance of constructivist epistemology among teachers. Airasian and Walsh (1997) suggest the following five reasons.

First, if students are constructors of their own knowledge rather than passive recipients of the knowledge of others, they will perhaps be in a better position to develop the 'higher-order' skills of generalising, analysing, synthesising and evaluating which will be needed to cope with the rapid expansion of information which is a feature of our contemporary world.

Second, constructivism offers teachers greater freedom to construct their own meanings and interpretations of classroom practice at a time when in other respects their hands appear to be tied by restrictive government legislation and guidance.

Third, the rhetoric of constructivism is seductive, stressing autonomy instead of obedience, construction of meaning as opposed to instruction and interest as opposed to reinforcement.

Fourth, constructivism is egalitarian in emphasising individualised learning and avoiding competition (cf. Lerman, 1994, p 61). It assumes that all students can and will learn and be actively and creatively involved in the building of personal knowledge and understanding.

Fifth, constructivism emphasises emancipation from outdated authority structures. In particular it is symbolically emancipatory for disempowered groups, for the different context in which their learning takes place will result in the construction of different knowledge, which in time will pose a challenge to the hegemony of the more powerful sections of society.

A constructivist epistemology influences classroom practice in at least three ways. First, it suggests that learning is most effective when the child is 'in control' of the process and when the curriculum is 'owned' by the child (Rowland, 1987), which can generate a powerful intrinsic motivation to learn. Children have experience almost from birth (perhaps even before that) of making sense of their environment by the interaction between previous knowledge and new experiences, and it is the task of the school to help to take this process forward (Jackson, 1987). Second, the role of the teacher is changed to more of a facilitator and collaborator than an instructor. The teacher facilitates children's construction of knowledge by interpreting and acting on what they say, by stimulating interest and encouraging reflection and by coordinating and critiquing the knowledge which they construct. Third, new teaching methods may be needed. In fact, this point must not be exaggerated. As we have already seen, the forms of knowledge thesis does not imply the superiority of direct instruction; Hirst is at pains to point out that guided discovery learning may sometimes be a more effective teaching method than direct instruction. Similarly, a constructivist approach to teaching does not imply that methods such as memorisation and rote learning are always and in all subjects useless. Clearly knowledge is something which can very effectively be shared, and there is no point in expecting each new generation to 'reinvent the wheel' (Mercer, 1995, p 1). Indeed, von Glasersfeld (1995, p 5), one of the leading advocates of constructivism in education, points out that 'there are... matters that can and perhaps must be learned in a purely mechanical way'. Nevertheless, according to Airasian and Walsh (1997, p 447), other things being equal, a constructivist approach will favour:

> methods that are likely to foster student construction of knowledge, primarily those that emphasise nonrote tasks and active student participation in the learning process (e.g., co-operative learning, performance assessments, product-oriented activities, and hands-on learning, as well as reciprocal teaching and initiation-reply-evaluation methods).

Constructivism is clearly compatible with a number of theoretical frameworks and strategies currently in use in values education, including values clarification, discussion, problem-solving, group work, pupil-directed research, peer mediation and philosophy for children (see below and Halstead and Taylor, 1998).

Activity B3

Consider the implications of a constructivist epistemology for your own specialist subject.

Comment on activity B3

I intend to restrict my comments here to a single subject, mathematics. One would expect to find that certain areas of the curriculum lend themselves more readily to a constructivist approach than others, notably those areas where creativity is most central, including the arts and physical education. It is therefore surprising to find that as much work has been done on constructivist approaches to teaching mathematics as on any other subject.

As Ernest (1994, p x) points out, the 'Euclidean paradigm of mathematics as an objective, absolute, incorrigible and rigidly hierarchical body of knowledge' has in recent years come increasingly under challenge. Philosophers of mathematics have broadened their area of interest to the social dimensions of mathematics, including the practices of mathematicians and the place of mathematics in human culture. Once mathematics is displaced as the 'secure cornerstone of absolutism' (*ibid.*, p xi) and reconceptualised as a social construction, this implies that we should examine the way that mathematics and mathematics education function in society. Does mathematics have a key role to play in the distribution of life chances in society? Think about the stipulation that entrants into several professions (including teaching) must have a minimum qualification of Grade C in GCSE Mathematics. Does mathematics act as 'a "critical filter" in depriving minority and women students of equal opportunities in employment' (*ibid.*)? Some mathematicians (for example, Thomas, 1994, p 35) have been led to suggest that mathematical knowledge needs the idea of constructivism as a counterbalance of the customary view of mathematics as 'truth pre-existing human rationality but miraculously commensurate with it'.

All this has a profound impact on the way mathematics can be taught, and has contributed among other things to the development of multicultural mathematics (Bishop, 1991, 1993) and feminist mathematics (Belenky *et al*, 1986). More attention has been paid to children's social interaction in learning mathematics (Steffe and Tzur, 1994) and their interaction with computers (Smith, 1994). The belief that children have an active role in their own learning leads teachers to pay more attention to children's mathematical language and to their personal concepts. What goes on in the learning process is not copying a file of the teacher's knowledge onto the pupil's mental disc; it is, more subtly, a modification of the pupil's existing knowledge as a result of interaction with the teacher. Steffe and Tzur (1994, p 12) suggest that when teaching children 'we base our interactions with them on schemes we observe the children use independently in mathematical activity'. Teachers observe children's mathematical activity so that they can learn to modify it and initiate productive interactions from which the children can develop new concepts and operations.

Critique of constructivism

Even in areas that seem to lend themselves most readily to a constructivist approach, some support more objective approaches to knowledge and education. Best (1996), for example, argues strongly for objectivity and rationality in the arts, Hirsch (1988) for the (pragmatic) need for all students in a country to be initiated into the same cultural knowledge, and others, as we shall see below, for universal fundamental concepts in the domain of moral education.

Activity B4

What difficulties are you aware of in the application of constructivism in classrooms?

Comment on activity B4

Airasian and Walsh (1997, pp 447-9) draw attention to several notes of caution as teachers attempt to implement constructivism in their classrooms.

First, it is difficult to derive teaching methods directly from a theory of knowledge, and there is much work still to be done on the appropriateness in different subject areas of those methods (like co-operative learning) which are most commonly associated with a constructivist approach.

Second, as already noted, it is not necessarily appropriate for all aspects of a subject to be taught in the same way, and even within a constructivist approach there may sometimes be room for more formal teaching.

Third, a constructivist classroom orientation may make very big demands on a teacher's time, energy and commitment. The teacher will not only have to create a safe, free, responsive environment which encourages disclosure of student constructions, and find a suitable balance between involvement and non-involvement in the process of learning, but will also have to be willing to expend considerable time in responding to students' individual constructions. Each individual construction will have to be reviewed separately, since one student may adopt a different frame of reference and underlying logic from another.

Fourth, teachers have to find acceptable ways of evaluating the wide diversity of possible individual constructions and must be aware that relying solely on personal meaning to justify constructions leads to rampant relativism in which standards and evaluation criteria become very difficult to establish. Clearly it is helpful if standards and criteria are constructed jointly by teachers and students, but the problem of guiding and evaluating students without undermining their constructivist activities remains a thorny one.

B4 Towards a middle path

The two views of knowledge which we have been discussing represent two extreme positions in which compromise seems unlikely. However, in his recent writings Hirst has moved away from what he calls the 'rationalist' position (which is implicit in the forms of knowledge thesis as set out above) to a position which is somewhat nearer in some respects to the constructivist approach. We shall conclude part one with a brief examination of Hirst's current thinking.

The main error in his earlier position, Hirst (1993, p 197) now maintains, was 'seeing theoretical knowledge as the logical foundation for the development of sound practical knowledge and rational personal development'. Logically coherent mastery of the distinct forms of knowledge was seen as fundamental to everything else in education. His current position, on the other hand, sees practical knowledge as much more important. Practical knowledge forms the foundation on which a proper understanding of the significance of theoretical knowledge is based; but what is important is not just the priority of practical knowledge in education, but

> the priority of personal development by initiation into a complex of specific, substantive social practices with all the knowledge, attitudes, feelings, virtues, skills, dispositions and relationships that that involves.

Hirst goes on to note that he therefore considers it necessary for the curriculum to be organised in terms of those significant practices.

In comparing Hirst's current position to constructivism, there are several points we can make.

First, the concept of initiation, even though it implies some degree of social interaction, is alien to constructivist thinking, because it gives too dominant a role to the teacher and too passive a role to the learner. However, Hirst makes clear that it is only at the start of education that the practices into which the child is initiated are determined by others (p 195). They are selected in the light of the emerging capacities of the child and the physical and social context. As the child develops, he or she takes responsibility increasingly for selecting or modifying the practices on which education is based.

Second, development is understood as concerned with wants, capacities and achievements. The development of practical knowledge starts, Hirst suggests, with the 'structuring of our natural wants into specific forms and patterns' (p 193), an idea which is clearly compatible with constructivist thought, but this should not be thought of in individualistic terms. The satisfaction of wants is dependent on social relations in a number of ways, not least because language and social interaction extend people's awareness of the possibilities open to them. In a fundamental sense, Hirst claims, persons are social constructions dependent on but also able to modify the social networks within which they live.

Third, the concept of 'practices' is clearly central to Hirst's current thinking, and this is a concept which occurred earlier in our discussion of constructivist approaches to mathematics. By the term, Hirst appears to mean patterns of activity (such as knowledge, judgements, values, skills, dispositions, virtues, feelings and actions) which may be engaged in individually or collectively and which have been socially developed or constructed. He now rejects the idea of the rational planning of education and argues instead that the content of education (which is itself a social practice) must be conceived as initiation into specific social practices. He identifies three distinguishable categories of these.

First are the basic practices which any individual needs in order to be viable in their everyday physical, personal and social lives. Second, there is a much wider range of optional practices which enable the individual to construct his or her own rational life. Third, there are practices of critical reflection, which may lead individuals to modify how they live their lives and pursue their desires.

It is interesting that Hirst includes both knowledge and values within the concept of 'practices'. For the purposes of this unit, however, they are being dealt with separately and it is suggested that they raise quite different issues. We must now turn to examine the notion of 'values' more closely.

B5 Values and education

Values are central to the work of schools in two ways.

First, schools and individual teachers are a major influence, alongside the family, the media and the peer group, on the developing values of children and young people. This is an inevitable process whether or not it is intentional and explicit: children *do* learn values at school - perhaps as much from relationships, everyday classroom interactions and the example set by the teachers as from more formal attempts to engage in values education.

Second, values permeate and underpin the whole management and organisation of the school, including, for example, decisions about budget allocation, admissions policies, approaches to behaviour management, grouping policies, equal opportunities, staff development and appraisal, curriculum policies and so on. Even the *minutiae* of classroom practice, such as seating arrangements and tone of voice, reflect implicit value judgements.

Of course the part schools play in the teaching of values and the part values play in the organisation of schools are closely connected. Schools generally both embody and transmit the values of the broader society (though, as we shall see, this becomes more problematic in a pluralist society) and children are quick to perceive, and respond negatively towards, any inconsistencies between the values they are being taught and the values which are reflected in school organisation and management.

Activity B5

Take ten minutes to think of as many approaches as possible to a problem of misbehaviour during school lunchtime. Then go back and make a note of what values underpin each of your proposed solutions to the problem.

Comment on activity B5

If you are familiar with the techniques of lateral thinking, you may have been able to have come up with a very substantial list of possibilities. I would expect you to mention:

- giving children a strict telling off;
- employing more lunchtime supervisors;
- talking to children about the problem in the next assembly;
- reducing the length of the lunchbreak;
- punishing the worst offenders;
- organising a wider range of supervised activities during the lunchbreak;
- encouraging children to talk through the problem and produce solutions;
- organising a circle time when children can express their feelings about the problem;
- helping children to produce their own list of rules for lunchtime;
- giving children specific responsibilities over the lunchtime, as part of a general policy of caring and social responsibility.

Underpinning such a diverse range of possibilities is an equally diverse range of values: discipline, cost-effectiveness, authority, control, justice, sense of fair play, care and concern for others, respect for others, fairness, co-operation, self-restraint and responsibility.

Reflecting on values

What you have just been doing is reflecting on the values which might underpin school decision-making. Schools have been encouraged as a result of recent legislation and guidance to reflect on and articulate their values with much greater clarity and openness than in the past, as part of a general drive to increase accountability and in response to a perceived 'moral decline' among young people.

However, once schools embark on this process of bringing values out into the open and articulating them, all sorts of problems emerge. What can schools do if staff do not all share the same values? Is it possible to please all parties with a legitimate claim to a stake in the educational process at the same time? Do schools need to have common values if they are to engage in values education? How can schools ensure that the values they proclaim do in fact underpin their practice? How can schools ensure that the values which their pupils develop are those which they intend? What preparation, guidance and resources do teachers need as values educators? Before any of these questions can be considered, however, we need to examine more closely what is meant by the term 'values'.

B6 Meaning and nature of values

In spite of the rapid growth of writing about values in education in the last decade and the increasing number of surveys concerned with moral and social values in Britain and Europe, there is still much disagreement over the precise meaning of the term 'values'. Values have been variously defined as things which are considered 'good' in themselves (such as beauty, truth, love, honesty and loyalty), as personal or social preferences, as emotional commitments and ideas about worth. Raths, Harmin and Simon (1966, p 28) describe values as 'beliefs, attitudes or feelings that an individual is proud of, is willing to publicly affirm, that have been chosen thoughtfully from alternatives without persuasion and are acted on repeatedly'. Beck (1990, p 2) defines values as 'those things (objects, activities, experiences, etc) which on balance promote human wellbeing'. Each of these descriptions is open to criticism. For example, the one offered by Raths *et al.* appears too narrowly individualistic: surely an important thing about some values at least is that they are *shared*. On the other hand, Beck's definition seems too broad: there may be many things which on balance promote human wellbeing (such as playing the lottery or the responsible use of condoms) which we would not want to describe as *values*.

Some of the confusion about the term arises from a desire to force too close a link between 'value' (singular) and 'values' (plural). To talk of the *value* of something (as in the phrase 'value-added') has always been to talk of its worth, and when we 'value' something we are making a high estimate of its worth. However, the term 'values' (in the plural) now seems to be used to refer to the criteria by which we make such value judgements, to the principles on which the value judgements are based. In the present text, the term 'values' is used in the sense of *those principles or fundamental convictions which act as general guides to behaviour or as points of reference in decision-making* (adapted from Halstead, 1996a, p 5).

Activity B6

What criticisms can you make of this definition? Read back over the previous sections to help you and feel free to range widely in your comments.

Comment on activity B6

You may have raised several points.

- The definition fails to make the connection clear between values and virtues, attitudes and commitments.

- It does not make clear whether values are to be considered as a subjective preference or whether they have an independent existence of their own.
- It leaves open the question of whether there is a distinction between private and public values.
- It also leaves open the question whether there are any absolute values, or only changing and relative ones.
- If values are socially constructed, there may be particular values (whether political, aesthetic, moral or religious) which have validity only within particular cultures or traditions.

Each of these points has important implications for the place of values in education. With regard to the first point, virtues are personal qualities such as honesty, generosity, perseverance and compassion, and when these qualities are the subject of reflection and are consciously chosen as the basis for behaviour they may be counted as values. Attitudes are predispositions or acquired tendencies to act towards a set of objects or experiences in a predictable manner, and attitudes such as openness, tolerance and respect may be considered values. Commitments involve accepting particular beliefs, principles or courses of action as binding; a commitment to truth and justice means accepting these as fundamental values. Carr (1991) provides a useful introduction to arguments that moral education should be based on the promotion of moral virtues.

With regard to the second point, some people treat values as things they just happen to have (like a preference for heavy metal music), whereas others reject this subjective approach, and consider values to have an objective reality or existence irrespective of whether people acknowledge it or not. The latter would consider that owning slaves was just as morally unjustifiable in first century Rome as it is today, whereas the former might say, 'They just had different values in those days, that's all; I have no right to judge what they did by my own values.' Fishkin (1984) offers a detailed critique of the subjectivist position.

With regard to the third point, there continues to be substantial debate as to whether the same moral principles apply to both public and private behaviour (cf. Hampshire, 1978). This question is of particular interest to lawyers wishing to establish whether there is a domain of private morality in which legal intervention is inappropriate. Hart (1961, p 179), for example, argues that 'morality has its private aspect, shown in the individual's recognition of ideals which he need not either share with others or regard as a source of criticism of others, still less of society as a whole', whereas, according to Smith and Hogan (1993, p 350), Viscount Simonds in a House of Lords judgement maintained that:

there remains in the courts of law a residual power... to conserve not only the safety and order but also the moral welfare of the state.

The question is also highly relevant to teachers who see the formation of children's character as part of their duty: is there a domain of private values in which teachers have no right to interfere?

Interest among educationalists in the fourth point has been revived as a result of recent initiatives by the Schools Curriculum and Assessment Authority (SCAA) (see Talbot and Tate, 1997; Talbot, 1998). Much hinges on what precisely is meant by the term 'absolute'. It may mean that the values apply *universally* and at all times, in other words, that they are not relative to any given cultural context. Or it may mean that the values can never be outweighed by other considerations. The second meaning is counter-intuitive, however, because it is easy to imagine circumstances when the value of truth-telling, for example, might lead to great harm, perhaps even the loss of life. But to argue that important values sometimes have to be balanced against each other is not necessarily to commit oneself to a full-blown relativism which claims that values are always dependent on a particular context or that no set of values can be shown to be better than another.

A response to the final point depends on the way values are classified, and we must now turn to this topic. Apart from the distinctions which have already been discussed, between subjective and objective and between relative and absolute values, there are two main ways in which values are commonly categorised: by subject matter or area of concern and by ideology.

Categorisation by subject matter

Values are often grouped together into distinct types according to their main focus of concern: thus we have moral values, aesthetic values, economic values, environmental values, spiritual values, intellectual values, family values, religious values, health values, social values, cultural values and so on. Of these, moral values are often taken to be the most fundamental, since the others (with the probable exception of the aesthetic) all seem to involve moral concepts. Moral values are the principles which guide our actions towards others, incorporating notions of right and wrong, obligations and responsibilities, the promotion of human wellbeing and the avoidance of harm.

Activity B7

Think about the disagreements among experts concerning the aims of sex education. For some, sex education is primarily about safer sex, and the effectiveness of a sex education programme is judged in terms of the extent to which it leads to increased condom use. For others, it is about reducing teenage pregnancy; or encouraging sexual abstinence among young people; or helping people to satisfy their sexual needs; or increasing understanding and acceptance of 'differences in sexual norms and practices'; or developing an appreciation of 'the value of stable family life, marriage and the responsibilities of parenthood'; or empowering young people by increasing their knowledge about sexuality; or enjoining 'chastity and virginity before marriage and faithfulness and loyalty within marriage'; or developing a greater sense of style, satisfaction or fun in sexual relations; or encouraging responsible sexual decision-making. All of these proposed aims are drawn from texts on sex education published over the last thirty years; you can find the full references in Halstead (1998).

What different kinds of values underpin this wide diversity of aims for school-based sex education? Which clashes of values are likely to generate the most disagreement in formulating school sex education policies?

Comment on activity B7

You could have mentioned any of the following areas of values.

First, there are *socio-economic* values. Controversial claims are often made about young single mothers being a burden on the welfare state and about links between absent fathers and growing crime rates. One of the basic assumptions underlying many sex education programmes is that such education can reduce adolescent pregnancy and thus alleviate the social and economic problems that have been blamed on teenage sexual activity.

Second, there are *health* values. The reduction of risk-taking behaviours such as exposure to disease, combined with a concern for psychological and emotional health and wellbeing is considered by many people to be the most important underlying value in sex education.

Third, there are *moral* values. These may include self-respect, honesty in relationships, personal responsibility, self-determination, control over one's own life and body, and the protection of individual rights, including freedom from corruption and invasive behaviour.

Fourth, there are *cultural* values. Values which belong only to certain cultures include values such as romantic love, the 'innocence' of children, various notions of family values, sexual pleasure, and virtues such as abstinence and self-control.

Fifth, there are *religious* values. Religions have given rise to a huge diversity of sexual values, and there is rarely a consensus on values even within a single religious tradition. Some traditions see marriage as a religious duty for everyone, whereas others see celibacy as an equally valid (or even superior) lifestyle. Some traditions find homosexuality totally unacceptable (cf. Halstead and Lewicka, 1998), whereas others urge acceptance as the only response which is in keeping with religious principles (Lenderyou and Porter, 1994, p 41f). Some traditions are certainly more prescriptive than others. Many traditions celebrate religious virtues such as purity, chastity, fidelity and self-discipline, but others have argued for a new vision of sexual relationships which is free from the 'patriarchal' attitudes and assumptions of the past (Thatcher, 1993, chapter 1). Many traditions would also probably emphasise the importance of love as the basis of meaningful relationships, the importance of the spiritual dimension in sexuality and the importance of seeing sexuality as a gift from God.

Of course, these five categories are neither mutually exclusive nor clear-cut in the distinctions they make, but the list does serve to draw attention both to the complexities of value frameworks and to the nature of disagreements about them. There are disagreements between conflicting values within each category as well as conflicts between the categories, and further disagreements about how the values should be interpreted. Perhaps the biggest disagreement in contemporary sex education is between those who prioritise health values and those who prioritise the moral values which are implicit in education itself. A health-oriented approach has the straightforward goals of reducing sexually transmitted diseases and reducing teenage pregnancy, and the only significant question is the most effective way of promoting these goals. Since any health campaign which is perceived to offer moral guidance is thought unlikely to have credibility among targeted groups, there is a conscious avoidance of moral guidance in sex education based on health values. On the other hand, a moral educational approach will put more emphasis on the balanced development of the whole person and will be based on values such as respect for others, honesty and non-exploitation in sexual relationships (see Halstead, 1998).

Categorisation by ideology

We often talk of conservative values, liberal values, humanist values, market values, utilitarian values, Christian values, and so on. Each of these ideologies provides an overarching framework within which formal education can be carried out. Objectivist approaches such as those which simply present values as God-given no longer carry much weight in public decision-making in the west, particularly with the decline of moral authority and certainty in the postmodern world. The dominant educational ideology in Britain over the last forty years or more has been the liberal democratic one. Central concepts in this ideology are the importance of social justice, the rights of individuals, equality of opportunity, religious neutrality, democracy, impartiality, the just resolution of conflict, the rule of law, the free market economy, respect for others and the freedom to make independent judgements and choices.

At the heart of the liberal democratic framework are two values which exist in a state of tension: first, individual liberty, i.e. freedom of action and freedom from constraint in the pursuit of one's own needs and interests; and second, equality of respect for all individuals within the structures and practices in society, i.e. non-discrimination on irrelevant grounds. The tension between these two values of freedom and equality gives rise to the need for a third, consistent rationality, i.e. basing decisions and actions on logically consistent rational justifications. It is the interaction of these three fundamental values that provides not only all the familiar liberal values which I have already mentioned, but also the vision of liberal education with its emphasis on critical openness, the autonomy of the academic disciplines, equality of opportunity, personal autonomy, rational morality, the avoidance of indoctrination, the refusal to side with any definitive conception of the good, citizenship, democratic values, the celebration of diversity and the recognition of children's rights. In recent years, economic liberalism has made some inroads into this democratic liberal vision of education by promoting market values and the enterprise culture and by redefining the success of a school in terms of its ability to attract 'customers' and to produce skilled manpower to meet the needs of industry (see Halstead, 1996b).

As we shall see in the next unit, Christian educational values, particularly within the Protestant tradition, have not found it hard by and large to live with democratic liberal values. Many Christian teachers are basically happy with the liberal framework, but would wish to give it a Christian gloss, for example, by emphasising an ethos of service, caring and Christian love; by interpreting the spiritual side of education in a distinctive religious way rather than from a humanist perspective; and by providing a context where faith and commitment can thrive. A bigger challenge to liberal values and liberal education comes from Marxism (cf. Harris, 1979; Matthews, 1980), radical feminism (cf. Graham, 1994), postmodernism (cf. Aronowitz and Giroux, 1991; Carr, 1995, chapter 9) and fundamentalist religion. To those committed to such views, liberal education may appear as just one more challengeable version of what is good for children. An Islamic worldview, for example, which is based on values drawn from divine revelation, produces an approach to education which is at odds at several crucial points with liberalism. In Islam, the ultimate goal of education is to nurture children in the faith, to make them good Muslims, and children are not encouraged to question the fundamentals of their faith but are expected to accept them on the authority of their elders. Some liberals consider this approach intolerable and suggest that the state should intervene to protect the rights of the children to be liberated from the constraints of their cultural environment and to grow up into personally autonomous adults (Raz, 1986, p 424). This response might be considered equally oppressive from a non-liberal perspective, however, since it might be seen as undermining particular religious traditions.

Amid all this diversity, schools find themselves in a very difficult position. On the one hand, as we have seen, they cannot avoid values and are under pressure to make more explicit the values which underpin school policy and the values they teach to children. On the other hand, it is hard in a pluralist society to find a set of values which is shared by all groups but which is also sufficiently substantial to act as a basis for education in the common school attended by pupils from a wide range of cultural and ideological backgrounds. It would seem unjust to minorities to base the values of the common school uncritically on those of the dominant cultural group; yet to give free rein to market forces might result in a diversity of provision which would prove socially divisive. Hence there have been attempts in recent years, notably by SCAA, to re-examine the values of British society to see if there might in fact be a greater consensus among the different sub-groups than had been thought. We must now look at these initiatives in more detail.

B7 Framework of shared values for schools

The 1988 Education Reform Act places a statutory duty on schools to promote, among other things, the spiritual, moral and cultural development of pupils and of society, and the 1992 Education (Schools) Act makes this an aspect of schools' work on which OFSTED inspectors must report. In the current *Framework for the Inspection of Schools*, pupils' spiritual, moral, social and cultural development is inspected as part of the 'Quality of Education Provided', and attention is directed towards 'the curriculum and life of the school; the example set for pupils by adults in the school; and the quality of collective worship' (OFSTED, 1994, p 19). Inspectors' judgements should be based on the extent to which the school:

- provides its pupils with knowledge and insight into values and beliefs and enables them to reflect on their experiences in a way which develops their spiritual awareness and self-knowledge;
- teaches the principles which distinguish right from wrong;
- encourages pupils to relate positively to others, take responsibility, participate fully in the community, and develop understanding of citizenship;

- teaches pupils to appreciate their own cultural traditions and the diversity and richness of other cultures.

Non-statutory curriculum guidance provided by the National Curriculum Council (NCC) on the five cross-curricular themes makes explicit reference to values. *Education for Citizenship*, for example, states that 'pupils should be helped to develop a personal moral code and to explore values and beliefs. Shared values, such as concern for others, industry and effort, self-respect and self-discipline, as well as moral qualities such as honesty and truthfulness, should be promoted' (NCC, 1990, p 4). The NCC also issued a discussion document in 1993 on spiritual and moral development (reissued by SCAA, 1995) which listed moral values schools should promote: 'telling the truth; keeping promises; respecting the rights and property of others; acting considerately towards others; helping those less fortunate and weaker than ourselves; taking personal responsibility for one's actions; self-discipline' (p 4). Schools should also reject 'bullying, cheating, deceit, cruelty, irresponsibility, and dishonesty' (p 4). Morally educated school leavers should be able to 'articulate their own attitudes and values... develop for themselves a set of socially acceptable values and principles, and set guidelines to cover their own behaviour' (p 5).

National forum

Concerned that these early initiatives were too directive and not demonstrably grounded in a broad values consensus, SCAA set up the *National Forum on Values in Education and the Community* in 1996. The Forum comprised 150 members drawn from business, youth groups, faith communities, the police, social services, various pressure groups and all levels of education, and was given the task of making recommendations on two points:

- whether there are any values upon which there is common agreement within society;
- how schools might be supported in the important task of contributing to pupils' spiritual, moral, social and cultural development.

The Forum identified a number of values on which members believed society would agree (though this did not imply a consensus either on the source of the values or on the way they should be applied). Extensive consultation (both in schools and among the general public through a Mori poll) showed that there was overwhelming agreement on the values. The statement of values which emerged from this process concentrated on four areas: self, relationships, society and environment.

Self

We value ourselves as unique human beings capable of spiritual, moral, intellectual and physical growth and development. On the basis of these values, we should:

- develop an understanding of our own characters, strengths and weaknesses;
- develop self-respect and self-discipline;
- clarify the meaning and purpose in our lives and decide, on the basis of this, how we believe that our lives should be lived;
- make responsible use of our talents, rights and opportunities;
- strive, throughout life, for knowledge, wisdom and understanding;
- take responsibility, within our capabilities, for our own lives.

Relationships

We value others for themselves, not only for what they have or what they can do for us. We value relationships as fundamental to the development and fulfilment of ourselves and others, and to the good of the community. On the basis of these values, we should:

- respect others, including children;
- care for others and exercise goodwill in our dealings with them;
- show others they are valued;
- earn loyalty, trust and confidence;
- work co-operatively with others;
- respect the privacy and property of others;
- resolve disputes peacefully.

Society

We value truth, freedom, justice, human rights, the rule of law and collective effort for the common good. In particular we value families as sources of love and support for all their members, and as the basis of a society in which people care for others. On the basis of these values, we should:

- understand and carry out our responsibilities as citizens;
- refuse to support values or actions that may be harmful to individuals or communities;
- support families in raising children and caring for dependants;
- support the institution of marriage;
- recognise that the love and commitment required for a secure and happy childhood can also be found in families of different kinds;
- help people to know about the law and legal processes;
- respect the rule of law and encourage others to do so;
- respect religious and cultural diversity;
- promote opportunities for all;

- support those who cannot, by themselves, sustain a dignified lifestyle;
- promote participation in the democratic process by all sectors of the community;
- contribute to, as well as benefit fairly from, economic and cultural resources;
- make truth, integrity, honesty and goodwill priorities in public and private life.

Environment

We value the environment, both natural and shaped by humanity, as the basis of life and a source of wonder and inspiration. On the basis of these values, we should:

- accept our responsibility to maintain a sustainable environment for future generations;
- understand the place of human beings within nature;
- understand our responsibilities for other species;
- ensure that development can be justified; preserve balance and diversity in nature wherever possible;
- preserve areas of beauty and interest for future generations;
- repair, wherever possible, habitats damaged by human development and other means.

Activity B8

Ask yourself what criticisms need to be made of SCAA's *Statement of Values*. For example, is it too general? Is it impractical? Can everyone agree with it?

Comment on activity B8

Among your criticisms you may have raised several of the following points.

First, the list of values is rather bland and uninspiring. The words used may mean different things to different people, and until there is a shared understanding of what is meant in practice by 'respecting others' or 'valuing freedom', for example, not much has been achieved. It is precisely when attempts are made to flesh out these principles that disagreements and conflicts will emerge. It is therefore simply ducking the issue for SCAA to suggest that 'it is for schools to decide, reflecting the range of views in the wider community, how these values should be interpreted and applied'.

Second, some of the generalisations may not always be appropriate. For example, there may be many occasions when it is not appropriate to value the environment which has been 'shaped by humanity' as 'a source of wonder and inspiration'. Similarly, it is not clear when the list says 'we value families as sources of love and support' whether it means that all families *are* sources of love and support (which is clearly not true) or whether all families are *potential* sources (which may be true), or whether it is the principle of family life which is being supported irrespective of the less attractive reality in many cases.

Third, it is not clear to whom the recurring phrase 'we should' refers. Does it refer to individuals or to society as a whole? Do all individuals have the duty to 'help people to know about the law'? (Interestingly, this is the only mention of promoting knowledge in the whole list.)

Fourth, the list appears to recommend both direct action ('repair damaged habitats...') and attitude change ('recognise that...'). It is also a mixture of the impossible ideal ('clarify the meaning and purpose in our lives...') and the practical ('help people to know about the law...'; 'preserve areas of beauty').

Fifth, there are some surprising omissions; for example, the terms 'equal' and 'equality' are noticeably absent, and there is a silence about gender issues.

The last point gets to the heart of the problem with the list, that in seeking to avoid controversy it simply ignores some of the values which many people hold most dearly. SCAA claims that the general agreement that has been shown upon the values it has listed means that 'schools which base their teaching and ethos' on them can expect 'the support and encouragement of society' in so doing. But schools cannot base their teaching and ethos on a partial list of values, on a list which ignores many important values simply because they are controversial. And if schools are left to sort out the controversial areas themselves, then they have not in fact been helped very much in their task of clarifying the values which inform their work.

School policy statements on values

In recent years schools have been encouraged to develop a values statement 'which sets out the values the school intends to promote and which it intends to demonstrate through all aspects of its life' (SCAA, 1995, p 7). SCAA is currently developing guidance for schools on the procedures which may be followed in agreeing goals for values education, reviewing current practice, planning and implementing change and evaluating school success in this area (QCA, 1997). A recent national survey indicates that about one-quarter of both primary and secondary schools currently claim to have a values statement (Taylor and Lines, 1998), but this figure is likely to increase as a result of school inspections and evidence that parents may favour schools with a strong values orientation (Marfleet, 1996). But the task facing schools of discussing and clarifying their values and making them public is a daunting one. As we have seen, they must pay attention to the diversity of values in the communities they serve (which are themselves in flux) as well as in society at large, and to the legitimate expectations of interested parties. They must examine their aims and their curriculum provision and practices to see what values lie embedded there and must reflect on the justifiability, appropriateness and coherence of these values. In the end, the statements of value that emerge may be ambiguous, provisional and less than totally clear (cf. McLaughlin, 1994, p 459), but it is hard to see how else a foundation can be provided for schools' vital and unavoidable work in values education.

B8 Education in values

The term 'values education' has a much shorter history in England and Wales than it has in North America, or even in Scotland. Nevertheless, a recent directory of research and resources in values education in the UK lists 113 entries, made up of research projects, organisations, publications and other initiatives (Taylor, 1994b). The establishment of the Values Education Council in the UK in 1995 may prove an important turning point; it aims to bring together organisations with a shared interest in values education, its purpose being 'the promotion and development of values in the context of education as a lifelong process, to help individuals develop as responsible and caring persons and live as participating members of a pluralist society'.

The emphasis here on personal and social values, moral values and democratic citizenship is not intended to exclude other values. Indeed, as we have seen, recent official publications tend to link moral with spiritual values, and strong claims are commonly made about links between moral and aesthetic values (cf. Jarrett, 1991) and between spiritual and aesthetic (Starkings, 1993). Other values frequently mentioned in the context of the school include values relating to cultural diversity, cultural identity and national consciousness; intellectual and academic values; peace, international understanding, human rights and environmental values; gender equality and antiracism; work and economic values; health; and common human values such as tolerance, solidarity and co-operation (cf. Taylor, 1994a).

In this section we shall explore theoretical approaches and strategies, examine the contribution made by the school ethos and the curriculum, consider a range of different methods for values education and finally discuss issues of evaluation and inspection.

Strategies for values education

There are two major debates about approaches to values education: whether schools should instil values in pupils or teach them to explore and develop their own values; and whether moral development is primarily a matter of developing increasingly sophisticated skills in moral reasoning or primarily a matter of developing certain dispositions, particularly caring. The first is a debate between the proponents of *character education* and those of *values clarification*; the second, a debate between the proponents of *moral reasoning* and those of *caring*. Each of these strategies has been defined and developed in North America, but has had a much wider influence.

Character education

Character education is based on the belief that adults have a duty to form the character of children by teaching them moral values directly, by shaping their behaviour and by seeking to develop good habits (Lickona, 1991). It was the dominant approach to moral education in the first half of the twentieth century and has enjoyed a significant revival in the USA over the last ten years. A number of techniques are associated with the approach, including the use of stories, teaching by example, direct instruction, developing a consistent learning environment, and habituation. Character education has been criticised for paying insufficient attention to the diversity of values in western societies and for involving the imposition of values.

Values clarification

Diametrically opposed to character education is the view that values education is centrally concerned with teaching children to explore and develop their own feelings and values. The values clarification approach, developed particularly by Raths *et al.* (1966) and Simon *et al.* (1972), is based on two assumptions: that children will care more about values which they have thought through and made their own than about values simply passed down by adults; and that it is wrong, particularly in a pluralist society, to seek to impose values. According to Raths *et al.* (1966), legitimate valuing involves seven criteria: values must be (1) chosen freely (2) from alternatives (3) after consideration of the consequences, and an individual must (4) cherish, (5) publicly affirm, and (6) act on, the value, and (7) do so repeatedly. Values clarification was a very popular approach in the 1960s and 1970s, and was undoubtedly successful in developing confidence and self-esteem, but it has been criticised widely for being rooted in a spurious relativism and for failing to recognise that it is possible to make mistakes in matters of value (cf. Kilpatrick, 1992, chapter 4). Values clarification has rarely been advocated openly in the UK, though the influence of its philosophy can be seen in the *Humanities Curriculum Project*

(Schools Council/Nuffield Humanities Project, 1970), and it may in fact underlie the approaches of many texts and materials in use in schools.

Moral reasoning

This approach is based on Kohlberg's (1981, 1984) influential theory of moral development. This posits six invariant stages of moral reasoning which characterise judgements about issues of distributive justice. The role of the teacher is thus to stimulate moral development by encouraging students to move to a higher stage of moral reasoning by presenting them with moral dilemmas and encouraging them to discuss them in a way which it is intended will help them to see the inadequacies of their current moral thinking (Blatt and Kohlberg, 1975). Kohlberg also developed the 'just community' approach, which is designed to help students to develop responsible moral behaviour by coming to share group norms and a sense of community. A community cluster within a school is made up of about one hundred students and five teachers who meet on a weekly basis to make rules and discipline and to plan community activities and policies. The aim is to introduce students to participatory democracy and to give them greater opportunities for self regulation and moral awareness (Kohlberg and Higgins, 1987).

Caring

Behind this approach lies the belief that one's intuitive sense of concern or caring for others is a better guide to moral behaviour than an ethical system such as Kohlberg's based on a set of rational principles (Gilligan, 1982; Noddings, 1984). Relationship networks generate feelings of connectedness and a developing sense of responsibility to others. Caring is presented as a more feminine approach to moral education, and the central task of the school is seen as encouraging children to develop into loving, caring adults.

Values education through school ethos

The ethos of the school is an imprecise term referring to the pervasive atmosphere, ambience or climate within a school, yet it has been identified by numerous researchers as an important element both in school effectiveness and in values education (Rutter, *et al.* 1979).

Activity B9

What does the term 'school ethos' encompass, and how are these features relevant to values education?

Comment on activity B9

Some of the main features encompassed by the term 'school ethos' in its broadest sense include:

- the nature of relationships within a school;
- the dominant forms of social interaction;
- the attitudes and expectations of teachers;
- the learning climate;
- the way that conflicts are resolved;
- the physical environment;
- links with parents and the local community;
- patterns of communication;
- the existence of school councils and other democratic structures;
- extra-curricular activities;
- the nature of pupil involvement in the school (for example, involvement in the formation of school rules and policies on discipline);
- anti-bullying and anti-racist policies;
- management styles;
- the school's underlying philosophy and aims.

All of these are rich in their potential to influence children's developing values (see Halstead and Taylor, 1998).

Closely related to the concept of the ethos of the school is the hidden curriculum. It has long been acknowledged that children learn things at school which are not planned by teachers as part of the overt curriculum, and values are perhaps particularly susceptible to being picked up in this way ('caught rather than taught'). Such learning might come from the peer group or from the example set by their teachers in their relationships, attitudes and teaching styles. However, even teaching by example is now being brought out into the open. The new Standards for the Award of Qualified Teacher Status (TTA, 1997) require evidence, among other things, that trainees 'set a good example to the pupils they teach, through their presentation and their personal and professional conduct'. Such requirements, combined with increasing general demands for public accountability, are forcing schools to articulate their underlying values more explicitly and to reflect on the way that the life of the school may contribute to the development of pupils' values.

Values education through curriculum

When values are developed through direct teaching, this necessarily involves the formal curriculum, i.e. the subjects of the National Curriculum, other compulsory or optional subjects and cross-curricular themes. The values which may be taught through the National Curriculum fall into two categories: those which are intrinsic to the subjects themselves, and those which, while not intrinsic, may be included in the teaching of the subjects. The teaching of the former is uncontroversial, but there is currently a debate between those who believe that opportunities must be taken to instil any moral lessons which can be drawn from the study of history or English literature, for example, and those who believe it is inauthentic to use such subjects as a vehicle for teaching moral or other values.

Religious education, on the other hand, has long been regarded as a major subject for the transmission of values, though too close a link between religion and morality should not be assumed. The contribution of religious education is perhaps best seen in terms of the opportunities it provides for discussion and reflection on questions of meaning and purpose and on the nature of beliefs and values. Values are clearly at the heart of personal and social education (PSE). Where it is a timetabled subject, it is likely to cover topics such as study skills, life skills, conflict resolution, human rights education, controversial issues, family life and personal relationships and responsibilities, as well as the cross-curricular themes of economic and industrial understanding, careers education and guidance, environmental education, health education and citizenship.

Methods of values education

While many methods are used for values education in schools, one in particular, *circle time*, has enjoyed remarkable growth in primary schools in Britain over the last ten years. This has often had as its overt goal the development of social skills and self-esteem, but teachers are increasingly recognising its potential for values development generally. Discussion-based approaches and other student-centred active learning strategies are also common, though Taylor (1994a, p 52) points out that more experiential and less didactic teaching and learning approaches may be associated in pupils' eyes with low-status studies.

Other methods for values education include drama, project work, practical activities, co-operative learning and group work, pupil-directed research, philosophy for children, peer mediation, role play, simulation exercises, educational games and theme-days. Explicit teaching and learning methods make up only part of a school's provision, however, and, as we have seen, the implicit values education which derives from the teacher as exemplar or from other aspects of the hidden curriculum must not be underestimated.

Assessment, evaluation and inspection

The assessment of change in pupils' values in a school context is both controversial and problematic, and many teachers have understandably been less than enthusiastic about it. Assessment may be considered narrowly in terms of tests and measurements or more broadly in terms of monitoring and evaluation. Teachers continuously make judgements of the latter kind about pupils' personal qualities, attitudes and behaviour and build up a picture of the individual pupil as a person. They become aware of change and development through this kind of informal evaluation, but formalising such assessments of attitudes and values (for example, in school reports) is more problematic.

OFSTED inspections review school effectiveness and the quality of education. Difficulties in assessing pupil outcomes in the values domain have led inspectors to focus on evaluating school provision for pupils' spiritual, moral, social and cultural development. Inspections also consider pupils' attitudes, behaviour and personal development, as demonstrated by attitudes to learning, behaviour, quality of relationships and contribution to community life (OFSTED, 1994). Evidence includes analysis of school aims, policies and values statements; scrutiny of work schemes, resources, cross-curricular audit; and discussion with heads, governors, parents, teachers, other adults and pupils. Observation has to cover personal and social education, religious education, values issues in curriculum subjects, school life, assembly, extra-curricular activities, the 'teachable moment', and also less tangible issues like relationships, expectations, welfare and caring, responsibility, consistency of application of the school's values, and coherence of experience. Some insight into how inspectors approach these tasks in practice is provided by Ungoed-Thomas (1994).

It is clear that inspectors face several challenges. First, there is the problem of defining terms so that schools have a shared understanding of precisely what is being inspected; at the same time, the temptation must be avoided of defining the spiritual, moral, social and cultural in measurable terms simply for the convenience of inspection. Second, there is the problem of ensuring that schools are treated fairly; not all schools start from the same base line, and it is possible that a school may not always get credit for what it achieves against the odds. Third, it is difficult to establish links between the educational provision of a school and changes in attitudes, values, beliefs and behaviour on the part of the student. This is because students will inevitably be subject to other social influences in addition to those of the school. Fourth, it seems ethically questionable to make formal judgements about the personal development of students at all, let alone in order to evaluate a school's educational provision (Merttens, 1996). In spite of these challenges, however, it is clear that the work of inspectors in this area has had a very significant influence on the recent upsurge of interest in values education.

B9 Note on tolerance and neutrality

Tolerance comes high on the list of values which most schools in the West would claim to promote. It is usually presented as a core liberal value, and is often contrasted with the desire of religious believers (particularly Muslims) to impose the principles of their religion on society. Sometimes it is suggested that tolerance is not a strong enough value, and that schools should be encouraging pupils to *celebrate* diversity, not just to *tolerate* it.

I am going to suggest that these claims are muddled, and in particular that:

- liberalism is not a particularly tolerant ideology, though it is neutral about many aspects of life on which other ideologies take a stand;
- religious belief provides a suitable context in which tolerance can be nurtured;
- the celebration of diversity has nothing to do with the principle of tolerance; and
- the widespread muddled thinking about tolerance, neutrality and impartiality lies behind the growth of moral and cultural relativism in recent years.

We need to start by clarifying some of the key concepts. 'Tolerance' implies a deliberate choice not to interfere with beliefs, actions or states of affairs of which one disapproves. It involves recognising the right of individuals to hold and pursue their own beliefs, and is thus linked to the fundamental values of freedom and respect for persons. 'Neutrality' means avoiding taking sides, avoiding any presupposition of the superiority of one belief or mode of life over another; it differs from 'tolerance' in that it implies no necessary dislike or disapproval. The 'celebration of diversity' is often presented as a more positive attitude to cultural and religious differences than mere tolerance, as if there is a continuum with intolerance at one end, tolerance in the middle and the celebration of diversity at the other end. But of course this does not make sense. What tolerance and intolerance have in common is a response to beliefs or conduct which are disliked or disapproved of, but the celebration of diversity does not share this common feature and therefore does not belong on the same continuum. To make a deliberate choice not to interfere with conduct of which one disapproves is quite rational, but to 'celebrate' such conduct would require a schizophrenic personality. The celebration of diversity clearly has something in common with neutrality, not with toleration. Without diversity, the exercise of personal autonomy (a central liberal value) would be restricted because people would not have a range of options from which to choose. Liberalism is neutral with regard to the different modes of life which are open to those committed to fundamental liberal values, and the fact that there *are* different modes of life is a matter for celebration because without them autonomy would not thrive.

Liberals often claim that liberalism is more tolerant than any other ideology, but how tolerant *is* liberalism? As already implied, there may be many different modes of life and conceptions of the good that are compatible with the fundamental values of liberalism, and the response of liberalism to this diversity within its boundaries is one of neutrality rather than tolerance. It does not side with any substantive view of the good life. Liberalism is thus a pluralist philosophy in the sense that it welcomes all those who share its basic values, irrespective of their religious beliefs, sexual orientations, cultural commitments and the like. But when it comes to beliefs and values that lie outside the fundamental liberal framework, the response is quite different. Fitzmaurice (in Horton, 1993), for example, argues that liberalism has good grounds to promote the liberal value of autonomy in the public sphere even in the face of opposition from non-liberals and that it cannot therefore adopt a position of even procedural neutrality towards world views which do not support autonomy. Raz (1986, p 424) conceives of circumstances where the compulsory assimilation of non-liberals into a liberal worldview - by force if necessary - may be 'the only humane course'. To sum up, liberalism is neutral, rather than tolerant, towards those diverse ways of life and conceptions of the good that are found within its boundaries and appears intolerant towards those outside. A better example of one ideology tolerating those outside its own framework of values is found in the 'millet' system of the Islamic Ottoman Empire which allowed full freedom to Jewish and Christian minorities to organise the life of their own communities in accordance with their own beliefs and practices (Halstead, 1995, p 264).

Where liberal tolerance is found most clearly is among individual liberals. The response of one liberal to another maintaining a different mode of life or a different conception of the good must be one of tolerance rather than neutrality. Having actually chosen one mode of life in preference to others, the individual liberal cannot at the same time claim to be personally neutral, but her tolerance is seen in her conscious choice not to interfere with the beliefs and practices of those who have chosen differently. Thus a liberal who is a pro-life campaigner should accept the right of a fellow liberal to support the pro-choice lobby, and the vegetarian liberal should tolerate fellow liberals who eat meat. It is worth noting that it is where there are strong convictions that there is most need for tolerance; indifference is not a sign of tolerance, but a sign that there is no need for it.

Tolerance at an individual level needs to be learned, and it is here that the school has an important role to play. Schools can encourage children to reflect on the need for tolerance in any given circumstances, and can also help them to develop a tolerant disposition. This quality of character does not imply moral indifference, uncertainty or apathy. On the contrary, it is perhaps best understood as grounded in two strong moral convictions: first, disapproval of a belief or practice; and second, the belief that since we are prone to make mistakes ourselves, we must be tolerant of those made by others. On this view, a tolerant disposition presupposes a clear understanding of right and wrong *and* an acknowledgement of human imperfectibility. It certainly need not imply the lack of certainty or the commitment to moral relativism which are now so widespread in our schools.

For a more conventional liberal interpretation of tolerance, see Horton (1993) and Haydon (1997).

Readers

You will find helpful 3.2, 3.3, 7.2, 8.2 and 11.2 among other sections in L.J. Francis and A. Thatcher (eds) (1990), *Christian Perspectives for Education*, Leominster, Gracewing. Similarly parts of section 2 and 3.2 in L.J. Francis and D.W. Lankshear (eds), *Christian Perspectives on Church Schools*, Leominster, Gracewing, deal with various aspects of values.

Bibliography

Airasian, P.W. and Walsh, M.E. (1997), Constructivist cautions, *Phi Delta Kappan*, 78, 444-449.

Aronowitz, S. and Giroux, H.A. (1991), *Postmodern Education: politics, culture and social criticism*, Minneapolis, Minnesota, University of Minneapolis Press.

Barrow, R. (1976), *Common Sense and the Curriculum*, London, Allen and Unwin.

Beck, C. (1990), *Better Schools: a values perspective*, Lewes, Falmer Press.

Belenky, M.F., Clinchy, B.M., Goldberger, N.R. and Tarule, J.M. (1986), *Women's Ways of Knowing*, New York, Basic Books.

Berger, P. and Luckmann, T. (1967), *The Social Construction of Reality*, London, Penguin.

Bernstein, B. (1977), *Class, Codes and Control*, Volume 3, London, Routledge and Kegan Paul.

Best, D. (1996), Values in the arts, in J.M. Halstead and M.J. Taylor (eds), *Values in Education and Education in Values*, London, Falmer Press, pp 79-91.

Bishop, A. (1991), *Mathematical Enculturation: a cultural perspective on mathematics education*, Dordrecht, Holland, Kluwer.

Bishop, A. (1993), Culturizing mathematics teaching, in A. King and M. Reiss (eds), *The Multicultural Dimension of the National Curriculum*, London, Falmer Press, pp 32-48.

Blatt, M.M. and Kohlberg, L. (1975), The effects of classroom moral discussion upon children's level of moral judgement, *Journal of Moral Education*, 4, 129-161.

Carr, D. (1991), *Educating the Virtues*, London, Routledge.

Carr, W. (1995), *For Education: towards critical educational enquiry*, Buckingham, Open University Press.

Ernest, P. (ed.) (1994), *Constructing Mathematical Knowledge: epistemology and mathematics education*, London, Falmer Press.

Fishkin, J.S. (1984), *Beyond Subjective Morality: ethical reasoning and political philosophy*, New Haven, Yale University Press.

Gilligan, C. (1982), *In Another Voice*, Cambridge, Massachusetts, Harvard University Press.

Graham, G. (1994), Liberal vs radical feminism revisited, *Journal of Applied Philosophy*, 11, 155-170.

Halstead, J.M. (1995), Voluntary apartheid? Problems of schooling for religious and other minorities in democratic societies, *Journal of Philosophy of Education*, 29, 257-272.

Halstead, J.M. (1996a), Values and values education in schools, in J.M. Halstead and M.J. Taylor (eds), *Values in Education and Education in Values*, London, Falmer Press, pp 3-14.

Halstead, J.M. (1996b), Liberal values and liberal education, in J.M. Halstead and M.J. Taylor (eds), *Values in Education and Education in Values*, London, Falmer Press, pp 17-32.

Halstead, J.M. (1998), Values and sex education in a multicultural society, *Muslim Education Quarterly*, 15 (2), in press.

Halstead, J.M. and Lewicka, K. (1998), 'Should homosexuality be taught as an acceptable alternative lifestyle? a Muslim perspective, *Cambridge Journal of Education*, 28 (2), 49-64.

Halstead, J.M. and Taylor, M.J. (eds) (1996), *Values in Education and Education in Values*, London, Falmer Press.

Halstead, J.M. and Taylor, M.J. (1998), *The Development of Values, Attitudes and Personal Qualities*, London, OFSTED.

Hampshire, S. (ed.) (1978), *Public and Private Morality*, Cambridge, Cambridge University Press.

Hart, H.L.A. (1961), *The Concept of Law*, Oxford, Clarendon Press.

Harris, K. (1979), *Education and Knowledge*, London, Routledge and Kegan Paul.

Haydon, G. (1997), *Teaching about Values: a new approach*, London, Cassell.

Hirsch, E.D. (1988), *Cultural Literacy: what every American needs to know*, New York, Vintage Books.

Hirst, P.H. (1974), *Knowledge and the Curriculum*, London, Routledge and Kegan Paul.

Hirst, P.H. (1993), Education, knowledge and practices, in R. Barrow and P. White (eds), *Beyond Liberal Education: essays in honour of Paul H. Hirst*, London, Routledge, pp 184-197.

Horton, J. (ed.) (1993), *Liberalism, Multiculturalism and Toleration*, London, Macmillan.

Jackson, M. (1987), Making sense of school, in A. Pollard (ed.), *Children and their Primary Schools: a new perspective*, London, Falmer Press, pp 74-87.

Jarrett, J.L. (1991), *The Teaching of Values: caring and appreciation*, London, Routledge.

John-Steiner, V. and Mahn, H. (1996), Sociocultural approaches to learning and development: a Vygotskyan framework, *Educational Psychologist*, 31, 191-206.

Kilpatrick, W. (1992), *Why Johnny Can't Tell Right from Wrong: and what we can do about it*, New York, Touchstone/Simon and Schuster.

Kleinig, J. (1982), *Philosophical Issues in Education*, London, Croom Helm.

Kohlberg, L. (1981, 1984), *Essays on Moral Development, Vols 1 and 2*, San Fransisco, Harper and Row.

Kohlberg, L. and Higgins, A. (1987), School democracy and social interaction, in W.M. Kurtines and J.L. Gewirtz, (eds), *Moral Development through Social Interaction*, New York, John Wiley and Sons, pp 102-128.

Lenderyou, G. and Porter, M. (1994), *Sex Education, Values and Morality*, London, Health Education Authority.

Lerman, S. (1994), Articulating theories of mathematics learning, in P. Ernest (ed.), *Constructing Mathematical Knowledge: epistemology and mathematics education*, London, Falmer Press, pp 41-49.

Lickona, T. (1991), *Educating for Character: how our schools can teach respect and responsibility*, New York, Bantam Books.

McLaughlin, T.H. (1994), Values, coherence and the school, *Cambridge Journal of Education*, 24, 253-270.

Marfleet, A. (1996), School mission statements and parental perceptions, in J.M. Halstead and M.J. Taylor (eds), *Values in Education and Education in Values*, London, Falmer Press, pp 155-166.

Matthews, M. (1980), *The Marxist Theory of Schooling*, London, Routledge and Kegan Paul.

Mercer, N. (1995), *The Guided Construction of Knowledge: talk amongst teachers and learners*, Clevedon, Multilingual Matters.

Merttens, R. (1996), Assessing children's personal development: the ethical implications, in J.M. Halstead and M.J. Taylor (eds), *Values in Education and Education in Values*, London, Falmer Press, pp 191-202.

National Curriculum Council (1990), *Education for Citizenship* (Curriculum Guidance 8), York, NCC.

Noddings, N. (1984), *Caring: a feminine approach to ethics and moral education* , Berkeley, California, University of California Press.

Oakeshott, M. (1967), Learning and teaching, in R.S. Peters (ed.), *The Concept of Education*, London, Routledge and Kegan Paul, pp 156-176.

Office for Standards in Education (1994), *Handbook for the Inspection of Schools (Consolidated Edition)*, London, OFSTED.

Phenix, P. (1964), *Realms of Meaning: a philosophy of the curriculum for general education*, New York, McGraw Hill.

Piaget, J. (1977), *The Principles of Genetic Epistemology*, London, Routledge and Kegan Paul.

Pring, R. (1976), *Knowledge and Schooling*, London, Open Books.

Quality and Curriculum Authority (1997), *The Promotion of Pupils' Spiritual, Moral, Social and Cultural Development: draft guidance for pilot work*, London, QCA.

Raths, L.E., Harmin, M. and Simon, S.B. (1966), *Values and Teaching: working with values in the classroom*, Columbus, Ohio, Charles E. Merrill.

Raz, J. (1986), *The Morality of Freedom*, Oxford, Clarendon Press.

Rowland, S. (1987), Child in control: towards an interpretive model of teaching and learning, in A. Pollard (ed.), *Children and their Primary Schools: a new perspective*, London, Falmer Press, pp 121-132.

Rutter, M., Maughan, B., Mortimore, P. and Ouston, J. (1979), *Fifteen Thousand Hours: secondary schools and their effects on children*, London, Open Books.

Schools Council/Nuffield Humanities Project (1970), *The Humanities Project: an introduction*, London, Heinemann.

School Curriculum and Assessment Authority (1995), *Spiritual and Moral Development: a discussion paper*, London, SCAA.

Searle, J.R. (1995), *The Construction of Social Reality*, London, Penguin.

Simon, S.B., Howe, L.W. and Kirschenbaum, H. (1972), *Values Clarification: a handbook of practical strategies for teachers and students*, New York, Hart.

Smith, E. (1994), Mathematics, computers and people: individual and social perspectives, in P. Ernest (ed.), *Constructing Mathematical Knowledge: epistemology and mathematics education*, London, Falmer Press, pp 73-91.

Smith, J.C. and Hogan, B. (1993), *Criminal Law: cases and materials* (fifth edition), London, Butterworths.

Starkings, D. (ed.) (1993), *Religion and the Arts in Education: dimensions of spirituality*, Sevenoaks, Hodder and Stoughton.

Steffe, L.P. and Tzur, R. (1994), Interaction and children's mathematics, in P. Ernest (ed.), *Constructing Mathematical Knowledge: epistemology and mathematics education*, London, Falmer Press, pp 8-32.

Talbot, M. (1998), Against relativism, in J.M. Halstead and T.H. McLaughlin (eds), *Education in Morality*, London, Routledge.

Talbot, M. and Tate, N. (1997), Shared values in a pluralist society? in R. Smith and P. Standish (eds), *Teaching Right and Wrong: moral education in the balance*, Stoke-on-Trent, Trentham Books, pp 1-14.

Taylor, M.J. (1994a), *Values Education in Europe: a comparative overview of a survey of 26 countries in 1993*, Dundee, CIDREE/UNESCO.

Taylor, M.J. (1994b), *Values Education in the UK: a directory of research and resources*, Slough, National Foundation for Educational Research.

Taylor, M.J. and Lines, A. (1998), *Values Education in Primary and Secondary Schools*, Slough, National Foundation for Educational Research.

Teacher Training Agency (1997), *Standards for the Award of Qualified Teacher Status*, London, TTA.

Thatcher, A. (1993), *Liberating Sex: a Christian sexual theology*, London, SPCK.

Thomas, R.S.D. (1994), Radical constructive criticisms of von Glasersfeld's radical constructivism, in P. Ernest (ed.), *Constructing Mathematical Knowledge: epistemology and mathematics education*, London, Falmer Press, pp 33-40.

Ungoed-Thomas, J. (1994), Inspecting spiritual, moral, social and cultural development, *Pastoral Care*, 12 (4), 21-25.

von Glasersfeld, E. (1995), A constructivist approach to teaching, in L.P. Steffe and J. Gale (eds), *Constructivism in Education*, Hillsdale, New Jersey, Erlbaum, pp 3-15.

Vygotsky, L.S. (1962), *Thought and Language*, Cambridge, Massachusetts, MIT Press.

Vygotsky, L.S. (1978), *Mind in Society*, Cambridge, Massachusetts, Harvard University Press.

Wertsch, J.V. (1985), *Vygotsky and the Social Formation of Mind*, Cambridge, Massachusetts, Harvard University Press.

White, J.P. (1973), *Towards a Compulsory Curriculum*, London, Routledge and Kegan Paul.

Christian Values and the Curriculum

Unit C

Christian values in the educational process

Gaynor Pollard

University College

Chester

Contents

Introduction

Aims

After working through this unit you should be able to:

- relate Christian doctrine to Christian values;
- relate Christian values to secular values;
- locate the place of values within the curriculum;
- analyse the place of values within the educational process.

Overview

Unit A of this module considered patterns and models of the curriculum. Unit B considered the nature of values and their description. This unit shows how values may be applied within the educational process, both in the curriculum and in the human relationships that schools necessarily embody. It is quite clear that schools bear the expectation of society that 'they are failing in their social duty if they do not promote schooling as a force for conformity to established values and behaviours' (Best, 1996, p3). The role of church schools in this area is to reflect upon established values and behaviours and to provide a Christian alternative if necessary. The purpose of this unit is to examine the role of Christian theology in values education and its application to the situation of the school.

We begin with a consideration of some important themes in Christian theology: a consideration of what it means to be a person, an examination of the Trinity and Christian attitudes towards the world. Section C2 is a reflection on the identification of distinctively Christian values, and the ways in which a school might formulate its aims in this area. Section C3 is an overview of Christian values across the whole curriculum, dealing with specific subject content. Section C4 contains a discussion of methods of analysis of values in the curriculum and the ethos of the school (see Shepherd, 1998). It also briefly considers the formation of values through socialisation.

C1 Christian theology and values

Schools face the challenge of promoting a set of values that will command a broad consensus, both within the school, but also in the local and wider society. As mentioned in the previous unit, they are assisted in this task by advice from the National Forum for Values in Education, and these values carry within them an implicit understanding that educational establishments functioning in a liberal democracy cannot be permitted to impose what are known as 'thick' views of values on their pupils. 'Thick' views might be understood as systems of belief and values that must be accepted in their entirety, without debate. In contrast, 'thin' views are regarded as appropriate to education, because they are attempts to present values in such a way that all people of goodwill might accept them (McLaughlin, 1996, pp 14-15).

For Church of England schools, the task of identifying and applying values that are appropriate to the foundation of the school is made both easier and also more difficult by the existence of a body of Christian belief and practice to which they may refer. It is easier because the tradition provides access to wisdom and revelation which can inform school practice, but also more difficult because the Christian tradition can present a challenge to the expectations of parents, society and government. We may recognise the inevitability of this by noticing that the Church of England, whilst regarding itself as Catholic and reformed, also stands firmly within the Protestant tradition. It therefore has a history and a present duty to protest, and to challenge the existing order when that order is perceived to be working against Christian values. An example of this might be in relation to those elements of our present climate which value educational success simply because it is a means to economic prosperity. Applying Christian values to the curriculum might mean providing a challenge to this philosophy when it clashes with the Christian belief that everybody is equally valued by God, even those who appear to make no economic contribution to society. In practice this might mean that a Church of England school may choose to pay particular attention to pupils with special educational needs, even when such a policy may result in a lower position in league tables.

Christian values are brought into play when individual policies are being considered, but also play a large part in forming the underlying assumptions that shape the educational philosophy and aims of individual teachers and the school as a whole.

In this section our reflection is organised into Christian theologies about:

- human nature;
- the God who is three-in-one;
- the world.

Human nature

The importance of Christian theology for education in values can be illustrated by a consideration of what it means to be human. Faced with a few hundred faces at assembly on a Monday morning, we might be tempted to ask the question: what kind of animal do I see before me? Are human beings indeed creatures, or are we random accidents in a morally neutral universe? Were we designed to be the way we are? Is it our nature to be basically evil or intrinsically good? Do we have free will to choose our destinies, or are the efforts of teachers superfluous, and is character already determined in the collections of DNA that sit in front of us? In terms of education for values the important issues are whether we encourage pupils to nurture the essential goodness of their nature, and to express that nature in action, or whether, instead, we convince them of the irredeemable fallenness of their characters, which may only be transformed by the grace of God.

These mutually exclusive beliefs have been articulated in the course of church history. The view that human beings are fallen, that their sin is of such seriousness and depravity that only the saving act of God in Christ can bring them to heaven, has been read from the epistle to the Romans and is prominent in the writing of Augustine[1]. Luther, who knew Augustine's writings intimately, even wrote a book, *The Bondage of the Will*, arguing that, so far as pleasing God was concerned, the human will was bound by sin and irretrievably bent towards wickedness[2]. Calvin, likewise, argued that human beings are so sinful that their efforts at performing righteous acts are flawed[3].

The alternative position, that human beings are made in the image of God and, despite their sinfulness, contain a vestige of original goodness has been advanced both by Pelagius (a British monk heavily criticised by Augustine[4]) and Erasmus[5] (a reformer heavily criticised by Luther). Orthodoxy has been firmly within the Augustinian, Lutheran and Calvinist frameworks, as a glance at the Thirty-Nine Articles or the Westminster Confession will show. In recent years, however, the Roman Catholic theologian Karl Rahner[6], among others, has revived the argument and attempted to re-balance theological opinion in favour of a more Pelagian and Erasmian position.

For the purposes of a school community it is as well to be aware that these fundamental differences exist, and to take advantage of the Anglican way of allowing and even encouraging a variety of standpoints to enrich the community, and to act as necessary correctives to each other. A teacher who wholeheartedly believes that the child is essentially good may be rather naive in dealing with pupils whose activities may well be criminal, whereas a teacher who sees the natural capacity for evil in each child may enforce a discipline that is harsh and unforgiving.

---

[1] E.g. in *The Treatise on Nature and Grace*, chapter 2.

[2] Similar views are expressed in Luther's *Smaller Catechism*.

[3] E.g. in book 3 of Calvin's *Institutes of the Christian Religion*.

[4] E.g. in his *Treatise on the Proceedings of Pelagius*.

[5] See R. Bainton, *Erasmus of Christendom* (London, Collins, 1970).

[6] Within his massive *Theological Investigations* (London, Darton, Longman and Todd, 1974).

Adrian Thatcher (1990) makes the case for Christian theology as a provider of resources for fulfilling the educational aim of learning to become a person. He begins, as Christians must, with the person of Jesus Christ, as the only authentic expression of what it means to be a person. He explains that the important feature of this argument is not the claim that Jesus was a full member of the human race, a debate that took up a lot of time and energy in the early church, but that '. . . in Jesus Christians claim to see what true humanness is, and what true personhood means' (Thatcher, 1990, p 75). Such a point of view is not without its difficulties, and Thatcher identifies two of them: first, that we are ignorant of much of the detail of the life of Jesus and, second, that we are unfamiliar with much of the culture of the first century. Despite these, Thatcher makes a case that we can draw on knowledge about the person of Christ, from history and also from the experiences of the church, contemporary as well as historical. He anticipates the criticism that the life and influence of Christ is no longer relevant to a largely secular society, but argues that our system of education has not been formed in a values vacuum, and much of what passes for secular values are drawn from the Christian tradition.

What does it mean to say that Jesus Christ shows us what it means to be truly human and truly a person? It means among other things that it is possible to integrate the spiritual, emotional, rational, moral and social sides of our being so that the spiritual does not prevent the emotional (Christ felt deep emotion) and the emotional does not rule out the rational (Christ spoke reasonably even when he stood before Pilate) while retaining his moral integrity. And these aspects of Christ's person allowed him to form social relationships (with the disciples, with Mary and Martha, for instance). Thus to 'achieve personhood' and to be 'truly human' is to achieve a rounded and harmonious character where all the powers and capacities in our being are drawn out.

In order to ground his thinking in the real world of the school curriculum, Thatcher applies some of these ideas to three very different areas: science, literature and physical education. In science he critiques a system of education which seems to direct its goals towards the supply of a good number of graduates to work in the arms industry, where it might be better employed in encouraging a sense of *reverence for all life*. In literature he deals with the area of poetry, stressing the importance of *self-expression, self-knowledge* and *empathy*, which are all critical in the business of learning how to become a person. In physical education he deals with the means through which respect for the whole person can be reached, and provides a training in *co-operation* and *self-expression*. All the italicised words are key values within the Christian faith. In considering love as a central value for educators Thatcher (1990, p 81) concludes:

The sort of love which it is appropriate to speak of in this context is the love which, for example, sees war as a sickness, nuclear weapons as unspeakable blasphemy, poverty as a crime, involuntary unemployment as a betrayal, and purely material values as the bankruptcy of spirit.

God who is three-in-one

The doctrine of the Trinity, recently and cogently examined and defended by Brown (1985), asserts the essential oneness and essential threeness of God. These assertions have sometimes been weighted towards oneness, as in the case of Augustine and at other times, as in the case of Gregory of Nyssa, towards threeness. But, if threeness grows out of a fundamental oneness or oneness is found in a fundamental threeness, the result may lead in different directions. If the oneness is the starting point then there is a danger that the timeless and static unity within the Trinity will put God out of the reach of the human condition. At least that, according to Moltmann (1981) and Boff (1988), is the implication. Both these theologians have taken the threeness of God as their starting point and found in the eternal society of Persons grounds for reformulating Trinitarian doctrine. In recent times, they, as well as Hodgson (1944), have argued for a 'social Trinity' which takes the social relations within the Trinity as the basis for a theoretical construct that determines an overall concept of God (Gresham, 1993). Used in this way the social Trinity becomes much more than an illustration. According to Gresham (1993, p 337) the social Trinity:

> envisions divine unity as a dynamic loving community of persons and the psychological analogy roots that community of persons within one divine being.

In the hands of the Brazilian Leonardo Boff it is important to pass from the logical mystery of the Trinity to the 'saving mystery' of the Trinity. In our struggles against oppression and injustice, we are not alone. Rather, 'we are called to enter into communion with the Trinity' in the knowledge that society is not permanently set in unjust and unequal power relations but is 'summoned to transform itself in the light of the open and egalitarian relationships that obtain in the communion of the Trinity' (Boff, 1988, p 157).

We may put this another way by saying that the social Trinity speaks not only of loving relationships between the persons of the Trinity but also of the saving purposes of God. The Father sends the Son to save, to redeem, to carry out a mission of justice. Thus the Trinity is viewed in Christian theology as the source of all interpersonal relationships and also as the source of all justice, for justice is to be found not only in the equitable distribution of material possessions but in perfect equality and perfect love between equal beings.

Moreover, the Trinity draws attention to the concept of personhood. If human beings are made in the image of a Trinitarian God, this tells us about what human beings should be, can be, and essentially are. A reflection on how the Trinity operates should be instructive in deciding on the values that might be encouraged in young people and children. Jurgen Moltmann (1981, p 75) points out one way God differentiates himself from himself[7]:

- the Father sends the Son through the Spirit;
- the Son comes from the Father in the power of the Spirit;
- the Spirit brings people into the fellowship of the Son with the Father.

The image is that of activity: sending, coming and bringing are central in this definition of the Trinity and therefore to an understanding of all persons. Others claim that God has no ontological content, no true being apart from communion (Zizioulas, 1993, p 17), which implies the necessity of relationships in the formation of human personhood.

This thought is taken up by LaCugna who underlines the importance of the relationality of the Trinity, stressing that the existence of humankind and of the world is a product of God's self-communication which therefore puts human beings in a relationship of fundamental dependence. God relates, not just within the Trinity, but pours out this relationship within the acts of creation, redemption and consummation (LaCugna, 1991, p 103). In turn there is an imperative for human beings to do the same, to express their personhood in relationships with others. This is a dynamic process rather than a static state and has less to do with observing and practising a list of virtues than perceiving the verbs that translate them into action. For instance, it might be appropriate sometimes to avoid speaking of 'values' and begin instead to practise 'valuing'. This area has been explored by the British theologian Mary Grey, who contrasts a method of learning that involves 'the memorising and reproduction of authorised words' with that of 'creative appropriation' (Grey, 1993, p 24). Grey produces what might result in a useful checklist for schools who would like to embark upon the process of 'creative appropriation' with their pupils. Grey (1993, p 130) introduces what she terms 'verbs of connection':

> hearing, listening, responding, communing, reaching out and touching, by the mutuality of committing, cherishing, remembering and healing.

The insights that might be gained from Christian theology in this instance are that God constitutes a Being-in-Relation, and those who wish to bring children and young people into fuller personhood should begin with the active and dynamic, rather than constructing a list of desirable qualities or values and pointing towards them for the pupils to appropriate in a passive way. Values

---

[7] Moltmann's view is of a divine society of distinct persons with one purpose. This is the model to be emulated by other societies, ecclesiastical, social, political. The point is that Moltmann rejects a monarchical Trinity where the Father commands, but embraces a co-operative society where each person delights to do the will of the other.

education then becomes less of an academic study and more an action plan for creative change in individuals and in society.

The world

Concern about the environment, although high on the list of issues that trouble young people (Francis and Kay, 1995, pp 69-81), has been slow to come to the forefront of Christian theological concern, despite the basic and long-standing belief that God is the uncreated creator. One reason for this has been a widely held presumption that this world is a temporary state of affairs, a proving ground for the life to come, which will culminate at the second coming of Christ and a new heaven and a new earth. At its worst these theological beliefs result in a notion that the present world may be exploited and used without any concern for sustainability. The exploitation of the world results in a theology of *dominion* taken from the passage in Genesis 1.26 where human beings are given control or dominion over the earth. The alternative position is found in a theology of *stewardship* where human beings are told to look after, cultivate and preserve the earth, and this is taken from Genesis 2.15.

A theology of dominion may well lead to industrialisation, pollution, and a sense that the world is a resource to be endlessly plundered and mined without any concern for its expendability. Such a theology has been attacked by White (1967) in a seminal paper which laid the blame for environmental problems firmly at the door of the kind of science and technology inspired by Christianity. A theology of stewardship, on the other hand, leads to a concern to preserve the world without, at the same time, treating the world as semi-divine or conscious or naturalistically holy.

Mainstream Christian theology has been nervous of the connection between environmentalism and New Age religion. Nevertheless 'green theology' in its various forms is now established as an important area for values. These values may all coincide though, depending on the shade of greenness of the theology, the justification for them will vary. The least controversial kind of green theology develops the stewardship notion outlined above and this has the advantage of making a clear distinction between human beings who have an obviously dominant and yet protective role towards the natural world and the natural world itself. In other words, a theology of stewardship does not produce a belief that the natural world is an object of worship and a living organism along the lines advocated by the Gaia hypothesis (Lovelock, 1988).

The principles put forward by the National Forum for Values in Education in 1996 are certainly compatible with a stewardship theology of the environment. The suggested principles for action to be considered by all schools included:

- preserving balance and diversity in nature wherever possible;
- accepting our responsibility to maintain a sustainable environment for future generations;
- ensuring that development can be justified;
- repairing habitats which have been damaged by human development and other means wherever possible;
- preserving areas of beauty and interest for future generations wherever possible;
- understanding the place of human beings within nature;
- understanding our responsibilities for other species.

The emphasis in these principles is on taking care of the earth and ensuring its present bio-diversity. In Christian theology this theme has been taken forward by Sallie McFague, who widens the scope of the perspective to take in concern for God and humanity as well as the natural world. The relationship between God and the world is viewed in the light of the model of God as the spirit of the body. In this model the universe becomes the Body of Christ, and anything we do to this body, we do to God (McFague, 1993, p 191).

One of the problems with McFague's view is that it advances the notion that God's mind can exist without God's body since the universe had a beginning in time but God did not[8]. To this extent, then, her view is only to be seen as an illustration or analogy of the relationship between God and world. Certainly there are theological reasons for treating the material world as an object of great value without resorting to this sort of reasoning, as Osborn (1993) points out. Moreover, the traditional doctrine implies with great force the *creaturely* and therefore relational nature of human beings. A creaturely being is one by definition related to a Creator, and the Trinity of Persons within the Creator implies the possibility of separate and yet non-contradictory relationships with the different Persons. But a creaturely being is one that may, through the potential relationship with Creator, also relate to other creatures.

In a later work McFague argues that the contemporary view of spirituality has encouraged a privatisation of belief, where spirituality is regarded as the opposite of ethics, and religious belief does not translate into ethical action. Instead of being a private sphere of self-improvement spirituality should be seen as a preparation for action (McFague, 1997, p 10). Such attitudes must include generosity towards the natural world, towards what Leonardo Boff calls 'social ecology' (Boff, 1995, p 88).

---

[8] Polkinghorne, J (1998, p 57) also points out a further difficulty, 'to put the matter bluntly, if the world is God's body, where is God's nervous system within it?', that is, how does God make it obedient in the way that a body is obedient to the brain.

McFague finds her justification for urging this worldview amongst Christians, not just in the integrity of the natural world itself, but in the life of Jesus, understood to be the incarnate God who is bodily and physical, just as the material world is bodily and physical. In addition, the biblical narratives of the ministry of Jesus show his concern for the healing of the human body, which again serves to underline the concern of God for the real, practical, physical everyday world (McFague, 1997, pp 14-15). Moreover, even the Old Testament perspective supports this view by showing King Solomon, famous for his wisdom, as an expert on plant life (1 Kings 4.33).

McFague is clear that this perspective must be recovered for young children, and she critiques the lack of direct experience of the natural world available to them. The methodologies she suggests include paying attention to the natural world, in order to see its variety, its many differences, and using the media of 'paintings, poetry, novels, sculpture, dance, music to help us to look at colours, sounds, bodies, events and characters with full attention' (McFague, 1997, pp 27-29). She characterises this method as learning to use the Loving Eye rather than the Arrogant Eye. Solidarity with that which is different is achieved by abandoning the duality of characterising everything in oppositional terms, either 'for me' or 'against me', so that we stop asking how something might benefit us and begin instead to appreciate it for its own sake.

Activity C1

Construct an 'action plan' for the youngest children in your school, containing verbs of action, such as those suggested by Mary Grey above. Then devise some activities which might promote such action, available both in and outside the curriculum.

Comment on activity C1

If you chose three of Grey's suggestions you might have devised a programme that included some of the following elements.

First, you might have identified *cherishing*. Pupils might be given the responsibility of care of a living thing, either plant or animal, be encouraged to research how to care responsibly, and to report their experiences to the rest of the class.

Second, you might have identified *listening*. Listening to what is communicated means paying full attention. As well as the normal work that pupils undertake in English, they might also be encouraged to practise empathy by listening to the feelings behind the words, noticing body language, and be able to identify emotions expressed in their own communication and those of others.

Third, you might have identified *responding*. Responses may take many different forms, and pupils should be encouraged to take initiatives when they see a need. Sometimes this help will be practical, sometimes befriending, and sometimes they will need to be strong enough to refuse to respond when provoked or encouraged into wrongdoing.

C2 An understanding of Christian values

I have suggested that Christian values are derived from Christian theology and that therefore what is distinctive about Christian theology contributes to what is distinctive about Christian values. Of course, Christian values overlap with non-Christian values, and not all Christians would agree about which values should be called distinctively Christian. As Mark Halstead has pointed out in the previous unit, values can be seen as 'principles or fundamental convictions which act as general guides to behaviour or as points of reference in decision-making'. To clarify this further we can enquire into the kinds of values there are. What we find is that they may be classified according to their main focus of concern, whether family, religion, or health, for example, but since our behaviour affects other people (because none of us lives in isolation), it is *moral* values which are most basic. Indeed Halstead suggests that our other values derive from our moral values.

When we try to derive our moral values from Christian theology, we find that some values have both a theological and a moral weight. For instance, the values of forgiveness, reconciliation, truth and faithfulness could all be seen as at the heart of the New Testament account of God's dealings with humanity. In the sense that forgiveness is human and divine it is both theological and moral. To the extent that truth is intrinsic to the New Testament presentation of God (cf. John 1.14; 15.26) and that truth is essential to human relationships, the same applies. If we are looking for *distinctive* Christian values, then, we shall find them at the place where Christian theology and morality intersect.

It is for this reason that we have devoted space to a discussion of human nature, the Trinity and the environment. In all these areas Christianity is distinct. It would, however, be a lengthy and probably fruitless exercise to try to make a long list of distinctively Christian values and then to try to apply them systematically to the educational process. This is partly because we cannot simply read values from theology or even from Christian practice. But it is mainly because values relate to each other in networks and hierarchies and then have to be applied to situations. Some values are more central than others. Some values supersede other values. For example, Christians would agree that the value of being concerned for the poor and underprivileged is more central than the value of keeping *exactly* to the speed limits on motorways. Similarly the value of caring for one's children supersedes the value of attending church every Sunday: if children are ill, parents stay at home to look after them.

Moreover, it is also helpful to think of values as having a particular range so that some values are wider than others. The value of telling the truth, it may be argued, should apply in every and any situation and at all stages in life. The value of being careful not to steal-by-finding, while important, could be said to have its limits. If you found a penny on the pavement in the middle of London, should you take it to the nearest police station? Presumably not. Thus, while truthfulness can apply to everything we˙ do, stealing-by-finding is more circumscribed.

The problem of applying values to education is one of deciding which value applies most strongly to a situation. Is it better to care for the environment or to care for dyslexic children? Is it better to spend resources retaining fewer older and more costly staff on the payroll, or would more younger and less expensive staff benefit children's education more? These are dilemmas caused by conflicts in values, even Christian values. And this conflict, of course, becomes more acute when Christian values have to compete with the wider, but less obviously Christian values that inform our liberal democracy. Should the objections of a Jehovah's Witness family to the celebration of Christmas be allowed to interfere with the school's carol service? On the one hand, children have a right not to have their religious consciences infringed (as in the case of the Jehovah's Witness family). On the other hand, children have a right to enjoy a carol service which Christians might feel was also important *religiously*.

Although we are concerned in this section with distinctively Christian values, it is helpful to turn attention to values that are common to a variety of philosophical views. These values may not be central to Christianity, and they may not be high in the Christian hierarchy of values but, nevertheless, they are compatible with Christian values and may lead to them.

In *The Philosophy of Christian Religious Education* Jeff Astley (1994, pp 137-139) discusses the nature of Christianity and its relationship to Christian religious education. He tackles the question of defining Christianity in such a way that it might be of benefit to educational practice and points out that much Christian theology is concerned with an analysis of what it means to be in a right relationship with God through Jesus Christ. For Christians this relationship is central to questions of values and ethical thinking. Astley proceeds to examine a multidimensional approach to religion, which includes a consideration of the ultimate value questions that impinge on our understanding of human life. He gives an account of the attitude-virtues of the Canadian philosopher Donald Evans who identifies eight 'normative attitude-virtues'. These are: basic trust, humility, self-acceptance, responsibility, self-commitment, friendliness, concern and contemplation (Evans, 1979, p 186-187). Since Evans believes that these are necessary conditions for the discernment of the divine in religious experience (Evans, 1979, p 171), it could be claimed that the formation of these attitude-virtues, all of which would feel at home in a secular world-view, might be regarded as an educational *precondition* of the religious learner's having an experience of God.

This seems a promising seam of thinking to mine for some church schools who recognise that their position within the maintained sector prevents evangelism even though the communication of Christian beliefs is their duty according to their Trust Deed. Concentration on the nurture of attitude-values that can be shown to enable recognition of the divine leaves the educational task (the primary responsibility of the Church school) complete, and entrusts revelation to God. This is good education and good theology. In this scheme of things the attitudes and values themselves may not be regarded as distinctively Christian, but may serve at least to predispose pupils to consider the validity of Christian claims.

Christian values and mainstream thought

> Do not be conformed to this world but be transformed by the renewal of your mind, that you may prove what is the will of God, what is good and acceptable and perfect. (Romans 12.2)

A more difficult nettle to grasp is the inhospitability of the current philosophical climate towards those values that could be described as Christian. I have argued that Christian values derive from Christian theology, but have noted that Christian values may overlap with values that derive from other theological or non-theological positions. There is no difficulty when the overlap occurs. In one sense it does not matter whether people care about the environment because they do so from a Christian value base or from a Buddhist value base. The problem occurs when the values that derive from one intellectual position cut across the values that derive from another. The case of abortion is one where the rights of the child (or the foetus) are in conflict with the rights of the mother. The rights of the child are supported by a large range of theological considerations drawn from the importance of individuals to God, the obligation to care about the weak and defenceless, and many others. The rights of the mother are supported by a range of theological and secular considerations drawn from the importance of choice, of control over one's own body, and many others.

Where there is this collision between sets of values, the most common position taken by Christians is that they should use their rights within a democracy to argue their case without forcing others to accept it. They should seek to persuade rather than to coerce (Stott, 1999). They may demonstrate and protest, but they should not prevent others exercising their lawful rights.

In the field of education, conflicts between Christian and secular values can take place and some of these conflicts may concern the place of religion in schools. These conflicts are easier to resolve than others because they concern the compatibility of religion with education. Other conflicts, for instance those revolving round the rights of human beings or the kinds of beings human beings are, become complex.

This sort of conflict is illustrated by Jasper Ungoed-Thomas (1996, pp 121-136) in his essay 'Respect for persons: a curricular crisis of identities'. He makes the argument that schools may sometimes find it difficult to maintain their sense of personal authenticity as a result of attacks on the view that individuals have any moral worth. Despite the arguments of post-modern philosophers, Ungoed-Thomas argues that schools must always hold the view that pupils have the capacity to achieve wholeness, both intellectual and moral. Their strategy must include an acceptance that:

- persons are able to improve in ways generally agreed to be worthwhile;
- different ideals can emerge, and that these have to be treated as potentially worthy of respect;
- persons have, in however limited a way, the capacity and freedom to choose their own moral and intellectual destinies;
- the way persons develop is open to influence.

These starting-points for values education are compatible with Christian theologies of human nature mentioned earlier, especially since most Christian moralists hold fast to the notion of free will, in the sense that the New Testament command to repent (e.g. Acts 17.30) presumes the possibility of moral improvement. Ungoed-Thomas deals with the problem of relative, and therefore conflicting, values by suggesting that the school may provide a 'centred base from which they can explore de-centredness'. In other words, it is necessary to hold a set of basic values before it is possible to explore variations in value systems.

He discusses four types of ideals that have influenced western thinking: Christian, Classical, Rational and Humanist. The Christian view regards persons as capable of wrongdoing, so that fulfilment must first be found in sanctification, in a growth in holiness. The Classical view, drawn from the

Greeks, emphasises the destructive power of the emotions, and the ideal person will be one who can control or sublimate the worse passions, whilst strengthening the virtues. This can be achieved by subjugating everything to reason, thus achieving wisdom through a knowledge of the true and the good and eventually achieving excellence. The Rational model, heavily influenced by the philosopher Descartes, puts the emphasis on the autonomy of the person and the capacity for choice. For the Humanist a person is always good and free from sin and persons are perceived as those who gain knowledge and understanding through experimental behaviour, rather than reason or revelation. In the light of these competing paradigms Ungoed-Thomas suggests that headteachers and governors need to elucidate their own beliefs about what persons should become and that schools need to be able to identify where the curriculum is promoting particular ideas of a person. Ungoed-Thomas (1996, p 134) writes as follows:

> Within the general sense of direction given by a feeling of common purpose, a school should become a forum where contrasting ideals of a person are clarified, common ground discovered and differences respected.

Activity C2

The quotation from Romans 12.2 with which the previous section begins, contrasts conforming to the values of this world with being transformed by the renewal of minds. In what ways may a Church school plan for transformation?

Comment on activity C2

The first task of a school planning for 'transformation' is to decide what the transforming takes place from, and where the transforming should lead. This will involve some wide-ranging discussions amongst staff and pupils. There must be accommodation for a range of views if the exercise is not to prove counter-productive and result in fracturing relationships within the school.

The second task is to state openly, clearly and succinctly the expectations of the school, the processes by which these expectations are to be realised and the process which will be put in place in order to monitor the success of the policy. Many schools have already undertaken this journey in their work on ethos statements, mission statements and behaviour policies.

The third task is to ensure that the model of transformative personal development is present in all areas of the school's work, and that there is consistency in the way the values of the school are expressed and applied across the curriculum, not just in relationships, although these are, of course, critical, but also in the way subject content and skills work is chosen.

A school that undertakes this exercise will ensure that its claim that the life of the school is underpinned by Christian values will not just be employing empty rhetoric, and could prove to be a way in which a strong Christian ethos could be further strengthened.

C3 Christian values in the curriculum

This section has been designed to look at curriculum subject areas to explore values that are implicit within their:

- characteristic content;
- academic discipline.

Once this has been done the connection between subject areas and Christian values can be more easily drawn.

Core subjects

For example, in relation to *content* (see here and in later examples, DfE, 1995), the study of poetry at Key Stages 1 and 2 helps pupils begin to learn about the range of emotions that are part of human life. They may for the first time begin to understand the sense of loss felt when a living thing dies or the mysteriousness of meetings and partings. The content of English implies that emotion in all its variety is something to value. Walter de la Mare, much anthologised, illustrates some of these feelings:

> 'Is there anybody there?' said the Traveller,
> Knocking at the moonlit door;
> And his horse in the silence champed the grasses
> Of the forest's ferny floor...
> 'Tell them I came, and no-one answered,
> that I kept my word', he said.
> Never the least stir made the listeners,
> Though every word he spake
> Fell echoing through the shadowiness of the still house
> From the one man left awake. (Walter de la Mare, *The Listeners*)

In reading novels and plays the same possibilities are present. Whether pupils read *Kes* (Barry Hines), *The Silver Sword* (Ian Serraillier), or a Shakespeare play, human actions and motives are disentangled or symbolised. For instance, pupils may begin to appreciate the value of moral courage, loyalty or patience. In relation to values within the *academic discipline* of English, pupils begin to learn precision in the use of language, clarity of expression and how to order their thoughts into a coherent sequence.

Mathematics is like a language with which to explore the world. In relation to *content*, mathematics allows pupils to see connections between things in terms of size, shape, space and ratio. Simple bar graphs showing height within a class help pupils to appreciate how numbers are distributed around an average. Simple grids showing multiplication tables help pupils appreciate patterns within numerical arrays. The flexibility and fluidity of mathematics makes its content hard to pin down but, in terms of the *academic discipline*, it enables pupils to appreciate precision and the power of deductive reasoning. In arithmetic there is one, and only one, answer to the sum the teacher sets, and in solving mathematical problems logical deductions have to be followed to reach the solution.

The *content* of science education tends to follow the basic divisions between biology (including botany and zoology) and physics and mechanics. Within biological investigations pupils discover the relationship between living things and their habitats, the characteristics of living things, their response to stimuli, their methods of metabolism and reproduction and their typical life cycles. Within physical and mechanical investigations pupils begin to discover about electricity, magnetism, forces, optics, levers, weights, pulleys, balance, friction and flotation. The values implicit within the content of these explorations, some of which also use mathematics, suggest order, cause and effect and interrelationship. These are values in the sense that they can inform our convictions of how the world should be. The values implicit within the *academic disciplines* of science suggest the importance of evidence and observation.

History

The *content* of history within schools has been diversified so that it now no longer includes merely political and military history but takes note of social history. What interests children is how people lived then, not whether this king came to the throne in this year or ten years later. Historical epochs and events have been selected to illustrate general themes (like travel, trade, houses, diet or emigration) and these themes have been related to other parts of the curriculum. The *academic discipline* of history is concerned with evidence (what it is, how it is evaluated) and with understanding and interpreting change.

There are, however, implications for values in historical studies. Gavin Baldwin in his essay 'Modern spirituality, moral education and the history curriculum' concentrates on the possibilities and problems inherent in widening the curriculum to include those who are very different from ourselves. He identifies three possible responses to a social situation of increasing complexity: religious fundamentalism, relativism and Enlightenment rationalism. (Baldwin, 1996, p 208). He cites the case of Fundamentalist Islam, as a response that is reacting to the complicated, shrinking modern world. This response is one among many. Another is to embrace the moral nihilism of relativism and the partial account of reality that he believes rationalism provides. Instead he considers Liberalism – particularly in respect of the doctrine of utilitarianism which 'holds that actions are right in proportion as they promote happiness, wrong as they tend to promote the reverse of happiness' - as providing an account of why people ought to be good (cf. J S Mill's 1863 book *Utilitarianism*). He argues that the role of history in ethical enquiry can be analysed by considering the process of historical investigation, the content of the history curriculum and the role of the history teacher as moral agent (Baldwin, 1996, p 211). History involves exploring the operation of different moral codes and through this children's own moral choices will be given greater substance. By careful consideration of the difference between moral analysis and judgement they may be better equipped to understand the moral positions of others in conflict with their own (Baldwin, 1996, p 214).

Environmental studies

The *content* of environmental studies falls partly within geography and partly within the science curriculum. Its values concern the perpetuation of balance within the biosphere, and this will involve both a study of relations between animals and their food supply and the effect of climatic and human intervention on the system. The value of the *academic discipline* of environmental studies concerns those found in the sciences.

John Smyth (1996) does not advocate the promotion of fixed agendas for values education in this area. Instead he regards its main task as equipping people with the knowledge and understanding that they require in order to operate as 'environmental citizens' (Smyth, 1996, p 63). He suggests that the Scottish strategy for environmental education is a good working model for schools to adopt. This includes the following characteristics:
- caring and responsible attitude to the well-being of the whole environment;
- critical attitude to received information including assumptions and personal interpretations;
- respect for other people's beliefs and for evidence and rational argument;
- sense of community with other people and other living things;
- sense of continuity with past and future;

- respect for human potential to work within environmental constraints while designing the future creatively;
- commitment to contribute personal talents to improving environmental quality.

Arts education

In regard to *content* art education focuses upon both expressing ideas and feelings and in the properties of line, tone, colour, shape and form. Clearly its values are analogous to those found in the English. In respect of its *academic discipline* art values elegance, style, originality, versatility with regard to its different media, a co-ordination between hand and eye and between idea and its non-verbal expression. The values implicit in art are hard to put into words (precisely because art is a non-verbal medium) and because art covers a spectrum of activities from craft (making useful objects) at one end to 'high art' (Rembrandt) at the other.

At a time when there is concern that education in the arts is being squeezed out of the curriculum, David Best (1996) reminds us that arts education can offer a major contribution to values, over and above its own integrity as a subject area. He argues that values in the arts are objective, rather than concerned with subjective aesthetics. The arts can lead pupils into a re-consideration of life-issues, and stimulate a new appraisal of moral and intellectual values. Those concerned with church schools might also be reminded that the arts have always flourished alongside the written and spoken word as a way of expressing a response to the divine. The visual and plastic arts, especially, express values: think of Epstein's statue of the archangel Michael triumphing over Satan on Coventry cathedral as a symbol of the power of good. Or, in the same building, think of the cross made from the twisted nails from the old bombed cathedral which show how suffering can be transformed into something beautiful.

Reflections on Christian values

Earlier analysis suggested that distinctively Christian values are found at the place where theology and morality intersect. The values derived from the content of the curriculum are ultimately derived from our personal, social or physical worlds. This is because the subject areas of the curriculum concern either human beings (biology, English, art) or society (history, art) or the natural world (environmental studies, science). Indeed, within environmental studies the scheme outlined could be recommended for use in any church school, with the possible addition of intercessory prayer for the environment, during the act of worship. In the sense that all curriculum subjects are related to human beings, their place in nature and the societies they have built, it follows that the big Christian doctrines mentioned earlier are relevant. The doctrine of the Trinity has implications for the nature of human beings and the nature of society; the theologies of human nature have implications for history and literature; beliefs about the natural world have implications for science and biology.

Similarly the values derived from the academic disciplines themselves are ultimately relevant to human behaviour and human nature. The values of order, precision, coherence, self-expression, deduction and evidence which we have identified have a moral and theological import. They point towards a God of order, precision, self-expression, coherence, and so on.

Moreover, if we step back and take a general view of the core subjects we can see how they harmonise with religion. Religion is about communication, deep emotion and the best way to organise human life. English, too, is about communication, emotions, elegance, verbal play and the social life of human beings. While religion is also about unity between people and with God, science is concerned with the *uni*verse, a word derived from unity or oneness. The holy grail of theoretical physicists and cosmologists today is to combine the four fundamental forces of nature into a unified theory of everything[9]. Science and religion have more in common than perhaps either would like to admit. It was the philosopher Voltaire who once remarked that he loved the man who sought truth but hated the man who claimed to have found it. The wooden claim of authority is lethal; it leads to stagnation and death in science, to bigotry and violence in religion and politics. Science is a superb example of the exploration of the human imaginative spirit. In that sense it is a spiritual enterprise. Certainly it is reasonable to argue, as Polkinghorne (1998, p xi) has recently done, for:

> a methodological comparison of science and theology that exhibits their common concern with the attainment of understanding through the search for motivated belief.

Activity C3

Using the mission statement and aims of your school as a starting point, write a short policy document on the Christian values that are represented across the curriculum areas of the school.

---

[9] The four forces are gravity (attraction only), magnetism (attraction and repulsion between magnetic poles), electricity (attraction and repulsion between electrical charges) and nuclear (the forces between subatomic particles).

Comment on activity C3

The worth of this exercise comes from the reflective process of considering the detail of the values education that the school provides. It also acts as a catalyst for the whole school teaching staff to consider their role in fulfilling the aims of the school, since this policy document will only fulfil its function if it is drafted after extensive consultation. It should contain a description of the present position and a plan for development, including in-service training.

C4 Values in the educational process

> Whatever is honourable, whatever is just, whatever is pure, whatever is lovely, whatever is gracious, if there is any excellence, if there is anything worthy of praise, think about these things. What you have learned and received and heard and seen in me, do; and the God of peace will be with you. (Philippians 4:8)

The words employed by Paul in Philippians are ordinary, everyday words in the original Greek. They serve as a reminder that values can be more pervasive than those found within the content or academic discipline of the curriculum. Values as we have suggested earlier not only have different ranges and areas of focus, but they also concern actions and activities. Or, to put this another way, they are concerned with process as well as content. Since the process of education involves human interaction, values will be evident in the relationships within the school. Priestley (1985, p 117) writes:

> the tendency to use 'curriculum' as if it were a synonym for 'education' has crept up on us so slowly that we have hardly noticed it. It is one of those small bewitchments of the language which may appear trivial but can have wide-ranging consequences. Curriculum is one half of the educational process: the other half is the people concerned in that process .

Relationships within schools have sometimes been explored by the use of sociograms (Lovell, 1968, pp 190f). Children are asked to write down who they would like to sit next to and the results are plotted on a chart. Arrows run from each child to the ones he or she wants to be next to. What happens is that some children turn out to be popular (everyone wants to sit next to them) and others turn out to be isolated. When the chart is examined it is possible to see the networks of friendships within the class and the way they tend to cluster round one or two individuals who are the natural leaders of the group. Similar explorations can be made of relationships among the teaching staff. The point of the exercise is to make clear what sort of friendship links develop in schools. This is one type of relationship, a type that is voluntary and within a peer group. Other types of relationships occur when a teacher interacts with a class of children. Here the relationships are involuntary and do not involve equals - the adult is older and in a position of authority over the children. The pattern of relationships among the children is mirrored by the pattern of relationships among the teaching staff. The relationship between teacher and children is, to some extent, mirrored by the relationship between headteacher and classroom teachers.

In voluntary relationships loose-knit networks tend to form spontaneously unless children (or staff) feel in need of protection - in which case they form gangs or cliques, groups that 'stick up' for each other. In involuntary relationships, authority within schools is given for a specific purpose: to facilitate the education of children. But it can be abused so that it becomes an end in itself, something that is exercised for personal gain or private pleasure. When Christian values are applied to relationships, the Golden Rule given by Jesus is 'so in everything, do to others what you would have them do to you, for this sums up the Law and the Prophets' (Matthew 7.12). The key question to ask, according to this rule is, what would you want this person to do if the roles were reversed? If I were a child and the child were a teacher? Or if I were the headteacher and the headteacher were a classteacher?

There are various factors that can prevent the rewarding development of relationships between staff and staff and pupils and staff in schools. In his essay 'The ambiguity of spiritual values' John Hull (1996, pp 33-44) examines some difficulties in the interpretation of spiritual values, the type of values that teachers in church schools often hope to exemplify in their relationships. He unpacks the complexity of the various interpretations of spiritual values before going on to describe how the origins of spirituality are to be found in social being: the way we conduct the concrete and material forms of our community life. Increasingly, the privatisation of spirituality has rendered us incapable of extending our religious values into the public realm, where the god Mammon holds sway, except in ambiguous and manipulative ways.

According to Hull's analysis education has suffered from this understanding of relationships as that which stands between the consumer and the provider. The pupil expects a teacher to provide a set of educative experiences, to 'deliver' a curriculum, and may resort to litigation if this service is found wanting. Hull makes it very clear that our present position of enthralment to money is idolatrous, which should make us think twice about advocating an education where relationships are based solely on the ability to deliver a product to a satisfactory standard. Our values will be evident in the quality, which in this case means the nearness they come to the Golden Rule, of the relationships within our school, whether we befriend and nurture young people, or whether we regard them as units of income, to be processed through to satisfactory results.

In respect of Special Educational Needs (SEN) relationships are problematic. The needs of SEN children must be balanced alongside the needs of all the children. Yet the Gospels show Jesus stretched out his hands to weaker members of society (whether children, Samaritans or lepers) and the early church continued this tradition by showing a marked concern for the poor (Galatians 2.10). Human relationships with weaker members of the school community have difficulty in becoming reciprocal (e.g. 'My duties to you are balanced by your obligations to me'). As a result relationships with SEN children are often one-sided. Stronger and abler members of the community must continuously give help to them while knowing that they will not receive help in return. This said, relationships with SEN children can and should be warm: intellectual handicaps do not prevent emotional responses.

We have been concerned here with relationships as the place where the process values of education can be expressed. But, in keeping with our earlier definition of values as 'general guides to behaviour or as points of reference in decision-making' it is obvious that values influence the decisions that are taken in schools about educational aims and the deployment of resources. Our values are shown by our decisions because values help order our priorities and inspire our plans. The educational process, then, so far as it is driven by general goals embodied in mission and ethos statements, must be a value-laden one.

Developing awareness of values

Examine the following model of an 'ideal school', by Brenda Watson and Elizabeth Ashton (Watson and Ashton, 1995, p 149). Any scheme for an ideal situation is bound to cause some controversy and argument, but the justification for this exercise is not to critique the scheme, but to practise skills of analysis and to use it as a starting point for your own vision.

They suggest that an ideal school can be schematised according to three basic concepts: appearance, atmosphere and integrity. The *appearance* of the school will be most obviously seen in the campus buildings and their interior. They will be attractive, free from clutter and litter and contain areas where children and teachers can work in different kinds of ways. Appearance will also be relevant to the staff since they will be aware of the influence of speech and dress. But more importantly, they will be aware that their behaviour should not appear to be critical about other people or pompous and dogmatic. Teaching methods will not appear to be stilted or inflexible. They will be varied throughout the day and individuality in lesson planning will be valued.

The *atmosphere* of the school will be lively but orderly and there will be an emphasis on the individual and on freedom to carry out personal projects. The head teacher will be enthusiastic and open to new ideas and be supportive of staff. In other words the social atmosphere will be friendly and creative. The organisational atmosphere will be similarly open and porous. Visits outside the school will be frequent and there will be a minimum of meetings and hierarchical control.

The *integrity* of the school will allow controversial issues to be discussed and for discussion to go beyond the superficial so that all areas of the curriculum will enjoy equal status. Pupils will be self-motivated and learn to plan their own activities. Integrity will therefore spread to the process of learning so that learning will not be forced, but will be valued for its own sake. Discipline will be based on reason and justice rather than coercion and there will be room for a sense of humour.

Before considering this model of an ideal school in detail consider two pieces of research which have a bearing on values. The first comes from Israel and compares pupils from religious and secular schools. The pupils were carefully matched and the difference between them simply concerned the kind of school, and therefore the kind of ethos and curriculum, they experienced. In the religious school the ethos was determined by the tradition of Jewish religious scholarship found in the *Torah* and the *Talmud*. There was intense study of Jewish texts and an insistence on correct clothing, diet and behaviour. In the secular school, the Jewish identity was not expressed in a religious way.

The researchers used a questionnaire for identifying values constructed by Schwartz (1992). This clustered values according to two opposed pairs, stimulation and self-direction versus security, conformity and tradition. The second pair positioned power, achievement and hedonism opposite universalism and benevolence. The religious and non-religious students were asked to rate what was important to them and their ratings were compared. It was found that the religious students placed greater emphasis on tradition (respect for tradition, devoutness, accepting one's lot in life, humility and moderation) and universalism (wisdom, social justice, unity with nature, protecting the environment) while the non-religious students placed greater emphasis on hedonism, achievement, self-direction and security (national and family security, health, cleanness and a sense of belonging).

The point to notice is that schools were able to influence the values (convictions, choice-making criteria) of pupils on a range of issues. The influence was predictable and largely intended. But this does illustrate the importance of being clear about what values the church school wishes its pupils to imbibe.

The second piece of research, concerning values in sub-cultures (Megargee, 1997, pp 601f), shows that values are a result of socialisation, that is, a result of the general processes of learning and conditioning. Simply by growing up in one kind of society rather than another, or one sub-culture rather than another, we take in values from the people we are with and from our parents. There are all kinds of psychological mechanisms at work here but it is fairly well established that where children are exposed to contradictions in value systems, where adults say one thing and do another, or where the agents of socialisation (home and school, particularly) are in disagreement, children have difficulty in forming a consistent set of values themselves. Where there is a situation of *anomie* or normlessness, children are more exposed to anti-social value systems and may more easily be drawn into crime or violence.

Activity C4

Consider the following three questions.

- What values can you detect embedded within Watson and Ashton's model of the ideal school?
- Using an action plan how would you have to change this model (if at all) if this were to describe an ideal church school?
- How would you identify the values held by pupils in a school?

Comment on activity C4

You might have noticed the two values of liberal education: autonomy, shown in the emphasis on independent learning and the importance of reason in the scheme. There is an emphasis on individuality and a reluctance to support a hierarchy.

In a church school you might consider whether all curriculum areas should be equally valued, or whether there is a case for strengthening the provision for religious education. You might also have added space and time for contemplation and reflection, a willingness to forgive and an extra concern for those pupils with special educational needs. A specific reference to particular Christian values that are important in the school would also normally be included.

Your action plan, to stand any chance of success, would need to be costed and set within a time span, with a designated person in charge of monitoring it. You may have suffered some qualms about planning for the 'ideal school', as it has a ring of finality that precludes any more development or improvement!

With regard to the identification of values, the best way seems to be by looking at choices that pupils make. This can be done by giving pupils hypothetical situations to consider (e.g. 'what would you do if you had to choose between saving a baby or your pet dog from a burning building?' or

'How would you decide whether to give money to help people affected by famine or to repair the roof of your local youth club?'). It can also be done by looking at aims and ideals since these are also relevant to the long-term decisions people make for their lives.

C5 Conclusion

Throughout the whole of the curriculum there is a drive for academic excellence and a hunger for success. We want to celebrate the joy of achievement, with the pupils' successes and also with our own. What is easily forgotten in the striving to achieve is that we also need to teach our children how to fail, sometimes by example, how to get it wrong, how to survive being silly, trivial, under par, disastrous, how to mend relationships, how to stay with problems we cannot immediately solve, in short how to be human. If we can do this then we may come closer to seeing what values education in a Church of England school should be like.

Readers

You will find helpful section 3 in L.J. Francis and A. Thatcher (eds) (1990), *Christian Perspectives for Education*, Leominster, Gracewing.

Bibliography

Astley, J. (1994), *The Philosophy of Christian Religious Education*, London, SPCK.

Astley, J. and Day, D. (eds) (1992), *The Contours of Christian Education*, Great Wakering, McCrimmons.

Baldwin, G. (1996), Modern spirituality, moral education and the history curriculum, in R. Best (ed.), *Education, Spirituality and the Whole Child*, London, Cassell, pp 206-221.

Best, D. (1996), Values in the arts, in J.M. Halstead and M.J. Taylor (eds), *Values in Education and Education in Values*, London, Falmer Press, pp 79-91.

Best, R. (ed.) (1996), *Education, Spirituality and the Whole Child*, London, Cassell.

Boff, L. (1988), *Trinity and Society*, Tunbridge Wells, Burns and Oates.

Boff, L. (1995), *Ecology and Liberation: a new paradigm*, New York, Orbis.

Brown, D. (1985), *The Divine Trinity*, London, Duckworth.

Department for Education (1995), *Key Stages 1 and 2 of the National Curriculum*, London, HMSO.

Evans, D. (1979), *Struggle and Fulfilment*, Cleveland, Collins.

Francis, L.J. and Kay, W.K. (1995), *Teenage Religion and Values*, Leominster, Gracewing.

Francis, L.J. and Thatcher, A. (eds) (1990), *Christian Perspectives for Education*, Leominster, Gracewing.

Gresham Jr, J.L. (1993), The social model of the Trinity and its critics, *Scottish Journal of Theology*, 46, 325-343.

Grey, M. (1993), *The Wisdom of Fools? seeking revelation for today*, London, SPCK.

Halstead J.M. and Taylor M.J. (eds) (1996), *Values in Education and Education in Values*, London, Falmer Press.

Hodgson, L (1944), *The Doctrine of the Trinity*, New York, Charles Scribners Sons.

Hull, J.M. (1996), The ambiguity of spiritual values, in J.M. Halstead and M.J. Taylor (eds), *Values in Education and Education in Values*, London, Falmer Press, pp 33-44.

LaCugna, C. (1991), *God For Us: the Trinity and Christian life*, San Francisco, Harper.

Lovell, K. (1968), *Educational Psychology and Children*, London, University of London Press.

Lovelock, J. (1988), *The Ages of Gaia: a biography of our living earth*, Oxford, Oxford University Press.

McFague, S. (1993), *The Body of God*, London, SCM.

McFague, S. (1997), *Super, Natural Christians*, London, SCM.

McLaughlin, T.H. (1996), Education of the whole child? in R. Best (ed.), *Education, Spirituality and the Whole Child*, London, Cassell, pp 9-19.

Megargee, E.I. (1997), Internal inhibitions and controls, in R. Hogan, J. Johnson and S. Briggs (eds), *Handbook of Personality Psychology*, London, Academic Press, pp 581-614.

Moltmann, J. (1981), *The Trinity and the Kingdom of God*, London, SCM.

Osborn, L. (1993), *Guardians of Creation*, Leicester, Apollos.

Peters, R. (1981), *Essays on Educators*, London, George Allen and Unwin.

Polkinghorne, J. (1998), *Belief in God in an Age of Science*, London, Yale University Press.

Priestley, J. (1985), Towards finding the hidden curriculum: a consideration of the spiritual dimension of experience in curriculum planning, *British Journal of Religious Education*, 7, 112-119.

Schwartz, S.H. (1992), Universals in the content and structure of values: theoretical and empirical tests in 20 countries, in M. Zana (ed.), *Advances in Experimental Social Psychology*, volume 25, Orlando, Florida, Academic Press, pp 1-65.

Shepherd, P. (1998), *Values for Church Schools*, London, National Society and Church House Publishing.

Smyth, J.C. (1996), Environmental values in education, in J.M. Halstead and M.J. Taylor (eds), *Values in Education and Education in Values*, London, Falmer Press, pp 54-67.

Stott, J.W.R. (1999), *Issues Facing Christians Today*, Basingstoke, Marshall Pickering.

Thatcher, A. (1990), Learning to become persons: a theological approach to educational aims, in L.J. Francis and A. Thatcher (eds), *Christian Perspectives for Education*, Leominster, Gracewing, pp 73-82.

Ungoed-Thomas, J. (1996), Respect for persons: a curricular crisis of identities, in R. Best (ed.), *Education, Spirituality and the Whole Child*, London, Cassell, pp 121-138.

Watson B. and Ashton E. (1995), *Education, Assumptions and Values*, London, David Fulton.

White, L. (1967), The historical roots of our ecologic crisis, *Science*, 155, 1203-1207.

Zizioulas, J. (1993), *Being As Communion*, New York, St Vladimir's Seminary Press.

Church School Management

Church School Management

Unit A

Concepts of management

Roger Goulden

Trinity and All Saints University College

Leeds

Contents

Introduction

Aims

After working through this unit you should be able to:

- understand the nature of management as a technical term;
- understand the nature of organisations;
- appreciate how managers achieve organisational purposes;
- reflect on assumptions underlying management theory;
- reflect on psychological theories as a basis for human resources.

Overview

According to Briault and West (1990, p 74) every teacher has a management role. This unit explores different definitions of management and will look at ways in which these may be applied to schools. The various forms of management theory give rise to different conceptions of the management process and lead eventually to a variety of aims depending on whether the needs of the organisation or of the people within it are put first.

A1 What does manage mean?

In everyday speech you might hear people say things like, 'Thanks for your help. I think I'll be able to manage now', or 'If I leave out a couple of things, I'll just about be able to manage.' *Managing* seems to be about making the most of whatever resources are called for, acquiring them in the first place or making them go round. The person who can *manage now, thank you* is ready to face the world. *Just managing,* in the second example, goes further than this and implies that there are difficult choices to be made.

In both scenes the word 'manage' gives the impression that the speaker is doing the managing, looking at the options before committing him or herself. But if we look again at the snippets, we notice that someone else is involved, providing direct assistance or a listening ear. *Managing* is not something you can do on your own; it involves other people.

In the classroom we could consider the following example of teacher as manager. Littlewood (1981, p 92) writes that:

> As classroom manager, the teacher is responsible for grouping activities into lessons and for ensuring that these are satisfactorily organised.

The manager is now in charge, making judgements and setting things up for others to do. Yet co-operation from pupils and their willingness to participate probably owe a great deal to the quality of relationships or to the motivation provided by the way the teacher initiates and organises the task in hand.

In the classroom, our attention is directed towards these human factors. Once inside the classroom management strategies take a back seat, since, during planning, solutions have been provided in advance to problems anticipated. As they develop their management roles, teachers are encouraged to leave *re*active responses to situations behind and to favour *pro*active planning strategies.

Financial management and the teacher

As classroom teachers, our attention tends to be taken up by responses to changing situations and pupil needs. Our ability to be proactive is diminished by the lack of time we have to think in the day-to-day life of the school. There is an analogy here between teachers and those who work in the world of business. When companies cannot afford financial resources to buy in stock before it is actually needed, 'just-in-time' management strategies have to be used.

When one can afford a stockpile, there is little need to exercise judgement. But where reserves of resources run low, just-in-time strategies have to be put into action and these demand the flexibility contained in the dictionary definition of management as simply 'the exercise of judgement'.

Despite the need for management strategies in the classroom, recognition of the importance of management in the field of education owes much to its use in the phrase 'local management of schools' (LMS). However, the notion of involving schools in management activities outside the classroom is not new. As long ago as 1959, a pamphlet published by the Bow Group Conservative Political Centre suggested:

> the governing body of a good school should receive a per capita grant.... The Governors would then draw up a budget for the school year.... In Hertfordshire a scheme similar to this has been operating since April 1950... the headmaster may order supplies from whatever source... and pays all bills.... The Hertfordshire Education Committee has particularly stressed the importance of the headmaster working in close consultation with (the) Governing Body.

This could be viewed as the 'simple model of school management'. We can describe relationships between the agencies in terms of levels as table 1 shows. In carrying out these financial transactions, the headteacher must learn to ensure that the correct financial procedures are followed. More strategically the headteacher's management tasks also involve projecting income and expenditure for the coming year and then monitoring what was planned against what actually happens. In this sense the headteacher must occupy two worlds: the world of the classroom where there is untidiness and immediacy and the world of financial planning where there is bureaucratic order.

Table 1: Simple model of school management

Level	Action
LEA	Provides finance
Whole school	Governors and headteacher set budget
Headteacher	Headteacher orders and pays for supplies

Since the Bow Group pamphlet was issued management in schools has changed its character considerably: it is no longer confined to the daily fabric. In contemporary education, management procedures involve a host of different agencies, many of them outside the immediate context of the school and each of which has specific responsibilities. This considerably complicates the task of management and creates many new management tasks. Within the school, the headteacher very frequently extends the process of financial management to other members of staff who are given responsibility for specific areas of school expenditure, as displayed in table 2.

In this way, as the simple model of school management is put into place, secondary school heads of department are likely to be required to buy books and equipment. In a primary school, there will be similar delegations, though not on a departmental basis. One clear benefit of this Simple Model is that younger staff gain experience and some of the skills of financial management needed for headship.

Table 2: Devolving responsibilities in a simple model of school management

Level	Action
Whole school	Headteacher provides allocation from school budget
School department	Responsible person sets own budget, orders and authorises payment

Viewed from above, this extension of management is an important step in the preparation of teachers for promotion. It also removes responsibility for making decisions about relatively small sums of money from the headteacher's desk.

Viewed from below, this extension of management ensures that a proportion of classroom teachers have a range of management tasks to perform. They must manage pupil learning and also finance. Overall and ultimate responsibility for proper spending of public money, however, will remain with the headteacher. He or she will need to put in place appropriate financial regulations for the school, monitor the impact on staff and pupils and inform the governors. This delegation of financial responsibility to staff coupled with monitoring of their handling of these responsibilities illustrates an important principle in the management process. Where responsibility is delegated, it must be monitored. Delegation, in other words, is not the handing over of responsibility. It is merely the lending of responsibility for day-to-day decision-making.

The simple model and its extension is at the heart of the successes of devolved responsibilities for schools. Nevertheless, whereas the original pamphlet looked *within* the school, a new theme runs through this unit: many initiatives in schools require senior managers of schools to look *outside* their organisations as well as inside them.

Activity A1

On the basis of this brief overview, you may now wish to explore your own understanding and experiences of management.

Brainstorm some of the qualities of management that have been raised in this section (such as making judgements, planning ahead, setting budgets, negotiation, reporting, monitoring, matching plans with outcomes).

Consider three management tasks you have undertaken. (You may wish to choose three that relate to different aspects of the manager's role.) You may also wish to consider the extent to which your current role contains management responsibilities and how they relate (if at all) to your role as a classroom teacher.

If you are considering possible future management roles, you may further wish to identify the levels of management within the school at which you currently operate, and how they relate (if at all) to your future roles.

Comment on activity A1

It is impossible to comment on your personal experience of management roles in any detail. You may have been involved in financial management or in the management of people, particularly pupils and staff. You may find it easy to cope with the first and hard to cope with the second. Your own preferences and skills will probably lead you in one direction or the other.

You may have noticed the way management seems to involves roles, procedures and schedules even when it consists of solving problems related entirely to people. In some respects management is entirely about 'objective' 'rational' decisions, for example, the application of reason to the distribution or rationing of resources. In other respects it is a matter of good human communications or of good will.

A2 Management theory

Much of what is written on management is determined by the assumptions we adopt. As Douglas McGregor (1960) wrote,

> it is not possible to reach a managerial decision or take a managerial action uninfluenced by assumptions... so long as the manager fails to question the validity of personal assumptions, he is unlikely to avail himself of what (information about the likely fit between management practices and intended outcomes) is available.

The next four sections will address management from each of four different perspectives adopted in standard management texts. The texts chosen are classics, and are frequently employed in management training for application in a wide variety of contexts. Many of the figures provided have been developed in order to contribute to the application of insights from general management theory to management in schools.

What do managers do?

This is the opening question in Henry Mintzberg's (1973, p3) classic text *The Nature of Managerial Work*. The question is expanded by others such as:

- What kinds of activities does the manager perform?
- To what extent can basic differences (between variations among managerial jobs) be attributed to the situation, the incumbent, the job, the organisation and the environment?
- To what extent is management a science?

Mintzberg's aim in his book is to develop a job description for a manager that will have meaning to those who believe that management can be approached as science. We shall be considering his first and second questions. The third question will not be answered directly but should be borne in mind as the context of Mintzberg's thinking. We take the view that, within schools, it is not practical to think of management as properly a science.

In order to address his questions, Mintzberg draws upon the work of earlier management studies. In doing so, he establishes a framework that will largely be followed here. Towards the end of this section, elements of his framework will be combined in order to facilitate their application to schools.

Mintzberg's initial literature review surveys clusters of management theory. The acronym POSDCORB comes from the classical cluster as a means of drawing attention to the various functional and administrative elements of the work of a chief executive in:

- planning;
- organising;
- staffing;
- directing;
- co-ordinating;
- reporting;
- budgeting.

As we saw from our own analysis of the management roles of teachers undertaken in activity A1, these words do not in fact describe the actual work of managers. Rather, they are a means of classifying what managers do.

In his survey of the literature Mintzberg (1973, p 9) considered the *decision theory* of management but regarded it as inadequate because managers are - in strict scientific terms - very untidy in view of

> Man's inability to cope with complex problems, the usual lack of information... and the difficulties of stating realistic goals... policy making is a never ending process of successive steps in which continual nibbling is a substitute for a good bite.

Many practical strategies are, of course, based on this reality of eating the elephant in bite-sized pieces. The theory makes explicit the way huge aims and objectives are broken down into smaller pieces. But it does not show exactly how larger tasks ought to be broken down or what sort of decisions need to be made at each stage.

An alternative theory of management looks at *leader effectiveness* and starts from a model that sets two polarised styles of leadership:

- autocratic (largely task-focused);
- participative (largely people-focused).

It soon recognises, however, that a single style of managing does not suit all occasions. As we attempt to apply the results of theory, it is useful to be aware that our own preferred leadership styles might be inappropriate in certain circumstances.

In addition to leader effectiveness, there is also the contaminating factor of *leader power*. It is arguable that the leader behaves in ways which allow him or her to control his or her own job and so exert power over others with the main purpose of creating or maintaining conditions for remaining in authority. For example, in the 'simple model' introduced earlier, both headteachers and departmental heads could use the budgeting and allocation cycles to build alliances and gain support within the school as a means of achieving their own goals.

How managers spend their time

In considering research evidence of the 1950s and 1960s, Mintzberg concluded that there was relentless pressure on managers during working hours. Whereas for many managers pressure abated outside work, for chief executives it continued beyond. Where managers are responsible for success, how can they - without turning that general desire into something specific - be certain that they have been successful? Unless they set precise targets, managers are continually striving for an unattainable ideal.

In considering how managers spent their time, Mintzberg noted variety and lack of predictability because of the need to move between the significant and the inconsequential. Managers appeared to prefer tasks that took up small amounts of time and to like being interrupted for concrete jobs - especially ones that were out of the ordinary. More time was devoted to chatty information and informal speculation rather than settling down to routine and to relatively formal reports. However time planning favoured the definite and the concrete, specifics rather than generics, and often failed to make room for responsiveness to live issues.

Differences between successful and unsuccessful managers appear to have more to do with what they spent their time *for*, rather than what they spent their time *on*. Those who simply spend time on managing tend to let the tasks dominate them, and drown in them. The successful managers consider what they spend time for, and, through their creativity, turn necessary tasks and problems into opportunities for achieving their own goals.

Roles managers perform

Through observing managers at work, Mintzberg developed what he calls a set of 10 roles. The choice of the word 'set' is important, as these roles are not really a combination of unrelated activities. He makes it clear that the labels themselves and the boundaries between them arise from looking at the full picture of what managers do. Management roles are, in effect, an integrated whole.

Formal authority and status underpins *impersonal roles*. These roles may be classified as:

- figurehead;
- leader of subordinates;
- liaison with external contacts.

The impersonal roles give rise to *information roles*, particularly those of:

- monitor, gathering information from external and internal agencies;
- disseminator of selected internal information;
- spokesperson to external audiences.

Finally there are *decisional roles* of:

- entrepreneur;
- disturbance handler;
- resource allocator;
- negotiator.

The manager within the organisation

Mintzberg then reconsiders this set of roles by relating them to the functions of the manager in respect of the organisation. The manager:

- ensures the organisation serves the ends of those who control it;
- makes a bridge between the organisation and its environment;
- secures an appropriate balance between organisational stability and change;
- maintains and represents the status of the organisation.

Mintzberg does not identify any managerial roles that are associated with the first set of functions, but he consider that the liaising and monitoring roles mentioned earlier help make a bridge between the organisation and its environment. The balance between stability and change is secured by the roles of leader, monitor and entrepreneur and the final set of functions are brought about by the figurehead, spokesperson and negotiator roles.

Many debates in education centre around the *control* of schools and measures such as league tables for establishing the *status* of a school. The two areas also have a great deal in common with two key areas of headship:

- Strategic Direction and
- Development of the School and Accountability.

The importance of these areas is confirmed in the fact that candidates for the National Professional Qualification for Headship are required to follow national training in both of them. Management of a school thus has a key component concerned with far-reaching external relationships that go well beyond governors and parents at the gate.

Within the context of church schools, it will also be appropriate to review the idea of serving the ends of the organisation so as to align it with the school's specific Christian mission as shaped by its theological understanding of itself. In the context of church schools, it will also be worth asking whether leadership functions might:

- serve as a beacon for values of organisation;
- identify pressures and influences.

In looking beyond the school gate, the leader of a church school may also need to consider the extent to which external pressures are, in fact, consistent with the fundamental purposes of the school.

Having established common principles underlying what managers do and the functions they perform, Mintzberg goes on to identify four sets of variables that determine how an individual manager performs. They, in effect, expand on what has already been discussed. These four sets of variables are:

- *Environment*, i.e. social context of the industry or organisation;
- *Job*, i.e. level and type of job within the organisation;
- *Person*, i.e. individual's personality and preferences;
- *Situation*, i.e. time, context.

If one of the functions of the manager is to serve as a bridge between the environment and the organisation, environmental variables will obviously influence the work to be done, and this sort of effect will be relevant to classroom teachers who are, of course, highly sensitive to their working environment.

Mintzberg also points out that smaller organisations demonstrate less formality and the manager's increasing concern to take on the leadership and information processing roles. Clearly, small organisations require individuals to fill more than one role. In large organisations there are sufficient people in post for the different roles to be shared out among them.

Mintzberg's scheme thus serves to uncover further layers of detail involved in his simple question 'What do managers do?' We may summarise the manager's tasks by the formula: *Role requirements + environmental, personal and situational characteristics = Individual manager's work*

A management model striving towards a 'neutral science' might, perhaps, simply allocate the explicit links to enduring Christian values of a church school as a further situational variable.

As his focus is on individual managers, Mintzberg looks at ways in which roles relate to each other and change over time. It is worth looking at these two areas in more detail as they begin to raise issues to do with the organisation that will be considered later. They also tend to point to the importance of management tasks rather than the individual manager *per se*.

Cyclical changes

Mintzberg points out that what managers do changes over time in two ways as a result of:

- cyclical patterns deriving from the work itself;
- stages in development depending on the time the manager has been in the post.

One of his main examples of cyclical patterns involves the work of a school superintendent. He points to the large number of social functions which are mainly figurehead activities at the end of the school year. The context is North American and may apply more to the custom of High School graduation ceremonies, but similar patterns occur in British schools over Christmas when normal educational activities tend to be eclipsed by a variety of social and religious events.

Other examples of cycles in the work of schools include: budget setting, reporting on test results, curriculum planning, and the longer pattern of OFSTED inspections. The time-related pattern of school activities has clear implications for the plans a manager might wish to draw up. The manager must not only prioritise tasks in order of importance but also ensure that tasks are done in the correct sequence and with a sufficient allowance of time for each. A newly appointed manager, therefore, will step on to a moving escalator and will initially gather information (monitoring the situation) before turning to entrepreneurial tasks (identifying opportunities for change).

Shared roles

When addressing person variables Mintzberg begins to identify ways in which management roles may be shared by managers working in partnership. He suggests that the single managerial job can be shared in a number of ways, including:

- specialised roles (to reflect personality and preferences of leader):
- two people split work (according to respective talents or the needs of long term planning/day to day management).

Within schools, such splitting of posts might well reflect the ways in which headteachers and deputies share the work of managing the school, and is one means of gathering evidence of management expertise.

Using Mintzberg's analysis of the manager, that concentrates on what managers do, we can identify the manager's various roles. In this framework, the starting point is the *status and authority conferred by the post*. The various roles are not really separate and can be seen to relate to different aspects of the job at particular points in time and reflect the priorities the manager has identified. The roles may in fact be seen as facets of a single task: the manager helps to *achieve the purposes of the organisation.*

Activity A2

Consider the roles outlined in the section 'The manager within the organisation' that would be appropriate at the levels of headteacher, section head and classroom teacher in a school with which you are associated. As you do so, you may wish to reflect on differences between levels. For example, some levels involve more roles than others.

Consider what a fly-on-the-wall would see you doing when exercising a particular role in a particular school at a defined level of management.

Now reflect on *changes* that might be seen if you were at: an early/middle/late stage in your post; in different school climates; in different forms of school organisation; with different colleagues with whom to share roles. Are changes associated with WHAT you do or HOW you do it (or both)?

Comment on activity A2

Each of the levels within the school has a series of roles associated with it. For example, there is bound to be a need for all members of staff to pass information to others (liaison). More senior staff are more likely to function as leaders (for initiating new activities and showing others what to do), monitors (in checking that the work of others has been done properly) and figureheads or spokespersons (in representing others at, for example, the board of governors). But even quite new staff might act as negotiators (in obtaining money for the school through local authority and other schemes). Though the headteacher is more likely to act as a figurehead than others, classteachers are also eligible to act as staff representatives on the governing body. In this role they may symbolise the presence of all other teaching staff. In a more complicated set of roles experienced classteachers may have to monitor newly qualified teachers while themselves being monitored by the headteacher or the deputy.

The changes brought about by the point in a person's career are interesting and show how much flexibility there is in any well defined role. For example, the headteacher a few months from retirement is unlikely to be too concerned with the long-term career implications of a forthcoming OFSTED inspection and may be quite prepared to tell inspectors what their shortcomings are or stand firm on major issues of principle. A young headteacher, by contrast, would find this a risky strategy. Age, then, may bring less restraint to interpersonal conduct. But there are other changes brought about by experience, which need to be brought into view. An experienced headteacher may have learnt how to handle argumentative staff or parents more diplomatically; how to balance the opinions of one person in a committee against another; how to ensure the budget is used for maximum efficiency; what the safety regulations are and how they should be applied, and so on. In other words, experience will bring greater *technical* competence and may also bring greater insight into conflicts between interest groups and personalities.

Different forms of school organisation will also change roles by creating some and abolishing others, but there may be more subtle changes as well. For instance, some forms of organisation may be more co-operative and less hierarchical and so allow disagreements to be resolved privately and quickly rather than publicly, slowly and formally.

Shared roles either promote good teamwork or alternatively provoke painful disagreements. In the end this is a matter of ensuring that the right people are paired together.

A3 What do organisations do?

This question might appear to suggest that it would provide specific answers such as 'teach children' or 'sell prawn sandwiches'. However, such specific answers are not very helpful to theorists, so the question is subtly redefined to become 'how organisations behave'. Further redefinition is brought about through limiting the scope of the question to processes within the organisation itself. Responses to the external environment will be briefly addressed within this section, but will be addressed more fully in the next section.

The classic text used in the first part of this section is *Organisation in Action* by James Thompson (1967). As with Mintzberg, Thompson's aim is also to contribute to the building of a science and he explicitly acknowledges that he borrows from other writers across many disciplines (p viii),

> selecting those concepts which appear fruitful for present purposes and omitting all others, no matter how widely they are used or how powerful they have proved to be for other purposes. Only those I could hook together have been used.

He first reviews the literature, considering tidiness and untidiness in organisations. In striving to establish a science, one would expect organisations to display tidy rules. Thompson points out that organisations are simultaneously both tidy and untidy; for example, within a complex organisation such as a school, aspects of the formal and informal organisation are simultaneously at work. In this way it is possible to distinguish between:

- things that happen because managers plan them (tidiness);
- unforeseen things that happen as a consequence of what managers plan (untidiness).

Thus, in the simple financial delegation model of the first section, the rational processes of deciding priorities and controlling expenditure would give rise to sentiments, cliques, social controls via informal norms, status and status striving and so on. These would, in Mintzberg's analysis, be situational variables, operating *within* the organisation. From the perspective of the organisational scientist, there is a coherence and a certainly about what at first appeared to be contradictory standpoints. The organisation is both tidy and untidy at the same time. The manager can now predict that rational decisions will have consequences, but the precise nature of those consequences is not fully clear. As they go about their business, managers thus need to have regard to both tidy and untidy dimensions of their work.

Levels in the organisation

Just as we used the term levels within the management of a school, Thompson introduces the American sociologist Talcott Parsons' three levels within an organisation:

- technical;

- managerial;
- institutional.

At the technical level, he places the conduct of classes by teachers and the processing of income-tax returns! The managerial level takes responsibility for providing the resources (books, paper etc.) needed to carry out the technical functions. It further determines the nature of the classes to be taken or the way in which forms are processed. The managerial level additionally mediates between conduct of classes by teachers and those who use its products, the pupils.

Thompson uses the above examples from schools in order to help define his scientific model of the nature of organisations. His levels operate within an organisation. Let us consider for a moment what goes on in the conduct of classes by teachers. Some aspects of the curriculum (the content but not the delivery) and some aspects of testing and reporting pupil achievement to parents are determined by national legislation. At the managerial level of the school, some aspects of funding and opportunities for staff development are determined by LEAs, funding councils or, in the case of church schools, by church resources.

In other words, Thompson's model would need an additional layer outside the organisation of the school for it to be applicable to all maintained schools in England and Wales. For schools in the non-maintained sector, it would of course require no modification, as the legislation referred to in the previous paragraph does not apply to them.

Dimensions of the organisation

Given the difficulty of generalising about ways in which national policies are translated into action within the school and the different forms of organisation adopted within schools, it may well be more appropriate for purposes of looking at schools to separate technical, managerial and institutional levels:

- the *technical* dimension is concerned for the effective performance of functions imposed by the nature of tasks and the kinds of co-operation necessary to succeed;
- the *managerial* dimension simply mediates between the technical dimension and the pupils and procures necessary resources;
- the *institutional* dimension is concerned with the overall philosophy of the organisation and its components.

The levels of headteacher, departmental or area head and class teacher are all in some sense responsible for all three dimensions.

Such a formulation appears consistent with Thompson's recognition of differences between Parsons' levels, so that although what is done in the managerial dimension is not the same management function being transmitted down the hierarchy for implementation, it is nevertheless clearly managerial in nature. Further, the use of vertical dimensions emphasises that for the whole organisation to function, all levels must work effectively with each other.

This formulation also recognises that schools may determine whether controls between levels are formal or informal. Informal controls between levels might be associated with the same staff exercising responsibilities in all three dimensions - institutional, managerial and technical. Formal controls might entail different staff or grades of staff exercising institutional, managerial and technical responsibilities. Decisions as to the formality of controls and the nature of staff appointed to exercise controls are taken in various ways and, in some respects, are a matter of style rather than of substance: what matters is that the organisation fulfils its purpose. In a small school, much of this would not apply because formality would be inappropriate. National policies, externally derived funding and classroom activity are more than enough to ensure teachers have little choice but to work closely together.

Activity A3

Links between the school and outside. In considering Thompson's model, we identified that some decisions in respect of schools are taken outside the organisation of the school itself. Brainstorm a list of policies set outside the school that determine what *really* happens in classrooms. Consider only those that are set by bodies with explicit responsibility for education; e.g. DfEE, the National Society, Dioceses, LEAs, Funding Councils, TTA, QCA. Look at the *detail* of the policy against the levels and dimensions. Does it contain anything that suggests a school might have greater control than might at first glance be assumed? Consider, for example, the statement that what really goes on in my classroom is totally determined by the National Curriculum. When might it be appropriate to identify those elements of external policy over which a school legitimately has control and those over which it has little to say?

Within the school. Try to recall how you spent your time during half a school term. Attempt to (crudely) identify proportions of time you spent on management tasks at each of the three levels of school organisation:

- headteacher;
- area head (e.g. co-ordinator, head of department, pastoral);
- classroom teacher.

Take *one* task at the level of classroom and identify rough proportions of time you spent on:

- determining policy;
- considering how to implement policy;
- actually implementing policy.

Is it possible to identify a pattern to the work you have undertaken?

Comment on activity A3

Links between the school and outside. Statements such as 'the National Curriculum leaves me with no space to make decisions about what and how to teach' would imply that curriculum implementation is conducted at the 'managerial' or 'technical' dimension.

Viewing curriculum change in this way is certainly more convenient administratively when faced with the scale of change created with the initial implementation of the National Curriculum, or the need to demonstrate impact over short timescales - as with current initiatives in literacy and numeracy. However, when the National Curriculum was first implemented, schools were advised to review their curriculum as a whole. Such advice recognised the key importance of the institutional dimension.

The National Curriculum documentation further suggested that *how* the curriculum was to be delivered should take into account the particular context of the school. Detailed arrangements for planning, content, assessment and record keeping - as 'new' activities - limited opportunities for teachers to consider the everyday concerns of 'how to teach'. How to teach is, of course, tied to Thompson's definition of the institutional dimension; i.e. 'the overall philosophy of the organisation and its components'.

In considering the three dimensions of the school, it is thus possible to see how pressures on one dimension inevitably squeeze out opportunities at other dimensions. Inspection evidence points to the importance of 'whole school' dimensions in securing success. In giving explicit attention to 'institutional dimensions' teachers should consider their own philosophies of how to best teach subjects. By doing this they will be in a better position to contribute to whole school policies on matters such as teaching and learning styles.

Within the school. In the previous section, a clear mismatch was identified between the intention of the National Curriculum to support the development of the curriculum in individual schools and the pressures created by implementation. It is highly likely that the same pattern can be seen in the work of individual teachers, whereby routine pressures predominate to the detriment of 'institutional' dimensions of management.

How are the purposes of the organisation achieved?

The organisation is seen as an agency that attempts to resolve problems it faces. Thompson establishes a set of *propositions* to account for the behaviour of organisations. These propositions appear to work in favour of the *status quo* and even suggest that much of what goes on works in direct opposition to the goals of the organisation.

Organisational responses such as anticipating and adapting to external change are thus set in a context of protecting core elements of the organisation from change. Similarly, the original demands on the organisation are turned into things with which the organisation can cope.

Thompson proposes that organisations, when looking to the future, will adopt minimalist strategies, rather than attempt to anticipate best possible outcomes. To do this, achieving good ratings on visible indicators is seen as particularly important. Yet, ominously, thirty years ago, in the United States, Thompson was pointing out that schools, particularly, measured themselves against external indicators, even though these indicators might have little real bearing on quality.

Rules and indicators as barriers to success

How then do organisations go about their business? In further propositions, Thompson suggested that organisations turn to external criteria when they believe information about what makes their organisation successful is generally lacking or hard to find.

In attempting to align themselves with external criteria organisations often set up rules of conduct or procedure. Unfortunately these rules tend to become ends in themselves. Judgements of success are then made according to how well assessable actions fit organisational rules The rules are usually measured 'in terms of (past) efficiency' and according to Thompson (1967, p 92):

> the use of extrinsic measures of fitness for the future has the special advantage that they can be employed selectively.

Even where groups such as 'instructional teams in schools' are mutually interdependent, the quality of the work done appears to matter less than 'confidence' expressed in one team by others.

Deviance from institutional procedures is discouraged since, if anything goes wrong with the institution's outcomes, it becomes hard to justify innovation. Safer to follow the rules and fail, then innovate and succeed. Deviant or innovative individuals may then be targeted and undermined for failing to follow the organisation's preferred method of obtaining success.

The notion of pursuing quality and standards within education, 'especially when it is difficult to score on intrinsic criteria' while good in itself could fall into the trap of degenerating into a set of rules and procedures, with easily definable outcomes, which actually do the opposite of what they intend.

A4 The organisation and the individual

When looking at the role of the individual within the organisation, it is often the case that the aims of the individual run counter to those of the organisation. A key concept of 'discretion' is introduced. In order for the institution to respond to change, it needs individuals capable of exercising discretion, yet 'organisations can thwart the exercise of discretion by establishing inappropriate structures'. For example, an individual with a high workload, given discretion over what to do, will choose activities promising better grades on assessment criteria (rather than doing what is best for the organisation). When given a choice, the individual will try to hide failure in favour of advertising success. The greater the degree of freedom, the greater will be the temptation to create a personal powerbase that balances or outweighs dependence on others.

Thompson also argues that individuals will develop strategies for accumulating power, for example by seeking coalitions. In consequence, changes in the organisation will have implications for existing coalitions and create opportunities for building new ones. Coalitions do not move the organisation forward, however. Coalitions are limited in power to ratifying existing areas of consensus, but not building new ones.

The organisation does, of course, have corresponding strategies: a key concept is the inner circle. Such a circle develops where power is distributed throughout the organisation and groups organise themselves covertly to resist change.

Thompson's propositions suggest that the goals of the individual and the organisation are frequently at variance. At times, the exercise of discretion on behalf of the organisation may entail considerable personal sacrifice for the individual. At other times, the organisation may be crippled or required to build around that individual. The 'organisations' to which Thompson refers are, by implication, large. Nevertheless, within the context of church schools, the concept of 'discretion' is perhaps even more significant for small schools. The capacity of schools to manage all aspects of curriculum implementation discussed in activity A3 is particularly relevant.

The leader within the organisation

Thompson's set of propositions about ways in which organisations work suggests that it is uniquely the job of the manager to help the organisation achieve its goals. Proposition 10.9 expresses this clearly:

> In the organisation with dispersed power, the central power figure is the individual who can manage the coalition.

Using Thompson, we have identified some of the processes at work in an organisation that a leader needs to take into account in order to make a difference. Tom Peters and Nancy Austin (1985) take up the theme of the importance of the leader in the organisation in *A Passion for Excellence*. They see the leader as a key individual who does make a difference.

The employee as leader

Peters' stories of employees do not fit Thompson's propositions which, truth to tell, lead us in the footsteps of the bland. One such story is of the long-term impact of a peppermint popped into a bag by a shop assistant. Peters and Austin were buying wine with a credit card. It took ages for authorisation to come through on the customary phone call to verify credit. In dropping the mint into the bag and apologising, instead of muttering about inadequacies in the credit card company, the salesperson was effectively managing the coalition. The simplest gesture created enough power to get into a management textbook while remaining within Thompson's technical dimension. Peters and Austin (1985, p 46) conclude in terms similar to findings of research into school effectiveness.

> Excellence is a game of inches, or millimetres. No one act is, per se, clinching. But a thousand things, a thousand thousand things, each done a tiny bit better, do add up to a memorable responsiveness and distinction.

The chief executive

But what does the *senior* manager do, then? Peters and Austin (1985, p 60) provide many examples of chief executives taking a decision about the direction to be followed by a company, and creating a physical environment that reflects intentions. They mention an upmarket organisation for servicing cars that is decorated daily with fresh flowers and has such spotlessly clean workshops that customers are encouraged to walk around it. Creating the right environment applies equally to employees. In the words of this service manager

> If we want our service people to act like the well-trained professionals they are, we must provide professional working conditions.

How does the manager achieve these ends? The simple answer is through training.

Peters and Austin (1985, p 222) tell another story about a retailer, running a store, who trained all her staff herself. This had a major impact on quality in the store, but was taking time away from other priorities. She began to consider writing a training manual or appointing a training manager. These solutions began to feel very different from her philosophy, so she approached her best staff, asking them if they would like to do some training. They did, and quality of training has improved.

Many of Peters and Austin's examples are from organisations that focus on people - just like schools - yet very different messages begin to emerge from the two books. Many of Thompson's examples are from schools and colleges, but Thompson is concerned with the manager who determines what the organisation does on the basis of the authority conferred by the post. By contrast, our reallocation of the technical to a *dimension* rather than the hierarchical *level* reflects the growing importance given in Peters and Austin to employees who actually *do* the company's work - teachers and salespeople.

Theory X and theory Y

Douglas McGregor (1960) was also concerned to identify the scientific bases of management. Writing forty years ago, he identified two main approaches to management, which he styled *theory X* and *theory Y*, knowing in advance which one we will prefer (despite the fact that many management practices are actually based on *theory X*!)

Douglas McGregor (1960) defined *theory X* as comprising the following characteristics:

* human beings dislike work and will avoid it wherever possible;
* organisations need to coerce, control, direct - even threaten punishment - to overcome human dislike for work in order to achieve their objectives;
* humans seek security above all else, have little ambition, wish to avoid responsibility and prefer to be directed.

In contrast *theory Y* is defined as comprising the following characteristics:

* human potential is only partly utilised;

- high level talents such as imagination, creativity and problem-solving are widely distributed;
- work is as natural as rest and play;
- conditions may turn work into a source of satisfaction (when it will be undertaken willingly) or a source of punishment (when it will be avoided);
- external controls and threats of punishment are not the ONLY means of encouraging effort to bring about organisational objectives;
- individuals will exercise self-control and self-direction to achieve objectives to which they are committed;
- efforts directed towards organisational goals can bring about personal satisfaction;
- under appropriate conditions, people learn to accept and eventually seek responsibility.

While *theory X* could be said to represent a sticks-and-carrots approach, *theory Y* provides managers with the challenge to create conditions in which individuals will recognise that the *best* way of achieving their individual goals is through working to achieve the aims of the organisation.

Stages in helping staff develop

Douglas McGregor (1960) describes one manager responding to disappointing performance by another in a familiar four-stage approach based on *theory X*:

- clarify overall requirements of the task to be undertaken;
- set precise targets within a limited timescale;
- give instructions to do it (with some help and guidance);
- review (including self appraisal).

By way of contrast, using *theory Y*, the manager does not set the overall requirements or targets of the task, but encourages and guides the underachieving manager to articulate them for himself. The underachieving manager is not left to do it alone nor prevented from making mistakes.

The review element is particularly revealing. McGregor provides an extensive critique of performance appraisal, outlining negative benefits and limitations. He then describes an engineering manager who makes performance appraisal properly beneficial. The chief engineer invites engineers to complete the standard appraisal proforma themselves instead of giving it to their superior. In other words he turns appraisal into self-appraisal. However, the superior also completes a proforma and compares the two. Any follow-up is based on points of agreement or disagreement.

Leadership as a relationship

It is not surprising that McGregor views leadership as a relationship, deriving at least in part from a combination of factors, including the:

- characteristics of the leader;
- characteristics of those for whom the leader has responsibility;
- characteristics of the organisation;
- general social and economic factors.

He also recognises that complexity of organisations means that individuals may exercise different leadership functions at different times and that leaders may need to come together to address issues jointly. His insight rests on the realisation that leaders must relate at a human level to those they lead. Without this kind of relationship, technical excellence in management will not inspire motivation.

An example of the kind of approach pioneered by McGregor may be taken from an amalgamation of two schools. The headteacher of the more prestigious school became the new headteacher of the combined institution. Staff who had been in the less prestigious institution under the other headteacher were worried about their positions. The new headteacher solved the problem by concentrating on the refurbishment of the staff room. New furniture and telephones were installed. The staff quickly felt that their new circumstances were an improvement on the old ones. Technical aspects of leadership were seen to be no more important than human concerns for the welfare of others.

Much of McGregor's work draws on intangibles - assumptions, attitudes, relationships. He points out, for example, that a manager's ability to remember subordinates' names does nothing to reduce a feeling of mistrust. Rather the success of the leader depends on the perceptions of others about what the leader is trying to achieve. Despite the behavioural scientist's professional distrust of intangibles, McGregor's (1960, p 242) vision for the future is built on them:

> It seems to me unlikely that the transition will be rapid from our conception of an organisation as a pattern of individual relationships to one of a pattern of relationships among groups.

In an attempt to talk about something concrete - observable behaviours - and remain faithful to his view that organisations are fundamentally complicated, he turns his attention to teams. This is because a successful team is both a place where personal relationships may flourish and where a group of people, each with a different function, work together for a common goal. McGregor ends by considering characteristics of effective and ineffective teams.

It turns out that effective teams display many of the features of lively classrooms. For example, they show:

- an informal, comfortable, relaxed atmosphere;
- virtually everyone participates in discussion and listens to each other;
- everyone understands and accepts the common task;
- follow up action is readily agreed and undertaken;
- feelings are openly expressed, ideas are shared and disagreements aired;
- constructive criticism is possible;
- the group considers its own ways of working and is not overly dependent on the chair.

Theory Y points clearly to the benefits of teamwork in both the daily routines of leaders and their continuing development.

Activity A4

In commenting on activity A3, we began to consider the contribution of *all* staff to the 'institutional' dimension. Read through the principles of *theory Y*. To what extent do you feel that *theory Y* implies that opportunities need to be provided for all staff to operate 'institutional dimension?'

Now review your feelings about the implications of *theory Y* against the realities of management tasks in school in which you have been involved. Bear in mind McGregor's comment 'our assumptions are frequently implicit, sometimes quite unconscious, often conflicting' and begin to list some of your own assumptions together with the conflicts they raise. Consider an element of management task in which was involved:

- real opportunities provided for staff to operate at institutional dimension;
- relevant statements from *theory Y*;
- your own assumptions about the task;
- assumptions that you might infer from the way the task was set up or managed;
- any areas of conflict identified e.g. timescale for task/competing claims for time or resources; specialist expertise demanded; perceived relevance of task; the need for managers to manage.

A number of factors identified during the section have been listed below. They may help in reviewing your own school prior to the start of a specific project. Ask yourself where you are *now* and what you might *do* to create conditions for individuals to recognise the best way of achieving individual goals through working to achieve the organisation's aims. What are the:

- characteristics of the leader;

- characteristics of those for whom the leader has responsibility;
- characteristics of the organisation;
- general social and economic factors?

Conclude with a review, including self appraisal.

Comment on activity A4

As we look back over activity A4, we see that it is largely concerned with assumptions, personal values and relationships. Even the apparently simple four steps need to be taken in a quite different way if they are to support the implementation of *theory Y*. No matter how hard we try, we can do little about some social and economic factors, and psychological theories suggest that it is really quite hard for individuals to change. A mechanical checklist may be a way forward, but it probably raises as many problems as it appears to solve. The faith and values of teachers in church schools reminds them of the imperative to act with the best interests of society in mind. But neither are these issues over which the manager can claim influence.

In concentrating on intangibles, we reinforce the notion that the manager seeks to identify key areas that suggest growth points and obstacles that need to be worked round. Even if we get it right for individuals, McGregor reminds us that our longer term goal must be to create conditions where effective working relationships come into existence for groups of people.

A5 Management theory and the school

Local Management of Schools (LMS) dominates our understanding of school management. What has happened since the 1988 Education Reform Act, when LMS became a legal reality, is that headteachers and other school managers in schools in England and Wales during the 1990s have come to experience the unrelenting pressures described by writers on American industry in the 1950s. And, among the many sources of pressure on teachers in England and Wales, are those connected with the management of change.

Managing change

In many of the examples we have considered, there is a clear implication that one of the functions of the manager is to bring about and to co-ordinate change. Evidence of research into industrial organisations suggests that different systems of management in commercial organisations were effective in different situations. In *Flexible Planning*, Mike Wallace (1992, p 151) suggests that, perhaps, it is not possible to make a direct transfer of the results of research on change in commerce or industry to schools:

> it may be significant that Spinks's collaborative planning cycle was developed incrementally over seven years in an isolated school in Tasmania which enjoyed a relatively stable environment.

Wallace (1992, p 155) includes a list of factors affecting planning for change including:

- the multiplicity of goals that planning must address;
- the rate at which these goals change;
- the sheer number of goals that compete for attention at any time;
- unpredictable crises and issues affecting innovations and other work alongside the predictability of most routine activity in school.

This description sounds very much like the daily work of the classroom teacher with which we began. Classroom management strategies distinguish between starting a new topic (with a heavy classteacher involvement) and routines that need little attention. Projects (in management as well as in the classroom) have different phases in their life cycles and each phase has different demands. Maintaining discipline is as important as recreating order from scratch. But as in all spheres, there are considerable long-term costs of neglected maintenance. Above all, if management is not allowed sufficient time for reflection, it is bound to overlook tasks that ought to demand attention.

In the classroom, multiplicity of goals and unpredictable crises are largely an internal matter, whereas at the level of the school, external factors tend to predominate. As we have seen, the annual cycle of school activity creates its own management demands, as does organisational structure. Not surprisingly, Wallace identified a group of key factors affecting school planning that arise from the scale of change over the past decade. These are given below and grouped according to a four-stage analysis of institutional or systemic change: innovation, implementation, maintenance and evaluation.

In the first phase, *innovation*, the following factors are identified as affecting planning:

- many initiatives compete for attention at the same time;
- unpredictable shifts in LEA and government policies;
- mix of clear, detailed arrangements for some initiatives and uncertainties over scope, timing and funding of others.

In the second phase, *implementation*, the following factors are identified as affecting planning:

- unpredictable demands of external initiatives compete with well established internal routines;
- mismatch between academic and financial years;
- lack of control in flow of external innovations coupled with high degree of control over internal workings of school restricts freedom to manoeuvre;
- number and scope of external demands dictates and adds to workloads;
- difficulty in securing resources (time and expertise).

In the third phase, *maintenance*, the following factors are identified as affecting ministry:

- innovations that don't last;
- routine planning skewed by external innovations;
- co-ordination of multiplicity of goals.

In the fourth phase, *evaluation*, the following factors are identified as affecting ministry:

- limited evaluation of progress on innovations;
- limited evaluation of outcomes of innovations;
- insufficient time and expertise to conduct evaluations;
- some innovations diffuse and difficult to evaluate.

Management implications of LMS

Many of the tasks facing schools were in consequence of the implementation of Local Management of Schools. An early book on the topic, *Effective Local Management of Schools* by Fidler and Bowles (1989), contains the following chapter headings:

- Background to the Education Reform Act;
- Strategic management in schools;
- Marketing and promotion;
- Economics and budgeting;
- Income generation;
- Aspects of personnel management;
- Management information systems;
- Increased responsibilities of governors;
- LMS and LEAs;
- A management plan for the school;
- On receiving a formula budget.

This approach contains its own health warning:

> The delivery of the curriculum is at the heart of the educational process and so must be the ultimate concern of school management.

Yet management has gathered so much power to itself that

> there is insufficient space here to do anything but point out the most obvious managerial concerns.

Whereas Peters and TQM (see next page) would suggest that the main business of the school is its curriculum, concentration on management seems to entail an implicit maxim: *look after the management and the curriculum will take care of itself*. This perhaps explains a conversation when I was in the offices of the National Curriculum Council (NCC) in York shortly before it was to be merged with School Examinations and Assessment Council to form School Curriculum and Assessment Authority (now itself merged with the National Council for Vocational Qualifications as QCA). An officer with considerable experience in national agencies responsible for the curriculum in schools was reflecting on the 1988 Education Reform Act. The Act had brought into being NCC itself, Local Management of Schools and the National Curriculum. He mused that the two certainties of 1988 had within a short time become one. As he put it, somewhat cynically:

> Schools did not then know how to manage the National Curriculum or how to make Local Management of Schools work. They're now very good at Local Management of Schools.

Despite international recognition of the strategic benefits of the coincidence of curriculum and management reform, integration of school management and school leadership within the school appeared to be under developed. Even a key text, such as *Leading the Self-managing School* by Caldwell and Spinks (1992) that identifies the qualities of an educational leader's role within the school, changes focus when faced with Local Management. Its section on achieving equity in resource allocation is written with reference to allocation of resources *to* schools rather than *within* them.

Managing change within the school

The tradition in management theory associated with Tom Peters would, of course, begin with the needs of the customer rather than management processes. Remember the salesperson with the peppermint who served Peters and Austin to the wine? That salesperson considered the impact of the *total* transaction (not just their own part) at the point of service.

Peters and Austin, among others, are effectively challenging managers to unlock the inertia in their organisations so as to encourage quality on the part of all members of the organisation. Such an approach leads naturally into Total Quality Management (TQM). This has been developed within education by Edward Sallis (1993) in *Total Quality Management in Schools*. Sallis re-lists

14 points set out by W Edwards Deming in 1982. Many of these points are direct exhortations to counteract the characteristics of organisations identified by Thompson. For example, 'break down barriers between departments' is reminiscent of the tendency for institutions to resist change simply because departments lack confidence in each other. The failure to identify the real issues is found in organisations which try to measure success only through performance indicators. And, in the warning that it is best to eliminate standards that prescribe numerical quotas, Sallis underlines the point that Deming's principles were developed in an American industrial setting which set great store by these kinds of figures.

Yet Thompson drew to our attention parallels in schools, particularly where the real issues are complex and only partially understood. Assumptions are no less important than verifiable facts. These warnings are important because they suggest the current climate in education in England and Wales, which in part stems from the prominence of business methods, may need to be adjusted. After all, if American business methods did not work in the field of commerce and industry in the 1950s and 1960s, is it likely they will work in the field of education in the 1990s and the 2000s?

It could be argued that such new philosophies are concerned with what the organisation does for its customers, rather than what the organisation does for itself or its managers. Total Quality Management (TQM) is an approach designed to put in place procedures to keep the organisation focused on its main purposes, and hinges on the concept of customer. In essence, the customer is anyone who receives a service from an organisation.

Given the importance of each part of the system, and the inertia created by internal competition among departments, TQM reminds us that customers can be inside the organisation as well as outside. Internal providers need to consider ways in which others depend on them and internal customers need in turn to consider ways in which they depend on others. In this way both customers and providers recognise their joint contributions and responsibilities.

The vision of the organisation is one in which every member has a key role to play. As Sallis (1993, p 40) points out:

> the standard of service provided to someone junior in the institution is as important as the service provided to the headteacher or the chair of governors.

Is it possible, then, to bring about management of change that respects the natural unfolding pattern of an institution? Much of the research discussed so far has been undertaken by social scientists in order to understand the nature of management. Action research is undertaken by practitioners themselves in order to develop theory and their own practice together (See *Religion in Education 1*, pages 351-368).

The *Management of Change* by Lomax (1989) is a collection of articles about ways in which teachers can use action research to improve their own practices of managing schools and classrooms. It focuses on schools and classrooms, and celebrates the involvement of practitioners in taking charge of their own agendas for joint programmes of school improvement and staff development. In his essay in this collection Rod Linter describes a process of investigating interaction within his own classroom. He has his own vision and he makes a direct reference to the environment outside the school by quoting from a Government-sponsored initiative:

> we need to encourage teachers to tackle the challenges of active learning in the classroom through team activities.

In the same collection Margaret Follows reports on her project to develop co-operative teaching in one area of the school in which she was deputy head. She concluded that the results have been impressive, both for the teachers and pupils concerned there and for the school as a whole. She admits that the success of her programme depends on the commitment of participants - a critical element in any change process - but recognises that in most schools this is not supported by the allocation of extra resources such as time.

In an essay in *Education Management for the 1990s*, edited by Davies, Ellison, Osborne and West-Burnham (1990), John West-Burnham identifies characteristics likely to be displayed by schools that have not responded effectively to change. Among them he includes:

- lack of leadership, an absence of explicit goals, recognition and empowering;
- underdeveloped middle managers i.e. no infrastructure to translate principle into action to ensure the development of individuals or to make the most effective and efficient use of resources;
- limited understanding and application of principles of planning, budgeting, managing, motivation and evaluating.

Almost all of the factors identified by West-Burnham have been addressed in this unit. Where Action Research is used as a method of simultaneously introducing and monitoring change, it is important that the intended aims of the research relate to the vision for the school as a whole.

A future strategy of school management?

Nearly all standard management theories recognise the management responsibilities of *all* members of a school community. This, of course, sounds like a cop-out. If management is everyone's responsibility, it is no one's responsibility. And, in practice, because schools are hierarchical institutions, it is fairly easy to identify who the managers are. Yet, the dissenting voices have a case to make. Peters devotes a section of a *Passion for Excellence* to school leadership. His own understanding of his mother's work as a teacher (and even working as her classroom assistant himself!) leads him to suggest that management in schools needs to be focused on the *learner*.

By contrast, thinking simply in management terms, Thompson assigned the conduct of classes to the low status of a technical activity. We chose to classify Thompson's 'technical', 'managerial' and 'institutional' as *dimensions* in order to remove suggestions of low status. It is perhaps now worth reconsidering the use of levels as used in tables 1 and 2. There we referred to the three levels within the organisation of the school: headteacher, area leader, and classroom teacher.

As levels could contain notions of hierarchy, it might be more appropriate to consider their functions so that responsibilities are seen to be different at each level. This representation is consistent with McGregor's theorising. It would be more in keeping with a TQM approach and would also reflect realities in schools!

Even in a large school, area leaders still work as class teachers. A primary school curriculum leader may well direct the work of the headteacher who also operates as a classroom teacher. The same frequently holds true of secondary school heads of department with the headteacher or other senior managers in their subject teams. In a small school, of course, the full range of functions is exercised by the same individuals, without necessarily being aware of the joins.

The leader's vision

Many writers include 'vision for the organisation' among the qualities of the leader. The term vision of course has a quasi-religious connotation and is best understood in this context as a large idea about the future shape and functioning of a school. Peters and Austin (1985, p 286) point out:

> the most effective leaders from all walks of life - the classroom, the battlefield, the corporation - have set down challenging but achievable visions.

The process of managing change on the basis of the vision for the school thus becomes a key task for the manager. Beare, Caldwell and Millikan (1989, p 118) in *Creating an Excellent School* identify two elements in vision:

• a desirable and achievable future state;
• a desirable process though which the change is achieved.

At this point, we can see considerable agreement over what might constitute the desirable and achievable state through Action Research and the work of

West-Burnham, Peters and TQM. Which of these approaches is right depends of course on the second element of the manager's vision for the organisation: the process by which the state is achieved. West-Burnham implies that change should be precisely managed according to existing structures and procedures of the school. Others take a different view.

Examples of Action Research programmes involve staff in a desirable process that is consistent with *theory Y* and follows evidence cited by Peters. From my personal perspective, what appears to be lacking in both is the headteacher's articulation of aims or vision. The only management action needed might have been to link a class teacher's work to a school policy initiative and to acknowledge the quality of work being undertaken. Similarly, a headteacher might simply need to recognise the match between his or her vision for the school and the work of the deputy headteacher. Management might amount merely to the provision of resources.

A third example provided in the set of action research articles would tend to confirm the importance of both a desirable future state *and* a desirable process by which to reach it. A deputy headteacher in a special school begins work on an Action Research project designed to integrate teaching of boys and girls. The headteacher is about to retire, and explicitly excludes the project from his vision for the school. Nevertheless, all staff react favourably to the proposals, suggesting alternatives and willingly discussing matters. When the new headteacher is appointed, she takes the initiative on board and presents it as a fixed policy without discussion. Consequently the staff bicker among themselves: it is not the aim, but the method of its announcement that caused discontent.

Achieving balance

The role of the manager is therefore to ensure that the desirable state and the desirable process are consistent with each other. Of course, where the desirable process requires a degree of control to co-ordinate competing and contradictory initiatives that do *not* flow from the institutional vision, West-Burnham's analysis would be appropriate. But this is an altogether more tricky scenario to manage.

Action research ideas correspond to what might be called 'internal agendas for change', and the school managers can plan to implement these agendas, as they are largely under their own control. The word to notice here, though, is 'largely', because these agendas are nonetheless part of the complex web of interrelationships between the individual teacher and forces outside the school.

We can also identify an agenda for change emanating from national educational agendas outside the organisation of the school. Action research is an appropriate means of implementation and may be welcomed by class teachers as being consistent with personal career plans. Thompson's notions of discretion are pertinent in this regard. If an LEA rejects initiatives as being inconsistent with its values, then internal agendas and national agendas may not make much impact on a school, even if the means for change are readily available. Thus, although Action Research may be under the control of individual teachers, it will achieve no impact unless it is consistent with whole school agendas and other educational agendas within the LEA and beyond.

Unfortunately, agendas for national educational change arising from legislation (changes to the curriculum, testing and reporting) do not necessarily lead to the satisfactory development of individual schools. Myers and Goldstein (1998, p 176) write as follows.

> Along with numerous other reform initiatives that have involved teachers learning, 'unlearning' and 'relearning' new curricula, new teaching strategies and new structures within in a very short period of time, some of these changes have fostered a climate of fear and retribution. For many heads and teachers, the combined effect of the changes and related pressures has had a negative impact on their morale, resilience and self esteem.

It is usually the task of the headteacher to distinguish short-term from long-term demands and to identify ways in which national policy agendas may be used to benefit their own schools. More research is needed to show how major policy initiatives can be translated into the lives of schools, but my personal experience suggests that study of outside educational agendas may help those responsible at local level to develop schools along beneficial lines.

Paul Clarke and Tom Christie (1997) describe 'typical examples of school response to externally imposed innovation, namely the assessment of pupils against the progressive learning scale in the National Curriculum'. They identify a set of five responses to a simple question: What use will this be to me?

- This change is of no use to me.
- This might be of some use to me.
- This is useful to me and I'll get involved.
- How has this been of use to me?
- Now we know what we can do, how can we develop it?

Their work is concerned with impact on class teachers, but has clear implications for the work of managers in building a learning organisation.

Harnessing external agendas

Expressed in these terms, any apparent inconsistencies in Thompson's Standard Model disappear. At institutional level, managers need to consider the external environment. The rate of social and technological change (not to mention national educational policies designed to respond to them) suggests that managers will increasingly have to initiate and embed changes within the school against the tendencies for inertia identified in classic organisational theories. The task of school managers is now to address *all questions* emanating from outside the school by asking in what ways their answers can be harnessed to achieve the school's own goals.

By approaching all external agendas in the same way rather than, for example, trying to spot orders that can be safely ignored or worked around, school managers may adopt a consistent educational strategy. These are the true tasks of management, the visionary tasks to continue this theme, as against the non-visionary and routine tasks which risk the snares of what has been called *administrivia*.

The successful classroom teacher knows that the way to reduce time spent on trivia is to reorganise administration by encouraging learners to support each other and organising resources so pupils can easily access them. Designing tasks that enhance pupil learning rather than simply reduce time spent on trivia is, of course, a management activity. Such considerations suggest a possible distinction between classroom management and classroom administration. The former ensures that pupil learning is the main priority of classroom activity. The latter ensures that what is done is carried out efficiently without duplication of effort or confusion. Some management issues in the classroom cannot be addressed by the class teacher without decisions in the institutional dimension. It is for this reason that whole school policies have to be adopted.

A6 A wider view of school structures

Earlier we appeared to be rejecting a hierarchical view of school management while stressing the importance of the headteacher's vision. One dimension of education management reforms that has so far received little mention is the role of governors.

Governors operate only in terms of the institutional dimension and are effectively another functional level in the school organisation. Baginsky, Baker and Cleave (1991) in *Towards Effective Partnerships in School Governance* point out that of the four potential models for governing bodies identified in a report published in 1984 the supportive, advisory and mediating roles are no longer sufficient. Legislation has provided them with additional responsibilities and rights that appear to cover almost all aspects of the school. Accountability is the one role remaining from the 1984 list, to which might be added setting and monitoring policy. The obvious term for the function of governors is governance, whose circular definition in my dictionary is probably a realistic one: it is the act, manner, fact or function of governing. Nevertheless Baginsky, Baker and Cleave (1991, p 44) warn:

> in an ideal world, it would be possible to distinguish governance from management to the satisfaction of all concerned.

Clearly, such a distinction is not really possible. Although some governors might view their roles in terms of the Board of Directors, the studies on management to which we have referred hardly address relationships between managers and Boards of Directors. There is an assumption that real power lies with the headteacher. There is clearly a great deal still to understand about relationships between headteachers and governing bodies, and that is nicely encapsulated in the formula 'working *with*' the governing body in the gloss on the Core Purpose of Headship with which the *National Standards for Headship* begin (Teacher Training Agency, 1997).

Importance of functional roles in school management

Although at the peak of the hierarchy, governors operate in the three dimensions of institutional, managerial and technical. Governors have an institutional task in the sense that they are representative of the institution as a whole and must ensure that its character is enhanced. In church schools such an institutional responsibility may be expressed in admissions policies, which shades evenly into the technical and managerial dimensions. Policies must be set out fairly in accordance with reputable criteria and applied impartially. More obviously technical details need to be correct since they are relevant to the inspectorial process. Governors of voluntary aided schools in particular have managerial responsibilities as employers and this means they must understand, for example, the relevant legislation on employment.

The complications of applying management theory to schools is, however, illustrated by the sharply hierarchical definitions of headteacher and class teachers which are given statutory representation in the *Pay and Conditions* document. Middle management is usually defined at the level of the school with reference to organisational structure and job descriptions. Where hierarchical definitions of management are assumed, it is usually because legal responsibilities are in view. From a legal standpoint, responsibility for the welfare of children must be located in a specific person or role although, from an educational standpoint, it is clear that all members of staff contribute to the effectiveness of a school and to pupils' progress in learning.

Pursuing this functional analysis of schools in terms of levels supported by legislation, our analysis is further confirmed by the fact that the teacher-governor is, of course, a proper governor in his or her own right, as well as being a teacher, and procedures are provided to help prevent conflicts of interest. Similar considerations apply to the headteacher who sits on a governing body.

We are now returning full circle to the first component in Mintzberg's model for management as presented in table 3 in which the roles of the manager stem from the formal authority and status of the post. By applying management theory to the school, our analysis suggests that formal authority and status belongs to all members of school from governors to teaching staff, or, perhaps, did in some lost golden age. Each member of the school might identify their particular management functions within the vision for the school as a whole. But where does that leave the management role of the headteacher?

Management role of the headteacher?

A clue is provided by Sammons, Hillman and Mortimore (1995) in their review of school effectiveness. They point out that an effective headteacher is in most cases not simply the most senior administrator or manager, but is in some senses a leading professional. Almost the same terminology is used by the Teacher Training Agency (1997) in its core purpose of headship: the headteacher is the leading professional in the school.

Our analysis has been based on classic management texts that can be applied to management of any kind. As we progressively refine these concepts for application to the context of a school, we begin to move further away from a model of a headteacher as a generic manager whose vision for quality management may be applied in any organisational context.

We have already seen that organisations are possibly too complex for the purposes of theory builders, and now appear to be adding yet another dimension to the work of the school's headteacher. We can also see that management responsibilities, while drawing upon the professional skills of the classroom teacher, are not classroom responsibilities writ large. The notion of leading professional is the key concept that distinguishes a headteacher from governors and which enables the headteacher to deploy specialist expertise honed in classrooms to improve quality of pupil experiences. It would be more appropriate in schools to see governors as 'generic managers', using their skills to help the headteacher mediate complex and frequently contradictory external agendas against the needs of the school.

The identification by Teacher Training Agency (TTA) of awards for headteachers, subject leaders and expert teachers gives explicit national recognition to the various management functions within the school. The importance of the three related but distinct functional levels of school organisation is confirmed in TTA consultation papers, in which TTA was at pains to stress that the recommended qualifications were not intended as a hierarchical ladder from class teacher through subject leader to headteacher. On the contrary, each aspect of the teaching role within school from the classroom teacher to the subject co-ordinator was intended to be a valuable job in its own right and not simply a step on the road to a headship.

We have already noticed that TTA has identified strategic management and accountability as critical elements in the professional development of the aspirant headteacher. Emerging proposals are for a training programme for serving headteachers (Teacher Training Agency, 1998):

> designed to determine the development needs of the headteacher and the school using a wide range of data including self diagnosis and the use of standardised diagnostic instruments by the headteacher, plus internal, LEA and national data about the performance of the school.

The glimmerings of an alternative definition of the role of headship for Catholic schools are beginning to show in the work of serving headteachers working on the third TTA Leadership programme, HEADLAMP, for newly appointed headteachers. A questionnaire was given to recently appointed headteachers and to serving headteachers working with them in a mentoring context and on a course (Goulden, 1998). Responses suggest that working with newly appointed headteachers has a powerful impact on serving headteachers both in defining the tasks of headship and in identifying distinctiveness of provision. When asked to comment on training to be provided by the group, the overwhelming preference was for:

- management skills necessary to address the Catholic character of schools;
- tasks to help schools sustain and develop their Catholic character.

In defining both experiences and needs in this manner, a group of headteachers in Catholic schools has created a very powerful congruence of interest between what might otherwise be competing agendas of national and LEA priorities and those of governors, trustees and school staff.

Activity A5

This activity takes phrases from the text that encapsulate management principles as a means of enabling you to develop your own management ideals.

- As you review your developing vision for a school and for its management, identify approaches that will enable you to ensure that you do not suffer from: lack of leadership, an absence of explicit goals, recognition or empowerment.
- To what extent do you agree that 'Management involves crucial processes like problem-solving, planning, decision-making and organising'?
- Can you identify at which points in: Innovation; Implementation; Maintenance, and Evaluation you might need to use 'management processes'?
- What strategies might you wish to put in place to ensure that your school does not suffer from underdeveloped middle management?
- Using your response to the second bullet point, 'unpack' the following limitations of unsuccessful schools identified in an early text on school management - 'limited understanding and application of principles of planning, budgeting, managing, motivation and evaluating' - to help clarify where you would wish to draw a distinction between 'higher order management activities' and the mechanical, routine support and maintenance of a system encapsulated in 'administration'.
- How might the work you undertake help all members of the school community move through a series of stages leading to empowerment?

Comment on activity A5

The activity was intended to help you develop your own vision and understanding on the basis of your own values and experiences. In serving as a review, it has provided an opportunity for you to refine your own ideas on the practicalities of management.

One important message from the early stages of Local Management of Schools is that the need to develop 'management' abilities is not necessarily tied explicitly to improving the experiences of pupils. This relationship is now better understood, and is being addressed in national policy-making. The re-emergence of a national dimension, but now intended to focus directly on the experiences and achievement of pupils, adds a further dimension of complexity to school management.

The comment on activity A4 drew attention to the key role of the leader of a school in working with groups of people. The uneasy threat of external pressures on schools has finally enabled us to see the pivotal role of governors in mediating between external pressures and the enduring values of a church school. Relationships between school leaders and governors will thus be crucial.

Management theories have had little to say on such relationships, much less on those enduring values - preferring to strive for a 'scientific' approach. Theories of management concentrate on outcomes, yet studies of effective schools point to the importance of evaluation in which outcomes are measured in part against the whole school context. Evidence from OFSTED inspections suggests that the values of church schools may be a contributory factor in their high 'outcome' scores.

The leader of a church school community needs to encourage all groups to follow a journey that will take each of them from the familiar to the unfamiliar, that draws on, but does not slavishly follow, all available insights and challenges and creates a balance between management and administration. Otherwise, there is a real danger that, like Topsy, management will have 'just growed'.

Bibliography

Baginsky, M., Baker, L., Cleave, S. (1991), *Towards Effective Partnerships in School Governance*, Slough, NFER.

Beare, H., Caldwell, B.J. and Millikan, R.H. (1989), *Creating an Excellent School: some new management techniques*, London, Routledge.

Bow Group Conservative Political Centre (1959), *Willingly to School*, London, Bow Group.

Briault, E. and West E. (1990), *Primary School Management: learning from experience*, Windsor, NFER.

Caldwell, B.J. and Spinks, J.M. (1992), *Leading the Self Managing School*, London, Falmer Press.

Clarke, P. and Christie, T. (1997) Mapping changes in primary schools: what are we doing and where are we going? *School Effectiveness and School Improvement*, 8, 354-368.

Davies, B., Ellison, L., Osborne, A., West-Burnham, J. (eds) (1990), *Education Management for the 1990s*, Harlow, Longman.

Fidler, B. and Bowles, G. (eds) (1989), *Effective Local Management of Schools*, Harlow, Longman.

Goulden, R. (1998), *Impact of Provision on Headteachers*, unpublished report.

Littlewood, W. (1981), *Communicative Language Teaching*, Cambridge, Cambridge University Press.

Lomax, P. (ed.) (1989), *The Management of Change*, Cleveden, Multilingual Matters.

McGregor, D. (1960), *The Human Side Of Enterprise*, New York, McGraw Hill.

Mintzberg, H. (1973), *The Nature of Managerial Work*, New York, Harper and Row.

Myers, K. and Goldstein, H. (1998), Who's failing? in L. Stoll and K. Myers (eds), *No Quick Fixes: perspectives on schools in difficulty*, London, Falmer Press, pp 175-188.

Owen, J. (1992), *Managing Education: the purpose and practice of good management in schools*, London, Longman.

Peters, T. and Austin, N. (1985), *A Passion for Excellence: the leadership difference*, New York, Random House.

Sallis, E. (1993), *Total Quality Management in Schools*, London, Kogan Page.

Sammons, P., Hillman, J., Mortimore, P. (1995), *Key Characteristics of Effective Schools*, London, Institute of Education University of London for OFSTED.

Stoll, L. and Myers, K. (1998), *No Quick Fixes: perspectives on schools in difficulty*, London, Falmer Press.

Teacher Training Agency (1997), *National Standards for Headteachers*, London, TTA.

Teacher Training Agency (1998), *The Leadership Programme for Serving Headteachers*, London, TTA.

Thompson, J. (1967), *Organisation in Action*, New York, McGraw Hill.

Wallace, M. (1992) Flexible Planning: a key to the management of multiple innovations, in N. Bennett, M. Crawford and C. Riches (eds), *Managing Change in Education*, London, Paul Chapman, pp 151-165.

Church School Management

Unit B

Christian values and the management of schools

Revd Professor Jeff Astley

North of England Institute for Christian Education

Durham

Contents

Introduction

Aims

After working through this unit you should be:

- able to understand more about the *status* of Christian values and their relationship to moral and spiritual values generally;
- better equipped to analyse the undergirding values, problems and possibilities of different styles of school management and leadership;
- better equipped to reflect on some gender issues in this area;
- able to come to a considered view on the value of a market philosophy in the management of schools.

Overview

We begin with some reflections on the means and ends of education and of educational management, relating this discussion to the central question of moral evaluation. We then look at the relationship between morality and Christianity, and say something about spiritual values. Section B3 focuses on the values underlying three different historical approaches to school management and the values of the school's hidden curriculum. It ends with some comments on moral education, which are taken up in section B4 which analyses different styles of leadership. Section B5 concludes the unit with a critique of some aspects of the application of market theory to schools.

B1 Means and ends of management

Terminology

The verb 'to manage' was classically defined over eighty years ago (by Henri Fayol) thus: 'to forecast and plan, to organise, to command, to co-ordinate and to control'. Although more recent accounts tend to temper these stark words with references to motivation, participation and leadership, the essence of the definition still stands. Basically, 'management' (and the somewhat broader term 'administration') may be defined as *the process of creating organisational means to achieve purposeful ends* (cf. McFarland, 1979, p 5).

This means-end language is worthy of further unpacking. It crops up again in descriptions of 'leadership', which might be thought of as the more inspirational aspect of management and has been defined as a 'dynamic process in a group whereby one individual influences the others to contribute voluntarily to the achievement of group tasks in a given situation' (Cole, 1996, p 51). We are concerned in this module, then, with the processes of creating, sustaining and intervening in an organisation's *means-to-an-end*.

Morality, means and ends

Education in this country began in an intimate relationship with the church (Durham, 1970, chapter 1). Secularisation has changed the picture considerably. It is arguable that the severing of most forms of education from its traditional religious roots has weakened the sense of moral and spiritual vision of many teachers and school administrators (Grace, 1995, pp 154-155). A number of writers on school management point out the dangers of neglecting the *moral dimension* of this activity. In his book *Educational Leadership: the moral art*, Christopher Hodgkinson describes administration as 'philosophy in action'. Such a phrase runs along with his notion of the educational leader as a 'practical idealist' who exercises a 'moral art' by seeking 'according to personal ideals, to prevent the bad from being born and the good from dying too soon' within the educational institution (Hodgkinson, 1991, pp 165). This involves both practical, technical ability *and* ethical reflection, in a way that is akin to more ancient notions of the exercise of moral wisdom.

Educational management has often been reduced to what Aristotle called a *techne* ('craft', 'skill', or 'art') or *deinotes* (mere 'cleverness'), the technical skill and calculating competence that makes things and contrives to get things done effectively. These dimensions are, of course, crucial; but they can exist in the absence of any complementary moral or spiritual insight or wisdom. Producing things (Aristotle's 'productive life') and finding the right means to particular end results are activities that any competent and clever rogue could perform. According to Aristotle, more is needed for us to call such activity 'good'.

Aristotle used the term *praxis* to label the practical life, which he saw as purposeful human conduct combining knowledge with values. For this life we need a *praxis* way of knowing, which is achieved by reflective engagement in action. This has been described as reflective-practice or 'conscious reflective intentional action'. The concept of praxis should encourage us to resist the claim that debates about management should be value-free: a matter of empirical study only, without reference to morality. 'Applied to administration, [praxis] would mean the combination of management science with ethics' (Hodgkinson, 1991, p 113). Hodgkinson thus follows Aristotle in recognising the unavoidability of the value dimension in matters of practice.

We may seek further help from Aristotle. This classical Greek philosopher also distinguishes between two types of wisdom. On the one hand, we need what we may call a *wisdom of ends*, which is a matter of having the right aims by possessing a proper insight and judgement about correct values and virtues. First, then, we need to know what is good: what we should aim at. On the other hand, we also need to know how to aim at it. So we need the deliberative reasoning of a *wisdom of means*, which includes knowing the empirical effects of different sorts of social behaviour, as well as the more conceptual knowledge of what counts as the proper expression of specific ends (e.g. how justice or compassion are best exhibited). Second, therefore, we also need to know the means by which we can 'produce the goods', in the sense of producing *the good*.

The wisdom of means is my phrase for Aristotle's *practical wisdom* (Greek, *phronesis*). For Aristotle this is the state of mind that develops from (and develops) *praxis*. It is a type of means-ends reasoning that takes the general form: A is good; B is the means to A; therefore do B[1]. A considerable part of management-type work is activity of this kind: Do this in order to create that (and prevent the other). That is why managers need to know something about social psychology, to help them assess the probable results of their own behaviour and that of others. They need to know what people are likely to do in different circumstances. And they need to know what counts as an expression of the ends they intend to achieve. But this wisdom of means, as Aristotle notes, *presupposes* knowledge of the good ends, hence 'it is impossible to be practically wise without being good'[2].

Let us leave Aristotelian scholarship to others at this point[3], and concentrate on the most obvious sense in which B is good as the 'means to A'. We say that something is *instrumentally* good (good as a means) only if it leads to what is *intrinsically* good (good as an end, good 'in and of itself'). Applying this to our topic, we may say that if management is to show a *full moral wisdom* it must concern itself with the moral status of the results - the products - of the exercise of management. While managers and others often agree about the proper practical ('pragmatic') means to facilitate certain ends, they and we may disagree in the moral evaluation of those ends. And people frequently do disagree about moral values.

So far, so good? Well, perhaps not. You may be comfortable with the language of ends and its ethical dimension. After all, education is all about ends, and 'good ends' at that. Education is a value-laden word, labelling a

---

[1] Aristotle, *Nicomachean Ethics*, various editions, 1112b 8-20.

[2] *Ibid.*, 1144a 36.

[3] I attempt here no further analysis of *Aristotle's* view on these matters, merely noting that he has such a wide concept of *eudaimonia* ('happiness') that the means to this good end appear to be a constituent part of it. In the text here, however, I am thinking of means that are more *external* to their ends.

'valuable' activity. It is itself regarded as a 'good thing', something of which we should approve. The ends of education are 'values' or valuable states (knowledge; intellectual and motor skills; discernment; wisdom; tolerance; moral, spiritual and physical development, etc.).

If educational management is about ends - and it is - then it is concerned with values. All that is unexceptionable. But shouldn't we be suspicious of the language of means? Of course, we do say that some situations are 'good' and some actions 'right' only insofar as they lead to good results. The surgeon's cutting and the dentist's drilling aren't good in and of themselves. They gain our moral commendation only as means to a better end: life and health, (eventual) cessation of pain, freedom to eat ice-lollies again, and so on. These ends may 'justify the means', but does it follow that *any means* are justified provided that the end is justified? Surely not. We must make a moral assessment of the means as well. Even the classic 'value-condition' of the normative concept of education, that connects it with the development of desirable qualities in a person, always assumed that this should take place in a morally unobjectionable manner[4].

Activity B1

Try a thought-experiment. Reflect on various management strategies which may apply in school or elsewhere that produce good results, but might themselves be ethically questionable. Can *these* means be justified by *those* ends? Perhaps you could rank them from 'clearly justifiable' means, through 'sometimes justifiable' means, to 'completely unjustifiable' means or 'never justifiable' means.

Comment on activity B1

It is worth trying to produce a really 'difficult case' of morally suspect means that produce laudable ends. A great deal of education in earlier days might fall into this category. My religious education teacher at secondary school thought that he could produce a more disciplined and religiously responsive class by keeping us in to write out the Sermon on the Mount! It is, of course, important here to distinguish (i) *factual* ('empirical') questions about whether this means does effect these ends, and (ii) *moral* evaluations of the means (and also of the ends themselves).

---

[4] See R.S. Peters, Aims of Education, in R.S. Peters (ed.), *The Philosophy of Education* (London, Oxford University Press, 1973) and R.S. Peters, What is an educational process? in R.S. Peters (ed.), *The Concept of Education* (London, Routledge and Kegan Paul, 1967, pp 1-23).

Another problem arises where an action that is a means to good ends *also* produces bad ends[5]. You bribe your children to work hard with gifts of sticky toffee. The test results improve, but their teeth and health do not (not to mention their understanding of the proper reasons for putting energy into learning). Do the ends justify the means? Well, you will have to calculate *all* the ends - all the consequences of your strategy - and then attempt some sort of moral calculus or cost-benefit analysis.

But is there a further problem? A major insight of many ethical traditions, and most definitively of the moral philosophy of Immanuel Kant (1724-1804), is the claim that actions are only right, not as means to any end, but as a function of the action itself - that it was done for the right reason. In particular, Kant argued that persons should always (also) be treated as 'ends in themselves', and never *merely* as a means[6]. As you reflect again on this exercise, ask yourself whether the management and educational means that you rejected were rejected because pupils or teachers were being treated simply as means to some end, and not also as ends-in-themselves. Bottery (1990, pp 126, 134) argues that much recent management literature is essentially *manipulative*, in treating pupils - and teachers - as means to an end. (To manipulate is to change people against their will and desires, see Astley, 1994a, pp 216-217.)

B2 Christianity and values

So far we have hardly mentioned *Christian* values. The omission should be remedied; but first it is important to try to get clear about the relationship between morality and religion in general, and moral values and Christian values in particular.

Morality and religion

Our first problem, however, is that this relationship is very far from being clear. There is a strong consensus that morality is autonomous and independent of religion. According to Kant, religion might offer additional motivation for obeying the moral law, but the moral law is itself grounded in universal rationality and not in particular revelations. Many others have followed Kant's lead, even if they have identified their grounding for morality in different non-

---

[5] Compare the 'Principle of double effect', which permits acts that are done for intended good results that also produce foreseen, but not directly intended, bad effects.
[6] See *The Moral Law*, a translation of Kant's 'Groundwork of the Metaphysics of Morals' by H. J. Paton (London, Hutchinson, 1948, especially pp 90-91).

religious sources: moral vision or intuition; human nature and human flourishing; social rules and prescriptions; or human attitudes, evaluations and feelings. By contrast, religious traditions appear to find their morality in revelations and/or experiences of God's will. They argue that our moral duty is our duty because God commands it, and our values are valuable because God values them.

We might attempt a reconciliation by noticing that the central core of morality lies in a claim about human beings - that 'persons matter' (cf. Kant's insistence that we treat other people as ends in themselves). *Virtues* are human attitudes of which we approve (which we 'value') that foster certain *values* that are recognised goals for individual and social human life, and fulfil certain recognised *duties and obligations* to people. According to Peter Baelz, these 'obligations, values and virtues are all rooted in some "vision" of what it is to be truly and fully human' (Baelz, 1996, p 37). But as God has created us with a nature such that we find human fulfilment in certain situations (which we then call 'good', and naturally so does God), even those who do not believe in God can share the same values, in that they have that same nature. Christians, other theists and atheists may thus all agree about morality.

Theists, however, make the additional claim that human beings, as God's creatures, are created *for* free caring relationships with one another, and free devotion to God. Christian ethics may also be seen as an account of the way of life that is *appropriate* to one who believes in this merciful, loving, dependable God: as 'the way in which anyone who genuinely and wholeheartedly believes in the heavenly Father will naturally tend to live' (Hick, 1983, p 63).

Note that many values may properly be designated 'Christian' even though they are not unique to Christianity. It is in the area of values particularly that the religions, and many secular world-views such as humanism, share most in common. Thus trustworthiness and compassion for the weak, suffering and oppressed are certainly 'characteristic' of Christianity, without being 'distinctive' of it. Other characteristic Christian values are those that promote (i) a full realisation of the potentials and needs of human beings, (ii) the furtherance of community (both in terms of the community of the institution and of the wider community), and (iii) a relationship of stewardship towards creation. These values may be applied to businesses (see Higginson, 1993, 1996) as well as to schools (see the papers by Sedgwick, Zipfel and Hulmes, in Astley and Day, 1992). Despite the apparent variety of moral codes in our plural society and across world cultures, there are striking similarities in their lists of basic moral principles and 'human goods' (Lewis, 1943, appendix; cf. Midgley, 1991, chapters 11 and 12). Some (particularly Catholic) moral theologians argue that this is explained by the existence of a 'natural law': a set of moral insights and injunctions that can be discerned by contemplating human nature as such with our unaided reason.

One understanding of the ambiguous phrase *Christian education* is in terms of a Christian approach to general schooling, which evaluates and directs the whole activity of the school in the light of Christian values (Astley and Day, 1992, chapter 1). This sort of Christian education might be described as a 'Christian approach' to general education or schooling. A Christian critique of the management aspect of schooling forms part of this. Does this critique have to be uniquely Christian? I think not, unless we restrict ourselves to the rather small set of values that are distinctive of, rather than merely characteristic of, Christianity.

Activity B2

Attempt at this point to list the set of 'moral' and 'spiritual' values ('goods') and virtues that you take to characterise Christianity. Mark any that you think are unique to Christianity

Comment on activity B2

Your list of moral virtues might have included, for example, honesty, compassion, trustworthiness, justice, prudence, temperance, fairness and co-operativeness. Lists of spiritual virtues usually include the 'theological virtues' of faith, hope and love, and the 'fruits of the spirit' of Galatians 5.22-23, including joy, peace, kindness, meekness and self-control[7]. Are any of these unique to Christianity?

Spiritual values?

Many of the values that religious people point to, as either characteristic or distinctive of their religion, are better labelled as 'spiritual' rather than 'moral' values. The relationship between spirituality and ethics is very close, for both areas arise from basic attitudes and values that find expression in moral actions ('good works') or religious actions (worship and prayer). According to

---

[7] On Christian ethics and moral and spiritual values, see also: R. C. Mortimer, *The Elements of Moral Theology* (London, A. and C. Black, 1953); E. Le Roy Long, *A Survey of Christian Ethics* (New York, Oxford University Press, 1967); K. Ward, *Ethics and Christianity* (London, Allen and Unwin, 1970); N.H.G. Robinson, *The Groundwork of Christian Ethics* (London, Collins, 1971); J.P. Wogaman, *A Christian Method of Moral Judgement* (London, SCM, 1976); P. Baelz, *Ethics and Belief* (London, Sheldon, 1977); E. Le Roy Long, *A Survey of Recent Christian Ethics* (New York, Oxford University Press, 1982); J. Macquarrie and J. Childress (eds), *A New Dictionary of Christian Ethics* (London, SCM, 1986); R. Preston, Christian ethics, in P. Singer (ed.), *A Companion to Ethics* (Oxford, Blackwell, 1993).

Gordon Wakefield (1983, p 549), spirituality comprises those attitudes, values, beliefs and practices that 'animate people's lives and help them to reach out towards super-sensible realities'. On this definition, our spirituality includes our deepest commitments: what matters most to us. Spirituality is not restricted to religion, however, although there may be particular spiritual values that are stressed in particular religions.

David Carr (1995, p 92; cf. 89) notes that spiritual virtues go beyond their moral counterparts. Thus 'hope' is more than 'courage', and 'asceticism' more than 'temperance'. They do this, he claims, in a way that is a function of their being 'orientated towards the extra-mundane dimension of human aspiration, to what lies beyond the purely temporal'. There have been similar, but less ontologically committed, accounts of the *transcending nature* - in a real sense the *religious nature* - of the spiritual perspective[8]. It is in this area of spirituality that we may find distinctively religious and Christian values, especially those relating to worship, devotion, obedience and vocation[9].

B3 School leadership, values and moral education

William Foster (1989, p 56) writes that leadership in general, and educational leadership in particular, must be thoroughly value-driven, i.e. 'ethically-based'. Thomas Sergiovanni shares this concern for an 'ethical focus' or moral dimension to educational leadership. He writes of the 'virtuous school' as an end in its own right (an interesting variation on our theme in section B1). He also notes 'that effective schools have virtuous qualities that account for a large measure of their success' (Sergiovanni, 1992, p 99), an empirical claim that we shall return to later. Shared positive values, especially caring and respect, mark out these virtuous schools; and 'servant leadership' and a strong concept of stewardship are the distinguishing features of the proper leader within them, according to Sergiovanni.

Such arguments usually specify a particular moral *content* in the purpose of the school. But other accounts claim to be more formal, in the sense of content-free, and are defended as implied by the very notion of education. Thus Bottery (1992, chapter 12) argues for a 'transformative or moral' model of leadership that is closely linked to his understanding of the ultimate moral purpose of the school. He identifies three dimensions of this style of leadership:

---

[8] See S.R. Sutherland, *God, Jesus and Belief* (Oxford, Blackwell, 1984, part II) and G. Moore, *Believing in God* (Edinburgh, T. and T. Clark, 1988, chapter 5.

[9] For a criticism of accounts of 'spiritual values' that are presented in isolation from particular religious traditions, see A. Thatcher, 'Policing the sublime': a wholly (holy?) ironic approach to the spiritual development of children, in J. Astley and L.J. Francis (eds), *Christian Theology and Religious Education: connections and contradictions*, London, SPCK, 1996, pp 117-139.

- possessing a vision of a good and just community (this is the 'culture' an organisation creates - mainly directly, but also indirectly in its influence on the wider society);
- enabling others to reach their full potential (including their moral education potential);
- empowering others to become leaders themselves.

You may care to reflect on how far you think that these are moral and/or Christian values.

Three ages of school management

Headteachers in particular have traditionally been expected to show not only pedagogical, but also moral leadership in their schools. In the past this moral leadership was usually closely related to religious authority and example, and was properly seen as a 'vocation'. It was routinely wedded to a particular social and political ordering of society (cf. Grace, 1995, pp 8-11, 28-30). Gerald Grace traces the shift from this understanding of educational leadership, 'firmly located in notions of class hierarchy and of class-cultural control', and defined by a sense of moral energy and purpose, to the more professional (but perhaps no less political) sort of leadership that was preferred during the period from the 1940s to the 1970s.

The new style of school leadership reflected the cultural changes of those times in its adoption of the language and values of social democracy, in particular a more equitable distribution of wealth and of power, and its recognition of the importance of government involvement in this 'public service' (Grace, 1995, pp 30-39; cf. Bottery, 1992, pp 71-76). Mostly, we should note, this was a period still innocent of the managerial rhetoric and practice that was later to distinguish the 'market management' era of the 1980s and 1990s, the last of the three stages identified by Grace. Cutting the cake slightly differently, Bottery (1990, chapter 2) distinguishes the first and last of these three periods in terms of the approaches they adopted to the teaching of morality in schools. Thus the period 1820-1960 was marked by the 'ruler and ruled code' (with the upper classes educating their children into a morality of the right and a duty to rule, while other classes were being socialised into accepting their position and fitting the needs of industry). Moral education from 1974 onwards, by contrast, was marked by 'the GNP code', with its stress on moral conformity, freedom of economic manoeuvre, and profiting from one's endeavours[10].

---

[10] According to Bottery (1990), 1960-1974 was marked by the 'self-chosen code' in moral education, which emphasised moral choice, 'values clarification' and ethical relativism, and tended towards a somewhat anarchistic, 'doing one's own thing' view of morality.

All three stages were undergirded by distinct values:

- the values of 'godliness and good learning', and of authority, obedience and control, in nineteenth and early twentieth century schooling;
- democratic, egalitarian and humane pastoral values, in the social democratic period of the mid-twentieth century;
- the more secular values of cost-efficient productivity, in the late twentieth century market culture.

As Grace (1995, pp 40-41) puts it:

> Education, regarded in the nineteenth century as primarily a moral and spiritual enterprise and regarded in the social democratic era as a professionally autonomous cultural service, has been recontextualized in the 1980s as a product of the market place.... If school leadership, in the person of the headteacher, was expected to provide and articulate a moral mission in the nineteenth century and a professional and pedagogically progressive mission in the social democratic era, then it seems that contemporary headteachers in England will increasingly be expected to articulate a market mission.

This language of 'mission' and values relates closely to the perceived ends of education. 'Mission statements', that is statements of 'an organisation's overriding purpose or vision' (Cole, 1996, p xi), are revealing in this context. A school's 'mission statement', if not simply an anodyne statement of being in favour of education (or of virtue!), should articulate the underlying vision of the aims of this particular school[11]. One revealing feature of documents of this nature is whether or not they contain references to a community that is wider than the school itself. General management theory is often willing to acknowledge that managerial responsibility is both a responsibility *for* the desired outcomes of management, and a responsibility *to* the groups that have a stake in the process, including society at large (McFarland, 1979, pp 55-56; Solomon, 1993). Schools need not therefore be shy of acknowledging *their* wider accountability (cf. Grace, 1995, p 209).

You may want to study your own school's 'mission statement' and note the values to which it declares its commitment. How many of them may be described as recognising an accountability to the wider community? How many are - at least characteristically - *Christian*?

The hidden curriculum of the school

The 'ethos', 'climate' or 'culture' of your school finds expression in a whole host of ways that are influenced by (and influence) its management. The so-

---

[11] For examples of mission statements from several major *companies*, see Higginson (1996, p 53). Higginson points out that the word 'integrity' crops up in many of them 'with intriguing regularity'.

called 'hidden curriculum' of a school comprises those experiences that effectively change the values and beliefs of pupils and teachers, but which are not explicitly labelled as 'learning experiences' (as they are in the 'manifest', 'overt' or 'official' curriculum).

If we are not alert to the learning that takes place in this tacit way, we will be ignorant of many of the effects of schooling. Schools have policies in a number of areas that contribute to the bulk of the 'learning iceberg' of schooling that lies below the waterline, ready to shipwreck the unwary. The areas include: its working environment; relationships among pupils (including the problem of bullying) and between staff and pupils; self-control and responsibility; order and consistency; clear goals, communication and feedback; rewards and punishments; homework; and race and gender issues (see Spooner, 1981; Reynolds, 1982, p 27; DES, 1985; McGuiness, 1993, chapter 7; Sammons *et al.*, 1995, pp 12-13, 19; Riley, 1994, pp 40-45, 59-70; Forster, 1997, chapter 3).

The hidden curriculum produces learning that we approve of, and learning of which we may strongly disapprove. We must be particularly alert to this 'negative learning', although we do not need to go as far as the 'deschoolers' in arguing that the existence of compulsory schooling as such provides a hidden curriculum where children mainly learn conformity, consumerism, how to cheat and how to fail[12].

The educational effect of this hidden curriculum is 'hidden' from the learners, and is perhaps the more powerful because of this. Only conspiracy theorists believe that this 'hiding' is deliberate. Indeed, unfortunately, the hidden curriculum is often equally well hidden from the teachers, as the 'forgotten curriculum' and the 'unrecognised curriculum' (Bottery, 1990, p 98). We may even speak of the 'null curriculum' of what is not taught and appears not to be worthy of mention - but from which children learn something[13].

One of the responsibilities of teachers and educational managers is surely to don their wetsuits and penetrate the murky waters to discover for themselves the hidden part of the iceberg: i.e. the learning effects of this more subtle side of their teaching and managing. This is part of our general responsibility to identify the effects of our actions, perhaps especially the unintended effects of those actions (Burbules, 1981; Gordon, 1980).

---

[12] See I. Illich, *Deschooling Society* (Harmondsworth, Penguin, 1971); E. Reimer, *School is Dead* (Harmondsworth, Penguin, 1971); I. Lister (ed.), *Deschooling: a reader* (Cambridge, Cambridge University Press, 1974).

[13] 'Not being educated in something skews and biases the options that lie before us, the perspectives from which we see, the alternatives from which we might choose' (Harris, 1987, p 100).

Activity B3

Bottery (1990, pp 98-100) offers us 70 'hidden curriculum questions'. I list a number of these below. In each case, ask yourself: What is the answer for my school? What are the moral educational effects of this practice? What do children learn from it? How would you morally evaluate this learning? Should the situation be changed, and if so how?

- Is the staff room for all members of the school or just the teaching members?
- What image of the Third World is presented in the school?
- Are children from ethnic minorities treated differently in disciplinary matters?
- Are boys and girls treated differently in disciplinary matters?
- What proportion of senior management posts are held by men/by women?
- How are letters home to parents addressed?
- What account is taken of parental expectations?
- How are visitors to the school treated?
- What proportion of time is spent on co-operative as opposed to competitive activities?
- What subjects are regarded as important, and why?
- In what areas are the staff least involved in decision-making?
- Does the school involve pupils in the decision-making process?
- When are rewards and punishments used?

Comment on activity B3

School management profoundly affects many of these means and ends of education. Would you expect a church school to offer different answers to these hidden curriculum questions from those provided by a 'state' (local authority or GM) school? If you would, is this because there are *distinctively Christian* values underlying your evaluation of the effects of this hidden learning?

Moral education and school management

Bottery and others argue that management theory should accept that moral education itself is one of the main responsibilities of the school. One might add that it is primarily the responsibility of parents, and also a responsibility of society in general. But it is, of course, a major obligation of the school also. (The moral obligation to spread, encourage and increase morality is perhaps fundamental to the very notion of having a morality or being moral.) Much moral education involves the *transmission* of, and *formation* of young people in, moral values and dispositions ('virtues'). Some of this will be done in the manifest or overt curriculum, i.e. through experiences that are labelled as learning experiences. But moral learning also happens through the learning experiences of the hidden curriculum. That is why we need to be especially clear about what personal values the school's management policies are teaching its pupils.

But there is more to moral education than moral formation through the overt and hidden curricula of the school. It is also the task of moral education to help the learner to *think for herself* morally: to develop, clarify, refine and grow into her own moral position, as well as to criticise and evaluate the received moral tradition. 'Genuine ethical commitment', Bottery writes, 'is more than the adoption of another's values; it is the constant striving to define one's own within the context of the community at large. This is the ultimate educational purpose of the school' (Bottery, 1992, p 52). This claim is of a piece with arguments about the importance of the development of autonomy in moral reasoning (cf. Wilson, 1990).

B4 Power, authority and leadership

I shall begin this section with a few definitions and some reflections on them. *Power* is the ability to implement actions. *Authority* is the legitimate power to act. In many discussions about management our main interest is in 'structural' authority: authority by virtue of the office a person holds. But leaders may also possess 'personal authority', which is a function of their personality; and teachers should always have 'sapiential authority', as a function of their knowledge and skills. You might like to reflect on whether there is something that might be called 'moral' or 'spiritual' authority, and what that is based on.

Responsibility is the obligation to act, coupled with an accountability for one's actions. *Delegation* assigns duties to others ('subordinates'). It involves a sharing of both responsibility (my obligation to perform certain functions) and authority (my legitimate power to act in certain ways), which nevertheless paradoxically leaves me with ultimate personal responsibility and authority (McFarland, 1979, pp 366-377)[14]. The notion of *decentralising authority* - placing authority and responsibility further down in an organisation - is a crucial concept in the field of management.

It is often said that the exercise of authority implicitly demands a voluntary acceptance of authority on the part of others. Without such acceptance, the

---

[14] Some argue, less paradoxically, that authority can be delegated but responsibility ('accountability') cannot. See Cole (1996, p 185 and chapter 23).

power of authority is lost. This rings interesting bells, of a political, moral and indeed religious timbre, in terms of concepts such as *government by consent*, *social contracts* and *covenant*. However, 'if authority were *purely* consensual, it is doubtful whether we would speak of power [being] exercised' at all (Fincham and Rhodes, 1992, p 437). With reference to the danger of the *abuse of power*, it should be noted that, if legitimate authority is not to be misused, authority must not exceed responsibility. On the other hand, where responsibility exceeds authority the management of organisations is disabled.

Task leadership and social leadership

John McGuiness finds in the social psychologist Michael Argyle a distinction between two complementary types of leadership: *task leadership* and *social leadership*[15]. Task leaders are experts who possess the ability to achieve their objectives - that is, to complete the task successfully. But social leadership is also needed in communities. This involves communicating an additional, motivating message: 'Follow me, not only because I know where to go; but also because you will be affirmed, respected, *valued.*' We manage best and teach best, McGuiness (1993, pp 19-28, 39) argues, when we communicate that message best - in a word, when we relate best. This is perhaps part of what has been called the 'aesthetic' dimension of leadership, which is a matter of capturing the imagination of others, offering a sense of direction, and engaging their feelings and aspirations. It requires a certain amount of sensitivity and even 'artistry'. It might lead us to think of the leader as 'poet', rather than as scientist or technologist (cf. Duke, 1986).

The management literature echoes this broad distinction between a leadership that is task oriented and one that is oriented to 'relationships', 'people' and 'socio-emotional needs' (cf. Cole, 1996, chapter 7; Fincham and Rhodes, 1992, chapter 8). A standard description of the key roles of the manager includes that of *friend*, alongside the role of *technician* (Herbert Sonthoff, quoted in McFarland, 1979, p 50). It is often said that efficiency ('productivity'), however scientifically plotted and technically facilitated, can easily suffer if relationships suffer. 'This is because people do not respond particularly to efficiency as an ideal, but rather to care, trust and responsibility' (Bottery, 1992, p 30).

But even if the effects were not counter-productive, from a values viewpoint we might claim that an organisation - especially a school - that did not strive to

---

[15] See M. Argyle, *The Psychology of Interpersonal Behaviour* (Harmondsworth, Penguin, 1983); M. Argyle, *Bodily Communication* (London, Methuen, 1988). Some would reserve the concept of *leadership* for the exercise of interpersonal skills, treating *management* as the activity of dealing with administrative tasks (see Higginson, 1996, p 26).

improve the quality of its relationships was failing *morally* and *spiritually*. The biblical tradition, although it is set in societies that are very different from our own, encourages us in this. In the Bible autocratic leadership was often not welcomed (cf. 1 Kings 12) and God's judgement on the powerful was fearlessly proclaimed (2 Samuel 12, 1 Kings 22, Micah 3). And even if slaves, children and wives had to obey; masters, parents and husbands were enjoined not to threaten or exasperate them, to treat them as beloved brothers, or to love them 'as Christ loved the church and gave himself up for her' (Philemon 16; Ephesians 5.21-33).

Democracy and autocracy

Communities arise only where there are shared values. 'Human valuations... lie at the basis of all moral judgements. We can live in societies because we share many of these judgements. We share them because we live in societies' (Astley, 1994b, p 46). If any organisation is to strive for and deserve the status of a community, there must be some sense in which there is a 'common unity' of values - a set of values that are shared among and between both the management and the 'managed' (cf. Solomon, 1993, p 358; Higginson, 1993, pp 49-51).

There is evidence that this may be regarded as a good thing at a number of levels. At one level, schools may be more effective when there is consensus among staff about the aims and values of the school (Sammons *et al.*, 1995, pp 11-12) or at least where teachers feel that their views are represented (Reynolds, 1982, p 27). The arguments for *participation by teachers* in the collaborative management of schools chimes in with language about 'participative management' in the general literature of management[16]. This often stresses the possible advantages for organisational effectiveness of such a decision-making and planning strategy (McFarland, 1979, p 94-95, 140-142), particularly through building and maintaining morale (McFarland, 1979, pp 502-507) and strengthening motivation (McGregor, 1960, pp 47-48; cf. Cole, 1996, chapters 5 and 6).

But there is a downside to democratic participation. We have all experienced situations where 'over-discussion' actually prevents things being done. The effectiveness criterion is vulnerable to empirical test: we really have to look and see whether managerial practice 'works' or not. Ethical arguments are in a different league, for they cannot in the same way be brought to the bar of experience. Bottery (1992, pp 170-177) suggests three such grounds for teacher participation. First, teachers ought to be involved in management

---

[16] All teachers are in a sense 'educational managers' - as managers of their pupils' learning.

because teachers give of their autonomy, individuality and self: they are indeed 'co-owners in the means of production'. Second, they ought to be involved because it is only through their participation that the teachers and their pupils will learn and understand citizenship. Third, teachers should be involved primarily because they are persons: 'ends in themselves', whose development and fulfilment is a proper moral concern of the school. Here we meet again the central Kantian moral principle about how people ought to be treated.

Participation by pupils in school management is a less popular option (at least among the teachers!), but similar justificatory arguments may be developed in terms of allowing pupils to exercise autonomy - i.e. treating them as moral ends in themselves - and giving them the appropriate experience and responsibility to enhance their moral and socio-political education. However, attempts to extend democratic decision-making in this way tend to run into well-worn arguments that would deny or severely limit the children's rights to decide their own actions, express their own opinions and be involved in institutional decisions. Bottery is critical of any arguments along these lines that are based on the children's lack of power and financial stake, or on their apathy and limited rationality. Bottery (1992, p 158) argues that there are strong epistemological and moral reasons for involving children in decisions about the curriculum and organisation of their schools:

> It is a child's right to be made aware of the differences of opinion, to know that an 'authority's' judgement is not the only one, and the acknowledgement of this right must inform the teaching of all subjects.... Not to consult children [about their own treatment] would specifically be a failure to educate them towards democratic involvement within the community as a whole.

Bottery (1992, p 66) argues that authority ought to be more dispersed in society so that more people can have the experience of exercising authority, and of being close to others who exercise it. Only in this way, he writes, can its mystique may be dissipated and the problems and fallibilities of people in authority better recognised.

Styles and structures of leadership and management

We defined leadership earlier in terms of the ability of one person to influence others to make that additional exertion that is often needed to achieve certain goals. The literature indicates that it is not possible to identify empirically any set of specific traits common to all successful leaders. The influence of the *authoritarian leader* may come down to his personality, but it may equally well derive from his exercise of coercive power by issuing threats or by relying on the prestige of his position. Authoritarian leaders get things done (their own things mainly, of course), and many people feel more secure under their leadership. But 'research indicates that in most situations the democratically led group is likely to be superior in accomplishment to a group led by an authoritarian' (McFarland, 1979, p 217; cf. Fincham and Rhodes, 1992, chapter 8). *Democratic leaders* - who are still *leaders*, let us remember - use persuasion and example rather than coercion or power. They consider the opinions and feelings of followers, and encourage self-control and participation in decision-making. By encouraging more group initiative, they strengthen the organisation itself.

Look again at McGregor's distinction between *theory X* and *theory Y* approaches to management (unit A of the module *Church School Management*). In his terms (McGregor, 1960) democratic leaders are more likely to adopt *theory Y* . These managers believe in their workers' capacity to grow and contribute to the organisation. They view people in a rather more favourable and optimistic light than the distrustful *theory X* managers, who see workers as essentially lazy, selfish and unambitious people who need to be controlled and coerced.

These characteristics of leaders may be used to describe organisations also. Thus 'authoritarian organisations' are those in which there is little or no participation from the members of that organisation to influence and contribute to decisions. Direction and control are 'top down' in such places. In 'democratically managed' organisations, however, many more people participate to a greater degree in making decisions[17]. Hierarchical structures of management are likely to lead to authoritarian management styles. By contrast, 'flatter' or net(work) organisational structures will be more attractive to democratic leaders than tall hierarchies.

There are educational implications in our choice of organisational structure. Bottery (1990, p 135) writes:

> What does a hierarchical structure in school tell the pupils? It tells them that in an age of cultural pluralism there is one person who is given the final say on matters of value, rather than these matters being discussed. It tells them that in terms of knowledge, even the expert must defer to the non-expert if this non-expert happens to have been granted a title of 'head'. It tells them that in the end their voice counts for nothing, nor does that of their teachers. They may be asked for their opinion, but it does not have to be accepted, as neither does the teachers'. In a democratic society, in *the* institution where democracy has a real chance of existence, it does not exist.

We noted above that if schools are *not* democratic, children will not learn the virtues and practices of democracy (cf. also Grace, 1995, pp 202-204). The present argument is different. It is that without democratic involvement the

---

[17] Lawton (1983, p 97) and others describe the less hierarchical and bureaucratic form of accountability of the network-structure of some organisations as 'democratic accountability'. In education this would involve most of the players (the head, teachers, parents, pupils, LEA, DfEE, public, industry etc.) being accountable to most of the others. Such a scenario is very unlike the present situation in schools.

pupils learn something else. They learn that democracy is not valued by adults, or at least not by the adults who run this particular institution.

Of course, 'democracy' may be adopted to varying degrees, and other moral and religious criticisms may be made of those schools that have enthusiastically embraced a one-person-one-vote democratic procedure in all matters. Some have even argued that democracy is not always a good thing anyway.

It has been said that 'the most important single factor in the success' of a school is 'the quality of leadership of the head' (DES, 1977, p 36). The traditional understanding of school leadership comes from the *autocratic headmaster* tradition, neatly articulated in Edward Thring's classic assertion of the head's authority: 'I am supreme here and I will brook no interference' (Peters, 1976, p 2). Today some argue for a democratic (even elected) educational leadership in schools that is a world away from this. The two types mark the extreme ends of a spectrum of models of headship. According to Pat White, *lynchpin heads* lead from the front, whereas *democratic heads* provide just those opportunities that we have already noted for staff and pupils to learn and develop, and to exercise their own rights and responsibilities as citizens (White, 1983). Interestingly, a recent report for OFSTED (Sammons *et al.*, 1995, p 10) amasses considerable research evidence for its advocacy of a middle way between extreme leadership styles, arguing that:

> Effective leadership requires clarity, avoidance of both autocratic and over-democratic ways of working, careful judgement of when to make an autonomous decision and when to involve others, and recognition of the efficacy of the leadership role at different levels of the school.

The traditional management distinction between *line-management and staff-management* structures may be of some relevance here. Line management authority is the controlling and directing backbone of most hierarchical organisations; it is based on the direct authority to act, decide, approve and control the work of others. Staff authority is more limited; for 'staff' managers usually often have no authority to direct or command, their task being rather to advise, monitor, plan and generally support. Whereas line-management fits a 'vertical' superior-subordinate relationship, staff structures appear 'to the side' of this up-and-down line structure, offering advice and sharing decision-making - exercising 'authority without responsibility' (Cole, 1996, pp 183-185; McFarland, 1979, pp 307-315, 361-366)[18]. At first sight staff management structures seem more suited to groups of professionals than do line structures; although many would argue that most organisations need some sort of line management, if only as something to fall back on.

---

[18] There are other forms of authority. *Functional* authority is subordinate to line-authority, but does have a limited right to command. Much staff authority in practice becomes functional authority.

It may be useful to summarise the notion of a *professional* at this point, with particular reference to teaching. A profession is usually thought to be marked by *self-regulation*, with the professional's competence being judged by fellow professionals and the profession controlling the selection, training and licensing of its own members. In these respects, it is often argued that teaching does not qualify as a profession. But two other traditional marks of a profession do apply to teaching, and they are more pertinent to our concerns here: 'professional work typically has a *service* element' and 'the professions are *ethical* occupations' (Fincham and Rhodes, 1992, p 283). With regard to the latter, theorists note such features as regulation by some code of ethics (in teaching, this is largely implicit)[19], the existence of a relationship of trust, and the assumption that the professional will act in the best interest of the 'client'. If professionals have these responsibilities and concerns, we may ask how far their work should be directed by others, even by others in the same profession? Such matters certainly can lead to tensions within a school staff when issues of management arise.

To conclude this section, we should note some *gender issues* relevant to management and leadership. Some contend that women approach managerial and leadership roles in ways that are very different from men. Thus women tend to be less hierarchical and are often more opposed to line management. They are more effective at interpersonal relationships, and therefore more attracted to co-operative modes of working, participatory teamwork and consultative decision-making. Men, on the other hand, tend to adopt more autocratic and directive styles of management (Sergiovanni, 1992, pp 135-138; Cole, 1996, pp 105-106. Cf. Gray, 1993; Grace, 1995, pp 60-62, chapter 10). These are additional possible sources of discontent within a school's management.

Activity B4

Reflect on your experience as a woman or man of managing, and being managed (by women and by men). Are there any particular *weaknesses and problems*, and any particular *strengths and possibilities*, that relate to gender?

Comment on activity B4

It has been argued that stereotypical masculine characteristics include: independence, assertiveness, risk-taking, dominance, ambition, self-reliance,

---

[19] 'Professional responsibility' is one aspect of this, and labels an area of responsibility *additional to* the moral accountability any one would have in relation to others (and particularly to children).

individualism and aggression; whereas stereotypical feminine characteristics include: sensitivity, compassion, warmth, loyalty and understanding. According to Sandra Bem (1981), 'competitiveness', 'leadership' and 'making decisions easily' are also viewed by the majority as 'masculine' traits.

On her view, however, 'masculine' traits may exist in women and 'feminine' traits in men. *Masculinity* and *femininity* are thus functions of one's personality, rather than of one's sex. If there is any relationship between management styles and gender, it may relate more closely to the masculinity/femininity than to the male/female distinction. Hence, the co-operative, caring male manager and the competitive, authoritarian female manager of your experience may not be such 'exceptions to the rule'. But perhaps there isn't a rule anyway. What do you think? And what should be the Christian view on this issue?

A Christian perspective?

Much of the above discussion falls under the heading of evaluation from a *characteristically* (rather than distinctively) Christian perspective. Can more be said? Richard Higginson (1996, pp 44-51) offers us three New Testament images of leadership: the leader as servant, shepherd and steward. (On the servant, see Luke 22.27, John 13.1-17, Philippians 2.6-8, Mark 10.42-45; on the shepherd: 1 Samuel 17.34-37, Isaiah 40.11, Psalms 23, John 10.11, Hebrews 13.20, John 21.15-19, 1 Peter 5.2, Acts 20.28; on the steward: Luke 12.42-48, 1 Corinthians 4.1, 1 Peter 4.10, Titus 1.7.)

- We have already noted the theme of *service*, and will return to it in the next section. 'Servant leadership' might include, according to Higginson, both willingness to delegate *and* the willingness to assume responsibility.
- The biblical metaphor of *shepherding* has connotations of hazard and exploration, as well as of tenderness and nurture, i.e. 'of courage, care, protection, discipline and establishing direction'. All these are dimensions of a true pastoral ministry, which may be exemplified in leadership and ad*ministration*.
- The third image of *stewardship* speaks of responsible authority owed to a higher authority, of one who is 'accountable to one's master for the management of resources'.

Like much religious language, the different metaphors are mutually qualifying. No one of them should be taken as a literal or complete picture of leadership. But they are suggestive in helping to articulate a Christian perspective on leadership, particularly in a school. You will note that they are routinely used in Christian pastoral and practical theology to describe ordained ministry and church leadership (which are not, perhaps, synonymous), and the wider ministry that belongs to all Christians. Nevertheless, they are not unique to understandings of *Christian* ministry.

B5 Commodities and persons

By the 1980s the dominant social democratic educational rhetoric began to face a number of challenges. It was exposed as vulnerable to criticisms about its economic effectiveness and to unease about the elements of social engineering involved in it. It was increasingly castigated for its failure properly to embrace the virtues of 'individual liberty, personal responsibility and self-reliance' (cf. Bottery, 1992, p 76) and for creating dependency or 'learned helplessness' (Bottery, 1990, p 28).

It was at this time that the 'discourse of the market' came to be heard more and more in the land with reference to schooling (cf. Grace, 1995, pp 39-47). The rhetoric of the market place found expression in the shibboleths of 'choice' and 'competition', and the battle-cries, 'If I can do it, so can you' and 'Avoid dependency'. These attitudes were later enfleshed in school reforms such as open enrolment, 'opting out' to grant-maintained status, LMS, and the publication of school results. Employers and parents became 'consumers', and teachers and schools the 'providers'. Increasingly children were spoken of as the 'products' of a 'value-added' educational process, and assessments made with the help of 'performance indicators' and 'league tables'. And all this was done with an eye to ensuring that the school-business kept and expanded its market share in *competition* with others.

Even the notion of accountability in schools has now become corporatist and consumerist, rather than democratic (Grace, 1995, p 200). Toughness, even a certain brutality, is thought to be a proper part of single-minded, entrepreneurial, realistic management in such a context. As a consequence, a different sort of professionalism is often expected of the head. This is the head as managing director, embracing *management* tasks enthusiastically; rather than a head t*eacher* who is most 'at home' back in the classroom (cf. Grace, 1995, p 23 and chapter 7).

But many have asked whether this is the appropriate language frame for 'education', if we understand by that word the facilitation of growth through learning of *persons*. Opponents of the market model in educational provision often also claim that education as a 'public good' cannot be left to markets, particularly with regard to the good end of equality of opportunity. Others contend that education is essentially subversive of authority, being predicated on criticism and reflection: educational outcomes that are ultimately unmarketisable. But defenders of the market have resisted such criticisms, arguing that markets *can* deliver even these goods, and that a just society is primarily one in which people are free to pursue their own ends without interference (see the debate in Bridges and McLaughlin, 1994; also Bottery, 1992, pp 77-80).

The Bottery critique

Mike Bottery is highly critical of the market paradigm for education (which he described in 1990 in terms of the 'GNP code' - see section B3 above)[20]. He rejects the market model's dual assumptions (a) that competition is natural to the human condition, rather than the product of 'artificial' market conditions, and (b) that human beings are basically selfish, arguing that selfishness is merely a potentiality - alongside altruism - that develops under particular social conditions (Bottery, 1992, pp 86-88). He further contends that the market model downgrades co-operation and empathy, makes people more selfish and judgmental, and results in organisations becoming more manipulative. More sweepingly, he criticises free-market theory as routinely ignoring issues of moral merit and evaluating everything solely in terms of 'price' and 'profit'. In the computation of the market place, social responsibility and the needs and desires of the child are bracketed out of the equation. According to Bottery (1992, p 88):

> A basic problem with the philosophy, then, is that it finds it hard to see people except as means to an end, the end being that of consumption. It tends to cheapen the quality of human relationships.

The sole criterion now becomes: Do I (or does my school) 'profit' from this action? 'The work of the teacher or the child is assessed in terms of effectiveness... how effective is the teacher in turning out the required product, how effective is the child at becoming what society wants him or her to become' (Bottery, 1990, p 29).

We have noted some of these ethical issues before. There is certainly a danger that in free market thinking moral virtues will become mere second-order principles, which may be over-ridden by the first-order principles of production, consumption and ownership. This will not do, if the ethical must come first. Others agree that one area in which the free market is deficient is that it does not pay sufficient attention to *merit*, 'where it is by no means guaranteed that virtue will be in sufficient demand so as to be rewarded'

---

[20] See also his earlier book for an excellent account of eleven arguments for and against competition in education (Bottery, 1990, chapter 9, chart on p 87). He concludes with the claim that competition is not inevitable in a school and asks, 'What is the point of a competitive environment when the same academic results can be gained by other means, and better social results can always be produced?'

(Solomon, 1993, p 359). This is surely a very important issue in education, as it is in ethics - and religion.

According to Oscar Wilde, it is the cynic 'who knows the price of everything and the value of nothing' (*Lady Windermere's Fan*, III), so perhaps we cannot be accused of cynicism in questioning market economics on this point. The issue is simply this: if we are talking about educational, ethical and/or spiritual *values*, then we are talking about what 'should exist', what '*ought* to be', what is *desirable*. We are not asking what the price of such activities actually *is*, or how much people are willing to pay for them, or even what people themselves in fact *desire*. Simply choosing a particular school or subject or learning experience can and should be distinguished from according it merit - i.e. thinking that it is morally or educationally a good thing. Merit, like virtue, is 'without price'.

In this context, Bottery offers four 'focuses of concern' for schools and society. They are:

- fostering the child's self-esteem;
- heightening the child's empathy;
- furthering co-operation between children;
- promoting rationality.

Activity B5

How might these four focuses of concern relate to the competitive culture of market forces?

Comment on activity B5

You may yourself be quite sympathetic to the demands of the market as they affect the management of schools. If you are, or indeed even if you are not, you may like to see how a critic of the free market in education would answer this question. Bottery relates these educational needs to the 'GNP code' and its effects, along the following lines (Bottery, 1990, pp 29-32, see also, pp 36-37). (The GNP code, Bottery argues, fails to recognise any problems in these areas.)

First, the fostering of the child's self-esteem is easily damaged by a culture of competitiveness and the concomitant, inevitable failure of many. (He adds that the insecure and unloved are less likely to help others and that the creation of 'a caring and supportive environment' is part of a school's moral duty.)

Second, the child's empathy needs heightening so as to combat an egocentric pre-occupation with the self, fostered by concentrating on one's own success. (He adds that tolerance and the appreciation of the suffering of others will not be created without it.)

Third, the furthering of co-operation between children is opposed to too much competition, which breeds suspicion and hostility. (He adds that violence and aggression often result from competitive sports, and asks: Do we *have* to teach children that co-operation will be 'punished' by society?)

Fourth, the promotion of rationality is always needed for complex judgements about the empirical facts of moral dilemmas and the effects of human actions, and for an imaginative understanding of the distress of others.

In both his books, Bottery adds a *pragmatic condition* to his ethical critique, arguing that the aspirations of the free market should be kept in check at least so as to prevent the undermining of the principle of choice that unbridled competition can produce. Examples of this would include the closure of less popular schools, with consequent restrictions on parental freedom of choice. Here again we come across an empirical argument that is independent of, but may be used to complement, an ethical critique.

Some conceptual issues

There are conceptual, as well as moral and pragmatic difficulties with the market model of schooling. Who are the *consumers* of the products of the educational enterprise? Are they the parents or the employers (or 'society' or 'the state')? Should parents be seen as 'partners' in the educational enterprise, rather than (solely) as customers (Bottery, 1992, pp 110-111)? At least in partnership there is a two-way dialogue. And why are the consumers not the children? (One author brackets 'parents, children, employers' together as 'customers': see Handy, 1984, p 28.) How else might we view the children on this philosophy: as *workers*, *clients* or *products* of some organisational process? Normal businesses do not seek to enhance the learning and development of those who are within them in quite the way that schools do (cf. Bottery, 1992, p 114). A further difficulty is that 'achievement' is more difficult to measure in educational processes, compared with those of the manufacturing industry[21].

---

[21] It would be helpful to read Bottery (1992, pp 115-127) for an account of nine 'business analogies' that find their way into educational management debate, together with his comments on their value.

Qualifications of the market model

Perhaps the market model can be redeemed somewhat by the recognition that the appropriate analogy for schools is not so much with the processes and products of *manufacturing* industry ('production') as with the *service* provided by business, commerce and the 'service industries'. Many teachers would prefer that language frame, even though it retains the metaphor (surely it is a metaphor?) of 'customers'. But we would then be only a short step away from the idea of a 'public service', and the free market reformers started by wanting to move away from that 'costly', 'inefficient' and 'socialist' notion. Defenders of public services often argue along the modest lines that 'not all services or initiatives can have their worth measured by profit or numbers or even popular success' (Hoggart, 1996, p 10). This seems an entirely reasonable, moderate - and self-evident - claim.

Another way to temper the apparent harshness of market language in school management is to draw on elements in management theory itself that have expanded the notion of organisational effectiveness ('achieving its objectives without undue strain, given its resources') to embrace wider concerns than just 'productivity' and 'efficiency', let alone 'profit'. After all, what is to count in the calculus of an organisation's effects is a conceptual issue, not an empirical one. We decide it, we don't discover it. Some have pleaded for 'softer' criteria of effectiveness (McFarland, 1979, chapter 24; cf. Solomon, 1993), including measures of social responsibility (e.g. improving human relationships inside the organisation and promoting the good of at least some sections of the society that lies outside it[22]) and environmental responsibility (e.g. the prudent and non-polluting use of natural resources and the rejection of animal testing programmes). This would appear to be a less contentious set of criteria for assessing schools.

It is refreshing to read that the purpose of a corporation, according to Robert Solomon, is to 'serve the public' (Solomon, 1993, p 361), rather than to serve itself alone. Solomon (1993, p 358) also helpfully criticises the rather overblown rhetoric about the role of competition in business:

> However competitive a particular industry may be, it always rests on a foundation of shared interests and mutually agreed-upon rules of conduct, and the competition takes place not in a jungle but in a community which it presumably both serves and depends upon. Business life is first of all fundamentally co-operative. It is only within the bounds of mutually shared concerns that competition is possible.

While we should not ignore the positive value of self-reliance and independent responsibility that a culture of competitiveness can also bring (Higginson,

---

[22] These are the so-called 'stakeholders' - 'all who have legitimate expectations and rights regarding the actions of the company' (Solomon, 1993, p 360). Solomon also inveighs against the foolishness of singling out 'profits' as the central aim of any business activity (p 357).

1997), it is clear that Christians must critique the *unqualified* endorsement of profit and competition that lies behind some of the assumptions of the market place.

A Christian critique?

Gerald Grace underscores the significance in the literature on Catholic schooling and educational leadership of the dimensions of moral and spiritual responsibility, commitment independent of rewards or status, and service and dedication. Grace (1995, p 66) writes, 'religious-educational cultures of many traditions carry messages about leadership which stand in a critical relation to those currently dominant or rising to dominance in secular culture'. Protestant critiques of different aspects of what has been called the 'commodification' of schooling include its stress on certain forms of assessment (those that 'erode self-esteem and the joy of learning': Hill, 1997, p 146) and its limited vision for humanity ('to train "cannon fodder" for the commerce of the future': Forster, 1997, p 10). Christians generally expect schools to serve the common good. The market philosophy, however, tends to undermine a commitment to the common good, because in a competitive ethos it is individual success that counts and those who wait to assist their weaker brethren are unlikely to win any race. Competition and inequality seem to be inextricably linked (Walford, 1993)[23].

Very many of those who are most vociferous in defence of the *ethical focus* of educational leadership refuse to reduce it to the deliberately amoral notions of marketing and industrial or commercial styles of management (Foster, 1989). We might argue that Christians in particular should commend a broader and more human vision for education (Forster, 1997, chapter 2). In writing elsewhere on this topic, I have expressed my concern that the impersonal language of production, manufacturing, retailing and commerce tempts us 'to see education in less than fully human terms, as a production line moulding people into the right shapes to fit empty holes in the economy'. According to Astley (1992, pp 319-320) this is too ruthless and 'macho' a model of education and of human maturity:

> If one of the aims of education is the person-making function, teaching me to be more fully human, then it needs to develop more than my technical skills and economically-valuable technological knowledge.... Something more is needed for that. It is something that is rather low-tech and difficult to quantify, and therefore embarrassing to mention in economic debates. But it is crucial to the development of mature personhood, and can only be provided by

---

[23] Gender issues arise here also, for research shows that women headteachers are less likely to celebrate either market values or the notion of 'winning' than are their male colleagues (e.g. Grace, 1995, chapter 10).

those who have attained a certain sort of maturity. It is *love*, and knowledge directed by love.

> The concept of Christian maturity is integrally related to the power and possibility of love: of growing up through love into love.... What is required is social support for the values of our true humanness. To put it bluntly: if Christianity is soft - if it is the expression of a soft model of maturity - then it needs soft societies to allow its full growth.

This is the point at which I would align myself with an alternative discourse, one that employs the personal language of relationships, vocations, needs and particularly *service*. The understanding of education as a 'public service', at the very least as a 'service industry', and of teaching as a vocation to serving the needs of people, is very different from the impersonal language of production and retailing. Service is a species of love - of *agape*, love-in-action, the promotion and procuring of the good of others.

Public services are, of course, dependent on the wealth creation of industry and commerce, 'parasitic on' them if you must. Where there is no profit, there is no business, no incomes, no taxes - and therefore no health or social services, and no education. All this is true. But there is another, more easily overlooked and less easily quantified dependency. Business and markets are themselves sustained by a substructure of comparatively lowly paid 'support' staff, without which no business would exist and no profits would be possible. And beyond them lies the whole fabric of our society, which rests on the *wholly unpaid* devotion, love and service of human relationships. I am thinking here particularly of parents, but also of the informal networks of human support and care (and 'production') that are provided by relatives, neighbours and friends. Only a myopic 'realistic' vision can fail to see and to value that contribution to the economy.

While we need to recognise that public services are parasitic on the 'business community', let us also acknowledge that those businesses are themselves parasitic on the 'private services' of a *real* community: a community that they did not create, do not pay for and have no moral right to control. People came first. People come first, and their loves make the world that is society go round, turning into the sun. So people have the right to come first.

Markets are not the only 'forces' that exist. They are just the easiest places in which to negotiate a price. Some expenditures of energy, though costly, are not bought and sold there. And others cannot be, for they would be dissipated in the transaction. Love can have no price.

Readers

A large part of L.J. Francis and D.W. Lankshear (eds) (1993), *Christian Perspectives on Church Schools*, Leominster, Gracewing, is indirectly relevant to the internal organisation of church schools. You will find helpful reference to church schools in section 5 of L.J. Francis and A. Thatcher (eds) (1990), *Christian Perspectives for Education*, Leominster, Gracewing.

Bibliography

Astley, J. (1992), Growing into Christ: the psychology and politics of Christian maturity, in J. Astley and D. Day (eds), *The Contours of Christian Education*, Great Wakering, McCrimmons, pp 307-322.

Astley, J. (1994a), *The Philosophy of Christian Religious Education*, London, SPCK.

Astley, J. (1994b), Communities, feelings and education, *Aspects of Education*, 51, 46-52.

Astley, J. and Day, D. (eds) (1992), *The Contours of Christian Education*, Great Wakering, McCrimmons.

Baelz, P. (1996), Morality and religion, *Dialogue*, 6, 36-39.

Bem, S. (1981), *Bem Sex Role Inventory: professional manual*, Palo Alto, California, Consulting Psychologists Press.

Bottery, M. (1990), *The Morality of the School: the theory and practice of values in education*, London, Cassell.

Bottery, M. (1992), *Ethics of Educational Management: personal, social and political perspectives on school organization*, London, Cassell.

Bridges, D. and McLaughlin, T.H. (eds) (1994), *Education and the Market Place*, London, Falmer.

Burbules, N.C. (1981), Who hides the hidden curriculum? in C.J.B. Macmillan (ed.), *Philosophy of Education 1980*, Normal, Illinois, Philosophy of Education Society, pp 281-291.

Carr, D. (1995), Towards a distinctive conception of spiritual education, *Oxford Review of Education*, 21, 83-98.

Cole, G.A. (1996[5]), *Management Theory and Practice*, London, Letts Educational.

Department of Education and Science (1977), *Ten Good Schools: a secondary school enquiry*, London, HMSO.

Department of Education and Science (1985), *Better Schools*, London, HMSO.

Duke, D.L. (1986), The aesthetics of leadership, *Educational Administration Quarterly*, 22, 7-27.

Durham, Bishop of (ed.) (1970), *The Fourth R: the report of the commission on religious education in schools*, London, National Society/SPCK.

Fincham, R. and Rhodes, P.S. (1992²), *The Individual, Work and Organization: behavioural studies for business and management*, London, Weidenfeld and Nicolson.

Forster, G. (1997), *Education: vision, ethos and 'values'*, Cambridge, Grove Books.

Foster, W. (1989), Toward a critical practice of leadership, in J. Smyth (ed.), *Critical Perspectives on Educational Leadership*, London, Falmer, pp 39-62.

Gordon, D. (1980), The immorality of the hidden curriculum, *Journal of Moral Education*, 10, 3-8.

Grace, G. (1995), *School Leadership: beyond education management: an essay in policy scholarship*, London, Falmer.

Gray, H. (1993), Gender issues in management training, in J. Ozga (ed.), *Women in Educational Management*, Buckingham, Open University Press, pp 106-115.

Handy, C. (1984), *Taken for Granted? looking at schools as organizations*, York, Longman.

Harris, M. (1987), *Teaching and Religious Imagination: an essay in the theology of teaching*, San Francisco, HarperCollins.

Hick, J. (1983), *The Second Christianity*, London, SCM.

Higginson, R. (1993), *Called to Account*, Guildford, Eagle.

Higginson, R. (1996), *Transforming Leadership: a Christian approach to management*, London, SPCK.

Higginson, R. (1997), *The Ethics of Business Competition: the law of the jungle?* Cambridge, Grove Books.

Hill, B.V. (1997), Evaluation and assessment: the tail that wags the dog? in J. Shortt and T. Cooling (eds), *Agenda for Educational Change*, Leicester, Apollos, pp 132-147.

Hodgkinson, C. (1991), *Educational Leadership: the moral art*, Albany, New York, State University of New York Press.

Hoggart, R. (1996), *The Way we Live Now*, London, Pimlico.

Lawton, D. (1983), *Curriculum Studies and Education Planning*, London, Routledge and Kegan Paul.

Lewis, C.S. (1943), *The Abolition of Man*, Oxford, Oxford University Press.

McFarland, D.E. (1979), *Management: foundations and practices*, New York, Macmillan.

McGregor, D. (1960), *The Human Side of Enterprise*, New York, McGraw-Hill.

McGuiness, J. (1993), *Teachers, Pupils and Behaviour: a managerial approach*, London, Cassell.

Midgley, M. (1991), *Can't We Make Moral Judgements?* Bristol, Bristol Classical Press.

Peters, R.S. (ed.) (1976), *The Role of the Head*, London, Routledge.

Reynolds, D. (1982), The search for effective schools, *School Organization*, 2, 215-237.

Riley, K.A. (1994), *Quality and Equality: promoting opportunities in schools*, London, Cassell.

Sammons, P., Hillman, J. and Mortimore, P. (1995), *Key Characteristics of Effective Schools: a review of school effectiveness research*, London, Institute of Education.

Sergiovanni, T.J. (1992), *Moral Leadership: getting to the heart of school improvement*, San Francisco, Jossey-Bass.

Solomon, R.C. (1993), Business ethics, in P. Singer (ed.), *A Companion to Ethics*, Oxford, Blackwell, pp 354-365.

Spooner, R. (1981), On leadership and ethos, *School Organization*, 1, 107-115.

Walford, G. (1993), Self-managing schools, choice and equity, in J. Smyth (ed.), *A Socially Critical View of the Self-Managing School*, London, Falmer, pp 229-244.

Wakefield, G.S. (1983), Spirituality, in A. Richardson and J. Bowden (eds), *A New Dictionary of Christian Theology*, London, SCM, pp 549-550.

White, P. (1983), *Beyond Domination: an essay in the political philosophy of education*, London, Routledge and Kegan Paul.

Wilson, J. (1990), *A New Introduction to Moral Education*, London, Cassell.

Church School Management

Unit C

Practicalities of church school management

David W. Lankshear

The National Society

London

Contents

Introduction

Aims

After working through this unit you should be able to:

- reflect on the issues raised by the challenge of managing a church school;
- reflect on and develop a management style appropriate to a church school;
- discuss the establishment of an ethos statement for a church school;
- translate an existing ethos statement into reality.

Overview

This unit builds on the work already undertaken in units A and B in this module. It presumes you have considered management concepts and the application of Christian values to these concepts. The focus in this unit is on the practical issues of management. The unit will have two intertwined lines of development. One will focus on the creation of a personal management style appropriate to the individual reader and to the context of a church school. The other will explore the issues raised by the challenge of managing a church school. This will be illustrated by considering the situation, experienced by several headteachers in the early 1990s, of taking over a failing county school and being required to change it into a successful church school.

C1 Challenges of church school management

The management of a church school is like the management of any other maintained school, but with an added church dimension. It is appropriate, therefore, to consider the summary of general research on school effectiveness that was commissioned by OFSTED in 1994 and reported in Sammons, Hillman and Mortimore (1995). They looked at a huge range of literature over at least thirty years and made use of international studies to report on the 'key determinants' of the effectiveness of primary and secondary schools.

School effectiveness

Their study concentrated on the effectiveness of schools, but they noted that it is difficult to disentangle school effectiveness from teacher effectiveness and other considerations like equality of opportunity, teaching methods, compensatory programmes to support ailing schools and economic studies of the schooling process. In addition, they noted that it is important to look at the connections between school factors (like policies, leadership and culture) and what goes on in the classroom. Effectiveness, if it is to be fully rounded, must show how good management leads to improved classroom performance by teachers and children.

Early studies of school effectiveness looked at exceptional schools, whether exceptionally good or exceptionally bad, and extrapolated from them. Sammons, Hillman and Mortimore's concern was broader. They wished to identify factors which led to the progress of all pupils, not just disadvantaged ones, over a period of time. They acknowledged that a proper estimate of a school's effectiveness in respect of all its pupils, and an estimate that was stable over several years, demanded sophisticated statistical techniques. In addition they noted from their search of the literature that 'individual student background characteristics' are more important than variations in the excellence or otherwise of schools. This implies that there are 'no quick fixes' for turning ineffective schools into effective ones. Nevertheless, given these qualifications and hesitations, they found 'a core of consistency across a variety of studies' which led them to conclude that there are institutional features that correlate with school effectiveness. On page 8 of their report they identify eleven factors for effective schools, listing specific components in each factor.

Professional leadership is seen to be:

- firm and purposeful;
- characterised by a participative approach;
- identified with a leading professional.

Shared visions and goals generate:

- unity of purpose;
- consistency of practice;
- collegiality and collaboration.

The learning environment provides:

- an orderly atmosphere;
- an attractive working environment.

Concentration on teaching and learning and learning provides:

- maximisation of learning time;
- academic emphasis;
- focus on achievement.

Purposeful teaching is seen through:

- efficient organisation;

- clarity of purpose;
- structured lessons;
- adaptive practice.

High expectations are reflected in:

- high expectations all round;
- communicating expectations;
- providing intellectual challenge.

Positive reinforcement provides:

- clear and fair discipline;
- feedback.

Monitoring progress leads to:

- monitoring pupil performance;
- evaluating school performance.

Pupil rights and responsibilities are reflected in:

- raising pupil self-esteem;
- positions of responsibility;
- control of work.

Home-school partnership is seen in:

- parental involvement in their children's learning.

A learning organisation provides:

- school-based staff development.

They take each of the eleven factors in turn and comment on them. All these factors are associated, to a greater or lesser extent, with the management of schools. The package of findings associated with *professional leadership* are among the most important ones here. Commenting on this group they write as follows.

> Leadership is not simply about the quality of individual leaders although it is, of course, important. It is also about the role that leaders play, their style of management, their relationship to the vision, values and goals of the school and their approach to change.

On the second sub-heading they point out that effective leaders are 'proactive', often in the 'selection and replacement' of teachers. This is the necessary condition for building a team. Once the right people are in place, the headteacher then has to ensure they relate to each other creatively and co-operatively and without dissension. At the same time there is evidence that good leaders can protect their schools from 'unhelpful change agents' by challenging 'externally-set guidelines' so as to increase the resources or autonomy of their institution.

The 'participative approach' indicates that effective headteachers delegate responsibility and involve their deputy heads in policy decisions. They also make use of departmental leaders to whom considerable freedom is given and avoid 'both autocratic and over-democratic ways of working'. Perhaps most telling, however, is the headteacher's competence as the 'leading professional'. He or she knows what goes on in the classroom, understands how children learn, what the curriculum implies, what steps ought to be taken to monitor pupil progress and is able to give practical assistance to struggling staff.

The second factor in the Sammons *et al* summary is to be found in 'shared visions and goals'. One of the strands of research brought into play here is that relating to Catholic schools. In the US context Lee, Bryk and Smith (1993) show that Catholic schools have a lower drop-out rate than other schools situated in similar socio-economic environments and other research (McLaughlin, O'Keefe and O'Keeffe, 1996), building on these findings, shows that the extended role of teachers in Catholic schools – not just teaching but having a pastoral concern for pupils and being prepared to offer out-of-school help in sport or drama – helps to link home and school together in a single value system centred on the well-being of the child.

Associated with this unity of purpose and method is a consistency of practice (which provides guidelines for the behaviour of pupils) and a sense of collegiality and collaboration. This produces the third factor, 'a learning environment'.

The purpose of the school, and the purpose of the management of the school, is to produce, first, an environment where learning naturally and easily takes place and, in the end, an organisation which is dedicated to learning for everyone who comes into contact with it, staff included.

Leaving the work of Sammons *et al* at this point in the unit, we turn to Brennan (1994) who, in his book *The Christian Management of Catholic Schools*, identifies six roles for the headteacher. His approach is concerned with what kinds of tasks the headteacher might expect to carry out. According to Brennan the tasks are described as:

- representative;
- selector;
- facilitator;
- enabler;
- encourager;
- initiator.

Activity C1

The role of the headteacher is clearly key to the delivery or creation of the type of school envisaged by Sammons, Hillman and Mortimore. Reflect on how Brennan's six roles relate to the eleven functions listed by Sammons, Hillman and Mortimore. Are there any of the roles that do not fit into the functions? You could also refer back to unit A to compare Mintzberg (1973) both with Sammons, Hillman and Mortimore (1995) and with Brennan (1994).

Comment on activity C1

The role of the headteacher as *representative* may not appear to relate closely to the vision of the effective school, but the point to emphasise here is that the role of the headteacher is expressed in what he or she does. The headteacher by representing the vision and values of the school either to the professional world of education (the local authority, for instance) or to the community (parents and prospective parents) helps to establish the reputation of the school and the expectations people have of it.

Similarly, at first glance the role of *selector* does not seem to fit comfortably with the type of school envisaged by Sammons *et al*. But, when it is remembered that the headteacher has a powerful voice in the selection of staff, it quickly becomes apparent that the headteacher's ability to make selections is an important managerial tool.

The roles of *facilitator*, *enabler* and *encourager* seem to fit more closely with several of the items included in the list of functions and are roles that many will recognise. They are roles that make considerable demands on the headteacher, as they require both a listening approach, which seeks to encourage others to develop their ideas, and a proactive approach, which seeks to set standards and goals for the whole school community. Many members of staff, particularly those who are strongly motivated, will find these roles supportive. Those colleagues will respect a leader whom they see as valuing their commitment and professional expertise. Those members of staff whose personalities respond more readily to clearly defined boundaries and roles may interpret a leadership style that is founded on facilitating, enabling and encouraging as lacking direction and authority.

For the headteacher with clear ideas about education the role of *initiator* has many attractions. It seems to fit comfortably with ideas of 'firm and purposeful leadership' and being the 'leading professional'. In essence this means that the headteacher begins projects or new directions for the school, even to the extent of suggesting new ways of doing old things and making sure that the resources of time, equipment and money are in place.

These reflections highlight one of the basic tensions in the management and leadership of schools. How can ideas of leadership be reconciled with ideas of enabling and facilitating? Although Brennan's book is clearly set in a Christian context, these tensions exist in every school. Within a church school, the dimension created by Christian beliefs must be included in any detailed consideration of leadership issues. Unit B in this module addresses these matters in general terms. Christian values are to be applied to both means (how things are achieved) and ends (what things are aimed for). In terms of means Astley (in unit B) criticises the conception of people and education as commodities, as part of the economic life of the country, and of education as an amoral process. Instead he aligns himself with the language of vocation, service and relationships. By making this alignment he highlights the purposes of education: to make people who care about other people, to foster knowledge directed by love.

If you tried to bring Mintzberg (1973), Sammons, Hillman and Mortimore (1995) and Brennan (1994) together, you might have referred back to the summary in unit A in this module. There you will have found the manager classified as figurehead, spokesperson and negotiator. You will see that there is an overlap here. The figurehead and the representative are very similar. In other words, there is a convergence between Brennan's analysis and that of Mintzberg. Similarly, the facilitating and enabling roles found in Brennan relate to the leading professional concept identified by Sammons, Hillman and Mortimore.

C2 Nature of the organisation (i)

In unit A of this module Roger Goulden drew attention to McGregor's analysis of two kinds of leadership. He drew attention to the 'characteristics of the organisation' as being relevant to management functions. For a school with a religious foundation some of the characteristics will be drawn from religious belief. Historically these have been enshrined in school Trust Deeds and have been informed by guidance prepared by national or diocesan bodies. The National Society has a particular responsibility for the preparation of such advice for the Church of England and for the Church in Wales. In recent years many church schools have sought to develop mission statements which have laid out the philosophy on which the school will be based. These will be considered in more detail in the next section. This section deals with a recent innovation which, in the long term, may change both the nature of mission statements and the basis on which school managers will undertake their tasks.

As a result of the School Standards and Framework Act 1998 all schools with a religious foundation will have to incorporate an *ethos statement* within their new instrument of government. This statement will have to be agreed by the governing body and will form the basis from which the religious aspects of the school's work will derive. This unit was written before the Act became law and before the Department of Education and Employment issued guidance. What follows is a copy of the first draft of guidance on how these statements might be prepared. It was prepared by the National Society, while the Bill was still in the House of Lords, long before it became an Act.

Ethos statements will function like Trust Deeds for any school which has misplaced its deed. If a school is in possession of its deed, the ethos statement must be compatible with it. In a sense this is a piece of legal 'tidying up' to ensure that the legal basis of all church schools is equally secure and equally clear. The problem has been that, because many church schools are well over a hundred years old, the Trust Deed which established their operations has been lost or thrown away. By insisting that each school should make use of an ethos statement (which is only a few lines long) and by relating this statement to an Act of Parliament there is now a linkage between statute law and local trust law.

Everything that happens in the school should flow from the ethos statement. The mission statement which, until now, has had an uncertain purpose and authority and has been mainly used to help parents decide what the school is offering, will probably become an expanded version of the ethos statement.

Developing an ethos statement

The ethos statement for an Anglican school must identify the Church of England or Church in Wales explicitly. It is not sufficient to mention Christian principles without identifying the denomination.

Where the school was created to provide education for a specific ecclesiastical parish or deanery this should also be mentioned.

Reference to the curriculum in general, religious education and school worship in particular and the general values that will inform the school's organisation and relationships may be helpful. The following three models of ethos statements have proved useful as models to assist headteachers and governors formulate an ethos statement for their own schools.

- St Gary's Church of England School provides education in accordance with the principles and practices of the Church of England for pupils whose parents are active members of the Church of England. Worship and the spiritual development of pupils and staff are at the heart of every aspect of the work of this school.

- St Kylie's Church of England school exists to provide education based on Christian principles to pupils living in the ecclesiastical parish of St Kylie's, Little Wondering. Religious education in this school provides the uniting themes for the whole curriculum.

- St Peggy-Sue's Church of England school provides education according to the principles and practices of the Church of England for pupils whose parents are either active members of an Anglican Church in the deanery of Lesser Pudding or who are resident in the ecclesiastical parish of St Peggy-Sue's, Greater Dripping. Within the school the delivery of the National Curriculum is informed by our understanding of the Christian gospel.

Activity C2

Consult with your church school to establish whether they have yet prepared their ethos statement. What guidance did they receive? How far does it relate to the first draft guidance that was prepared by the National Society? What process did they follow in order to develop their own ethos statement? If they have not yet prepared their own ethos statement develop a plan which would enable them to do this.

Comment on activity C2

For most people this will have been an investigation to discover what happened. If a plan for the development of an ethos statement was prepared from scratch it should have contained, or been informed by, the following elements:

- investigation into what is required and what advice is available;
- preliminary session to alert governors and staff to these requirements;
- meeting at which the draft wording is discussed in detail;
- formal confirmation of the final text;
- incorporation of the text within the Instrument of Government;
- review policy statements to ensure that they are in line with the text;
- implementation of the principles enunciated by the ethos statement.

Each of the stages in this process needs to be undertaken. The length of time given to each stage can be revealing of the management style of the person given responsibility for co-ordinating the task. In particular the balance of time given to preparation of the task and the discussion process is a very important indicator of the commitment of the manager to genuine consultation.

C3 Nature of the organisation (ii)

The ethos statements incorporated within the Instrument of Government of the school provide a basis from which the other policies of the school can be derived. The problem with ethos statements, however, is that they may not provide sufficient detail for this purpose. In order to expand them staff often fall back on a more detailed list of the characteristics which they believe should be important features in their school.

Mission statement

These characteristics are often presented in summary form in the mission statement of the school. In *Mission, Management and Appraisal*, Louden and Urwin, writing mainly for school governors suggested an exercise to help governors develop a church school mission statement. The following statements are provided as examples. The church school:

- is distinguished by the support of all its staff for its Christian foundation;
- co-operates actively with other church schools as part of the diocesan family;
- community is based on the model of a Christian family;
- exerts no pressure to believe yet Christian values are built into the ethos and teaching;
- gives high priority to the spiritual development of everyone in the school community;
- attaches high priority to strong links between school, home and parish;
- is distinguished by the quality of care extended to all its members;
- maintains an effective balance between the twin aims of service to the church and service to the community;
- is distinguished by the excellence and special character of its religious education;
- places collective worship at the centre of the school's daily life.

I have selected ten from the original list of thirty-six. Some of those that I have omitted were more negative. A number of these statements find echoes in the work of Sammons *et al* reported above. It is a simple exercise to draw together the eleven factors of Sammons *et al* and to place these in relation to the mission statement points above. The reason for doing this, of course, is that we would expect that effective leaders of church schools would ensure that mission statements become a reality within schools' practices and procedures.

In the following points we give the Sammons, Hillman and Mortimore (1995) factor in italics first and the mission statement second.

- *Professional leadership* is consonant with the support of all its staff for its Christian Foundation and with the excellence and special character of its religious education.
- *Shared vision and goals* is consonant with the support of all its staff for its Christian Foundation, the quality of care extended to all its members and the placing of collective worship at the centre of the school's daily life.
- *A learning environment* is fostered by a community that is based on the model of a Christian family and yet exerts no pressure to believe while Christian values are built into the ethos and teaching.
- *Concentrating on teaching and learning, purposeful teaching* and *high expectations* result in the excellence and special character of its religious education, and the latter will also produce high quality of care for all its members.
- *Positive reinforcement* will help to maintain an effective balance between the twin aims of service to the church and service to the community.
- *Monitoring progress* will result in the excellence and special character of its religious education.
- *Pupil rights and responsibilities* are supported by the use of the model of a Christian family which nevertheless exerts no pressure to believe.
- *A home-school partnership* and the ethos of *a learning* organisation will help reinforce the quality of religious education.

You may wish to fit the components together differently, but the point of the exercise is to show that ethos statements and school effectiveness can coincide. What this highlights is that a key element in management is the attitude the manager has to the people in his or her institution. Are other people seen as automata to be cajoled along a pathway chosen by their superiors or can motivation be inspired by less coercive means? Obviously the answer to this question must be that staff and pupils can and should be inspired to do what is in their own best interests, to *want* what education has to offer. And, as Astley in unit B of this module suggests, it is a democratic method of management that is most likely in the long run to internalise motivation because, when people contribute to decisions, they are most likely to support them.

These considerations can be most sharply worked out on the demanding occasions when a county school has been closed and a church school opened in the same premises, with the same pupils and with most of the same staff. The reason for the change has often been the need to give the school a fresh start. The only immediate and concrete changes are in the *expectations* of the institution. For the new headteacher in such circumstances the challenge is to present an example of Christian leadership and to develop the characteristics of the school that will enable it to be identified as a Christian school.

Activity C3

Given the ten characteristics described by Louden and Urwin, which three of them would you pursue first if you were in the situation described in the paragraph above? How would you set about initiating the necessary changes, bearing in mind the demands to lead the school towards those characteristics of an effective school identified by Sammons, Hillman and Mortimore.

Comment on activity C3

Any headteacher taking on this task will be subject to moments when the task seems impossible! It is very difficult. In the first instance the ability of the headteacher to listen to the concerns of the staff and to respond to them will be crucial. It may be that one of two strategies will need to be followed after listening.

Strategy one (probably used where the staff are generally supportive but suspicious of change): begin with some slight changes which command general support from the staff, like the following three statements from the list:

- giving high priority to the spiritual development of everyone in the school;
- attaching high priority to strong links between school, home and parish;
- emphasising the quality of care extended to all its members.

All three might emphasise that characteristic of an effective school that has to do with shared values and purpose and good links between home and school. Most staff should feel these emphases provide a step in the right direction. But they do not completely represent the key elements either of an effective school or a good church school. More progress would be needed. By introducing such changes the headteacher might be identified as working in an enabling or facilitating mode.

Strategy two (probably used where there is a need to demonstrate that the school is changing swiftly): begin with some clear changes from past practice. Pursue:

- co-operating actively with other church schools as part of the diocesan family;
- being distinguished by the excellence and special character of religious education;
- placing collective worship at the centre of the school's daily life.

This strategy, with the possible implication that new staff will need to be appointed to achieve it, provides an example of firm leadership and the setting of high expectations. It is also likely to attract swift support from church quarters, but might lead to some dissent in the staff room. In practice most headteachers faced with this task have worked on a variant of strategy one rather than strategy two.

You will probably have disagreed with my suggestions. In a real situation you would have much more information to work on, in fact you might have so much information and advice that the task of sifting through it all can delay taking action.

C4 Professional development for school managers

Those who are involved in the management of Anglican schools need to ensure that they make time and energy available for their own professional (and some would argue spiritual) development. This is both because it is important that they maintain a lively approach to their work that is stimulated by participation in such activities, and because it sets an example to other colleagues. They also need to know what is available to colleagues at all levels of development in order to be able to provide advice and encouragement to them.

The government is implementing a number of developments intended to provide a new and more complete structure within which the professional development of teachers can be placed. At the time of writing this section, these structures are beginning to emerge but many of the details are still to be developed. Therefore an aspect of the task for this unit will be to compare what is in place when you read this with what I am anticipating.

All teachers

In future all teachers will have to be registered with the General Teaching Council. In order to register they will have to be able to demonstrate that they have reached the basic level of competence required for Qualified Teacher Status (QTS) and have developed within their first year of teaching. Having satisfactorily completed their probationary year and become established within their school, teachers will be able to begin to work towards a number of steps in professional development. These will include qualification as a subject leader, a special educational needs co-ordinator and for the very best of practitioners in the classroom an advanced skills teacher. None of these qualifications will be specific to church schools, although teachers working towards them in church schools should be encouraged to reflect on and use the present context of their teaching. The Teacher Training Agency (TTA) lays down the structure of these stages in professional development.

For many teachers preparation for headship will be the most significant stage of professional development. The Teacher Training Agency has created a programme of training to assist teachers who have reached this stage of their careers. The first part of this is selection for training for the National Professional Qualification for Headship (NPQH). This training is skills based and at the time of writing does not contain elements that are specific to church schools. It is hoped that, as this programme is developed, there will be material, drawing attention to the issues that are important for headteachers in Anglican schools. Following NPQH, there is a programme of training designed to support headteachers in their first two years in post. This programme is called Headlamp and, because it can be delivered by a number of different providers, it is possible for headteachers of church schools to find courses within this scheme that address the challenges of headship in a church school. The TTA are also proposing to provide training suitable to the needs of headteachers who have been in post for more than five years.

Most of the training offered under the auspices of the TTA is skills based and not context specific. For those who are planning to serve for a substantial part of their career in church schools this will need to be supplemented by some professional development which is context specific.

Teachers in church schools

In recent years the National Society working on behalf of the Anglican church has developed or encouraged a number of programmes which provide opportunities for teachers and governors in church schools to undertake training and development activities which relate to the context of their work. Many Anglican dioceses also offer such activities. You will already be familiar with many of the Society's publications through your work on this material. Working with the Anglican Colleges of Higher Education the society has seen a significant growth in the Church Colleges Certificate in Church School Studies programme and the material that you are presently studying is of course another part of these developments. By making appropriate use of these national initiatives and the opportunities provided by dioceses, all teachers in church schools should be able to undertake professional development related to the specific needs of the school in which they are working.

There will be many teachers who have obtained the qualifications that they wish or need and for whom professional development means being aware of research and development in their field of interest. The creation of the College of Teachers and its commitment to research, including teacher led research, is an important avenue for those teachers who are reaching that level of professional development. This college should provide a new impetus for many whose professional development is not promotion orientated. The National Society and the church colleges have been active in promoting research into church school issues. The Ethos and Education Network[1], which provides international links with research into schools with a religious foundation world-wide, offers an important resource for teachers working in church schools.

Spiritual development

For those teachers who have chosen to work in church schools out of a sense of Christian vocation, spiritual development will be an important issue. Many will find that their needs are served within the context of their local Christian congregation. Some will seek other opportunities. It should not be surprising to learn that amongst the activities organised by the Anglican Association of Secondary School headteachers are annual retreats for headteachers and deputies. Some church schools provide activities for their staff to support their spiritual development. I have known many church schools that have had celebrations of the eucharist specifically for the staff of the school, perhaps most commonly at the beginning of a school year. I have known a few church schools where staff met regularly for prayer and bible study. Where school worship is well prepared and conducted there are many staff who find that this also contributes to their spiritual development. Those responsible for church school management need to consider how the school will provide for and encourage the spiritual development of the staff.

Activity C4

How far has the development of the initiatives and ideas outlined in this section been achieved? Given that context, how would you plan a programme of professional development for yourself after you have completed this course? How would you plan a programme for a teacher joining your school staff having successfully completed their probationary year in a community school?

Comment on activity C4

Inevitably, the context for professional development will have changed somewhat between the time when I wrote this section and the time that you have read this. Your response to the activity needs to reflect those changes.

---

[1] Information about membership of the Education and Ethos Network and subscriptions to the journal *Education and Ethos: studies in religiously affiliated schools, colleges and universities* can be obtained by writing to the Education and Ethos Membership Secretary, The National Society, Church House, Great Smith Street, London SW1 3NZ.

If you successfully complete this course one of the elements within your further development will need to be how you link into research either in your own subject or phase or within the church school context. Will you become involved in the College of Teachers or The Ethos and Education Network? Will you seek to develop links with a local Institute of Higher Education that is involved in research issues that interest you?

There may be a need to focus back on to your main responsibilities at school and take a year or so to apply the insights that you have gained from this course to those circumstances. You might also wish to give more time to aspects of your spiritual development, which may have been neglected while you were focused on these studies.

For new colleagues, once they have established themselves in the school and are working effectively within the policies and practices of the school, there will be a number of choices to be made. Are they going to prepare for the role of subject leader or special educational needs co-ordinator? Do they need to study for the Church Colleges Certificate in Church School Studies? Are there other needs that can be addressed by making use of local courses or facilities? The key issue for them, as for you, may be appraisal.

Appraisal should offer the opportunity to reflect with a senior colleague or line manager on your professional development needs and how these needs might be met. As with so many aspects of this section, appraisal is both a vital aspect of professional development and one which is, at the time of writing, subject to review.

For church school managers, their own professional development and the professional development of their colleagues is a vital aspect of school performance. Without interested, committed and growing professionals a school withers. With lively professionals committed to their own growth there is every opportunity for the school to grow as well.

C5 Worked examples for church schools

The National Society provides a training course for those wishing to inspect Anglican schools under Section 23 of the Schools Inspection Act 1996. One part of one of the exercises on this course contains the following scenario[2] in a section about the ethos of a church school and the way in which an inspector may obtain evidence about the extent to which Christian love and support is demonstrated in the school.

---

[2] In this section all the scenarios are based on real incidents in Anglican primary schools.

> The headteacher is about to speak to a lazy member of staff, whose punctuality and preparation are well known to be poor. Just as the headteacher is warming to the theme the teacher interrupts with the question, 'Can't we handle this like Christians?'

Reflect for a moment on what your response might be to such a comment and analyse with care the implications of the language used. Some of the issues in this scenario go to the heart of the leadership challenge that church schools offer. The following analysis only begins to tackle the issues, but should stimulate you to further reflection.

* The description 'lazy teacher' raises issues of motivating staff and knowing individuals in the community.
* The problem of 'poor punctuality' may demonstrate a lack of discipline.
* The problem of 'poor preparation' may point to professional incompetence.
* The fact that all this is 'well known' raised the question as to why no previous action has been taken.
* The way in which the teacher 'interrupts' displays a lack of courtesy.
* The request to handle the issue 'like Christians' may mean a variety of things. Is it a plea to tolerate poor performance, a cry for understanding, a suggestion that Christians avoid unpleasantness, or a ploy to avoid being called to account?

Like so many stories the scenario begins to have two sides and two possible titles. Is it 'the tale of the poor teacher and the exploited headteacher' or is it 'the tale of an ineffective manager and a professional in need of training'? It could be both of these. The implication is clearly that the teacher is not meeting professional standards. Has the teacher received help, support and training appropriate to the professional task? If not, the headteacher may be at fault by failing to ensure the professional development of staff. If the teacher has received the support but has not benefited, is this because the support was badly targeted or is it because the teacher has declined to take advice, follow guidance or in the last resort do what he or she has been told?

The headteacher seems to have been slow to pick up the issue, unless, of course, the guidance and support of the teacher had been delegated to a deputy or senior colleague. The headteacher may have a style of leadership that relies on example, goodwill and commitment. Such a style assumes that if the headteacher sets the example other colleagues will follow it. A style like this is vulnerable to colleagues who do not perceive what is required or will not follow the lead.

The analysis has focused on a scenario which involved two professionals, both of whom had received training and preparation for their work. This means that there are shared professional expectations and training which ought to allow the headteacher and the other teacher to come to an agreement. The plea to treat the situation like Christians could suggest that the headteacher behaves in the way required in Matthew 18.15, that is, to treat the matter privately without making a public incident of it. On the other hand, it could be a plea from the classteacher for forgiveness and an opportunity to 'repent', to do better in future and to be given another chance. These possibilities need to be explored by the headteacher. However, headteachers do not only have to deal with trained staff in the privacy of their offices. Here are three further scenarios. The first of these three scenarios involves a dinner supervisor.

> There is a crisis in the dining room. A dinner supervisor is behaving very aggressively with a child. It appears that some food has been spilt and the supervisor has interpreted this as having been done deliberately. The child is distressed, the dinner supervisor is over-heated and the rest of the school is watching with interest.

The second scenario involves parents and their children.

> A member of staff is put in charge of the football team in a junior school. He is given the task of selecting and training the children to be in the team and of organising matches. A parent decides to take a holiday during the school term and so her child, Mario, is forced to miss a match. When the family returns Mario is annoyed to discover that he has been dropped from the team and is now no longer needed. Another child, Freddie, has proved a suitable replacement. The parent goes to see the classteacher and demands that Mario be reinstated. The classteacher explains that he has been put in charge of this particular team and that Freddie has proved to be a better player than Mario. The mother goes to see the headteacher and complains that Mario has been unfairly treated because, if he had not been away from school, he would not have lost his place in the team. The headteacher assures the parent that Mario will be put back in the team for the next match.

The third scenario poses a management problem for the headteacher.

> John comes to school one day with marks in the shape of a hand on his face. The headteacher in consultation with the classteacher decides that the social services must be informed in case John is being abused at home. The social services investigate but find no wrongdoing. However, the mother is angered by what the school has done.

> Later her daughter, Jill, is a member of the class going on a school trip. At the end of the day, when the coach stops at a motorway service station, the children are told to go to the toilet. An hour later the coach stops again to let some children living in a village get off. Jill asks to be allowed to go to the toilet but is refused permission by the teacher because of the previous stop and because the coach will be stopping in five minutes at the school. Jill, who is aged ten years old, wets herself on the coach. When the coach eventually arrives at the school, the mother hears what has happened and accuses the teacher on the coach of treating Jill cruelly. She writes an official letter of complaint to the governors and to the local education authority. She wants the teacher on the coach to be sacked. How should the headteacher react in this situation?

Activity C5

Analyse the issues that arise for school leadership from the three scenarios. In particular where are Christian teaching and leading by example relevant in this? Comment on what the headteacher should do in the first scenario and what the headteacher actually did in the last two scenarios.

Comment on activity C5

The story of the dinner supervisor introduces two elements. The member of staff involved does not have the same level of professional background as the headteacher and is within a group who are often overlooked during staff discussions and training. On the other hand the incident takes place in public. It will be seen as an example of whether the school management is serious about its statements on discipline and relationships. For clarification we could lay out the issues in this scenario in the following way:

- The phrase 'behaving very aggressively' raises a question about school policy. Is there a school policy, explicit or implicit about the way in which staff and pupils should interrelate? Is such behaviour within the limits of this policy?
- The supervisor's interpretation that the child has spilt the food deliberately raises an issue of fact. Is the supervisor's interpretation correct? Or is the child's interpretation correct?
- The observation that the child is distressed raises the issue of pastoral care. How will the child be calmed, cared for and if necessary corrected or reassured?
- The observation that the supervisor is overheated raises another issue of pastoral concern and also of management style. How will the supervisor be calmed, cared for and if necessary corrected or reassured?
- The fact that the rest of the school is watching is also of significance. How will the pupils and staff be calmed and reassured? What will they have learned from the incident?
- The whole scenario focuses the key problem of how Christian teaching interacts with this kind of practical management issue. There may be issues of repentance, forgiveness and reconciliation in the way in which either the child or the supervisor is dealt with. The future relationship between the two will be dependent on it
- The way in which the headteacher deals with this issue also provides evidence of 'leading by example'. What kind of learning experience are being provided for the whole school?

The other two scenarios also involve actions by a headteacher. The football scenario concerns the issues of delegation to a member of staff and relationships with parents. This scenario raises the following questions. Has the headteacher made a correct decision? What will the classteacher say to (a) Freddie, (b) the headteacher? Should the classteacher resign from the responsibility of looking after the football team? On the other hand, has the headteacher, by acting in this way, prevented trouble at a future PTFA meeting and smoothed relationships between home and school? We do not know the basis for the delegation, but the assumption must be that when a headteacher makes a classteacher responsible for an aspect of school life, this responsibility is genuine and has decision-making powers implicit in it. If this were not so, the delegation would be a sham. Thus we need to ask how the headteacher should override the classteacher's decision. It seems reasonable to suggest that consultation should be involved and that a unilateral decision by the headteacher in these circumstances is almost invariably incorrect. It may be, for instance, that the parent is not telling the whole truth to the headteacher. In any event the headteacher, as the leading *professional*, should respect the *professional* conduct of a colleague. By acting as he has done the headteacher has placed the classteacher in a difficult position in relation to Freddie. Moreover, what will the headteacher do if Freddie's mother appears and complains? In the scenario as it has been described Christian values do not appear to have informed the behaviour of the headteacher and nothing has been done to ensure a 'participative' approach to decisions or the possibility of 'consistency of practice' (the first two points in the list provided by Sammons, Hillman and Mortimore, 1995.)

In the last scenario the headteacher again has the choice of supporting or effectively undermining a member of staff. Other factors, however, intervene here to make this a very complex matter. Amongst the most important of these are the requirements of formal legal procedures. In the first paragraph the school will have had to follow local authority required procedures on suspected child abuse. An issue then arises about the quality of communication between Social Services, the school and the parents. There are unresolved issues of reconciliation implied by this paragraph, which may not be totally within the headteacher's abilities to conclude satisfactorily.

In the second paragraph again formal procedures affect the headteacher's freedom of action. A formal complaint has been made. This must be dealt with in the context of the procedures laid down in the teacher's contract of employment. The headteacher must be sure that he or she has sought and have followed guidance from those who are employed to provide it (for example the local education authority's personnel officer). Knowing when to seek and use external help is an important feature of a good manager. Within this context the headteacher has to investigate the situation. Were the children given adequate opportunity to go to the toilet at the motorway service station? Was Jill refused an opportunity to go to the toilet reasonably when they stopped in the village? Should a ten year old be able to control her bladder? Is the parent acting unreasonably because of the previous reporting to the social services? If, after investigating the matter, and hearing all sides the appropriate body (possibly the headteacher but also possibly a sub committee of the governors) concludes that the teacher acted appropriately, the decision and the reasons for it should be conveyed to the teacher and to the parent in writing. Reconciliation after such an incident will be a significant challenge to the headteacher, the teacher and the parent.

It may be of interest to know that what actually happened was that the parent carried out her complaint vigorously. The governors and local authority supported the teacher on the coach and the parent eventually removed her child to another school.

C6 Challenge of leading a church school

In the first edition of *School Matters*, a publication produced by a company offering consultancy services to religious schools in the United States, Redmon (1997) offered a series of questions to help leaders in schools reflect on their management styles. In particular he was concerned to assist school leaders to examine how their management styles and their ethical beliefs interact. The questions reflected a context in which religious schools are all in the independent sector. I have adapted the original questions in his article to reflect more of the British context in the following seven issues.

- What is the nature of your commitment to the school and its values?
- Given the legal and administrative framework for your school, how do you ensure that the values of the school are clearly demonstrated?
- How far is your school part of 'an education service' for the area? How far is it part of the 'mission of the church'? In what ways do you express your commitment to these ideas?
- Can you identify how the respect that you hold for the value and dignity of individual pupils, members of staff, governors and parents is made clear in your actions?
- How do you show commitment to tolerance, diversity and social justice in your daily decisions?
- How do others describe the openness of your approach to management?
- How are the values to which the school is committed demonstrated in your management of the school's resources, particularly people, ideas, money and buildings?

Each of these questions contains a series of challenges to those in leadership positions in church schools. The following list supplies some of the locations within school policies and activity where these challenges may lie.

Your commitment to the school values may be located in:

- your sense of vocation for work in this school;
- your willingness to commit time to your work beyond that normally expected.

Demonstrating school values may be located in:

- reflecting on how new procedures demanded by law will affect the ethos of the school;
- ensuring that the school brochure does not just carry the legal minimum information but also makes a clear statement about the ethos of the school.

Service to community/ mission of the church may be located in:

- relationships with headteachers of non-church schools;
- contact with children's workers in the parish.

Respect may be located in:

- discipline policies;
- making time for people and giving them the courtesy of attention.

Tolerance may be located in:

- celebrating the variety of tradition and cultures represented in the school and the community;
- engaging the school in charitable work and issues of justice and fair trade.

Openness may be located in:

- ensuring that letters and other communications with parents provide full explanations;
- sharing financial information with all staff.

Management of resources may be located in:

- ensuring that every member of the community is able to make suggestions;
- ensuring the maintenance of school premises reflects good stewardship.

Activity C6

The preceding list has given two examples for each of the seven questions. Given the situation outlined in activity C3 (above), how would you expect the headteacher, attempting to create a church school ethos in a former county school, to identify further examples from their work?

Comment on activity C6

For any member of a school management team the management of change is a crucial task. The characteristics of openness, commitment and the ability to think beyond current practice and legal requirements into what it is desirable or essential to achieve in the short or medium term, will be crucial to success. I would expect that you would have identified significant issues in the rows, which reflect these key characteristics.

C7 Inspection and accountability

Considerable guidance is available to all those involved with church education on the subject of inspection. Your school will probably have a copy of the OFSTED framework document and also some at least of the range of publications from the National Society on the subject of Section 23 inspections. If you are not familiar with these publications you should take time to study them as they form the background to both this section and the next section of this unit. Most of the documentation on inspection has been written for the inspectors. It is assumed that school managers can interpret the implications of the documents for their school and for their role.

Both Section 10 and Section 23 inspections assume that there is high quality leadership in the school and reports will be critical if this appears to be lacking. Inspectors will gather evidence both from their observation of the schools management in action and from the way in which governors, teachers, support staff and pupils respond to it. They will be looking for signs of competence and forethought.

The school management team will have given careful thought to the whole process; they will mentally have rehearsed it to remove possible sources of trouble. In particular the team will have ensured that the administration of the school is well organised so those administrative problems do not interfere with the good running of the school at this time of particular tension within the community.

The team will have time during the week to be available to staff and to the inspectors. They will have ensured, as far as possible, that everything has been done to make their own performance in the classroom or in any other aspect of the school's work of the highest quality. In other words, the management team will lead by example.

To put it more humorously, they will be giving their best interpretation of a swan swimming against the flow of the river, appearing calm, graceful and in control on the surface, no matter how hard they may be paddling underwater!

Activity C7

What are the key characteristics of leadership the headteacher of a church school will need to demonstrate during the course of a school inspection?

Comment on activity C7

From your readings of the OFSTED Guidance and the National Society *Handbook* you will have identified the importance of the headteacher being clear about the process of inspection. He or she will need to be able to demonstrate a grasp of the school ethos statement and its implications for every aspect of the school's activity. For example, the management of the curriculum (including religious education) and of school worship will be effective.

The care of the school building and any grounds surrounding it will illustrate how the school seeks to convey its teaching about the stewardship of creation by example. The staff on whom this work principally falls will be valued and have an appropriate understanding of what they are doing and why they are doing it. The headteacher will have established effective management in this area of the school's life.

The support staff will know how their work contributes to the overall ethos of the school and will have received training to help them establish such an understanding. The headteacher will be able to demonstrate how this has been managed.

None of these understandings will have been developed overnight. Many will have been created by informal contacts and by the way in which the headteacher and other members of the school management team relate to staff and to each other. Particularly the extent to which every member of staff and every child knows that they and their work are valued will be a key factor in creating the appropriate atmosphere from which the ethos of the school will flow.

Staffing

In all of section C6 the issue of communicating the vision to all the staff of the school seemed to be fundamental to success. Much of the task of the headteacher and other school managers centres round communication. The skills of communication may not be the only skills that a manager needs but they are an essential tool.

Headteachers must have a clear vision of how their schools should be operating. Such vision will be informed and will reflect the ethos statements and other school policies. Having the vision however is not sufficient. It must be communicated to, and received by, all the staff and pupils. Opportunities to communicate the vision to staff exist in:

- staff meetings;
- school assembly;
- policy documents;
- interviews;
- induction programmes;
- in-service training;
- departmental meetings;
- informal conversations.

You could probably add many more to the list. Attention is often given to the first seven of the opportunities on my list but sometimes the last one is left to chance or neglected. It can be the most powerful.

In addition the headteacher needs to come out of the office and look at what is going on in the school. He or she may appear to be wandering about, but the underlying message being given here is of interest in every aspect of the school's life. 'Management by wandering about' is, oddly enough, an effective management technique in a small institution. It seems to be the antithesis of good organisation and use of time. One of the points in justification for the style is that it focuses on management not administration. The manager has deliberately created time to be around the school, to be able to see and hear what is going on and to be in contact with the individuals whose work enables the school to operate. In others words it creates the opportunity for informal contact. The headteacher, in the course of a 'wander' could:

- praise a child;
- correct a child;
- create informal contact with the dinner supervisors;
- thank the cleaners for the cleanliness of the building on Monday morning following the weekend's activities in the school;
- make note of incidents or issues that might be the subject of discussion or comment with teachers when they are not busy with their class;
- spot repair or maintenance issues that need to be discussed with the school buildings supervisor or caretaker.

Of course, 'wandering about' which is purposeless or which is followed only by a list of complaints or harangues is counter-productive. Crucial to the success of the approach is the quality of relationships that it develops and sustains. During times of pressure in the school, for example during an inspection, this informal contact could be particularly important.

Activity C8

I have provided a justification for 'management by wandering about' in terms of the importance of creating opportunities for informal conversation and contact. What are the weaknesses of 'management by wandering about'? How would you convince inspectors that such a style was purposeful?

Comment on activity C8

Taken to extremes the style can be an excuse for avoiding administrative tasks and formal decision making. 'The headteacher is never there when she is wanted' could be a telling criticism of the approach. Without a strong understanding of the desired ethos of the school it can be difficult to ensure that the informal conversations are contributing to progress and communicating the vision.

Good use of time requires the creation of space to think or reflect as well as to be responding to situations as they arise. Administrative tasks, meetings, teaching and planning all have to be allocated appropriate time. The challenge to any headteacher is to establish an appropriate balance and to stay in control of that balance when others create pressures.

Inspectors will only be convinced about the value of the management style when they observe a school that is running effectively and enabling staff and pupils to achieve the best of which they are capable. Managers must be prepared to keep their style of work under constant review until the organisation for which they are responsible is running perfectly at maximum efficiency. When this is achieved they should leave.

In this unit the emphasis has been to a large extent on reflection. There is no right or wrong way to manage a school. The combination of the aims of the school, the personalities of the staff and pupils and the level of resources available interact with the personality of the headteacher in a unique way in every individual school. These circumstances vary from one year to the next even in a school with 'a stable staff', or a well resourced and maintained environment. Therefore there are no right or wrong answers, there are only ideas and strategies that have worked for others in different circumstances. It is for each headteacher to wrestle with the issues. Support and understanding from governors, advisers and colleagues are very important if success in this area is to be achieved and sustained.

Bibliography

Brennan, J. (1994), *The Christian Management of Catholic Schools*, Northampton, The Beckett Press.

Brown, A.S. and Lankshear, D.W. (1997), *Inspection Handbook: for Section 23 inspectors in schools of the Church of England and Church in Wales*, London, The National Society.

Lee, V., Bryk, A. and Smith, J. (1993), The organisation of effective secondary schools, in L. Darling-Hammond (ed.), *Review of Research in Education: 19*, Washington, DC, American Educational Research Association, pp 171-226.

Louden, L.M.R and Urwin, D.S. (1992), *Mission, Management and Appraisal*, London, The National Society.

McGregor, D. (1960), *The Human Side of Enterprise*, London, McGraw Hill.

McLaughlin, T., O'Keefe, J. and O'Keeffe, B. (eds) (1996), *The Contemporary Catholic School*, London, Falmer Press.

Mintzberg, H. (1973), *The Nature of Managerial Work*, New York, Harper and Row.

OFSTED (1995), *Guidance on the Inspection of Secondary Schools*, London, The Stationery Office.

OFSTED (1995), *Guidance on the Inspection of Nursery and Primary Schools*, London, The Stationery Office.

OFSTED (1995), *Guidance on the Inspection of Special Schools*, London, The Stationery Office.

Redmon, T. (1997), Aggressive ethical behaviour: a new paradigm for school leaders, *School Matters*, 1 (1), 2.

Sammons, P., Hillman, J. and Mortimore, P. (1995), *Key Characteristics of Effective Schools*, London, The Stationery Office.

Index of names

Index of subjects